Collections Management

Collections Management

Edited by
Anne Fahy

London and New York

First published 1995
by Routledge
11 New Fetter Lane, London EC4P 4EE

Simultaneously published in the USA and Canada
by Routledge
29 West 35th Street, New York, NY 10001

Reprinted 1998, 1999, 2002, 2003

Routledge is an imprint of the Taylor & Francis Group

Editorial matter © 1995 Anne Fahy
Individual contributions © 1995 individual contributors

Typeset in Sabon by
Florencetype Ltd, Stoodleigh, Devon
Printed and bound in Great Britain by
T.J. International, Padstow, Cornwall

British Library Cataloguing in Publication Data
A catalogue record for this book is available from the British Library

Library of Congress Cataloging in Publication Data
A catalog record for this book is available from the Library of Congress

ISBN 0–415–11282–6 (hbk)
ISBN 0–415–11283–4 (pbk)

Contents

Figures

Tables

Series preface

Museums are established institutions, but they exist in a changing world. The modern notion of a museum and its collections runs back into the sixteenth or even fifteenth centuries, and the origins of the earliest surviving museums belong to the period soon after. Since then museums have always been and continue to be founded along these well-understood lines. But the end of the second millennium AD and the advent of the third one point up the new needs and preoccupations of contemporary society. These are many, but some can be picked out as particularly significant here. Access is crucially important: access to information, the decision-making process and resources like gallery space, and access by children, ethnic minorities, women and the disadvantaged and underprivileged. Similarly, the nature of museum work itself needs to be examined, so that we can come to a clearer idea of the nature of the institution and its material, of what museum professionalism means, and how the issues of management and collection management affect outcomes. Running across all these debates is the recurrent theme of the relationship between theory and practice in what is, in the final analysis, an important area of work.

New needs mean fresh efforts at information gathering and understanding, and the best possible access to important literature for teaching and study. It is this need that the *Leicester Readers in Museum Studies* series addresses. The series as a whole breaks new ground by bringing together, for the first time, an important body of published work, much of it very recent, much of it taken from journals which few libraries carry, and all of it representing fresh approaches to the study of the museum operation.

The series has been divided into six volumes, each of which covers a significant aspect of museum studies. These six topics bear a generic relationship to the modular arrangement of the Leicester Department of Museum Studies post-graduate course in Museum Studies, but, more fundamentally, they reflect current thinking about museums and their study. Within each volume, each editor has been responsible for his or her choice of papers. Each volume reflects the approach of its own editor, and the different feel of the various traditions and discourses upon which it draws. The range of individual emphases and the diversity of points of view is as important as the overarching theme in which each volume finds its place.

It is our intention to produce a new edition of the volumes in the series every three years, so that the selection of papers for inclusion is a continuing process and the contemporary stance of the series is maintained. All the editors of the series are happy to receive suggestions for inclusions (or exclusions), and details of newly published material.

Acknowledgements

The publishers and editors would like to thank the following people and organizations for permission to reproduce copyright material:

'Collection management policies' by Marie Malaro, reprinted from *A Legal Primer on Managing Museum Collections* by Marie C. Malaro (Washington, D.C.: Smithsonian Institution Press), pp. 45–51, 276–89, 327–34, © 1985, by permission of the Smithsoian Institution. 'Evolving a policy manual' by Arminta Neal, Kristine Haglund and Elizabeth Webb reprinted, with permission, from *Museum News* 56(3) (Jan./Feb. 1978), pp. 26–30. 'Guidelines for a Registration Scheme for museums in the United Kingdom' (1988), reprinted by permission of the Museums and Galleries Commission. 'A framework for management' reprinted from *The Cost of Collecting. Collection Management in UK Museums* by B. Lord, G.D. Lord and J. Nicks (London: HMSO 1989), pp. 61–75, by permission of the Controller of Her Majesty's Stationery Office. 'Museums and the horrors of war' by M. Lachs reprinted from *Museum* No. 147, © UNESCO 1985, pp. 167–8. 'Export Licensing Unit, 1993: UK export licensing system for works of art, antiques, collectors' items, etc.' paper by the Department of National Heritage, reprinted in entirety with the permission of the Controller of Her Majesty's Stationery Office. 'UNESCO Convention on the means of prohibiting and preventing the illicit import, export and transfer of ownership of cultural property. Appendix D' in M. Malaro *A Legal Primer on Managing Museum Collections* (Washington, D.C.: Smithsonian Institution Press 1985) by permission of the Smithsonian Institution. 'Law and diplomacy in cultural property matters' by Anne McC. Sullivan. This article was first published in *Museum Management and Curatorship* 10(3) (Sept. 1991), pp. 219–43, and is reproduced here with the permission of Butterworth-Heinemann, Oxford, UK. 'Collecting for the twenty-first century' by J. Kenyon reprinted from *A Survey of Industrial and Social History Collections in the Museums of Yorkshire and Humberside* (Yorkshire and Humberside Museums Council 1992) with permission. 'Hambledon Cricket Club Account Book: one of six offers the government accepts in lieu of tax' (press release 1992) reprinted by permission of the Department of National Heritage. 'Acceptance in lieu' leaflet (1990), reprinted by permission of the Museums and Galleries Commission. 'Legislation relating to the acquisition and disposal of museum collections in the United Kingdom' (internal publication of the Department of Museum Studies, University of Leicester 1988/1992) reprinted by permission of the authors. 'The Bowes Museum Canaletto Appeal: a case study' by G. Stansfield reprinted by permission of the author and the curator of the Bowes Museum, Barnard Castle, Co. Durham. 'Preservation of Industrial and Scientific Material (PRISM) Grant Fund' leaflet (1993), reprinted by permission of the Museums and Galleries Commission. 'The Science Museum Fund' by John Robinson, reprinted from *Science Museum Review* (London: Science Museum 1989) with permission of the Science Museum, London. 'Victoria

& Albert Museum 1992 Purchase Grant Fund' (1992) reprinted by permission of the Museums and Galleries Commission. 'Disposals from museum collections: a note on legal considerations in England and Wales' by Adrian Babbidge. This article was first published in *Museum Management and Curatorship* 10(3) (Sept. 1991), pp. 255–61, and is reproduced here with the permission of Butterworth-Heinemann, Oxford, UK. 'Infamous de-accessions' by Iain Robertson, reprinted from *Museums Journal*, 90(3) (March 1990), by permission of the Museums Association. 'Attitudes to disposal from museum collections' by Geoffrey Lewis. This article was first published in *Museum Management and Curatorship* 11(1) (March 1992), pp. 19–28, and is reproduced here with the permission of Butterworth-Heinemann, Oxford, UK. 'Scottish sense' by Robert Clark, reprinted from *Museums Journal* 91(9) (1991), pp. 34–5, by permission of the Museums Association. 'Why museum computer projects fail' by Lenore Sarasan, reprinted, with permission, from *Museum News* 59(4) (Jan./Feb. 1981), pp. 40–9. 'Museum information systems: the case for computerization' by Pnina Wentz. This article was first published in *The International Journal of Museum Management and Curatorship* 8(3) (Sept. 1989), pp. 313–25, and is reproduced here with the permission of Butterworth-Heinemann, Oxford, UK. 'Cataloguing collections – erratic starts and eventual success: a case study' by P.E. Rivard and S. Miller, reprinted from *Curator* 34(2) (1991), by permission of the authors and *Curator*. 'Foreign Ethnographic Collections Research Programme' by Elizabeth Kwasnik, reprinted from *Scottish Museum News* 8(3) (Edinburgh: Scottish Museums Council 1992), p. 2, by permission of the author and the Scottish Museums Council. Elizabeth Kwasnik has asserted her moral right to be identified as the author of this work. 'Scholarship and the public' by Neil MacGregor. This article was first published in *Museum Management and Curatorship* 9(4) (Dec. 1990), pp. 361–6, and is reproduced here with the permission of the author and Butterworth-Heinemann, Oxford, UK. 'Collections research: local, national and international perspectives' by Alexander Fenton reprinted from Thompson, John M.A. (ed.) *Manual of Curatorship. A Guide to Museum Practice* (Oxford: Butterworth-Heinemann 1992) by permission of Butterworth-Heinemann. 'Security is everybody's business' (1992) pp. 1–5, reprinted by permission of the Museums and Galleries Commission. 'Museum and gallery security' (1992) pp. 1–8, reprinted by permission of the Museums and Galleries Commission. 'A case study of a museum thief' by Don Steward, reprinted from *Museums Journal* 86(2) (1986) pp. 74–77, by permission of the Museums Association. 'Protection, security and conservation of collections' by ICOM and the International Security Committee reprinted from ICOM and ICMS *Museum Security and Protection* (London: Routledge 1993) by permission of Routledge. 'Liability risk management for museums' by Elizabeth A. Griffith reprinted from F. Howie, *Safety in Museums and Galleries* (Oxford: Butterworth-Heinemann 1987) by permission of the author. 'Insurance and indemnity' by G. Stansfield, originally produced as part of the Collection Management Course Handbook of the Department of Museum Studies, University of Leicester and reprinted with the permission of the author. 'Indemnity arrangements for local museums, galleries and other non-governmental bodies' (London: Office of Arts and Libraries 1989), pp. 1–6, including Annexe A, Annexe B and Annexe C. Reprinted by permission of the Department of National Heritage.

Every attempt has been made to obtain permission to reproduce copyright material. If any proper acknowledgement has not been made, we would invite copyright holders to inform us of the oversight.

Introduction

Anne Fahy

This reader, through the selection of articles and extracts from books and this essay, attempts to highlight contemporary issues which have an effect upon collections management and policy-making in national and non-national museums, within the context of the following eight themes:

1 Developing collections management policies.
2 The movement and protection of cultural property and the role of museums.
3 Acquisition policies and methods of acquisition, including the costs of collecting.
4 De-accessioning and disposal – including legal and ethical issues.
5 Museum documentation and current national and international initiatives in documentation.
6 Researching collections and disseminating information about them.
7 Museum security.
8 Insurance and government indemnity schemes.

The themes follow the outline of the Collections Management Course at the University of Leicester and the split between the themes in this book and the second collections management reader does not reflect any system, other than that included in the Leicester courses. Although each aspect is not dealt with in detail in this discussion, I have tried to emphasize current concerns as they relate to them. Whilst an international perspective is aimed for, inevitably the emphasis of the reader is based on concerns and issues in the United Kingdom. Readers from overseas, however, should find much that is appropriate and applicable to their own situations, as the general principles are universal.

The second volume about collections management in the series considers the museum environment, care and handling of collections, transportation, packing, storage and disaster preparedness.

Within the series, the two volumes that deal with collections management attempt to cover the main aspects of the subject, though inevitably there are some areas of overlap and exclusion. The reader is not advised to see each volume in the series in isolation from the others, as there are many links between them. Decisions made about objects, from a collections management perspective, may impact upon how the museum develops its communication policy or educational policies, or the special needs of specific collections may influence managerial decisions relating to the use of existing resources. Similarly, the history and philosophy of museums and the history of collecting have a direct influence upon many of the collections management decisions taken by today's curators. The historical development of the collections and the ways in which they are managed affect all other activities in which the museum is involved. The reader should attempt, first, to make connections between all the volumes in the series, by looking for areas of comparability and also difference; and second, to think about how museum finance or marketing programmes may affect the collections and to consider how the ways in which curators approach objects and interpret them can influence collecting decisions, display decisions and even disposal decisions.

Finally, collections management has often been perceived as being a deeply practical aspect of museum work, and on a day-to-day basis it is. However, it is essential to recognize that an understanding of the principles of collections management is critical to the development of good practice. Without a knowledge of the development of collections and of material culture, it is impossible to construct new ways of collections development and understand the role of museums in contemporary society.

CONTEXT: CONTEMPORARY ISSUES

This section will look at some of the external issues affecting collections management in museums today. The Museums Association defines a museum as 'an institution which collects, documents, preserves, exhibits and interprets material evidence and associated information for the public benefit' (Museums Association 1992). Within this definition lies the heart of museums: the collection, recording, preservation and exhibition, with all that it entails, of material evidence – objects. Whether a museum collects natural historical, military, archaeological or fine art material, it is the objects that make the museum unique from other heritage attractions, and from the collections that curators and museum managers generate their publications, research programmes, exhibition and educational programmes, and so on. All museum programmes, from visitor services, educational services, publication, etc., have the collections at their core in that they provide the source material for such programmes. In order to carry out all of these activities, the museum relies upon the collections being stored appropriately to prevent deterioration, and being protected against breakage and damage and exposure to harmful environmental conditions, fire, theft and disaster. In addition, objects must be recorded to a standard, so that the museum is able to account, locate and provide information about them. Objects must be accessible, via public exhibition, information services and loans, and finally, they must be legally accounted for, to ensure that the museum behaves in a responsible and ethical fashion.

But what is collections management? It is a blanket term applied to the physical care and documentation of collections. Because it is so broad, it effectively encompasses a wide range of activities which may at times appear to be disparate. What they have in common is the objective of protecting the collections and their associated information from degradation, theft and destruction, and permitting physical and intellectual access to the objects. Such activities are not new, and have formed part of basic curatorial care for many years.

The development of standards

Since the mid-1980s public attention has been focused upon the management of collections as a result of published surveys and reports which have been critical of standards of collections management in national and non-national museums in the United Kingdom.

The National Audit Office Report on the *Management of the Collections of the English National Museums* (National Audit Office 1988) expressed direct concern about standards of inventory control and storage in some national museums. Reports in the non-national sector have expressed similar concerns (Ramer 1989; Kenyon 1992) and all these have compounded to present an image of museums in a state of disarray, unable to account for their collections and incapable of caring for them appropriately.

In order to counter such problems, there has been a proliferation of schemes and incentives to improve collections care, co-ordinated by the Museums and Galleries Commission and the Area Museum Councils. All of these have the general aim of improving knowledge and understanding of collections management in practical terms, through the provision of grant aid for specific projects aimed at raising standards, and through the dissemination of knowledge, via training courses and publications.

By far the most significant scheme in the United Kingdom has been the Museums and Galleries Commission's National Registration Scheme (Museums and Galleries Commission 1988). Through setting minimum standards for collections care and public service, museums are able to improve standards or use the scheme as a means for obtaining funds to implement projects to raise standards. Achieving registered status brings access to Museums and Galleries Commission and Area Museum Council funds, along with a 'kite mark' of approval to encourage public confidence in the museum. Indeed, one of the stated aims of the scheme has been to foster public confidence in museums. In addition the scheme has also won support from other grant-giving agencies, such as the National Heritage Memorial Fund, who will also limit its aid to those museums that have achieved registered status.

Undoubtedly, the National Registration Scheme has raised standards in museums, but there remains the concern for those museums who have either failed to achieve registered status, or who have chosen not to participate in the scheme. Will museums in the future consist of the haves and have-nots? Of those museums that are registered, with all that it encompasses, and those that are not? What will it mean for those museums in the future in terms of levels of care, and access to advice and support?

The Registration Scheme is to continue into its second phase and all museums will be invited to apply to register in 1995. No museum is guaranteed registered status, even if it achieved it in the first phase. Each phase will build upon and expand existing criteria and it is possible that some museums may consider the benefits of registration to be insufficient to merit the effort required to go through to the next phase, particularly if major capital expenditure is required to meet the new standards.

Hand in hand with the Registration Scheme have been other standards initiatives. The Area Museum Councils have used the grant-in-aid schemes to encourage museums to improve standards of management through the development of collections management policies, and grant-aid has been focused upon physically improving collections care.

On the policy side, the Registration Scheme requires that each museum should have a fully thought out and approved acquisition and disposals policy, and some Area Museum Councils have gone further by including the development of collections management policies as part of their requirements for grant aid. A collections management policy has been defined by Malaro as 'a detailed written statement that explains why a museum is in operation and how it goes about its business, and it articulates the museum's professional standards regarding objects left in its care' (Malaro 1985: 43). Whilst the development of an acquisitions and disposal policy is a significant step for a museum's policy-making, a fully developed collections management policy – which incorporates all aspects of collections management, (from acquisition, disposal, incoming and out-going loans, storage, documentation, insurance, security and inventories, to packing and transportation) – allows museum management to demonstrate that consideration has been given to the museum's position on all collection-related activities. Thus, the museum should be able to provide clear and workable guidelines for staff about how to respond in situations where a decision may be required, the correct procedures to follow for acquisition, disposal, etc., to avoid giving offence to those who have requests to make of the museum which may be contrary to policy, and to openly demonstrate that the museum is behaving in a legal and ethical manner in all its collection activities. Once developed, the policy should be implemented through procedural manuals and it should be reviewed to ensure that it is consistent with the museum's changing aims and objectives. It could be regarded as a case for concern that the MGC Registration Scheme requirement at present limits itself to the development of acquisition and disposal policies, whereas museums need to consider the whole range of their collections management activities.

Improved collections management has also been the aim of a number of publications which have addressed the practicalities of collections care. Publications such as *Museum Basics* (Ambrose and Paine 1993), the revised edition of the *Manual of Curatorship* (Thompson 1992), the ICOM Security Committee's publication *Museum Security. A Handbook* (ICOM and the International Committee on Museum Security 1993) have attempted to provide the museum sector with up-to-date information about good collections management on the policy side, as well as providing practical information. Particularly significant has been the series of publications on standards in the care of collections produced by the Museums and Galleries Commission, which addresses the individual needs of specific types of collections. So far, three standards have been produced, for archaeological, geological and biological collections, with others planned. They provide guidelines for museums relating to the policy and practical aspects of looking after collections.

Within individual areas, standards work is also underway. The Museums Security Adviser, based at the Museums and Galleries Commission, has also done much to improve standards of security in museums and to raise awareness of security issues in museums in the United Kingdom. The Security Adviser advises museums about security matters and ensures that all museums receiving Government Indemnity meet specific standards of security. This ongoing work is complemented by that of ICOM and the International Committee on Museum Security, whose publication was mentioned briefly above, but who also retain an overview on international security matters.

The Government Indemnity Scheme has now broadened its requirements to include standards for environmental control and monitoring in venues. The gradual introduction of higher standards for security and environmental controls has meant that museums have been able to phase in the necessary improvements in buildings over time, and many organizations have been aided by the provision of grants from the Museums and Galleries Improvement Fund.

Recent trends in museum documentation have also focused heavily upon the development of standards. The Museum Documentation Association has embarked upon an ambitious programme with the UK Museum Documentation Standard to provide a procedural standard for all aspects of documentation, along with a guide to the fields of information the museum should record to meet the standard. The UK Museum Documentation Standard has the aim of improving standards in documentation through the provision of guidelines and examples of good practice, firmly based within the existing legal and ethical context. Eventually, the standard should encourage the exchange of information between museums and other organizations. The work of the MDA UK Museum Documentation Standard is firmly linked with international standards development work under the auspices of CIDOC, the international documentation committee of the

International Council of Museums. At the same time, other US-based initiatives, such as the Computer Interchange of Museum Information Committee (CIMI), a project to develop a technical framework for the exchange of electronic information, independent of existing systems (Perkins 1992), the Art Information Task Force, which is developing a standard for recording art-historical information (Hansen 1991), and the American Association for State and Local History's Common Agenda programme to develop a History Museum Standard for recording social history objects (Sander 1991), are all indicators of the general concern with developing common standards.

The development of standards in many aspects of collections management, accompanied by the link with central government funds, will eventually improve standards of care and raise awareness in some museums. Other benefits of increased standardization in collections care and documentation practices are the potential for increased mobility between museum staff, who will not have to learn new systems in every museum they work in; in the field of documentation, museums may be able to exchange information between each other more readily and easily than they have hitherto. This is an exciting prospect and may have profound implications upon the ways in which museums disseminate information about their collections.

One element that has pervaded the growth in standards has been the recognition that museums are publicly accountable organizations. This has to some extent been forced upon museums, as central government policy has affected both local government and national museums through local government review and reorganization and control over funding. However, accountability has become the watchword of museums as they have tried to demonstrate that they are worthy of public funds, through their public programmes, and that they are well-managed organizations, through improved collections care and greater accessibility to collections information.

CULTURAL PROPERTY CONCERNS

Events in the world have brought renewed fears about how countries can effectively protect important cultural items. First, the removal of trade barriers on 1 January 1993 between the twelve member states of the European Union raised questions about how the member states would be able to prevent the export of important cultural items once the trade barriers were removed. Second, the collapse of the Eastern Bloc has meant that new opportunities have opened up for both the legal and illegal trade in cultural property from these cash-hungry but culturally rich states. Finally, conflict in Kuwait, the former Yugoslavia and other parts of the world has demonstrated that cultural property is vulnerable to removal and destruction, even when 'protected' by the 1954 Hague Convention for the Protection of Cultural Property in the Event of Armed Conflict.

Let us consider the European Union first. The Treaty of Rome, which founded the EEC in 1957, included the freedom of movement of goods, services, capital and people within the European Community. In terms of protecting cultural property, Article 36 of the Treaty of Rome would appear to be the key mechanism, as it permits the member states to protect any national treasures that contain artistic, archaeological or historic value. In this way, the member states are allowed to protect their cultural property against export. As a result, they have used Article 36 to maintain their own national export restrictions, and this pack contains an example from the United Kingdom. In addition, the EU is also developing mechanisms for the return of material that has been removed in contravention of the protective measures of the member states.

The European Union has twelve members and Article 36 is applicable only to those member states. What then is the situation on a global scale?

Throughout the twentieth century there has been in operation a highly profitable legal trade in cultural material. Equally, there has been a thriving illegal trade of items which have either been stolen from their owners or from archaeological and other sorts of sites, or which have been removed in direct contravention of the prevailing legislation of the country of origin. The illegal trade in cultural property can result in the whole-sale destruction of archaeological sites, with the commensurate loss of information about the object and its provenance; it may encourage crime and may even result in the eventual loss of the cultural inheritance of ethnic groups in vulnerable areas.

To protect themselves against such losses and to control the movement of cultural material via the legal trade, many states have introduced mechanisms to control the movement of cultural property within their borders (in some cases) and beyond. In states where it may be considered that there have been major losses in the past, to such an extent that the cultural heritage is diminished, stringent regulations may be in force that prohibit the exportation of cultural material (for example, Italy, Greece and Turkey). Other states operate systems of selective export, screening only to retain the most important objects, whilst at the same time maintaining free trade (such as the UK, Canada, Denmark and Japan). Some states, such as France, also keep lists of items of such national importance that they cannot be exported, whilst others, such as Mexico, have declared national ownership of specific groups of material. In Mexico, such has been the concern over the loss of Pre-Columbian items that the state has declared national ownership of this group of material, which places restrictions over its ownership and movement.

To varying degrees, all of these systems attempt to protect and control the movement of cultural property. However, in spite of such measures, objects do find their way on to the black market and emerge in states other than their country of origin. Once this has occurred how can a state recover the material which has been illegally removed?

The answer will depend upon whether the state from which the object originated and the state to which it has been removed are members of the EU, or if they are signatories of the UNESCO Convention on the Means of Prohibiting and Preventing the Illicit Import, Export and Transfer of Ownership of Cultural Property, 1970. If both states are members of the EU then the mechanisms being set up by the EEC will come into play. If they are signatories of the 1970 Convention, then it will apply. If they are neither, then they may encounter serious difficulties.

The UNESCO Convention is significant because it has the greatest number of signatories, including the USA, Italy and Canada. It aims to establish international co-operation to fight the illegal traffic in cultural property, through the recognition that the illicit traffic is a major cause of the impoverishment of the cultural heritage of many states. The Convention places reciprocal obligations on its members and requires them, amongst other things, to introduce mechanisms to oppose the illegal movement of cultural property between states.

Within the Convention, museums and other similar institutions are prevented from acquiring illegally exported material, and the spirit of the Convention is enshrined in the codes of conduct and ethics of museums associations across the world, in that they emphasize that museums should be certain that any items they acquire have not been stolen, illegally imported or exported from their country of origin, or illegally collected through removal from a protected site or habitat, or that the items themselves are protected by law.

Through international co-operation, under the auspices of the International Council of Museums, museums can reaffirm their commitment to the acquisition of only fully provenanced material, by making every effort they can to ensure that the objects they collect are legally acquired. Equally, they should refuse to collect any item of uncertain provenance and should attempt to educate public opinion about the effects of the illegal trade. They can also inform each other about losses from their countries and organizations via the network of national and international organizations that are concerned with security and cultural property matters.

THE COSTS OF COLLECTING

With the recent emphasis upon the development of acquisition policies, there has also been a growth in interest in the actual costs of collecting. Indeed, it could be argued that the two go hand in hand; as museums develop responsible policies for acquisition, they need to examine the costs involved with collecting to ensure that their policy is appropriate to the organization.

A report written by Lord, Lord and Nicks (1989) produced an analysis of the actual costs of acquisition, including the initial costs of acquiring an object and ongoing operating costs associated with caring for, protecting and documenting collections. The study showed that there are always financial implications in acquisition; even if the object is being given to the museum, the museum will have devoted resources in terms of staff and time. There may even be packing and transportation costs (which may be significant for large items), along with carrying out initial conservation assessment to establish the exact condition of the object and research into the item to ensure that it is appropriate for the organization. Most museums do not quantify such commitment of time, staff and resources, but if they were to do so, they would consider that in some circumstances the cost of the acquisition has been considerable.

Once the museum has acquired an object, it must be documented, it may require conservation, and it will need secure, appropriate storage. Throughout its history with the museum resources will be allocated to it to ensure its survival, and these must be considered at the time of acquisition, particularly if the object has special requirements that may involve the museum in additional expenditure (for example, special lifting equipment).

Research into the costs of collecting will become increasingly important to museums if they have diminishing acquisition funds and restricted budgets to run their services. It is only sensible that acquisitions are made in the full knowledge of the ways in which the object can be used in the collections (via the collections policy) and the real cost of the acquisition to the museum. Using both of these tools, the museum should be able to make decisions relating to acquisitions, which reflect its aims and objectives, secure in the knowledge that they are able to give the object the care and resources it requires. In addition, they are able to demonstrate the wise use of diminishing resources in an efficient and cost-effective manner.

Linked with a more responsible approach to acquisition has been the recognition that there are occasions when a museum may need to remove items from the collections and dispose of them. Museum disposals is a very emotive and legally complex subject that has divided museum opinion for many years. However, disposal, if it is to be undertaken, must be within the context of a fully considered disposals policy, which has been approved by the museum's governing body. Furthermore, it must be implemented in strict accordance with the organization's procedures, in order to avoid adverse publicity and legal difficulties.

In the United Kingdom, there has always been a strong presumption against disposal, which is incorporated into the Museums Association's *Code of Practice for Museum Authorities* (Museums Association 1992) and also the Registration Scheme (Museums and Galleries Commission 1988), on the principle that museums hold objects in trust for the future and thus, if disposal should take place, the disposing museum should try to keep the object in the public domain, by gift, sale or exchange with another museum. Attitudes vary in other countries, with many museum professionals regarding disposal as a means of keeping collections dynamic. The papers included in this reader attempt to give both perspectives. Regardless of attitudes towards disposal, it is imperative that policy and procedures are developed and adhered to in order for the museum to demonstrate that it is operating legally and ethically.

CONCLUSION

In each of the sections of this chapter, an attempt has been made to present an overview of some of the main issues that have an impact upon collections management. They are not exhaustive and it is likely that some issues will remain prominent for some years, whilst others will become a thing of the past. Equally, there are concerns specific to particular groups of museums and regions that it has been impossible to include. Collections management is a fundamental part of museum work and it is hoped that this Reader in Museum Studies will provide the student of museum studies, or the new museum worker with an introduction to some aspects of collections management.

REFERENCES

Ambrose, T. and Paine, C. (1993) *Museum Basics*, London: Routledge.

Hansen, H. J. (1991) *Art Information Task Force*, CIDOC Newsletter, Vol. 3.

ICOM and the International Committee on Museum Security (1993) *Museum Security and Protection. A Handbook for Cultural Heritage Institutions*, London and New York: ICOM in conjunction with Routledge.

Kenyon, J. (1992) 'Collecting for the twenty-first century', *A Survey of Industrial and Social History Collections in the Museums of Yorkshire and Humberside*, Yorkshire and Humberside Museums Council.

Lord, B., Lord, G.D., and Nicks, J. (1989) *The Cost of Collecting. Collection Management in UK Museums*, a report commissioned by the Office of Arts and Libraries, London: HMSO.

Malaro, M. (1985) *A Legal Primer on Managing Museum Collections*, Washington, D.C.: Smithsonian Institution Press.

Museums Association (1992) *Code of Practice for Museum Authorities. Museums Yearbook 1992/1993*, London: Museums Association.

Museums and Galleries Commission (1988) *Guidelines for a Registration Scheme for Museums in the United Kingdom*, London: Museums and Galleries Commission.

National Audit Office (1988) *Management of the Collections of the English National Museums and Galleries*, London: HMSO.

Perkins, J. (1992) 'CIMI's data movement', *Museum News* 71(4):24–6.

Ramer, B. (1989) *A Conservation Survey of Museum Collections in Scotland*, Edinburgh: Scottish Museums Council.

Sander, M. (1991) 'The Philadelphia story', *History News* 46(4):7–10.

Thompson, J.M. (ed.) (1992) *The Manual of Curatorship*, Oxford: Butterworth-Heinemann.

Part 1
Collections management policies

1

Collection management policies

Marie Malaro

Marie Malaro has been one of the major contributors on the subject of the law and collections management. One tool she advocates, the collections management policy, articulates the museum's activities in its collections care, demonstrating that the museum is behaving legally and responsibly towards its collections. This chapter from her book A Legal Primer on Managing Museum Collections *clearly sets out the reasons why a museum should consider developing a collections management policy and how to prepare one.*

A. Why a Collection Management Policy?

B. Guidelines for Preparing a Collection Management Policy

A. WHY A COLLECTION MANAGEMENT POLICY?

- 'Our museum has quite a few objects that we have had for years, but we aren't sure if we own them. We would like to dispose of the objects, can we?'
- 'Every year, our museum ends up taking objects we don't really want. How can we control this?'
- 'Frequently, staff members are asked to provide appraisals for donors. We oblige but feel uneasy about it. How should these situations be handled?'

These are common questions from the museum community and the queries themselves reflect a degree of uncertainty regarding the role of the museum and the responsibilities of its officers and staff. Without clear direction, poor decisions are bound to be made and for a museum many such 'mistakes' have no easy solutions. The best approach is prevention, and a suggested technique is the adoption of a collection management policy.

A collection management policy is a detailed written statement that explains why a museum is in operation and how it goes about its business, and it articulates the museum's professional standards regarding objects left in its care. The policy serves as a guide for the staff and as a source of information for the public.

A good collection management policy covers a broad range of topics:

1 The purpose of the museum and its collection goals.
2 The method of acquiring objects for the collections.
3 The method of disposing of objects from the collections.

4   Incoming and outgoing loan policies.
5   The handling of objects left in the custody of the museum.
6   The care and control of collection objects generally.
7   Access to collection objects.
8   Insurance procedures relating to collection objects.
9   The records that are to be kept of collection activities, when these records are to be made, and where they are to be maintained.

Each of the above-mentioned topics raises a host of issues that must be considered if comprehensive and practical guidance is to be offered in the policy itself. Many of these issue are listed in the 'Guidelines for preparing a collection management policy', which follows this section. The very exercise of reviewing and coming to terms with these issues provides a worthwhile educational opportunity for museum officers and staff. All who participate cannot help but emerge with a better appreciation of their respective roles and with a firmer grasp of important basic principles.

The guidelines should not be viewed as a rigid format for the preparation of a collection management policy. Their purpose is to provoke thought and discussion. The form and content of any policy rests essentially with the individual museum, and it should be tailored to the needs of the museum. A collection management policy is not unlike a pair of eyeglasses; both are effective aids to perception only if individually prescribed and faithfully used.

Drafting a collection management policy is not an easy task. It requires much communication among staff members and frank discussion between staff and board members. Areas of uncertainty or disagreement must be resolved and adjustments made. The objective in drafting the policy is not to attempt to solve all possible problems, but to define areas of responsibility and to set forth guidelines for those charged with making certain decisions. The completed policy should be approved by the board or entity charged with overall governance of the museum and, once in effect, the policy should serve as a formal delegation of responsibilities.

As noted in the Preface, one of the objectives of [*A Legal Primer on Managing Museum Collections*] is to stress 'prevention' and for this reason, it is urged that the book be used as a tool for drafting or perfecting a collection management policy.[1] Each chapter serves this end. Chapters I and II, on the nature of a museum and its accountability, provide essential background material for understanding the role of a museum, the duties of governing boards and the obligations owed the public. Chapter III . . . introduces the general topic of collection management and provides guidelines for drafting a collection management policy. Subsequent chapters discuss specific collection-related problems, but these should not be read in isolation. They presuppose an understanding of the material in the preceding chapters.

B. GUIDELINES FOR PREPARING A COLLECTION MANAGEMENT POLICY[2]

These guidelines are offered as a checklist for the museum interested in drafting or revising a collection management policy. Most of the issues raised in the guidelines are treated in detail in the following chapters. Chapters I and II, which concern the legal nature of a museum and its accountability, are suggested as useful preliminaries before work on a policy is begun.

1 General comments

A collection management policy is a comprehensive written statement that sets forth the goals of a museum and explains how these goals are pursued through collection activity. One of the main functions of the policy is to guide staff members in carrying out their responsibilities. The policy, therefore, must be detailed enough to provide useful instruction and yet avoid procedural minutiae. (The latter are subject to frequent revision and are more appropriately handled in supplementary documents.) Flexibility is essential also in order to permit prudent *ad hoc* decisions. These objectives can be achieved by bearing in mind the following:

- Define areas of responsibility clearly.
- Where possible, delegate final decision-making authority to one individual or group.
- Establish policy but, where appropriate, permit decision-making authorities to grant exceptions in unusual circumstances.
- Stress the maintenance of complete, written records regarding all collection-related decisions.[3]

2 Definitions

As used in these guidelines:

- A *collection object* is an item that has been or is in the process of being accessioned into the collections.
- *Accessioning* is the formal process used to accept and record an item as a collection object.
- *De-accessioning* is the formal process used to remove permanently an object from the collections.[4]
- *Loans* are temporary assignments of collection objects from the museum or temporary assignments of similar objects to the museum for stated museum purposes, such as exhibition and research. These assignments do not involve a change in ownership.
- *Objects placed in the custody of the museum* are items that are not owned by the museum but are left temporarily in the museum for other than loan purposes, such as for attribution, identification or examination for possible gift or purchase.

3 Drafting the policy

(a) Statement of purpose and description of collections

The introductory 'statement of purpose' should be written so that it sets forth such basic information as:

- The purpose of the museum.
- The present scope and uses of the museum's collections.
- The more immediate goals of the museum as they relate to the collections.

Statutes and legal documents pertinent to the establishment of the museum should be explained as well as the role of any museum boards or committees involved in collection procedures.[5] If the museum maintains more than one type of collection (for example, permanent collection, study collection, school collection), the 'statement of purpose' section may be a convenient place to describe each type and its rationale. When a museum lists more than one type of collection, differences in the handling of these collections, if any, then should be noted appropriately in its collections policy.

13

The drafting of the statement of purpose can prove to be a challenge, especially for the small organization with very limited financial resources. How focused must collecting be in order to assure sufficient depth? What portions of time and money should be allocated to collecting? to exhibits? to educational outreach? Has there been a realistic appraisal of the resources it takes to support a collection (record-keeping, storage, conservation, exhibits)? Each of these questions, and others, must be considered before a realistic statement of purpose can be produced. One article which describes a particular historical society's efforts to draft a statement of purpose puts it this way:

> What the committee was actually wrestling with was a question of finding a comfortable middle ground between the ideal and carelessness. ... Few, if any, historical organizations have the personnel or funding to pursue the ideal. What is necessary is to have an understanding of professional standards and then to develop a plan that best approaches the ideal, based on the organization's resources.[6]

Because the statement of purpose is a very crucial element in any collection management policy, it is a prudent step to go back and thoughtfully re-examine the articulated purpose after the entire policy has been drafted. What has been learned in the drafting process should provide a basis for more critical review.

(b) Acquisition of objects

Objects may be added to collections by means of gifts, bequests, purchases, exchanges, field work acquisitions, or any other transactions by which title to the objects passes to the museum. In stating criteria for determining whether an object should be added to a collection, some basic considerations are:

- Is the object consistent with the collections goals of the museum?
- Is the object so unusual that it presents an exceptional opportunity for the museum and thus should be given preferential consideration?
- If the object is offered for sale, might it or a comparable object be obtained by gift or bequest?
- Can the proper care be given to the object?
- Is the object something which probably should be refused because it is of marginal value or interest?
- Will the object be used in the foreseeable future and is there a good faith intention to keep it in the museum's collection for the foreseeable future?
- Is the provenance of the object satisfactory and how is this decision made?
- Is the object encumbered with conditions set by the donor (for example, a requirement that it be permanently displayed)? How are decisions made on such matters and by whom?
- Is the use of the object restricted or encumbered by (1) an intellectual property (copyright, patent, trademark, or trade name) or (2) by its nature (for example, obscene,[7] defamatory, potentially an invasion of privacy, physically hazardous)? How are decisions made on matters of this nature and by whom?
- Will the acceptance of the object, in all probability, result in major future expenses for the museum (for example, for conservation, maintenance, or because it opens a new area of collecting)?

The policy should state clearly the procedures to be followed in accessioning, who makes the final decision, what records must be made of the process, when the records are to be made and by whom, and where the records are to be maintained.

In determining the procedure and the appropriate level of authority for accepting items for the collections, distinctions may have to be made on the basis of such factors as size or extent of the objects, value, cost of maintenance, restrictions on use.

As a general rule, objects should not be accepted unless they are destined for particular collections for the foreseeable future. Exceptions to this rule should be permitted only with the knowledge of the donors and with due consideration to the satisfactory disposition of unwanted objects.[8]

Advice should be given regarding the appraisal of objects by the staff in response to outside requests. As a rule, museums avoid doing formal appraisals, especially at the request of donors or prospective donors. Deviations from the museum's standard practice should require the approval of an appropriate museum official.[9]

(c) De-accessioning

As a general rule, collection objects may be de-accessioned unless there are specific restrictions to the contrary. In stating criteria for determining whether an object should be removed from a collection, some basic considerations are:

- Are there any restrictions which may prohibit removal? What is the procedure for resolving such questions?
- Is the object no longer relevant and useful to the purposes and activities of the museum?
- Is there danger of not being able to preserve the object properly?
- Has the object deteriorated beyond usefulness?
- Is it doubtful that the object can be used in the foreseeable future?
- Is there a need to weed out redundant items?
- Is there a need to improve or strengthen another area of the collections in order to further the goals of the museum?
- Have the interests and reactions of the public been considered?

The policy should state clearly the procedures to be followed in de-accessioning, such as who makes the final decision, what records must be made of the process, when the records are to be made and by whom, and when the type and value of the object under consideration may dictate such additional precautions as a higher level of approval than ordinarily required and the need for outside appraisals.

The issue of acceptable methods of disposal also may be addressed. Some basic considerations are:

- May objects be disposed of by exchange, donation or sale?
- Will preference be given to any particular method(s) of disposal?
- Will scholarly or cultural organizations be preferred as recipients rather than private individuals or commercial entities?
- Will local or national interests be given weight in deciding on the recipient?
- If an object has seriously deteriorated, may it be designated for other uses or destroyed?
- If donors of items to be de-accessioned are alive, as a matter of courtesy are they to be notified of the intent to de-accession?
- How are funds realized from de-accession sales to be used?

(d) Loans

1 Outgoing loans

In general, museums expect to lend objects only to similar institutions. The major reasons for this practice are to afford the loaned object adequate environmental protection, to assure adequate safety precautions, to encourage research on and public enjoyment of the object, and to avoid use of the object for private gain. In drafting loan statements, these reasons should be borne in mind. Also, it is recognized that justifiable distinctions can be made between the loan of a painting and, say, the loan of a plant specimen. Following are some of the matters which should be addressed:

- When are loans from the collection made and for what purposes? To whom will loans be made?
- Who has the authority to approve loans from the collection?
- If unusual restrictions are to be placed on a proposed outgoing loan, who must approve the loan?
- Will items be lent if there is a question whether they can withstand travel, extra handling or climate changes? How are such matters resolved?
- To ensure proper accounting, should all loans be made for specified periods of time (with options for renewal)?
- What procedures must be followed by the staff in proposing and processing a loan? What is the museum's policy regarding facilities reports on prospective borrowers? What records are necessary, when must they be made and by whom, and where are these records to be maintained?
- Who has the responsibility for monitoring a loan? What procedures are to be followed in connection with a loan whose period is about to expire or when a loan is overdue?

2 Incoming loans

The following questions, some of which are identical to those applying to outgoing loans, should be addressed in connection with incoming loans:

- When are objects borrowed and for what purposes? From whom may objects be borrowed?
- Who has the authority to approve an incoming loan?
- If a prospective lender places unusual restrictions on a proposed loan, who in the museum must approve the loan and assure compliance?
- How are decisions arrived at concerning the provenance of an item that may be the subject of an incoming loan? (The mere possession of an object of doubtful provenance can have ethical ramifications and/or legal consequences.)[10]
- Will items be borrowed if there is a question whether they can withstand travel, extra handling or climate changes? How are such matters to be resolved?
- What procedures must be followed by the staff in proposing and processing an incoming loan? What records are necessary, when must they be made and by whom, and where are these records to be maintained?
- Who has the responsibility for monitoring a loan? For packing and shipping the material when it is to be returned?

(e) Objects left in the custody of the museum

It is prudent for a museum to record in some predetermined manner and within a reasonable time every object which is placed in its care. This means there should also be a registration method for objects, other than loans, left temporarily in the custody of the museum for such purposes as attribution, examination and identification. In addition, the registration method should be designed to encourage periodic review of these objects to ensure expeditious handling. Existing museum practices should be reviewed with these considerations in mind.

Authority to accept objects placed in the custody of the museum should be clearly delegated to specific individuals.

(f) Care of the collections

Guidance on the topic of care of the collections should touch on a range of issues, such as the following:

1   At all times, staff members should be aware of their responsibilities to preserve and protect collection objects. This rather obvious point might warrant repetition in the collection management policy.
2   Are the collections, whether on exhibition or in storage, adequately protected against fire, theft, vandalism and natural disaster? Are there established procedures for handling such emergencies? Who in the museum has oversight responsibilities in these areas?
3   Conservation of collection items is a continuing responsibility. Should there be a delegation of responsibilities to appropriate staff members to monitor conservation needs?
4   Appropriate attention should be given to the packing and shipping of collection items moving in or out of the museum. Who bears the responsibility for monitoring this?
5   Ideally, no collection item should ever leave its assigned collecting unit unless a written record of such movement is made and the record centrally filed.

(g) Records

The following comments may be helpful in judging the adequacy of a museum's record systems:

1   Each museum should have established systems for preservation of data on collections. Collection records may be divided into two general categories. The first includes records which are commonly associated with registration functions. These primarily document the legal status of an object within the museum or on loan from the museum, and that object's movement and care while under the control of the museum. The second category includes records associated with curatorial functions. These provide a broad body of information about an object which establishes the object's proper place and importance within its cultural or scientific sphere.
2   Good registration records normally include a descriptive catalogue record as well as evidence of legal ownership or possession of all objects. These record systems should relate to objects by a unique museum number (for example, accession number, loan number) and should provide for easy retrieval of object information as well as current object locations. Records of accessioned objects should further reflect the prior history of ownership of each object and all activity of such objects (loan, exhibit, restoration, de-accession). Records of objects on loan to the museum should reflect all activity of such objects while under the control of the museum.
3   Collection records should be timely made, housed in secure locations and physically preserved by proper handling and storage methods.

4   If possible, a duplicate copy of registration records (for example, microfiche) should be made and stored outside the museum as a security precaution.

(h) Insurance

Some questions concerning insurance that may be addressed are:

1   If funds are limited, what is the proper role of insurance versus, for instance, protection, conservation, packing and transportation requirements?
2   Is insurance to be carried on the museum's collections when these collections are in the custody of the museum? If so, are collections insured at full value or at a fraction of value?
3   Must outgoing loans be insured? If so, by whom? Who pays?
4   Must incoming loans be insured? If so, by whom? Who pays?
5   Are objects left in the custody of the museum insured?
6   What records must be kept regarding insurance and by whom?
7   Who has authority to approve deviations from established insurance procedures?

(i) Inventories

In order to police collection activities, a museum should establish inventory procedures. These procedures may address such topics as:

1   Uniform method of maintaining inventory records.
2   Periodic comprehensive inventories.
3   Spot-check inventories.
4   Procedures to be followed if collection items appear to be missing.

(j) Access to the collections

This section may cover such topics as:

1   Who has access to the collections? (Actual physical access as well as the obtaining of copies of collection or collection-related material.)
2   When can access be denied and by whom?
3   Are fees to be charged for record reproduction work? Before answering these questions, any 'freedom of information' and/or 'privacy' laws in effect in the locality should be reviewed. (A government-controlled museum may have more complex problems in the area of access.)

C. THE ROLE OF INSURANCE

Insurance should not be used as a cure-all for poor management. The 'don't worry, we're insured' approach may be the simplest, but it hardly comports with responsibilities to care for and preserve cultural objects. If viewed from the proper perspective, insurance, as a rule, should be the last resort for the museum manager. Prevention rather than reimbursement should be the primary goal.

The term 'risk management' is in vogue, and fundamentally it is the application of analysis and common sense to perceived risks. Museum officials responsible for advising on insurance needs should be familiar with the risk management technique, because it puts insurance in its proper place. Risk management deals with the identification, analysis and the evaluation of risk, and the selection of the most advantageous methods for handling it. It is an aggressive approach that seeks first to avoid, control, reduce or accept an identified risk before insuring against it. For example, if a museum has many valuable small objects in its collections and the question is whether they should be insured on-premises, the risk manager looks at such things as storage security, exhibit procedures, display cases, detection equipment, crowd control, inventory and record procedures, all with an eye to avoiding or reducing possible loss or damage. Such a review might demonstrate that museum time and funds are better spent on improving preventive procedures and equipment rather than on insurance coverage. Similarly, if the museum is experiencing a high rate of loss for incoming loans, the risk manager does not automatically budget more for insurance. First there is an investigation of why losses are increasing. Are too fragile objects being accepted? Are unpacking and packing procedures at fault? Are condition reports being done routinely so there is certainty as to when loss or damage occurs? An elevated loss rate is accepted only when the risk manager is satisfied that reasonable care has been taken down the line to avoid or control the situation. The general risk management approach is inherent in any prudent review of a museum's collection procedures, with the insurance programme viewed as the last bastion in the defence.

D. SELECTING A POLICY

An insurance policy amounts to a contractual arrangement between the museum and the insurance company with regard to specified risks. Having identified the types of risks it wishes to cover, a museum should be able to bargain intelligently regarding the terms of its insurance contracts. Effective bargaining requires some comprehension of the factors that will be weighed by the insurance company in deciding whether it will accept a risk (and at what price), otherwise the museum cannot hope to put its best foot forward.[11] Effective bargaining also requires the museum to accept only a policy which meets its precise needs and which does not strain staff capabilities.

According to Patricia Nauert and Caroline Black, authors of *Fine Arts Insurance, A Handbook for Art Museums*,[12] the committee of the Inland Marine Underwriters Association specializing in fine arts insurance considers the following to be the most common problems encountered when evaluating a museum risk.[13]

1 *Record-keeping*. The museum's records do not reflect accurately what is in storage, what is on display or what is on loan. As a result, insurance is either insufficient or excessive.
2 *Security*. There may be little protection against theft.
3 *Valuation*. There can be a range of problems associated with setting values and keeping them current.[14]

Other experts such as Irving Pfeffer list the following as significant risk factors for museums:[15]

1 *Hazards*. Fire and the related perils of smoke and water damage.
2 *Storage*. Careless placement of artefacts in storage containers as well as poor storage areas.
3 *Transportation*. Packing and shipping methods frequently are negligent.[16]

A museum preparing to bargain for insurance coverage is well-advised to review its situation with regard to the above, compile needed statistics, and, if necessary, initiate corrective measures that improve its attractiveness as a risk. Once again, the museum's collection management policy can come into play as a means of implementing good internal procedures and of demonstrating to a prospective insurer that management in the museum is not left to chance. Armed with relevant facts and figures on its operation, the museum is in a better position to bargain realistically (that is, sell its risk, not buy insurance) for the insurance it actually needs.

Any insurance policy that is under discussion should be reviewed carefully to be sure that it offers adequate protection and that it does not impose unrealistic demands upon the museum.[17] A wise precaution is to involve museum staff who will bear the burden of implementing policy requirements in the review. These points warrant special scrutiny:

1   Does the coverage clearly define the property the museum wishes to cover? For example, if a museum maintains several types of collections (permanent, study, education), is it clear which are covered? Is it clear which incoming and outgoing loan situations are covered and when coverage goes into effect? Are partial gift situations, jointly held property, remainder interest in property, and so on, covered? Are frames, display cases, and other auxiliary materials covered?

2   Are the territorial limits of coverage adequate, and what is the most economical method for obtaining coverage for occasional shipments beyond normal traffic areas?

3   Are the perils insured against and the exclusions realistic? Most policies are 'all risks' with named exclusions. This is a more advantageous approach for museums because it is easier to evaluate specified exclusions than it is to list all possible perils. There is some leeway in negotiating certain exclusions, with corresponding rate adjustments, but the exclusions that usually survive in an 'all risk' policy are:
   • Wear and tear, gradual deterioration, insect, vermin, inherent defects (sometimes referred to as inherent vice) or damages caused by repairing, restoration or retouching.
   • War, insurrection rebellion, revolution or civil war.
   • Nuclear damage.
   • Shipments by mail, unless registered, first-class or insured parcel post (and with possible limitations on dollar value).[18]

4   Are the procedures for establishing valuations realistic? For example, if valuation is based on the fair market value at the time of loss, there is no critical pressure to constantly readjust book valuations. But what if a claim is for a borrowed object with an insurance value preset by the owner under the terms of the loan agreement? It may be necessary to distinguish between procedures used in valuing objects loaned to the museum and those used in valuing the museum's own objects. In any event, the museum should understand clearly the policy terms in this area and make sure that its internal methods for setting values mesh.

5   A 'pairs and sets' clause can be important. Such a clause provides that if any of the pieces which make up a pair or set is lost, the insured has the option to claim a total loss for the pair or set. However, it should be borne in mind that if total loss is paid, the remainder of the pair or set (as with an object declared a total loss) becomes the property of the insurance company.

6   Consider, also, a 'buy back' provision. This gives the insured the right to buy back from the insurance company a lost or stolen item that is recovered after the claim has been paid.

7   Is it prudent to include deductibles or franchises in order to reduce premiums? With a deductible, no claim is made if the loss is less than the stated deductible. With a franchise, the insurance pays the entire amount if the loss equals or exceeds the amount of the franchise. In deciding whether such clauses are prudent, the museum must consider its ability to respond with museum funds to cover losses or repairs falling below these limitations.

A museum purchasing insurance coverage for collection objects can be faced with a variety of proposals. Selection can be difficult because there is no standard collections insurance policy presently in use. Efforts have been made to draft model forms but only recently has one such proposal begun to attract considerable attention.[19] That proposal, the work of Phillip Babcock and Marr Haack can serve as a useful checklist when evaluating insurance proposals,[20] and, in addition, the model purposely was written in 'plain English' so that it can be understood even by the novice. In time, if a standard policy is adopted by the museum community, most questions between borrower and lender concerning the adequacy of insurance coverage should disappear.

NOTES

1 As of 1984, the Accreditation Commission of the American Association of Museums considers a written collection policy an essential for a museum seeking accreditation.
2 This section is based on presentations made by the author in 1979 and 1981 to the American Law Institute–American Bar Association seminars on 'Legal problems of museum administration'. Copyright 1979 and 1981 by the American Law Institute. The substantial reprinting of these presentations is with the concurrence of the American Law Institute–American Bar Association Committee on Continuing Professional Education.
3 An article, 'The future of museum registration', by Richard Porter, *Museum News* 5 (August 1984), discusses the growing importance to a museum of a skilled registrar.
4 The term is generally accepted in the museum community though not found in the dictionary. It is postulated that it is a corruption of 'decess', but many would explain it as an amalgamation of 'de' (to do the opposite of) and 'accession'.
5 Care should be taken to assure that the activities of the museum are in accord with its articles of incorporation or charter, etc. See, for example, *Queen of Angels* v. *Younger*, 66 Cal. App. 3rd 366, 136 Cal. Rptr. 36 (1977); *Holt* v. *College of Osteopathic Physicians and Surgeons*, 61 Cal. 2d 750, 394 P.2d 932, 40 Cal. Rptr. 244 (1964); *Rowan* v. *Pasadena Art Museum*, No. C 322817 (Cal. Sup. Ct., L.A. County, Sept. 22, 1981).
6 Broenneke and Petersen, (1984) 'Planning for change', 39 *History News* 12 at 14 (No. 8, August).
7 This text does not cover the topic of obscenity. See, however, Chapter 3 of Merryman, J. and Elsen, A. (1979) *Law, Ethics and the Visual Arts*, New York: Matthew Bender; Chapter 7B of Feldman, F. and Weil, S. (1974) *Art Works: Law, Policy, Practice*, New York: Practising Law Institute; and Reisman, 'The legal obsession with obscenity: why are the courts still being challenged?', *Journal of Arts Management and Law* 54 (Fall 1983).
8 See Chapter IV, 'The meaning of the word accession', and Chapter XII, 'Tax considerations relevant to gifts.' [Refers to chapters in original book.]
9 See Chapter XIII, 'Appraisals and authentications.' [Refers to chapters in original book.]
10 See discussion in Chapter IV [in the original book] on 'Circumstances that can affect the quality of title'.
11 It is the insurance underwriter who actually evaluates the risk and decides whether the company should accept certain coverage and at what rates. Naturally, a museum wants its circumstances to be presented to the underwriter in a favourable light.
12 Published in 1979 by AAMD and distributed by the American Association of Museums.
13 Fine arts insurance is a form of inland marine insurance.
14 Nauert, P. and Black, C. (1979) *Fine Arts Insurance: A Handbook for Art Museums* 27.
15 Pfeffer, I. (1976) 'Insuring museum exhibitions', 27 *Hastings L. J.* 1123.
16 One well-known insurance broker, Huntington Block, cites as the number one cause of museum collection claims 'accidents while objects are being handled or transported'. See Chapter 9 of Dudley, D. *et al.* (1979) *Museum Registration Methods*, Washington, D.C: American Association of Museums.
17 For example, if the policy calls for the museum to 'warrant' or 'guarantee' that something will be done, it is worth requesting that this be changed to read that the museum 'to the best of its ability' will, etc. Time limits should be checked for reasonableness and, rather than have to do something 'immediately', the museum might request a change to 'as soon as practicable'. With regard to 'proof of loss' provisions, see *Insurance Co. of America* v. *University of Alaska*, 669 P.2d. 954 (Ala. 1983).
18 Dudley, D. *et al.*, (1979) *Museum Registration Methods* 144.
19 See form prepared by John Lawton in Keck, C. *et al.* (1966) *A Primer on Museum Security* 26–30.

See also Vance, 'A proposed standard insurance policy', *Museum News* 21 (Sept. 1969), and Babcock, P. and Haack, M. (1981) 'Plain English collections insurance', *Museum News* 22 (July–August): 282–7.

20 This model policy has been endorsed by the American Association of State and Local History. It is reproduced in this text with the approval of the authors.

APPENDIX I: SAMPLE MODEL POLICY

Coverage features*

The Museum Collections form (see Figure 1.1) contains three insuring agreements, relating to permanent collections, loan collections, and legal liability for loan collections in the insured's care. The permanent collection can be insured for different amounts while on premises, in transit, and at other locations. The loan collections agreement provides 'wall-to-wall' coverage on borrowed collections the insured has agreed to insure, regardless of the duration of the loan. This agreement also applies to property owned by the insured that has been loaned to others. As with the permanent collection agreement, separate amounts can be arranged for loan collections on premises, in transit and at other locations. The legal liability agreement applies to the insured's liability (and related defence costs) for loss to collectibles in the insured's care when the insured has been instructed *not* to insure the property.

Coverage under all agreements is on an *all risks* basis, with the usual exclusions of wear and tear, gradual deterioration, insect or animal damage, inherent vice, nuclear risks and war. In addition, loss by extremes of temperature or humidity (mould or mildew, for example) are excluded if the property is not protected by environmental controls, unless loss results from another covered peril. Especially pertinent to museum exposures, loss resulting from repairing, restoration or retouching processes is also excluded. There are also exclusions of loss due to inventory shortage, loss to property shipped under an 'on deck' bill of lading, and loss to property sent by mail, (other than first-class or registered mail – see sample form).

Finally, there is an exclusion of loss caused by dishonest acts of officers or employees – an often underestimated loss exposure faced by museums. However, the form does cover such losses to the extent they exceed the museum's Fidelity bond limit or the Fidelity coverage deductible shown in the declarations. In other words, the policy can be written to provide excess Fidelity coverage.

Valuation of lost or damaged property is stated to be fair market value at the time of loss not to exceed the applicable limit of liability. There are a number of special provisions that apply to valuation in some instances, however. Loaned property, for example, is valued at the amount agreed upon by the lender and borrower. If there is no agreement, the amount of loss is valued at fair market value at the time of loss. Another special provision states that if the lost or damaged property is contemporary art that was designed by an artist and then constructed by the artist or a technician, the insurer may pay only for the cost of repair or replacement if the work can be repaired or replaced to the artist's specifications. Another clause permits the museum to buy back property for whose loss the insurer has already paid the museum. The terms of this provision are clearly stated in the sample form under 'Buy-back option'. The form also contains a 'Pairs and sets' clause.

*This introductory summary was first published in F.C. & S. Bulletins, August 1981

Of special interest is a condition stipulating that insured property will be packed and unpacked only by trained packers. There is also a clause entitled 'Conflicting terms' stating that the terms and conditions of the Museum Collections form prevail whenever they are in conflict with any other terms or conditions of the museum's policy. This refers to the fact that the Museum Collections form is not a free-standing document and is intended to be attached to the museum's regular Property insurance policy or, perhaps, the insurer's skeleton form for Inland Marine coverages.

Endorsements

The drafters have prepared two endorsements for use with the policy. One provides for reporting of values on either a monthly or an annual basis, and the other provides international coverage for property in transit or at another location. Without the latter endorsement, the regular policy territory is the continental United States, Alaska, Hawaii, and Canada, including losses occurring in transit between these places.

Fig. 1.1 Sample model policy form

Museum Collections Coverage

This agreement is designed to protect museum collections against all risks of direct physical loss or damage with some limitations.

Coverage Summary	Limits of coverage
Permanent Collections – locations	
1.	$
2.	$
• All other locations	$
• In transit	$
Loan Collection – locations	
1.	$
2.	$
• All other locations	$
• In transit	$
Legal Liability.	
International Coverage. This coverage applies only if a limit is shown and the International Coverage Endorsement is attached.	$
All Loss From any One Event. This is the most we'll pay for all loss from any one event no matter how many protected persons, property owners or financial interests are involved. This applies to all losses, expenses and salvage charges combined. Any amount we pay for a loss won't reduce this limit for loss from other events.	$

Deductibles.

$ Permanent collection

$ Loan collection

$ Fidelity Coverage

If we issue this agreement after the date your policy takes effect, we must complete these spaces and our representative must sign below.

Authorized representative

Reporting. If the museum Collection Reporting Endorsement is attached, we'll figure your premium on the basis of written reports you make to us. You'll report on a monthly or annual basis and pay the rate as indicated below.

☐   Monthly – Rate   per $100

☐   Annual – Rate   per $100

Policy issued to

Agreement takes effect

Policy number

What This Agreement Covers

This agreement protects museum collections indicated in your Coverage Summary against all risks of direct physical loss or damage. By museum collections we mean property of rarity or of artistic, scientific or historical significance. This includes property such as paintings, statuary, ancient artifacts and other property normally exhibited in museums. Frames, glasses, shadow boxes and other protective enclosures used to display the property are also covered.

Of course, there are some limitations to your coverage which will be explained later in this agreement.

Permanent collection. Your permanent collection consists of property you own and is covered on your premises. It's also covered while in transit to and from another location and while it's temporarily kept at that location for repair, restoration or storage.

We'll cover your permanent collection up to the separate limits shown in your Coverage Summary for premises, other locations and in transit.

Loan collection. Your loan collection consists of property of others loaned to you which you've been instructed to insure (verbally or in writing) and property owned by you which you've loaned to others. Your loan collection includes property on extended loan of six months or more as well as temporary loans. We'll cover this property on a 'wall to wall' basis, whether on exhibition or not. 'Wall to wall' means that we cover from the time Insured property is removed for shipping from the place it's normally kept, until it's returned there. Coverage also applies during transit and all phases of shipping and exhibition. If, before the return shipment, the owner specified that the property be returned elsewhere, we'll cover the property until it's returned to that place;

We'll cover your loan collection up to the separate limits shown in your Coverage Summary for premises, other locations and in transit.

Legal liability. If a limit is shown in the Coverage Summary for legal liability, we'll defend any suit brought against you for loss or damage to other people's collectibles in your care. This coverage applies when the owners of the property have instructed you not to insure it. Of course, if you have a signed release of liability from the owner, this coverage doesn't apply.

The limit shown in the Coverage Summary is the most we'll pay for defense costs and any judgment in any one loss.

Who's protected under this agreement. While this agreement is in effect, we'll cover your interest and the interest of the owners of covered property. We'll also cover the interest of temporary borrowers you've given custody of the property. But we won't cover the interest of transportation carriers, packers, or shippers. Nor will we cover the interest of others having temporary custody of property for storage or for any repairing, retouching or restoring process.

Where We Cover

We'll cover losses that occur in the continental United States, Alaska, Hawaii and in Canada. We'll also cover losses that occur in transit between these places.

If the International Coverage Endorsement is attached we will also cover losses according to that endorsement.

Exclusions – Losses We Won't Cover

Wear – deterioration – pests. We won't cover loss or damage resulting from any of the following causes:

- Wear and tear;
- Gradual deterioration; or
- Insect or animal pests like termites, moths or mice.

Inherent nature. We won't cover loss or damage resulting from the inherent nature of the property. By inherent nature we mean a quality in the property that causes it to deteriorate or to destroy itself.

Extremes of temperature or humidity. We won't cover loss or damage that results because covered property is kept at a location that isn't protected from extremes of humidity or temperature, unless the loss or damage results directly from another covered peril. For example, if your museum doesn't have the environmental controls to prevent excessive humidity, we won't cover mold or mildew damage to a painting unless that damage was directly caused by flooding or a leaking water pipe.

Repair. We won't cover loss or damage resulting from any repairing, restoration or retouching process if the loss results from this work. But if the work results in a loss that would otherwise be covered, we'll pay for the loss that results directly from the covered peril.

Mail. We won't cover loss or damage to property sent by mail unless it's sent by registered or by first class mail. But property sent by first class mail isn't covered if its value is more than $1,000.

Inventory shortage. We won't cover loss resulting from inventory shortage. Inventory shortage means a loss reflected in your records, but it can't be determined where, when or how the loss occurred.

Fidelity. We won't cover loss caused by any fraudulent, dishonest, or criminal act or series of related acts committed by your officers or employees even if there are others involved. However, we'll cover this loss once it exceeds your fidelity bond limit or the fidelity coverage deductible shown in the Coverage Summary, whichever is greater.

'On deck' shipments. We won't cover loss or damage to property shipped under an 'on deck' Bill of Lading.

Nuclear activity. We won't cover any loss caused by nuclear reaction, nuclear radiation, or radioactive contamination. And we don't intend these causes of loss to be considered fire, smoke, explosion, or any other insured peril. But we will cover direct loss by fire resulting from nuclear reaction, nuclear radiation or radioactive contamination if the loss

25

would otherwise be covered under this agreement.

War and government seizure. We won't cover any loss, damage or injury caused by: war (declared or undeclared), invasion, insurrection, rebellion, revolution, civil war, seizure of power, or anything done to hinder or defend against these actions. We won't cover seizure or destruction of your property under quarantine or Customs regulations, or confiscation by any government or public authority. Nor will we cover illegal transportation or trade.

Setting A Value On Property

If there's a covered loss, we'll consider the value of covered property to be the fair market value of your interest in the property at the time of loss. But in no case will we pay more than the applicable limits shown in the Coverage Summary.

The following special rules apply.

Loaned property. Property loaned to you which you've been instructed to insure or for which you may be liable will be valued at the amount agreed upon by you and the owner. If you and the owner didn't agree upon a value in advance, you and we will agree upon a value based on the fair market value at the time of loss.

Pairs and sets. There may be a total loss of one or more articles which are part of a pair or set. If you choose, we'll pay you the fair market value of the pair or set up to the limits of your coverage. If you choose this option, you'll give us whatever remains of the pair or set.

Contemporary art. Some contemporary art is designed by artists and then constructed by them or by technicians. If such a work is damaged and can be repaired or replaced to the artist's specifications, we'll pay only the cost of repair or replacement.

Buy-back option. If we recover property for which we have already paid you, you have the right to buy the property back from us. If the property is not damaged,

you'll pay the same amount we paid you, plus an amount for loss adjustment, recovery expenses and interest. The interest will be computed at 1% above the prime rate during the period between the date we paid you and the date you chose to re-purchase.

If we paid you for a total loss on damaged property, you have the right to buy back the damaged property. You'll pay the fair market value of the damaged property at the time of re-purchase.

We'll make every effort to notify you of your right to buy back damaged or recovered property. You'll have 60 days from the time you receive our notice to re-purchase the property.

Who We'll Pay

We'll adjust any loss with you or with the owners of the covered property. Our payments for losses will be made to you or any other person or organization you name.

Your Deductible

Your Coverage Summary may show deductibles for your permanent and your loan collections or for fidelity loss. If so, you'll be responsible up to that amount for each loss. We'll pay the rest of your covered loss up to the applicable limit of your coverage.

Other Insurance

Other insurance may be available to cover a loss. If so, we'll pay the amount of your loss that's left after the other insurance has been used up. But we won't pay more than the applicable limit of coverage under this agreement.

This section doesn't apply to insurance that the owners of property loaned to you may have. And the existence of the owners' insurance won't affect our responsibility to pay for a covered loss.

Of course, we won't pay a loss if you or the owner have already collected the loss from others.

Excess insurance. You agree not to purchase excess insurance without our permission. Excess insurance is insurance that applies after the limits of coverage under this agreement are used up.

Other Rules For This Agreement

Packing. You agree that the insured property will be packed and unpacked by trained packers.

Preserving your rights. You must do all you can to preserve any rights you have to recover your loss from others. If you do anything to impair these rights, we won't pay for your loss. You can, however, accept ordinary bills of lading from a shipper, even if they limit the carrier's liability for losses.

We won't attempt to recover any loss from museums or any other place borrowing covered property for exhibition. However, we must give our permission before you give a written release from responsibility of loss to any person or organization other than a museum.

Conflicting terms. The terms and conditions of this agreement apply whenever they are in conflict with any other terms or conditions in your policy, such as the General Rules or Conditions.

Expenses for reducing loss. When a covered loss occurs, you must do everything possible to protect the property from further damage. Keep a record of your expenses. We'll pay our share of reasonable and necessary expenses incurred to reduce the loss or protect covered property from further damage. We'll figure our share and your share of these expenses in the same proportion as each of us will benefit from them.

Insurance for your benefit. This insurance is for your benefit. No third party having temporary possession of the property, such as a transportation company, can benefit directly or indirectly from it.

Certificate of insurance. We may issue certificates of insurance to you. You'll have the authority to give these certificates to others.

Museum Collections Reporting Endorsement

This endorsement changes your Museum Collections Coverage

How Your Coverage Is Changed

Your Coverage Summary indicates that your premium is based on either annual or monthly written reports you make to us. We'll figure your premium by applying the rate shown for monthly or annual reporting to the values you report. You agree to keep accurate records of the location of covered property for the purpose of these reports.

Monthly reporting. Based on your records, you agree to make monthly reports to us in writing. Each month you'll report the total values of your loan collection (loans of less than 6 months durations) that were covered the previous month. Your reports are due within ten days after the last day of each month.

If the international Endorsement is attached, these conditions also apply to it. You'll also report the total values of your loan collection, that were covered while in international transit and at international locations during the previous month.

Annual reporting. Based on your records, you agree to make an annual report to us in writing. Each year you'll report the total values of your loan collection that were covered during each month. Your annual report is due within thirty days after the anniversary date of your policy or whenever your policy ends.

Other Terms
All other terms of your policy remain the same.

International Coverage Endorsement

This endorsement changes your Museum Collections Coverage

If a limit is shown for International Coverage in your Coverage Summary, we'll cover losses that occur at locations outside the continental United States, Alaska, Hawaii and Canada, except as noted below.

We'll also cover losses that occur while in transit to and from these locations.

Reporting Terms. The terms of the Museum Collection Reporting Endorsement also apply to International Coverage. You'll report on a monthly basis and pay the rate as indicated.

International Transit rate per shipment:

Airborne Shipments	per $100
Waterborne Shipments	per $100

International Locations

Rate per month	per $100

Where We Won't Cover. We won't cover losses that occur in transit to and from or at locations in:

Ocean Marine Terms. International Coverage as provided in this endorsement is also subject to the following American Institute Clauses:

- Delay
- Marine Extension Clauses

All other terms and conditions of the Policy not in conflict with the foregoing remain unchanged, it being particularly understood and agreed that the F.C. & S. clause remains in full force and effect, and that nothing in the foregoing shall be construed as extending this insurance to cover any risks of war or consequences of hostilities.

2

Evolving a policy manual

Arminta Neal, Kristine Haglund and
Elizabeth Webb

In this chapter the authors present well-argued reasons for defining museum policy and describe how one museum, the Denver Museum of National History, wrote its own policy manual.

Over the past twenty years, public servants in the United States have been increasingly called to account for their actions. Virtually every branch and level of government has been discussing and implementing codes of ethics that define the limits of activity of the individual in relation to his public service job. The impact of Watergate on the interest of both the private and public sectors in matters concerning the public trust cannot be overestimated. Inevitably, this interest now extends to those museums supported to any degree by public tax monies. Many museum professionals foresee that private institutions will become subject to the same kinds of ethical constraints that now operate in public institutions as federal support of museums increases through the National Endowments for the Arts and the Humanities, the National Museum Act and the Museum Services Act.

It is important to define in writing the standards by which the staff, administration and board of directors of a museum are guided. In response to a need expressed within the profession, a committee of the AAM is now revising the professional code of ethics written twenty-five years ago. The American Museum of Natural History, the Metropolitan Museum of Art, The Field Museum of Natural History and the New York State Association of Museums are some of the institutions that have developed formal, consistent and detailed policies and procedures that help to guarantee the proper stewardship of collections.

The Denver Museum of Natural History has followed suit. In August 1974, the director, Charles T. Crockett, established a collections policy committee composed of curatorial and administrative staff to formulate collections policies and procedures. The result is a fairly detailed but highly workable manual. Requests to borrow the manual have come from museums across the United States as well as from institutions in Canada, Sweden, Poland, Iran, Japan, Finland, Germany, Bulgaria and Kenya, reflecting an increasing worldwide concern for professional collections management. Reference copies of the manual are available in the AAM offices and the Office of Museum Programs at the Smithsonian Institution.

Portions of our manual have been adapted from written policies of other institutions, principally the American Museum of Natural History and the Field Museum, while other portions have been the result of our own particular circumstances. The manual is flexible and the Collections Policy Committee, a permanent group operating within the museum's hierarchy, provides recommendations to the director on any new or revised policies, procedures and guidelines, both general and departmental. The manual is divided into two major sections, the first of which deals with general policies. The second deals with specific departmental policies and procedures occasioned by the diversity of the museum's collections.

Different museums obviously have different needs, but some of the broad policy areas that may be successfully adapted by many museums are those that follow, summarized from the Denver Museum of Natural History manual.

ACQUISITIONS

Since the quality and relevance of collections are vital to the usefulness of a museum, acquisitions to the museum's collections should meet certain conditions:

- They should be relevant to the purposes and priorities of the museum.
- The museum must be able to provide the proper storage and care of the objects and insure their availability for research, education and exhibition purposes

The Denver Museum of Natural History observes United States and international laws on acquiring imported objects and will not accept objects collected under exploitive, irresponsible or illegal circumstances. Title to objects should be obtained free and clear of restrictions and qualifications of any type or manner. Every museum employee in a position to acquire objects for the collections should be reasonably assured that the museum can acquire valid and legal title to them.

If restrictions on the use of objects are unavoidable, every effort should be made to impose a reasonable limit on the time for which they shall apply and to define the conditions under which their force may terminate. It is extremely important that a notation of any restrictions remains as part of an object's permanent documentation.

Upon receipt of a donation, the Denver Museum of Natural History prepares signed copies of a donation record form, which is filed with the permanent records. The form includes the donor's name, address, phone number, date donation received, accession number and donation description, and requires the donor to certify that he has the legal capacity to convey the property to the museum.

DE-ACCESSION AND LOAN POLICIES

Objects in the collections should be retained permanently if they continue to be relevant and useful to the museum's purposes and activities, and if they can be properly stored, preserved and used. Objects may be removed from the collections by loan, sale, exchange, gift or disposal by intentional destruction only when certain conditions are met. Objects removed permanently from the collections, where there is a transfer of ownership involved, are de-accessioned.

- Curators may exchange or dispose of specimens or objects in the interest of improving the collections or when they no longer have relevance for the museum's purposes. Curators may lend them when public education and research can best be served.
- No outgoing loan, exchange or disposal of unique or extraordinary objects occurs without review by the Collections Policy Committee and approval of the director. At the Denver Museum of Natural History, extinct zoological specimens, type-specimens

and significant specimens figured, published or photographed in a professional or scientific reference fall into this category

Before de-accessioning any object from the collections, reasonable efforts are made to ascertain that the museum is free to do so legally. Objects to which restrictions of use or disposition apply are not de-accessioned until reasonable efforts are made to comply with the restriction conditions. Any questions concerning restrictions on or disposition of objects are referred to the museum's attorney.

Objects removed from the collections permanently are disposed of in accordance with the following principles:

- The manner of disposition chosen will be in the best interests of the museum, the public it serves, the public trust it represents in owning the collections, and the scholarly and scientific communities it represents.
- Historical, cultural or scientific material of a state or country should remain with the state or country respectively.
- Primary consideration will be given to transferring the objects to the museum's education department, and then through gift, exchange or sale to another tax-exempt public institution wherein they may serve a valid purpose in research, education or exhibitions. Under no condition will the museum remove from the public trust by sale or any other means, any item, man-made or nature-formed, which is of prime historical, cultural or scientific value

If objects superfluous to the museum's objectives are offered for sale, preference is given for sale at public auction or to the public market-place in a manner that best protects the interests, objectives and legal status of the museum.

- It is recommended that the proceeds realized from the sales be allocated to the purchase of materials for the collections or to otherwise support acquisition, management or preservation of collections.
- Objects will not be given or sold privately to museum staff, volunteers, members of the board of trustees or to their representatives

Exchange contracts and loan forms signed by both parties fully document each transaction.

Regarding incoming loans, no objects are borrowed for long-term use from any other institution or individual without a review by the Collections Policy Committee and approval of the director. This is due to the expense involved in housing, handling, maintaining, insuring and exhibiting these objects. Such objects, if approved, may or may not be insured by the museum against theft, loss or damage of any kind, and are handled in accordance with accepted museum procedures. Short-term loans to the museum for reference, comparison, photography or travelling exhibits are permissible. The curator must, of course, have full legal documentation regarding all arrangements. All travelling exhibits must be insured, the responsibility for the policy to be negotiated as part of the loan agreement. Other loan materials may be insured when deemed necessary.

APPRAISALS AND DONOR TAX DEDUCTIONS

Donations to the museum are tax-deductible as a charitable contribution for the value of the property as determined by an appraisal, receipt or other valid documentation.

In order to avoid any conflict of interest, staff members do not provide appraisals for donations. The donor should hire a professional appraiser and receive from him a written statement with a description of the items and his valuation; this must be received at the time of the donation. If in place of a professional appraisal, the donor has a valid receipt of purchase, the museum can provide a letter of acceptance from this information.

UNITED STATES AND INTERNATIONAL REGULATIONS

The Denver Museum of Natural History and its staff abide by all US and international laws and regulations concerning transfer of ownership and transportation of objects across political boundaries. Our museum's collections policy manual forbids the acceptance or acquisition of any object that is illegally imported into or illegally collected in the USA, or that is collected or recovered under circumstances that would support or encourage irresponsible damage to or destruction of biota, collecting sites, cultural or natural monuments or human burial places. However, the museum may accept objects that have been confiscated and offered to the museum by government authorities.

In 1970, 29 institutions signed the *Guidelines for Biological Field Studies*. These guidelines, among other things, identified to a degree the responsibility and ethics that should be observed by museums and their staffs in collecting biological specimens. Import and export laws in individual countries can and do become quite complex and confusing, and problems not covered by the *Guidelines for Biological Field Studies* still must be reckoned with in the fields of archaeology, ethnology, palaeontology and mineralogy.

PHOTOGRAPHIC POLICIES

The Denver Museum of Natural History does allow photographs to be taken in the galleries, although many museums do not afford their visitors this privilege. The museum does ask that photographs not be taken of an object that is the subject of copyright restriction. Also, photographs taken by visiting photographers may not be published without written permission from the director. If permission is granted, acknowledgement to the Denver Museum of Natural History must be given in the publication. Application may be made departmentally for permission to photograph specimens in the collections.

OBJECTS BROUGHT IN FOR EXAMINATION

The museum staff will examine objects for visitors or other agencies free of charge for identification, but *not* appraisal. Examination is on a daily basis by appointment only. When leaving objects for any period of time, a request for identification form must be completed and signed by the owner of the object. Objects brought in for identification will be considered abandoned if not retrieved within three months of the first date of acknowledgement of identifications; they then become the full legal property of the museum and may be accessioned or disposed of. These requirements must be understood and agreed upon by the owner before signing the request for identification. This requirement was initiated in order to prevent reclamation of property that has been housed for long periods of time in the museum. The museum waives all responsibility for loss or damage to objects during their stay in the museum.

SELLING OBJECTS IN THE MUSEUM GIFT SHOPS

The following policy refers both to objects purchased commercially for resale by the gift shops and to items determined to be superfluous to museum holdings.

The curatorial staff does not condone the sale in the museum sales counters of natural history, archaeological and ethnological objects of significant scientific or historical value, including but not necessarily limited to, rare specimens of butterflies and shells, fossils, prehistoric artefacts and pre-Columbian art. Sale of such materials tends to aggravate the commercial exploitation of natural resources by creating dubious market values for these items, and encourages the destruction of prime collecting sites and cultural monuments with an associated loss of essential data.

The gift counter inventory is reviewed periodically by a curatorial committee to determine the appropriateness of natural history objects offered for sale. The committee's recommendations, which are not binding upon the shop manager, are submitted to the director who is the final administrative authority. Review may also be requested by a committee member or the shop manager.

Upon the recommendation of the curator of the collection involved, objects not covered by these restrictions or other restrictions set forth in the policies, and with the approval of the curatorial review committee, may be sold at the current market value. Prior to disposal, all markings of ownership affixed to the object must be removed.

LIBRARY HOLDINGS

The library is a collection and is generally governed by the same polices that apply to the other collections of the museum. The library's subject areas, delineated by the disciplines covered within the museum, serve as a primary information source for the museum staff in their research.

In considering the informational needs of the staff, the primary objectives of the library are:

- To build a collection which will fill the majority of the research needs of the staff.
- To provide reference materials in both written and non-written forms for staff study, research and use in exhibition preparation and other educational activities.
- To assist the staff in their own educational endeavours in the fields of knowledge related to the museum, whether through structured academic programmes or self-initiated study.
- To encourage the exchange of information between the Denver Museum of Natural History and other institutions of a similar nature.
- To preserve those publications of extreme value or rarity in the library collection

As part of a publicly supported institution, the library has certain obligations to the community:

- To serve the community as an information centre in specific subject areas.
- To permit interested and qualified persons, under appropriate supervision, to use the museum's rare and valuable written resources in their research.
- To encourage both the scientific and lay communities to deepen their understanding of nature, past, present and future, and to provide them with the tools to do so

PRIVATE COLLECTIONS

No staff member is permitted to start a collection that may be in conflict with the museum's interests. Where such collections already exist, the museum is to be given serious consideration as the final repository. If a staff member is offered an item known to be desired for the museum's collections, the museum's option to acquire the item *must* be considered paramount over the individual's opportunity to acquire the object. Only if the museum is not interested in securing the object may the individual acquire it without being considered in conflict of interest.

PACKING AND SHIPPING PROCEDURES

Proper care and handling and transportation of objects are essential for the prevention of deterioration and irreversible damage. While a standardization of procedures is difficult, it is a curatorial responsibility to set extremely high standards for packing, according to the nature of the collection.

CONCLUSION

Our manual is still in a state of development, and major additions are being made with a considerable degree of frequency. We still must deal with such issues as the formulation of acquisition and conservation priorities, and the development of emergency procedures. We know periodic reviews of policies, procedures and guidelines will always be necessary to keep pace with changing laws and any refinements in philosophy which will inevitably occur within the museum community. But we feel that we have at least begun to develop a consistent and ethical approach to the stewardship of our collections.

3

Guidelines for a Registration Scheme for museums in the United Kingdom

Museums and Galleries Commission

The Museums and Galleries Commission's Registration Scheme is the single most important scheme in the UK aimed at raising standards in museums and fostering public confidence. The requirements for the scheme are set out here to provide the reader with a firm knowledge of the requirements of the first phase.

INTRODUCTION – THE ADVANTAGES AND KEY REQUIREMENTS OF REGISTRATION

1 The experience of museum[1] development in this century has led to the evolution of a broadly accepted philosophy of how a museum and its functions may be defined. This philosophy centres around the responsibilities a museum owes to its collections and to its public. Although museums in the UK are run by a wide variety of bodies – national and local authorities, universities, charitable societies and private individuals – they hold these responsibilities in common.

2 The Museums Association's *Code of Practice for Museum Authorities* (1977) and *Code of Practice for Curators* (1983) represented the first attempts to define these ideas formally in writing. The Museums and Galleries Commission (MGC) now hopes to take this process a stage further by offering registration to all museums which conform to the guidelines set out in this document. They have been drawn up after wide consultation over a two-year period (see 6 below) and represent common standards and aims which may apply to the very largest and to the very smallest museum. We emphasize that they are *guidelines*, and that they will be interpreted in the light of what is reasonable and appropriate in the case of each individual museum. We trust that they will prove to be of positive assistance to small museums and to new museum projects in providing information about the factors to be considered in museum development. At the same time it should be recognized that the guidelines are concerned with minimum standards; it is hoped that most museums will eventually go on to develop their operations far beyond this baseline.

3 Provisional registration will be available to museums which are striving to reach the required standard, and provisionally registered museums will continue to be eligible for grant-aid and subsidized services. The cost implications for most museums will be minimal and there will be no administrative charge associated with registration applications.

4 The advantages of registration can be summarized as follows:

(a) Eligibility for MGC and Area Museum Council (AMC) grant-aid and subsidized services (see also 39 below).

(b) The fostering of confidence among other funding agencies (e.g. tourist boards, charitable foundations and local authorities), that a registered museum is, in principle, worthy of support.

(c) The fostering of confidence among potential providers of material for a museum's collection that a registered museum is, in principle, a suitable repository.

(d) The opportunity for a museum to publicize itself as an organization which provides a basic range of services for the benefit of its visitors and other users.

5 The key requirements of registration are:

(a) Accordance with the Museums Association definition of a museum or, if appropriate, the MGC definition of a 'national' museum (see 7–10 below).

(b) An acceptable constitution and financial basis, and compliance with all legal and planning requirements (see 12–16 below).

(c) Publication of an acceptable statement of collection management policy (see 17–21 below).

(d) Provision of a range of public services/facilities appropriate to the nature, scale and location of the museum (see 22–24 below).

(e) Access to professional curatorial advice (see 25 and 26 below).

6 The registration scheme as described here has been developed after discussions with the Museums Association, the Association of Independent Museums and the AMCs. It was tested on a pilot basis in the north of England during 1986 and further refined after a national consultation exercise. The MGC decision to implement the scheme on a national basis has been widely supported by Government and interested government agencies, the local authority associations, grant-giving bodies and museum bodies.

DEFINITION OF A MUSEUM

7 The definition adopted at the Museums Association AGM 1984 was: 'A museum is an institution which collects, documents, preserves, exhibits and interprets material evidence and associated information for the public benefit.' The following guidelines will apply when interpreting this definition for the purposes of the registration scheme.

(a) *Institution* implies an establishment which has a formal governing instrument and a long-term purpose. Museums and collections privately owned by individuals are not eligible for registration (see also 12–15 and 17–19 below).

(b) *Collects* embraces all means of acquisition. It should also imply the museum's possession of, or intention to acquire, substantial permanent collections in relation to its stated objectives (see also 17–19 below).

(c) *Documents* emphasizes the obligation to maintain records (see also 20 below).

(d) *Preserves* includes all aspects of conservation and security (see also 21 below).

(e) *Exhibits* confirms the expectation of visitors that they will be able to see at least a representative selection of objects in the collections. It should also imply that the museum opens to a public at appropriate times and periods (see also 22–24).

(f) *Interprets* covers such diverse fields as display, education, research and publication (see also 22–24 below).

(g) *Material* indicates something that is tangible, while *evidence* indicates its authenticity as the 'real thing'.

(h) *Associated information* represents the knowledge which prevents a museum object being merely a curio and also includes all records relating to its past history, acquisition and subsequent usage.

(i) *For the public benefit* is deliberately open-ended and is intended to reflect the current thinking, both within the museum profession and outside it, that museums are the servants of society. It also implies that a museum should not be a profit-distributing institution, i.e. it should not distribute profits to shareholders (see also 12 below).

DEFINITION OF A 'NATIONAL' MUSEUM

8 To be eligible for registration, a museum wishing to use the word 'national' or equivalent in its title (see below for list of terms) should conform with the following points:

(a) It should conform with the registration scheme.

(b) The policy and practice of the museum should be to collect a range of objects of national importance and associated archival material in its particular fields.

(c) It should *already* have a substantial collection in relation to its stated objectives and the museum display policy should reflect the full range of its collections.

(d) It should provide professional and authoritative expertise and advice in all its fields to the public and other museums.

(e) It should provide study and research facilities for the public.

Museums constituted as charitable companies should note that the Companies Act, 1985 provides statutory constraints to the use of terms such as 'national' in company names.

9 The following names should be regarded as equivalent to 'national' and therefore subject to the above-mentioned criteria: International; World; Nation; Europe; European; United Kingdom; Great Britain; Britain; British; England; English; Scotland; Scottish; Wales; Welsh; Ulster; Northern Ireland; Northern Irish.

10 *Exceptions*: there are institutions which have the term 'National', 'British', etc., incorporated into their titles by statute or Royal Charter. If one of these establishes a museum, it may of right use its official title in the name of its museum, e.g. British Telecom Museum.

INSTITUTIONS INELIGIBLE FOR INDEPENDENT REGISTRATION BUT ELIGIBLE FOR REGISTRATION AS PART OF A BROADLY BASED MUSEUM SERVICE

11 The following categories of institution will not be deemed eligible for registration unless they form part of a broadly based museum service which conforms with the registration guidelines:

(a) Science centres and planetaria.

(b) Natural, archaeological, historical and industrial monuments and sites, not having associated museum collections.

(c) Institutions displaying live specimens, e.g. zoos and aquaria.

(d) Educational loan services.

(e) Record offices.

(f) Venues for temporary exhibitions.

(g) Biological and environmental record centres.

CONSTITUTIONS

12 The following constitutions will be deemed acceptable:

(a) Those based on Local Government Acts and forming the subject of a Local Authority Resolution.
(b) Those based on any other Act of Parliament.
(c) Those based on the formal decision of any public body.
(d) Those based on the formal decision of a university senate or council.
(e) Those based on an *acceptable* memorandum and articles of a charitable company.
(f) Those based on an *acceptable* deed of trust of a charitable Trust.
(g) Any other constitution which is acceptable to the MGC and which meets the criteria set out in this document, including the non-distribution of any profits. Commercial and company museums will be eligible provided that any profits made by the museum are retained within the museum.

13 With reference to categories (e) and (f), examples of acceptable formats are:

(a) Conformance with the specimen drafts published in the Association of Independent Museums Guideline No. 3, 'Charitable status for museums' (both versions: i. Scotland; ii. Rest of UK).
(b) Conformance with the specimen trust deed published by the Army Museums Ogilby Trust.

14 It is recognized that these specimen trust deeds (13 (a) and (b)) do not adequately provide for the safeguarding of museum collections. To counter this deficiency it is necessary for a museum's governing body formally to adopt the clauses in the registration guidelines which refer to the disposal of collections (see 18 (f)–(j) below).

FINANCES

15 A museum should be able to demonstrate that it has a sound financial basis and a copy of the current annual budget should be provided. Independent museums should also submit financial accounts for the two most recent financial years; these should include income and expenditure accounts and a balance sheet, and distinguish between annual operating costs/income, and details of commitments undertaken and financial resources available to meet development costs. Accounts must either be audited or, in the case of private trusts not legally required to provide audited accounts, certified appropriately. A museum should be sufficiently well supported and financially viable irrespective of any valuation placed on the items in its collection. In no circumstances should those items be mortgaged or in any way held as security for any loan. Information concerning the status of the museum building or site housing the collections should also be provided (e.g. leasehold, freehold).

LEGAL, SAFETY AND PLANNING REQUIREMENTS

16 Museum governing bodies are required to undertake that they have ensured and will continue to ensure that all relevant legal, safety and planning requirements are complied with.

COLLECTION MANAGEMENT POLICY

17 The policy statement should provide the following information:

   (a) Details of the museum's acquisition and disposal policy.
   (b) The nature of the museum's existing collection.
   (c) Details concerning the documentation of the collection.
   (d) Access to professional conservation advice.

Acquisition and disposal policy

18 A museum's acquisition and disposal policy must be formally approved by the governing body. *Sub-paragraphs (b) to (j) inclusive (below), or equivalent wording, should be incorporated within the policy.* They are based upon a section of the Museums Association's *Code of Practice for Museum Authorities.* Evidence of formal approval should be supplied in the form of a committee minute signed by a properly authorized person. This person should be the chief executive or proper officer authorized by the governing body (local authority museums); the chairman, secretary or other person authorized by the governing body (independent and national museums); the vice-chancellor, registrar or other person authorized by the governing body (university museums).

   (a) Reference should be made to the nature of the collections and the criteria used to define their scope. The criteria should normally include the following: the subjects or themes of the collection; the period of time and/or geographical area from which the collection is derived; the limitations on collecting imposed by such factors as inadequate staffing, storage and conservation. Due account should be taken of the collecting policies of other museums in order to avoid unnecessary duplication and waste of resources.
   (b) The acquisition policy should be published and reviewed from time to time, at least once every five years. Acquisitions outside the current stated policy should only be made in very exceptional circumstances, and then only after proper consideration by the governing body of the museum itself, having regard to the interests of other museums. The AMC should be notified of any changes to the acquisitions policy.
   (c) A museum should not acquire, whether by purchase, gift, bequest or exchange, any work of art or object unless the governing body or responsible officer is satisfied that the museum can acquire a valid title to the specimen in question, and that in particular it has not been acquired in, or exported from, its country of origin (or any intermediate country in which it may have been legally owned) in violation of that country's laws. (For the purpose of this paragraph 'country of origin' includes the United Kingdom).
   (d) So far as biological and geological material is concerned, a museum should not acquire by any direct or indirect means any specimen that has been collected, sold or otherwise transferred in contravention of any national or international wildlife protection or natural history conservation law or treaty of the United Kingdom or any other country, except with the express consent of an appropriate outside authority (e.g. a British court in the case of a specimen seized from a third party under the Protection of Birds Acts).
   (e) So far as British or foreign archaeological antiquities (including excavated ceramics) are concerned, in addition to the safeguards under sub-paragraph (c) above, the museum should not acquire by purchase objects in any case where

the governing body or responsible officer has reasonable cause to believe that the circumstances of their recovery involved the recent unscientific or intentional destruction or damage of ancient monuments or other known archaeological sites, or involved a failure to disclose the finds to the owner or occupier of the land, or to the proper authorities in the case of a possible Treasure Trove (in England and Wales) or *bona vacantia* (Scotland).

(f) By definition (see 7 above), a museum should have a long-term purpose and possess (or intend to acquire) substantial permanent collections in relation to its stated objectives. Each museum authority must accept the principle that there is a strong presumption against the disposal of any items in the museum's collection except as set out below.

(g) In those cases where a museum is free to dispose of an item (e.g. by virtue of an Act of Parliament or of permission from the High Court or the Charity Commissioners), it should be agreed that any decision to sell or dispose of material from the collections should be taken only after due consideration by the museum's governing body, and such material should be offered first, by loan, exchange, gift or sale to registered museums before sale to other interested individuals or organizations is considered.

(h) In cases in which an arrangement for the exchange, gift or private treaty sale of material is not being made with an individual museum, the museum community at large must be advised of the intention to dispose of material. This should normally be through an announcement in the Museums Association's *Museum Bulletin*. The announcement should indicate the number of specimens involved, the prime objects concerned and the basis on which the material would be transferred to another institution. A period of at least two months must be allowed for an interest in acquiring the material to be expressed.

(i) A decision to dispose of a specimen or work of art, whether by exchange, sale, gift or destruction (in the case of an item too badly damaged or deteriorated to be of any use for the purposes of the collections), should be the responsibility of the governing body of the museum acting on the advice of professional curatorial staff, and not of the curator of the collection concerned acting alone. Full records should be kept of all such decisions and the specimens involved and proper arrangements made for the preservation and/or transfer, as appropriate, of the documentation relating to the object concerned, including photographic records where practicable.

(j) Any monies received by a governing body from the disposal of specimens or works of art should be applied for the benefit of the museum collections. This should normally mean the purchase of exhibits for the collections but in exceptional cases improvements relating to the care of collections may be justifiable. Advice on these cases may be sought from the MGC.

Nature of the museum's existing collection

19 Details should be provided of the *existing* collection, indicating the proportion of items on loan to the museum.

Documentation of the collection

20 Details of the museum's documentation system should be provided. The minimum requirement is as follows:

(a) The maintenance of entry records of all items deposited in the museum, e.g. as enquiries, loans or potential acquisitions.

(b) The maintenance of a register with records about all accessions and long-term loans, each including an accession or inventory number and sufficient information for collections management purposes.

(c) The marking or labelling of each accession and (where appropriate) each individual object with a unique accession or inventory number.

(d) The maintenance of one or more indexes or equivalent information retrieval facilities, including (where appropriate) subject, donor and location lists.

(e) If documentation of the collection has not been completed as set out above, a statement of the museum's policy to eliminate this backlog within a stated timescale should be provided.

Conservation of the collections

21 Minimum standards are not proposed *at this stage*, but all reasonable steps should be taken to preserve the collections. Access to professional conservation advice is essential and details of the person(s)/organization(s) normally consulted should be provided (see also 25 and 26 below relating to curatorial advice).

PUBLIC SERVICES

22 The museum should provide a range of public services appropriate to its nature and scale relating to the interpretation of its collections, e.g. temporary exhibitions, educational activities and publications. Details should be provided.

23 In addition, the museum should provide or have available in the immediate vicinity a reasonable range of visitor facilities appropriate to the scale, location and nature of the museum, e.g. parking, toilet, catering and disabled access facilities. Details should be provided.

24 A museum should normally be open to the general public. If the museum's public is restricted, this must be defined, but will not automatically rule out acceptance for registration. Details should be provided of opening hours or other arrangements for access, and the means by which this information is advertised.

STAFFING AND ACCESS TO PROFESSIONAL CURATORIAL ADVICE

25 The governing body has a special obligation to ensure that the museum has staff sufficient in both number and kind to ensure that the museum is able to meet its responsibilities. Proper arrangements should be made for the museum to meet its obligations in relation to the care of the collections, public access and services, research and security. The size of the staff, and its nature (whether paid or unpaid, permanent or temporary), will depend on the size of the museum, its collections and its responsibilities.

26 A formal statement will be required which conforms with the following guidelines:

(a) A museum's governing body should normally have the services of a professionally trained and/or experienced curator, i.e. someone holding a degree and/or the

Diploma of the Museums Association or equivalent qualifications and/or substantial relevant experience. Full details should be submitted. (Interpretation of 'equivalent qualifications and/or substantial relevant experience' will be determined by the MGC in the light of case studies derived from the pilot registration scheme 1985–86.) There should be an efficient line of communication between the curator and the appropriate committee of the museum's governing body. We would normally expect that the senior museum professional is allowed direct access to the appropriate committee at least when estimates are presented and museum policy discussed. Details of these arrangements should be submitted

(b) In the case of a *small* museum which does not have the services of a professionally trained and/or experienced curator (as described above), the museum's governing body should make arrangements to receive curatorial advice from such a person on a regular basis. Normally, this would be done by appointing such a person to be a full member of the governing body. Alternatively, a curatorial adviser may be appointed (the AMC will be able to advise on potential curatorial advisers). Evidence of the formal appointment of a curatorial adviser by a museum's governing body should be provided in the form of a committee minute signed by a properly authorized person (see 18 above). All minutes and papers for meetings of the governing body should be sent to the curatorial adviser who should also be offered the opportunity to attend such meetings. The curatorial adviser (or the board member who fulfils this role) will be expected to endorse the registration application and make an annual report to the AMC concerning the operation of the museum and its continued conformance with the registration criteria. Normally, only the smallest museums should find it necessary to take advantage of these arrangements and interpretation of 'small' will be determined by the MGC in the light of case studies derived from the pilot registration scheme.

REGISTRATION AND APPEALS PROCEDURE

27 Registration application forms should be completed and returned to the Area Museum Council within six months from the start of the scheme as advised by the MGC (see also 35 below).

28 Within a further six-month period the director of the AMC will send all applications to the MGC.

29 Applicants will be considered by a registration committee drawn from a pool of nominated members. Any meeting of the committee will comprise:

(a) Two representatives of the MGC, drawn from a group which will comprise two commissioners (one of whom will be the committee's official chairman), the secretary, and the deputy secretary; any one of these four shall be entitled to take the chair at a meeting.

(b) A museum professional appointed after consultation with the president of the Museums Association.

(c) A museum professional appointed after consultation with the chairman of the Association of Independent Museums.

(d) A representative of the relevant AMC.

30 The registration committee will be able to co-opt expert advisers on an *ad hoc* basis when specialist advice on particular categories of museum is required.

31 The MGC will notify museums of their registration or the reasons for their rejection. Provisional registration may be offered to museums which are striving to reach registration standard, subject to annual review, e.g. museums at an early stage of development.

32 Museums which fail to qualify for registration will be notified of their right to appeal. Any appeals must be received by the MGC within six months of the date of the rejection letter. The appeals committee will comprise two commissioners and a museum professional nominated by the Museums Association, none of them previously involved in the decision to reject the applicant.

33 Whilst registration confers eligibility to receive funds from the MGC and the AMC, the acceptance of a museum under the registration scheme does not commit the MGC or any AMC to provide funding or to accept any responsibility for the management of the museum concerned.

34 Registered museums will be allocated a unique registration number which can be quoted on all published material. A certificate will also be provided.

35 Late applicants will not be excluded from the registration scheme but the processing of their application forms may be delayed. New museums established after the initial registration period may apply to be registered at any time.

ACCESS TO THE REGISTER AND MAINTENANCE

36 The register of museums will be maintained at the MGC. Copies will be made available to AMCs, to other agencies concerned with the funding of museums, and to the Museums Association and the Association of Independent Museums. All copies of the register will be available for inspection by enquirers with a *bona fide* interest.

37 The MGC reserves the right to remove a museum from the register at any time if it can be shown that it no longer conforms with the criteria in the guidelines. Such decisions will be made after an appropriate period of written notice and subject to the normal appeals procedure. A museum may also request that it be removed from the register if it so desires.

38 Registered museums will be expected to make an annual statistical return to their AMC confirming/amending previously submitted particulars. Museums will be expected to renew their applications for registration at five-yearly intervals, commencing from the initial registration date.

OTHER ORGANIZATIONS ELIGIBLE FOR MGC AND AMC FUNDING

39 The following categories of organization providing specialist services of repute for museums will be deemed eligible for financial support from the MGC and AMCs notwithstanding their ineligibility for registration:

(a) Countywide, regional and nationwide museum advisory services.
(b) Reputable conservation services.

    (c) Reputable museum-related training centres.

    (d) Museum education services.

    (e) Touring exhibition services.

1 March 1989

MUSEUM REGISTRATION: GUIDANCE NOTES FOR MUSEUMS

These guidance notes have been issued to supplement the *Guidelines for a Registration Scheme* in the UK and to provide practical assistance in completing the application form.

1 This is a voluntary scheme which is intended to benefit all museums, and to provide guidance to those who seek to assist them in their work. It takes a professionally-agreed definition of a museum (see Guideline 7) and asks each applicant institution to demonstrate that it conforms to this definition. Almost all the questions which you will be asked to answer stem from this definition. The criteria are such that they may be met equally by a national museum and by a village museum run by volunteers. Registration is not concerned with the scale of a museum's operation, nor with making detailed qualitative judgements about each museum's activities.

2 There is nothing revolutionary or new about the criteria contained in the *Registration Guidelines*. Most museums will be able to demonstrate that they have been fulfilling them for years. But even large and long-established museums may find that registration provides a valuable opportunity to review their basic functions and to translate good practices into written policies. There will be others, perhaps part of larger organizations which exist primarily to do other things, or very small museums at an early stage of development, for whom registration will provide an important stimulus to sorting out what their collections are for, and the future basis upon which they will be maintained and developed.

3 The first two years of implementation (1988–90) have confirmed our expectations that 'registered museums' can come in every conceivable shape and size. They may not even include the word 'museum' in their title. They are united by the possession of a substantial collection of historic objects, works of art or scientific specimens which have been gathered together to provide a long-term public benefit. If the ownership, preservation and interpretation of such a collection forms a key element of your organization's activities then registration will be appropriate for you. If, after studying these notes and the *Guidelines*, you are still unsure whether your institution comes within the remit of the scheme, your Area Museum Council (AMC) or the Museums and Galleries Commission (MGC) will be able to advise you.

4 The scheme is being implemented on a phased basis because there are well over 2,500 potential applicants in the United Kingdom. It is being introduced over four years, between April 1988 and March 1992. The regional timetable is shown at Appendix I. The Commission is being assisted in this task by the nine AMCs in England, Scotland and Wales, listed with their addresses at Appendix II. Their expertise and local knowledge will ensure that individual museums will have immediate access to any advice and assistance they may require.

5 Once your museum is registered, we will write to you again once a year for three years to ask whether the information which you initially supplied has changed in any way. In the fourth year we will ask you to submit a new application, but by that time we trust that all museums will be familiar with the procedure and that this will not involve much time or work on your part.

6 In future registration will provide basic eligibility for grant-aid and subsidized services provided by AMCs and the MGC, and this will normally take effect in the financial year following the year of registration. Registered status will also be taken into account by a wide variety of other funding agencies when they consider grant applications from museums. A list of the agencies which have already agreed to support the scheme is given at Appendix III.

7 If a museum is unable to meet all the registration criteria immediately, but can demonstrate willingness and intention to work towards achieving what is required within a reasonable period, the registration committee will be able to award the status of *provisional registration*. This can be a recognition of achievements to date and represents an interim stage on the way to full registration. Provisionally registered museums will still be generally eligible for grant-aid and subsidized services and their progress towards full registration will be monitored through the process of annual review described above.

Applying for registration

8 Please begin by reading through the *Registration Guidelines* carefully. Each question on the application form refers to a paragraph of the *Guidelines*. In completing the form the most important point to bear in mind is that the registration committee should be easily able to gain a picture of your museum's structure and operation. Do not feel unduly constrained by the spaces available for your responses. If necessary use separate sheets marked with the relevant question number, indicating that you have done this on the form itself. You may also wish to supply additional material (within reason!) such as a general publicity leaflet or events programme in connection with Question 15.

9 At the start of the registration process in any region, an AMC will usually provide a number of introductory seminars at which the *Guidelines* can be discussed. If you are completely unsure how to proceed, it would probably be sensible for a representative of your museum to attend one of these seminars before you put pen to paper. If this isn't possible, AMC staff will be ready and willing to deal with enquiries on a day-to-day basis by letter or telephone, or by arranging to visit you.

10 If you are a museum service running more than one museum, please supply an application form for each (additional copies are available from your AMC if we have not sent you enough). Information common to all museums, such as details of constitution or finances, need only be given on one form, and reference made to it on the others.

11 All completed application forms should be returned to your AMC as soon as possible but *no later than* six months after first receiving the forms. Each AMC will notify their museums of the closing date for the region. If you can complete your form well before that date it will be immensely helpful to us, and will enable earlier assessment of your application. You may gain the distinction of being the first registered museum in your area.

12 As soon as the registration committee has considered your application we will write to you directly to inform you of the decision. Registered museums will subsequently receive a registration certificate bearing their registered museum number.

Notes on the application form

Question 6: formal constitution

13 'Describe the museum's relationship to its governing body': this relationship is not always obvious; for example, collections may be owned by one organization but managed by another. Other examples of what might be indicated here are: the relationship of a university museum to the university as a whole; the relationship of a commercial museum to a parent company; the directorate, service or committee responsible for the administration of a local authority museum.

14 We recognize that it may be difficult for some local authority or university museums to supply copies of constitutional documents because it proves impossible to locate the original committee minutes relating to the foundation of a museum. The relevant minute for local authority museums may date from local government reorganization. (Do not worry unduly if you cannot trace these: it is generally obvious under which powers a local authority is providing a museum service.) All other museums, however, must supply copies of their constitutional documents, whether it be a deed of trust, the memorandum and articles of a company limited by guarantee, or other relevant management agreement. Where one organization is managing a collection owned by another organization, the registration committee will expect that the arrangement is made the subject of written agreement.

15 In supplying information about your museum's constitution, it will be helpful for you t › bear in mind the kind of questions which the registration committee will be asking:

(a) Who owns the bulk of the collections?
(b) Are these collections established in the public domain? (A collection entirely owned by a private individual is not eligible.)
(c) Who manages the collection? Is the answer to this the same as (a)?
(d) Is there a long-term intention to hold and maintain the collections?
(e) Are the collections treated as disposable assets? (This may be apparent from the balance sheet rather than from the written constitution.)
(f) What would happen to the collections if the organization that owned them ceased to exist?
(g) Are the collections used to generate income for non-income purposes, or as collateral for loans?

Some of the answers to questions like these will be found in your responses to Question 9 (financial details) and Question 11 (acquisition and disposal policy). They may not be entirely covered by the constitutional documents which you are able to supply.

Question 9: financial details

16 We are not looking for any particular account formats; we accept that these will vary greatly. Try to ensure that the various pieces of financial information listed in Guideline 15 are covered. It is recognized that some (mainly local authority) museums will not be able to provide a balance sheet.

17 In the case of independent museums, the registration committee will be looking for evidence of financial stability. Risk of bankruptcy implies risk to the collections. The constitutional documents of independent museums should, ideally, make reference to transfer of the collection to another public museum in the event of closure or winding up. Museum collections should *not* be included as fixed assets in balance sheets. If this practice has been followed up to now, the museum's auditor or accountant should be referred to paragraph 52 of the Accounting Standards Committee's *Statement of Recommended Practice 2: 'Accounting for Charities'*, which advises that a charity need not capitalize assets which are 'inalienable or historic'.

18 In the case of trusts or societies not legally required to provide audited accounts, 'certified appropriately' is likely to mean by a chartered accountant, or by a treasurer.

19 If your museum's budget is consolidated within a larger organizational or departmental budget, please do your best to supply an estimated summary of museum expenditure.

20 Information concerning the 'status of buildings or sites housing the collections' (Question 10) refers to freehold or leasehold arrangements. It is intended to assist the committee in determining the long-term security of the museum, a factor not always apparent from financial information alone.

Question 11: acquisition and disposal policy

21 There are two ways of responding to this question, which are outlined below. The first is the easiest, and represents the minimum statement which the committee will accept; the second requires a bit more time, but is strongly recommended and all museums will be expected to achieve it in due course. Whichever way you make this statement, it must be formally approved by your governing body, and evidence of this approval supplied (see the box at the bottom of this question).

22 The first method is to write a brief statement of your acquisition policy on the form, under the space for Question 11. The points you should cover in this statement are listed in Guideline 18a. In this space, of course, you will probably only be able to indicate broad subject areas and make general statements of intent, but this can constitute an adequate first attempt at an acquisition policy for a small museum. As time goes on, you can consider how to expand your statement and at that stage you will need to produce a separate document. You must, in any case, review your policy at least once every five years. Your governing body must now be asked formally to adopt this acquisition policy and, additionally, should be asked to adopt all the paragraphs of Guideline 18 as a general policy to which it will henceforward subscribe.

23 The second method is to produce a separate document incorporating both your acquisition policy (based on the points in Guideline 18a) and disposal policy (based on paragraphs (b)–(j) of guideline 18). This is highly recommended because your policy can never properly be made public if it only exists in the form of a series of committee minutes (Guideline 18b). You can tailor the wording of the Guideline 18 paragraphs so that they make specific reference to your museum and your governing body, but *you should not alter the disposal paragraphs in such a way as to change their meaning*. You may, of course, adopt a stricter disposal policy if you so wish, and some museums have chosen to do this. The *Guidelines* represent the most permissive statement which is acceptable.

24 It is important to emphasize that disposal of items from museum collections is not being ruled out where there are sound curatorial reasons for pursuing this course. But unless each museum governing body accepts the principle of 'strong presumption against disposal', the whole purpose of the museum is called into question (see Guideline 7a and 7b).

25 In responding to the question on disposal policy many museums cite the fact that their governing body has already adopted the Museums Association's *Code of Practice*, which covers this issue. This is entirely acceptable so long as it is the updated (1987) code which has been adopted. The earlier code (1977) contained a less detailed statement regarding disposals.

26 Please note that registration does not require that the full disposal procedure is followed (e.g. advertisement in the *Museums Journal*) in cases where a museum decides to transfer an item to another registered museum, although we would expect that such transfers were agreed by your governing body, and that full records were kept.

27 Some industrial and transport museums will wish to make the reasonable point that not all their items are acquired with a view to permanent retention: they may be used to provide parts for restoring other machinery or vehicles, or the museum may wish to 'trade-up' to acquire better examples of the same machinery or models. This argues the case for not 'accessioning' certain types of material which are acquired, but recording them in some other way which reflects the museum's intentions towards them. The same principle applies in the case of school loan or 'handling' collections which all kinds of museums create. They should not be treated as part of the permanent collection because there is an intention to use them in such a way that preservation cannot be guaranteed. It is therefore sensible to record these outside the main accession record.

28 If your museum does periodically acquire and dispose of certain types of material for the kind of specialist reasons outlined in 27, this should be clearly stated in your written disposal policy.

Question 12: your museum's existing collection

29 Please provide a brief summary of the subject areas covered, with approximate numbers of items, or rough proportions of types of material. The subjects covered by your existing collections may differ slightly from your present acquisition policy, particularly in long-established museums. The proportion of items on loan can be a significant factor. For example, if 70 per cent of a museums collection were owned by one private individual, and the items on loan could theoretically be withdrawn at any time, the museum's future could be in jeopardy. The registration committee will wish to look carefully at such cases, and will always expect that such loans are at least subject to written agreements. In cases where one organization is managing a collection owned by another organization (see also 13, 14, 15 above) acquisition and disposal policies should be approved both by the museum's governing body and by the body which owns the collection.

30 If you are writing your acquisition and disposal policy as a separate document, it is sensible to commence with details of your existing collections.

Question 13: documentation

31 The following brief notes are intended to provide immediate guidance to small museums without professional curatorial staff. Area Museum Council staff will also

be able to advise on basic documentation standards. For more detailed information, you are recommended to consult the following Museum Documentation Association publications: *Practical Museum Documentation* (1980) and *Planning the Documentation of Museum Collections* (1985). The Museum Documentation Association is based at:

Building 0, 347 Cherry Hinton Road, Cambridge CB1 4DH. Tel: (0223) 242848.

MDA runs training seminars on all aspects of documentation around the UK and its staff are also available to deal with enquiries from individual museums.

32 Documentation embraces all the records and information associated with museum collections. A museum without any documentation is useless: it cannot legally prove that it owns any of its collections; it cannot account to donors for what has been given, or to auditors for what has been bought; it cannot maintain proper security; and it has probably destroyed most of the historical and scientific value of its collections. Hopefully, there are not many museums in quite such a dire state. But we know that there are many where documentation is not taken as seriously as it ought to be, where not all the minimum forms of record required by registration are maintained, or where there are large backlogs of work. Documentation is time-consuming, and because it is not an area of work that has any immediate effect on a museum's public face, it tends to be given low priority. Registration is intended to encourage museums to give documentation much higher priority.

33 *Entry records* must be kept of every item entering (and by the same token, leaving) the museum premises, for whatever reason. We have all heard stories of items brought in for identification being lost, or members of the public turning up ten years later to reclaim items 'on loan' which the museum believed it owned. Museums just cannot afford to be sloppy about keeping records; they are in the business of looking after objects. However superfluous it may seem at times, you must scrupulously maintain entry records.

34 The entry record must consist of at least the following information:

(a) The name of the museum.
(b) Full name and address of the donor/owner/lender.
(c) A brief description of the item or items, sufficient to allow someone else to identify it if necessary.
(d) The reason why it has been brought into the museum, e.g. for identification/for temporary exhibition/as a gift/as a long-term loan/purchased.
(e) The date the item entered the museum.
(f) The signature of the donor/owner/lender and the signature of the museum representative who has taken the item in; lenders' signatures should also be obtained when an item is returned to them.
(g) It is sensible to record information which donors provide about objects as part of the entry record.

It is advisable to use these points as pre-prepared headings in whatever form of document or book you are using as an entry record, to remind staff of what they should record. The MDA can supply triplicate, write-through entry forms, which are highly recommended as they provide a copy which can be immediately given to the depositor.

35 Give each entry record a number of some kind so that a label bearing this number can be attached to the object. These numbers are not the same as accession numbers

(see below) because they are being used to identify objects you intend to keep as well as those which you may only hold for a week or so. A common way of providing an entry number system is E1, E2, E3, etc. The entry number should be unique to each item or group of items relating to an individual depositor on a particular day.

36 By their very nature, entry records cannot really be created retrospectively. If your museum hasn't kept such records up to now you should introduce a system forthwith, and include a statement to this effect in your answer to Question 13.

37 The accession register is the formal record of items which have been incorporated into your permanent collection. Accession records should be created as soon as possible after a decision has been made to retain an item for your permanent collection. The accession register is a record of things which your museum now legally owns, although some museums also record long-term loans in the same register. This is acceptable, so long as loans are clearly distinguished from gifts and purchases. The accession register is also used to record the number which will in future uniquely identify each item in your collection.

It should be a securely-bound book (such as a company minutes book) printed on substantial paper which is unlikely to deteriorate with time. Loose-leaf records, or records on index cards, are not acceptable. Fully automated documentation systems should be backed up by a paper accessions register which may be in the form of a bound hard copy output. This must be updated at regular intervals.

38 The following *minimum* information should be recorded in the accession register: item number, date of entry into museum and entry number; donor's name and address (or person from whom purchased); brief physical identifying description. If you are not yet maintaining a catalogue of the collection over and above the accession register, it will also be necessary to record unique information associated with an item's history and use. The usual method of numbering items in an accession register is to use a running sequence in combination with the year, e.g. 1988:1, 1988:2, 1988:3. Do not attempt to incorporate a classification system into this number sequence (e.g. A1988:1 for an art object). This is a good recipe for getting into a muddle later. Classifications can change over time and should be imposed at another level, for example, through indexes and catalogues.

39 As the accession register constitutes the long-term legal record of your permanent collections, you should periodically make copies of new entries and store these securely in another building. Original registers should be kept in secure conditions, ideally in a fire-proof cabinet.

40 *Marking or labelling* items with their unique accession numbers ensures that they will never become disassociated from the information in the relevant accession and entry records. We recognize that it may not always be possible or appropriate to mark small items such as coins, stamps or insects individually, but these should be stored in such a way that individual holders or cabinets can be clearly marked with accession numbers. Methods of marking should be permanent enough not to rub off, fade, or become unintentionally detached, but at the same time they should not damage the appearance of the item or endanger its physical condition.

41 There are many kinds of index which a museum can produce to facilitate use of its collections. Even the smallest museum should aim to produce some kind of search alternative to the numerical accession number sequence provided by the register. An *index of donors* is important because it reinforces your ability to account for objects

to your public and to your auditors, and a *location index* will help you to find items readily and to carry out inventory checks. The *subject indexes* which you use will depend upon the nature of your collections. Whether you use name indexes or classified subject indexes, you should work to an agreed convention. There are a number of standard published classification systems and name lists which may be appropriate to your collections (further information on these is available from the MDA). If you are using your own subject classification systems and standard names, make sure these are written down so that the same rules are always followed.

42 *Policy to eliminate backlog.* The registration committee will not be surprised to see that museums have documentation backlogs, but it will expect museums to make an honest and realistic assessment of the work involved and show some intention to tackle the problem. Finding extra staff and new resources for this purpose is not likely to be an option open to every museum, and this makes it all the more important that existing personnel commit some of their time to the problem, even if it is only two hours per week on a regular basis. The important principle is that backlogs should diminish: an increasing backlog should be viewed with alarm. Area Museum Council advisory staff may be able to assist you in formulating policies to eliminate backlogs.

43 We have already said that entry records cannot be created retrospectively and in a sense this will affect your ability to create accession records retrospectively. An un-accessioned item may have lost any associated information which told how the museum acquired it, and why. You will not be able retrospectively to record such an item as a 'gift' in your accession register if you have no written evidence that this was the case. If all attempts to trace associated information and donors or lenders fail, the item can be recorded in the accession register as 'source and status unknown'. It is this type of problem that the maintenance of proper entry and accession records is intended to avoid in the future.

44 Your policy to achieve documentation requirements (Question 13c) should demonstrate that you have realistically identified your problems; that you understand how they should be tackled; and that you intend to tackle them within the shortest time-span that resources will allow. Some museums will have to face the fact that their documentation problems will require additional resources. A documentation backlog need not be a bar to full registration if the registration committee is satisfied that the museum is willing and able to take problems in hand. Very substantial backlogs, particularly of basic accessioning, are likely to be made the subject of provisional registration.

Question 14: access to professional conservation advice

45 Preventative conservation (i.e. providing proper conditions for storage and display of museum collections) is an important element of collections care. Please provide details of who advises you in matters of preventative conservation (particularly in the case of small museums without professionally trained staff); who provides advice on specialist conservation treatments which objects in your collections may require; and who undertakes such treatments where they are carried out. It will also be helpful to indicate whether your museum has a budget for conservation work.

Question 15, 16, 17: public services

46 It should be emphasized that the fact that 'public services' only warrant three paragraphs in the *Guidelines* does not mean that they are considered to be of less

importance than the other aspects (although by implication all the guidelines are concerned with proper management of collections in public or charitable collections under public or charitable funding). It would have been difficult to make strictures in these areas because not all forms of interpretation or of visitor facility are appropriate to each museum. The registration committee will be adding the information given here to the overall picture of the museum and they will want to be assured that the museum is alive to its responsibilities to the public.

47 To give some hypothetical cases: the registration committee would probably look askance at a large local authority museum without any form of educational provision. On the other hand, it would be unreasonable to insist that a village museum run by volunteers should have a regular temporary exhibition programme. The committee would hope that museums on green-field sites would provide toilets and somewhere to park, but it would not be reasonable to insist that museums in the centre of towns should provide car parking.

48 Under Guideline 22, although not mentioned in the list of examples, 'permanent exhibitions' are of course one element of interpretation; other services which might be included here are guided tours, special events, lecture programmes, talks given outside the museum, etc.

49 *Opening hours and public access*: a collection only accessible by written appointment would be eligible if the committee were satisfied that these arrangements were appropriate to the nature of the institution and were well-publicized, and that the museum were able to respond to such requests regularly enough to permit steady access, not just, for example, three or four visits per year. In the case of museums with restricted access it will be useful to indicate average annual visitor numbers. Some specialist museums, despite restricted access, annually deal with a high number of written and telephone enquiries which in themselves constitute a form of public access. You should note this factor if it is relevant. It is useful to make reference to advertising, signposting, etc. in answering Question 17.

Question 20, 21, 22: access to professional curatorial advice

Does the museum employ a curator? (Question 20)

50 We accept that job titles will vary. The senior staff member responsible for day-to-day management of your museum may be called director, keeper, manager, administrator or secretary. This question is designed to ascertain whether among those responsible for running your museum is someone who has received training in, or who has had long experience of, the range of skills particularly associated with the management and care of museum collections. These skills do not simply imply familiarity with the subject areas dealt with by the museum: it is possible to be a first-rate engineer, ornithologist or military historian and still not have much familiarity with the general principles of collections management. It is certainly the case, however, that many museum staff acquire these skills through in-service training and by implementing professional advice provided by those outside the museum organization. The committee will certainly take account of such factors where post-holders have no formal museum qualification, and you are encouraged to provide this kind of additional information where appropriate. If you feel that existing personnel could be assisted by the opportunity to receive outside professional advice on a regular basis, you should additionally consider the appointment of a trustee or a board member with curatorial expertise, or a curatorial adviser (see 52 below).

Access to the managing committee (Question 21)

51 Local authority museums should note that the *Registration Guidelines* have received formal endorsement from all the local authority associations, and that access to committee was a point which was particularly discussed with these organizations at the consultation stage. All agreed that there should be no reason why a curator responsible for the management of a museum service should not normally be present when the relevant committee considered items concerning museum policy and estimates. In other types of museum, this question is only likely to pose problems when the museum is part of a much larger organization such as a university or a public utility and there is no intermediate governing committee to oversee the organization's museum function. In these cases it may be useful to consider the formation of such a committee and in this your AMC will be ready to advise.

Curatorial advisers

52 Where there is a lack of curatorial expertise (see paragraph 50 above) among existing staff of small museums, or where a small museum is essentially run on a voluntary basis, it will still be eligible for registration if the governing body receives regular professional curatorial advice, either because a trained and/or experienced curator is a member of the governing body, or because the museum has formally appointed such a person as a curatorial adviser. The appropriate arrangements will depend upon the structure of the museum's governing body. It is not possible for us to lay down strict criteria as to what will constitute a 'small' museum in the registration committee's terms of reference, but the size and importance of the collections and the museum's annual income are the kind of factors which will inevitably be taken into account. Many small museums already seek advice from local museum professionals on occasion and have welcomed the opportunity to formalize this relationship. It would not be expected that a curatorial adviser would interfere with, or be held responsible for, the ability of the museum's governing body to take independent action; he or she would be there to provide advice and information on specialist museum issues as required, particularly care of collections. The particular responsibilities of curatorial advisers are outlined in Guideline 26b and your AMC will be able to provide you with a copy of the Commission's more detailed *Guidance Notes on Curatorial Advisers* on request.

53 While AMC staff will be able to advise museums about potential curatorial advisers, they will not be able to act in this capacity themselves. For various reasons, it may not be possible in the short term to identify suitable individuals to act as curatorial advisers for particular museums. However, if these museums have expressed a willingness to follow such an arrangement when circumstances permit, provisional registration can be allocated until such time as a local solution is found.

Declaration

54 The final page of the application form constitutes a declaration that the information supplied is correct; that, to the best of their belief, museum governing bodies have complied with all legal, planning and safety requirements; and that they will continue to do so. The person who signs the form at 24 will, for local authority museums, usually be the chief executive or a chief officer and for independent museums, the chairman or secretary of the governing body.[2] It can be the person who completed the form, for example, the curator, but the museum's governing body must, under such circumstances, explicitly accept that the form is being signed

on its behalf. Where a museum has appointed a curatorial adviser, this person should also sign the form at 25.

55 Finally, if your regional closing date arrives before your governing body has had an opportunity to consider your policy documents, you can still submit your application. Enclose the draft policy documents and indicate the date on which they will be considered. The registration committee will be able to take an 'in principle' decision, subject only to confirmation that policies have been adopted. Remember that your application should be sent in the first instance to your AMC who will check that all the relevant documents are enclosed and that there are no points which require further clarification.

Museums and Galleries Commission
August 1990

MUSEUM REGISTRATION: GUIDANCE NOTES FOR MUSEUMS IN SCOTLAND

These guidance notes have been issued to supplement the *Guidelines for a Registration Scheme* **in the UK and to provide practical assistance in completing the application form.**

1 This is a voluntary scheme which is intended to benefit all museums, and to provide guidance to those who seek to assist them in their work. It takes a professionally-agreed definition of a museum (see Guideline 7) and asks each applicant institution to demonstrate that it conforms to this definition. Almost all the questions which you will be asked to answer stem from this definition. The criteria are such that they may be met equally by a national museum and by a village museum run by volunteers. Registration is not concerned with the scale of a museum's operation, nor with making detailed qualitative judgements about each museum's activities.

2 There is nothing revolutionary or new about the criteria contained in the *Registration Guidelines*. Most museums will be able to demonstrate that they have been fulfilling them for years. But even large and long-established museums may find that registration provides a valuable opportunity to review their basic functions and to translate good practices into written policies. There will be others, perhaps part of larger organizations which exist primarily to do other things, or very small museums at an early stage of development, for which registration will provide an important stimulus to sorting out what their collections are for, and the future basis upon which they will be maintained and developed.

3 The first two years of implementation (1988–90) have confirmed our expectations that 'registered museums' can come in every conceivable shape and size. They may not even include the word 'museum' in their title. They are united by the possession of a substantial collection of historic objects, works of art or scientific specimens which have been gathered together to provide a long-term public benefit. If the ownership, preservation and interpretation of such a collection forms a key element of your organization's activities then registration will be appropriate for you. If, after studying these notes and the *Guidelines*, you are still unsure whether your institution comes within the remit of the scheme, the Scottish Museums Council (AMC) or the Museums and Galleries Commission (MGC) will be able to advise you.

4 The scheme is being implemented on a phased basis throughout the United Kingdom. In Scotland, the Commission is being assisted in this task by the Scottish Museums Council. Their expertise and local knowledge will ensure that individual museums will have immediate access to any advice and assistance they may require.

5 Once your museum is registered, we will write to you again once a year for three years to ask whether the information which you initially supplied has changed in any way. In the fourth year we will ask you to submit a new application, but by that time we trust that all museums will be familiar with the procedure and that this will not involve much time or work on your part.

6 In future registration will provide basic eligibility for grant-aid and subsidized services provided by the Scottish Museums Council and the MGC, and this will take effect from 1992/93. Registered status will also be taken into account by a wide variety of other funding agencies when they consider grant applications from museums. A list of the agencies which have already agreed to support the scheme is given at Appendix I, and this list is growing all the time.

7 If a museum is unable to meet all the registration criteria immediately, but can demonstrate willingness and intention to work towards achieving what is required within a reasonable period, the registration committee will be able to award the status of *provisional registration*. This can be a recognition of achievements to date and represents an interim stage on the way to full registration. Provisionally registered museums will still be generally eligible for grant-aid and subsidized services and their progress towards full registration will be monitored through the process of annual review described above.

Applying for registration

8 Please begin by reading through the *Registration Guidelines* carefully. Each question on the application form refers to a paragraph of the *Guidelines*. In completing the form the most important point to bear in mind is that the registration committee should be easily able to gain a picture of your museum's structure and operation. Do not feel unduly constrained by the spaces available for your responses. If necessary, use separate sheets marked with the relevant question number, indicating that you have done this on the form itself. You may also wish to supply additional material (within reason!) such as a general publicity leaflet or an events programme in connection with Question 15.

9 A series of seminars on registration were held in Scotland between 1988 and 1990. As a result, it is anticipated that local authorities, and independent museums with appropriately experienced curators, should have little difficulty in preparing their applications. If, however, you are unsure of any point, staff at the SMC will be ready and willing to deal with enquiries by letter or telephone, or by arranging to visit you. If you are a museum service running more than one museum, please supply an application form for each. (Additional copies are available from SMC if we have not sent you enough.) Information common to all museums, such as details of constitution or finances, need only be given on one form, and reference made to it on the others.

10 In order to help the many small independent museums run by volunteers, or by specialists in other fields, such as many university or armed services collections, the Scottish Museums Council has appointed a network of professional curators to be

registration advisers. The name and address of the registration adviser covering your area is given in the letter from the Museums and Galleries Commission which accompanies these notes, and they will be in contact with you very soon. Their task is to help you work out-what your museum needs to do in order to be sure of meeting the criteria for registration at the first attempt, and to provide free specialist advice to you in certain key areas like the constitution, collecting policies and obtaining curatorial advice. If for any reason this arrangement proves impracticable, staff at the SMC will be only too pleased to help, direct.

11 Local authority museums and the larger independent museums which employ curators are being asked to return their completed application forms to the Scottish Museums Council *no later than* 31 March 1991. Applications from all other museums should be submitted to the SMC through their registration adviser no later than 30 September 1991.

12 As soon as the registration committee has considered your application we will write to you directly to inform you of the decision. Registered museums will subsequently receive a registration certificate bearing their registered museum number.

Notes on the application form

Question 6: formal constitution

13 'Describe the museum's relationship to its governing body'; this relationship is not always obvious; for example, collections may be owned by one organization but managed by another. Other examples of what might be indicated here are: the relationship of a university museum to the university as a whole; the relationship of a commercial museum to a parent company; the directorate, service or committee responsible for the administration of a local authority museum.

14 We recognize that it may be difficult for some local authority or university museums to supply copies of constitutional documents because it proves impossible to locate original committee minutes relating to the foundation of a museum. The relevant minute for local authority museums may date from local government reorganization. (Do not worry unduly if you cannot trace these: it is generally obvious under which powers a local authority is providing a museums service.) All other museums, however, must supply copies of their constitutional documents, whether it be a deed of trust, the memorandum and articles of a company limited by guarantee, or other relevant management agreement. Where one organization is managing a collection owned by another organization, the registration committee will expect that the arrangement is made the subject of written agreement.

15 Guideline 6 indicates that an 'acceptable' constitution is required, and refers to several published models, principally the booklet *Charitable Status for Museums (Scotland)* published by the Association of Independent Museums. A revised edition of this will be published in late 1990 and copies will be available through the SMC. In the meanwhile, your registration adviser should be able to tell you whether or not your existing constitution is likely to be acceptable, and to discuss any changes that may be appropriate. In many cases, they may be able to supply a model deed of trust in draft form. In order to meet the broad criteria of acceptability, your museum will almost certainly need to be operating under the terms of a deed of trust registered in the Books of the Council and Session, or the memorandum and articles of a company limited by guarantee, that is recognized as charitable by the Inland Revenue. It is

thought very unlikely that a museum constituted as a society in Scotland would be capable of meeting the criteria, although the final decision in any individual case will rest with the registration committee.

16 In supplying information about your museum's constitution, it will be helpful for you to bear in mind the kind of questions which the registration committee will be asking:

(a) Who owns the bulk of the collections?

(b) Are these collections established in the public domain? (A collection entirely owned by a private individual is not eligible.)

(c) Who manages the collections? Is the answer to this the same as (a)?

(d) Does the constitution contain a long-term intention to hold and maintain the collections?

(e) Are the collections treated as disposable assets? (This may be apparent from the balance sheet, rather than the written constitution.)

(f) What would happen to the collections if the organization which owned them ceased to exist?

(g) Are the collections used to generate income for non-museum purposes, or as collateral for loans?

Some of the answers to questions like these will be found in your responses to Question 9 (financial details) and Question 11 (acquisition and disposal policy). They may not be entirely covered by the constitutional documents which you are able to supply.

Question 9: financial details

17 We are not looking for any particular account formats; we accept that these will vary greatly. Try to ensure that the various pieces of financial information listed in Guideline 15 are covered. It is recognized that some (mainly local authority) museums will not be able to provide a balance sheet.

18 In the case of independent museums, the registration committee will be looking for evidence of financial stability. Risk of bankruptcy implies risk to the collections. The constitutional documents of independent museums should, ideally, make reference to transfer of the collections to another public museum in the event of closure or winding up. Museum collections should *not* be included as fixed assets in balance sheets and if this has been the practice up to this date, the registration committee will request that a change is made to future accounts. In the case of trusts not legally required to provide audited accounts, 'certified appropriately' is likely to mean by a chartered accountant, or by a treasurer.

19 If your museum's budget is consolidated within a larger organizational or departmental budget, please do your best to supply an estimated summary of museum expenditure.

20 Information concerning the 'status of buildings or sites housing the collections' (Question 10) refers to freehold or leasehold arrangements. It is intended to assist the committee in determining the long-term security of the museum, a factor not always apparent from financial information alone.

Question 11: acquisition and disposal policy

21 There are two ways of responding to this question, which are outlined below. The first is the easiest, and represents the minimum statement which the committee will

accept; the second requires a bit more time, but is strongly recommended and all museums will be expected to achieve this in due course. In either case, you will find the SMC's Factsheet 'Collections and disposal policies for museums', available from the Scottish Museums Council or your registration adviser, to be useful reading. Whichever way you make this statement, it must be formally approved by your governing body, and evidence of this approval supplied (see the box at the bottom of this question).

22 The first method is to write a brief statement of your acquisition policy on the form, under the space for Question 11. The points you should cover in this statement are listed in Guideline 18a. In this space, of course, you will probably only be able to indicate broad subject areas and make general statements of intent, but this can constitute an adequate first attempt at an acquisition policy. As time goes on, you can consider how to expand your statement and at that stage you will need to produce a separate document. (You must, in any case, review your policy at least once every five years.) Your governing body must now be asked formally to adopt this acquisition policy and, additionally, should be asked to adopt all the paragraphs of Guideline 18 as a general policy to which it will henceforward subscribe.

23 The second method is to produce a separate document incorporating both your acquisition policy (based on the points in Guideline 18a) and disposal policy (based on paragraphs (b) to (j) of Guideline 18). This is more highly recommended because your policy can never properly be made public if it only exists in the form of a series of committee minutes (see Guideline 18b). You can tailor the wording of the Guideline 18 paragraphs so that they make specific reference to your museum and your governing body but *you should not alter the disposal paragraphs in such a way as to change their meaning.* You may, of course, adopt a stricter disposal policy if you so wish, and some museums have chosen to do this. The *Guidelines* represent the most permissive statement which is acceptable.

24 It is important to emphasize that disposal of items from museum collections is not being ruled out where there are sound curatorial reasons for pursuing this course. But unless each museum governing body accepts the principle of 'strong presumption against disposal', the long-term purpose of the museum is called into question (see Guideline 7a and 7b).

25 In responding to the question on disposal policy many museums cite the fact that their governing body has already adopted the Museums Association's *Code of Practice*, which covers this issue. This is entirely acceptable so long as it is the updated (1987) code which has been adopted. The earlier code (1977) contained a less detailed statement regarding disposals.

26 Please note that registration does not require that the full disposal procedure is followed (e.g. advertisement in the *Museums Journal*) in cases where a museum decides to transfer 'ownership' of an item to another registered museum, although we would expect that such transfers were agreed by a museum's governing body, and that full records were kept.

27 Some industrial and transport museums will wish to make the reasonable point that not all their items are acquired with a view to permanent retention: they may be used to provide parts for restoring other machinery or vehicles, or the museum may wish to 'trade-up' to acquire better examples of the same machinery or models. This argues the case for not 'accessioning' certain types of material which are acquired, but recording them in some other way which reflects the museum's intentions

towards them. The same principle applies in the case of school loan or 'handling' collections which all kinds of museums create. It is advisable not to treat these as part of the permanent collection because there is an intention to use them in such a way that preservation cannot be guaranteed. It is therefore sensible to record these outside the main accession record.

28 If your museum does periodically acquire and dispose of certain types of material for the kind of specialist reasons outlined above, this should be clearly stated in your written disposal policy.

Question 12: your museum's existing collection

29 Please provide a brief summary of the subject areas covered, with approximate numbers of items, or rough proportions of types of material. The subjects covered by your existing collections may differ slightly from your present acquisition policy, particularly in long-established museums. The proportion of items on loan can be a significant factor. For example, if 70 per cent of a museum's collection were owned by one private individual, and the items on loan could theoretically be withdrawn at any time, the museum's future could be in jeopardy. The registration committee will wish to look carefully at such cases, and will always expect that such loans are at least subject to written agreements. In cases where one organization is managing a collection owned by another organization (see also 13, 14 and 16 above) acquisition and disposal policies should be approved both by the museum's governing body and by the body which owns the collection. Again, the registration committee would hope to see such arrangements covered by written agreements.

30 If you are writing your acquisition and disposal policy as a separate document, it is sensible to commence with details of the existing collections.

Question 13: documentation

31 The following brief notes are intended to provide immediate guidance to small museums without professional curatorial staff. Staff at the Scottish Museums Council will always be able to advise on basic documentation standards, whilst more detailed guidance is available free of charge from the Scottish Museums Documentation Adviser, who is based in the National Museums of Scotland Documentation Unit at the Royal Museum of Scotland, Chambers Street, Edinburgh. Alternatively, you can contact the Museum Documentation Association, based at Building 0, 347 Cherry Hinton Road, Cambridge: they run training seminars on all aspects of documentation throughout the UK, and can also deal with enquiries from individual museums. Three useful publications for you to consult are:

Wimps, Worms and Winchesters (RMS)
Practical Museum Documentation (MDA (1980))
Planning the Documentation of Museum Collections (MDA (1985))

32 Documentation embraces all the records and information associated with museum collections. A museum without any documentation is useless: it cannot legally prove that it owns any of its collections; it cannot account to donors for what has been given, or to auditors for what has been bought; it cannot maintain proper security; and it has probably destroyed most of the historical and scientific value of its collections. Hopefully, there are not many museums in quite such a dire state. But we know that there are many where documentation is not taken as seriously as it ought to be; where not all the minimum forms of record required by registration are

maintained, or where there are large backlogs of work. Documentation is time-consuming, and because it is not an area of work that has any immediate effect on a museum's public face, it tends to be given low priority. Registration is intended to encourage museums to give documentation much higher priority.

33 *Entry records* must be kept of every item entering (and by the same token, leaving) the museum premises, for whatever reason. We have all heard stories of items brought in for identification being lost, or members of the public turning up ten years later to reclaim items 'on loan' which the museum believed it owned. Museums just can't afford to be sloppy about keeping records; they are in the business of looking after objects. However superfluous it may seem at times, you must scrupulously maintain entry records.

34 The entry record must consist of at least the following information:

   (a) The name of the museum.
   (b) Full name and address of the donor/owner/lender.
   (c) A brief description of the item or items, sufficient to allow someone else to identify it if necessary.
   (d) The reason why it has been brought into the museum – e.g. for identification/for temporary exhibition/as a gift/as a long-term loan/purchased.
   (e) The date the item entered the museum.
   (f) The signature of the donor/owner/lender and the signature of the museum representative who has taken the item in. Lenders' signatures should also be obtained when an item is returned to them.
   (g) It is advisable to record information which donors provide about objects as part of the entry record.

   It is sensible to use these points as pre-prepared headings in whatever form of document or book you are using as an entry record, to remind staff of what they should record. The MDA sells pads of triplicate, write-through entry forms, which are recommended as they provide a copy which can be immediately given to the depositor, but there are many other acceptable methods, provided the above data is recorded in some way.

35 Give each entry record a number of some kind so that a label bearing this number can be attached to the object. These numbers are not the same as accession numbers (see below) because they are being used to identify objects you intend to keep as well as those which you may only hold for a week or so. A common way of providing an entry number system is E1, E2, E3, etc. The entry number should be unique to each item or group of items relating to an individual depositor on a particular day.

36 By their very nature, entry records can't really be created retrospectively. If your museum hasn't kept such records up to now you should introduce a system forthwith, and include a statement to this effect in your answer to Question 13.

37 The accession register is the formal record of items which have been incorporated into your permanent collection. Accession records should be created as soon as possible after a decision has been made to retain an item for your permanent collection. The accession register is a record of items which your museum now legally owns, although some museums also record long-term loans in the same register. This is acceptable, so long as loans are clearly distinguished from gifts and purchases. The accession register is also used to record the number which will in future uniquely identify each item in your collection. It should be a securely-bound book (such as a

company minutes book) printed on substantial paper which is unlikely to deteriorate with time. Loose-leaf records, or records on index cards, are not acceptable. Fully automated documentation systems should be backed up by an accessions register which may be in the form of a bound hard copy output. This must be updated at regular intervals.

38 The following *minimum* information should be recorded in the accession register: item number; date of entry into museum and entry number; donor's name and address (or person from whom purchased); brief physical identifying description. If you are not yet maintaining a catalogue of the collection over and above the accession register, it will also be necessary to record unique information associated with an item's history and use. The usual method of numbering items in an accession register is to use a running sequence in combination with the year, e.g. 1988:1, 1988:2, 1988:3, although other methods are acceptable. Do not attempt to incorporate a classification system into this number sequence (e.g. A1988:1 for an art object). This is a good recipe for getting into a muddle later. Classifications can change over time and should be imposed at another level, for example, through indexes and catalogues.

39 As the accession register constitutes the long-term legal record of your permanent collections, you should periodically make copies of new entries and store these securely in another building. Original registers should be kept in secure conditions, ideally in a fire-proof cabinet.

40 *Marking or labelling* items with their unique accession numbers ensures that they will never become disassociated from the information in the relevant accession and entry records. We recognize that it may not always be possible or appropriate to mark small items such as coins, stamps or insects individually but these should be stored in such a way that individual holders or cabinets can be clearly marked with accession numbers. Methods of marking should be permanent enough not to rub off, fade, or become unintentionally detached, but at the same time they should not damage the appearance of the item or endanger its physical condition. If you are unsure on how to go about marking and labelling specimens, the SMC's Factsheet on 'Labelling and marking' is available from the Council's headquarters or through your registration adviser, and will prove very useful.

41 There are many kinds of index which a museum can produce to facilitate use of its collections. Even the smallest museum should aim to produce some kind of search alternative to the numerical accession number sequence provided by the register. An *index of donors* is important because it reinforces your ability to account for objects to your public and to your auditors, and a *location index* will help you to find items readily and to carry out inventory checks. The *subject indexes* which you will use depend upon the nature of your collections. Whether you use name indexes or classified subject indexes, you should work to an agreed convention. There are a number of standard published classification systems and name lists which may be appropriate to your collections (further information on these is available from the NMS Documentation Service or the MDA). If you are using your own subject classification systems and standard names, make sure these are written down so that the same rules are always followed by everyone involved.

42 *Policy to eliminate backlog.* The registration committee will not be surprised to see that museums have documentation backlogs, but it will expect museums to make an honest and realistic assessment of the work involved and to show some intention to

tackle the problem. Finding extra staff and new resources for this purpose is not likely to be an option open to every museum, and this makes it all the more important that existing personnel commit some of their time to the problem, even if it is only two hours a week on a regular basis. The important principle is that backlogs should diminish: an increasing backlog should be viewed with alarm. Your registration adviser will be able to assist you in formulating policies to eliminate backlogs.

43 We have already said that entry records cannot be created retrospectively and in a sense this will affect your ability to create accession records retrospectively. An un-accessioned item may have lost any associated information which told how the museum acquired it, and why. You will not be able retrospectively to record such an item as a 'gift' in your accession register if you have no written evidence that this was the case. If all attempts to trace associated information and donors or lenders fail, the item can be recorded in the accession register as 'source and status unknown'. It is this type of problem that the maintenance of proper entry and accession records is intended to avoid in future.

44 Your policy to achieve documentation requirements (Question 13c) should demonstrate that you have realistically identified your problems; that you understand how they should be tackled; and that you intend to tackle them within the shortest time-span that resources will allow. Some museums will have to face the fact that their documentation problems will require additional resources. A documentation backlog need not be a bar to full registration if the registration committee is satisfied that the museum is willing and able to take problems in hand.

Question 14: access to professional conservation advice

45 Preventative conservation (i.e. providing proper conditions for storage and display of museum collections) is an important element of collections care. Please provide details of who advises you in matters of preventative conservation (particularly in the case of small museums without professionally trained staff); who provides advice on specialist conservation treatments which objects in your collections may require; and who undertakes such treatments where they are carried out. It will also be helpful to indicate whether your museum has a budget for conservation work.

Question 15, 16, 17: public services

46 It should be emphasized that the fact that 'public services' only warrant three paragraphs in the *Guidelines* does not mean that they are considered to be of less importance than the other aspects (although by implication all the guidelines are concerned with proper management of public or charitable collections under public or charitable funding). It would have been difficult to make strictures in these areas because not all forms of interpretation or of visitor facility are appropriate to each museum. The registration committee will be adding the information given here to the overall picture of the museum and will want to be assured that the museum is alive to its responsibilities to the public.

47 To give some hypothetical cases: the registration committee would probably look askance at a large local authority museum without any form of educational provision. On the other hand, it would be unreasonable to insist that a village museum run by volunteers should have a regular temporary exhibition programme. The committee would hope that museums on green-field sites would provide toilets

and somewhere to park, but could not insist that museums in the centre of towns should provide car parking.

48 Under Guideline 22, although not mentioned in the list of examples, 'permanent exhibitions' are of course one element of interpretation; other services which might be included here are guided tours, special events, lecture programmes, talks given outside museum, etc.

49 *Opening hours and public access*: a collection only accessible by written appointment would be eligible if the committee were satisfied that these arrangements were appropriate to the nature of the institution and were well-publicized, and that the museum were able to respond to such requests regularly enough to permit steady access, not just, for example, three or four visits a year. In the case of museums with restricted access it will be useful to indicate average annual visitor numbers. Some specialist museums, despite restricted access, annually deal with a high number of written and telephone enquiries which in themselves constitute a form of public access. You should note this factor if it is relevant. It is useful to make reference to advertising, signposting, etc. in answering Question 17.

Question 20, 21, 22: access to professional curatorial advice

Does the museum employ a curator? (Question 20)

50 We accept that job titles will vary. The senior staff member responsible for day-to-day management of your museum may be called director, keeper, manager, administrator or secretary. This question is designed to ascertain whether among those responsible for running your museum there is someone who has received training in, or who has long experience of, the range of skills particularly associated with collections management and care. These skills do not simply imply familiarity with the subject areas dealt with by the museum: it is possible to be a first-rate engineer, ornithologist or military historian and still not have much familiarity with the general principles of collections management. It is certainly the case, however, that many museum staff acquire these skills through in-service training and by implementing professional advice provided by those outside the museum organization. The committee always takes account of such factors where post-holders have no formal museum qualification, and you are encouraged to provide this kind of additional information where appropriate. If you feel that existing personnel could be assisted by the opportunity to receive outside professional advice on a regular basis, you should additionally consider the appointment of a trustee or a board member with curatorial expertise, or a curatorial adviser (see 52 below).

Access to the managing committee (Question 21)

51 District and regional councils in Scotland running museums should note that the *Registration Guidelines* have received formal endorsement from the Convention of Scottish Local Authorities, and that access to committee was a point which was particularly discussed with all local authority associations in the UK at the consultation stage.

All agreed that there should be no reason why a curator responsible for the management of a museum service should not normally be present when the relevant committee considered items concerning museum policy and estimates. In other types of museum, this question is only likely to pose problems when the museum is part of a much larger organization such as a university or a public utility and there is no intermediate governing committee to oversee the organization's museum function. In these cases it may be useful to consider the formation of such a committee and in this the Scottish Museums Council will be ready to advise.

Curatorial advisers

52 Where there is a lack of curatorial expertise (see paragraph 50 above) among existing staff of small museums, or where a small museum is essentially run on a voluntary basis, it will still be eligible for registration if the governing body receives professional curatorial advice on a regular basis, either because a trained and/or experienced curator is a member of the governing body, or because the museum has formally appointed such a person as a curatorial adviser. The appropriate arrangement will depend upon the structure of the museum's governing body. It is not possible for us to lay down strict criteria as to what will constitute a 'small' museum in the registration committee's terms of reference, but the size and importance of the collections and the museum's annual income are the kind of factors which will inevitably be taken into account. Many small museums already have good working relationships with the local district curator or staff in the local museum, and this offers an opportunity to formalize this relationship. It would not be expected that a curatorial adviser would interfere with, or be held responsible for, the ability of the museum's governing body to take independent action; he or she would be there to provide advice and information on specialist museum issues as required, particularly care of collections. The particular responsibilities of curatorial advisers are outlined in Guideline 26b and your registration adviser will be able to provide you with a copy of the Commission's more detailed *Guidance Notes on Curatorial Advisers* on request.

53 Your registration adviser or the Scottish Museums Council will be able to advise museums about potential curatorial advisers. In many cases, your registration adviser may be willing and able to accept appointment as your curatorial adviser, but the professional staff of the Scottish Museums Council will not themselves be able to act in this capacity. In some cases, particularly in more remote areas, it may not always be possible to immediately identify a suitable individual to act as curatorial adviser. However, if there is a demonstrated willingness to appoint an adviser when circumstances permit, provisional registration can be allocated until the situation is resolved.

Declaration

54 The final page of the application form constitutes a declaration that the information supplied is correct and that, to the best of their belief, museum governing bodies have complied with all legal, planning and safety requirements and will continue to do so. The person who signs the form at 24 will, for local authority museums, usually be the chief executive or a chief officer and for independent museums, the chairman or secretary of the governing body.[3] It can be the person who completed the form, for example, the curator, but the museum's governing body must, under such circumstances, explicitly accept that the form is being signed on their behalf. Where a museum has appointed a curatorial adviser, this person should also sign the form at 25.

55 If for any reason it looks as though you might be unable to meet the closing date set out in 11 above, for example, because your governing body has not had an opportunity to consider your policy documents, you may still be able to submit your

application. In such circumstances, you should contact the Scottish Museums Council as soon as you know that you may need to submit a late application, and they will advise you on what action to take.

Museums and Galleries Commission
August 1990

NOTES

1 Throughout this document the term 'museum' is used to subsume 'gallery'.
2 We apologise for the printing error in this section of the application form: the reference here should be to Guideline 18 – the introductory paragraph.
3 We apologise for the printing error in this section of the application form: the reference here should be to Guideline 18 – the introductory paragraph.

APPENDIX 1

Funding agencies in Scotland, England, Wales and Northern Ireland which have agreed to support the Museums Registration Scheme

(The list is not exhaustive or final)

Army Museums Ogilby Trust
Arts Council of Great Britain
Association of County Councils
Association of District Councils
Association of Metropolitan Boroughs
Carnegie UK Trust
Convention of Scottish Local Authorities
Council of Regional Arts Associations
Countryside Commission
Crafts Council
Department of Education, Northern Ireland
Department of the Environment
English Tourist Board
Highlands and Islands Development Board
National Art-Collections Fund
National Heritage Memorial Fund
National Trust for Scotland
Office of Arts and Libraries
Pilgrim Trust
Regional Tourist Boards (England)
Scottish Development Agency
Scottish Education Department
Scottish Tourist Board
Training Agency
Welsh Office

4

A *framework for management*
B. Lord, G. D. Lord and J. Nicks

This chapter presents some of the main findings of a survey of museums' collecting practices and the factors which affect collecting and collections. It also proposes a framework for calculating the actual costs of acquisition, which extend beyond the initial acquisition. In short, there is no such thing as a free gift.

This chapter reviews some of the main findings of the study and suggests a way in which they may be used to establish a framework for identifying the nature and scope of collection costs. This framework is presented in the hope that it will assist museums in predicting costs more accurately and therefore lay the foundation for more effective allocation of the resources assigned to collection care and management. Other practical applications of the study are also noted:

The discussion is divided into four sections:

- cost categories
- cost variables
- cost projections
- practical applications

COST CATEGORIES

Among factors for consideration are acquisition costs, and both direct and indirect costs of collection care.

Acquisition costs

The most basic cost which can be attributed to the cost of collecting is the cost of acquisition, whether it be by purchase, donation or as a product of research. For the purposes of this study, these costs are considered to be nil. In this analysis we have been considering only the operating cost categories which need to be understood as a basis for establishing a framework for allocating museum resources for the management and care of collections.

Nevertheless, it is useful to consider the scale of expenditure on acquisition by purchase. Most museums receive annual acquisition funds or grants. To this may be added endowed funds, special purchase funds raised by support organizations, and the major national purchase funds such as the National Heritage Memorial Fund. The median annual expenditure of acquisition funds from all of these sources for the sixty-one museums in the study sample was £12,000.

This can be compared with the median operating costs, which averaged £475,000 for all museums, ranging from £165,000 for independent museums to £491,000 for local authority museums to £2,291,000 for the national and university museums. Expressed as a proportion of operating costs, the annual expenditure on collection purchases is only 2.5 per cent for all museums, ranging from 1.2 per cent in the independent museums to 5.5 per cent with the national museums.

Operating cost categories

Data from the survey and case studies have been used to examine the operating cost categories identified in the early stages of the study on the basis of expert interviews and literature research. These have been analysed under the following headings:

- general curatorial functions
- documentation
- conservation
- stock-taking
- research
- security
- building maintenance and repair
- administration
- library
- education
- exhibits
- other public activities
- other

The average apportionment of costs by museums in the study sample was:

	%	%
All curatorial functions		24
Curatorial programmes	13	
Documentation	4	
Conservation	4	
Research	2	
Stock-taking	1	
Administration		19
Maintenance		18
All public activities		14
Exhibits	7	
Education	4	
Other public activities	3	
Security		14
Library		2
Other		9
Total operating costs		100

Operating costs directly attributable to collecting

Costs directly attributable to caring for the collection would include the curatorial and security categories:

	%
All curatorial functions	24
Security	14
Direct collection care costs	38

By type of governance, these direct collection costs range from an average of almost 60 per cent among the national museums in the study sample to less than 30 per cent among the independent museums, with the local authority museums being close to the average for all museums.

Indirect operating costs of collecting

While these percentages may be used to provide a general notion of the direct costs for maintaining collections, they do not provide a complete indication of costs related to collection management and care as they do not include any provision for a proportion of the general maintenance and administration charges.

Although it might be possible to ascertain a 'true' basis for allocating such costs by undertaking a detailed audit of expenditures and staff time, it would be useful to develop a rule-of-thumb method for estimating them.

A realistic estimate can be made by using a formula which takes account of both the space occupied by collections and the proportion of the annual budget allocated to collection management and care. Where:

a = proportion of operating budget allotted to collection management and care directly

b = proportion of space permanently occupied by collections (stores and permanent exhibitions)

c = operating costs for building repair and maintenance, heat, light and power

I = indirect cost for collection care

The formula for estimating indirect costs may then be stated in the following way:

$(100 - (a + c)) \times a = d$

$b \times c = e$

$d + e = I$

An example of the formula's use is presented here using the following round figures based on the data presented in detail in appendix C:

a (direct costs above)	= 38%
c (maintenance costs above)	= 18%
a + c =	56%

The first line of the formula therefore reads:

(100 − 56) x 38% = 16.72% (d)

Since we have determined that the proportion of space permanently occupied by collections in our survey group is 64.3% (= b), the second line of the formula will be:

64.3% x 18 = 11.57% (e)

Indirect costs of collecting may therefore be calculated in the third line of the formula as the sum of the first two lines:

%

d = 16.72

e = 11.75

I = 28.47

Total direct and indirect cost of collecting

The total cost of collecting, exclusive of acquisition costs, may then be calculated as the total of direct and indirect costs:

%

Direct costs = 38

Indirect costs = 28.47

Total costs = 66.47

This figure is likely to provide a close approximation of the percentage of costs actually invested in collection management and care.

If the calculation above is applied to statistics derived from the different categories of museums by governance, the following picture emerges, in rounded figures:

Table 4.1 Total direct and indirect costs for collection management and care

	%
National and university	83
Local authority	70
Independent	59

Before accepting these figures at face value it is important to consider what sources of error there may be.

In chapter 3 [not included in the present text], evidence was presented to indicate that the study sample is generally representative of the whole museum population with the exception of the fact that national museums were over-represented. However, the study sample is a small one, especially when it is segmented into different categories of museums. It is important, therefore, that the figures presented here should be interpreted with caution.

Information from the case studies has indicated the nature of some of the precautions that should be taken.

The most important concern is that the figures should not be interpreted as ideal or target figures. At best they represent a fair approximation of the current state of affairs with respect to collection management and care.

As other studies discussed during the literature review have thoroughly demonstrated, there are many serious areas of concern in collection care that remain to be addressed in all categories of museum. Some have primarily capital cost implications like the need for improved environmental controls and facilities for storage and conservation laboratories. Others may reflect more directly on operating requirements like the need to deal with the documentation and conservation backlogs and to find a suitable way of filling the labour requirements formerly met by widespread use of MSC programmes. If anything, the figures presented here may be lower than they would be if actual standards of collection management and care were to match ideal standards.

Despite these cautions, however, the basic trend indicated by this analysis is probably accurate. On average, two-thirds of the operating costs of museums are attributable to the cost of managing and caring for their collections. National museums tend to allocate more of their resources to collection management and care than museums under other governance; and the independent museums tend to spend the least in proportion to their means.

COST VARIABLES

Museum directors indicated that the most significant variables were likely to be:

- condition of the collection
- building type, condition
- type of collection

This was a different order of priorities than had been suggested by a panel of experts consulted during the research design phase of the study. They had suggested that the most important variable was likely to be the type of collection, particularly with respect to the materials in the collection and the size of the objects. They advised that the type and governance of the museum was not likely to be a decisive variable.

The analysis of the survey data has indicated to the contrary, that museum governance appears to be a significant variable affecting the structure of costs related to collections. It would be dangerous, however, to ascribe any causality to this relationship. The reasons may lie more in the different mandates of the museums than their type of governance.

In this section we address in turn the following variables:

- condition of the collections
- building type and condition
- type of collection
- museum governance

Condition of the collection

Observations by the study team during the case studies tends to support the contention that this is a significant variable. In addition, recent conservation surveys like *Conservation in Hertfordshire Museums* by Laura Drysdale (1988) and *A Conservation Survey* of *Museum Collections in Scotland* by Brian Ramer (1989) have indicated that collections in many local government and independent museums can be described as being in fair to poor condition with a large proportion in need of some treatment. The NAO Report on the *Management of the Collections of the English National Museums and Galleries* (1988) and subsequent committee hearings have indicated that some of the national collections are also in need of a major and expensive conservation effort. Unfortunately, without a consistent method of measuring relative conditions of collections, it was not possible in this study to ascertain the relative significance of collection condition as a cost variable. We are convinced, however, that this is a significant variable which needs to be brought into a calculation of future costs. The ultimate cost of neglect would be the destruction of the collection base itself.

Building type and condition

Building type and condition is also a significant factor. During case-study visits it was observed that listed buildings imposed limits on the level of climatic control that could be achieved. Poor buildings endanger collections housed in them, leading to a loss through deterioration of the core asset of the museum, and an obligation to make capital expenditures in order to upgrade or repair the inadequate space. These cost implications are easily disguised, and often deferred, but they are none the less real. Further, in a number of cases, conservation of a listed building is counter-productive to conservation of the collection it houses. On the other hand, there was no indication in the survey data that showed a direct cost relationship with the age of buildings or other easily identified parameters. As a consequence, it was not possible to test the validity of this proposition with quantitative analysis. This is an important variable which would appear likely to reward further study.

Type of collection

The type of collection is a variable that logically ought to be very significant, and by some calculations it can be shown to be so. Large industrial objects are usually much more costly to store and conserve than coins or small archaeological finds because of their size and complexity, although security requirements of smaller objects may offset the size factor. Textiles and costumes require more costly storage and treatment than collections of glass or ceramics. Unfortunately, it proved difficult to demonstrate a clear relationship between either collection size or material with costs by using information from the study database. This was partially due to the small size of the database, but it also reflects the complexity of the data occasioned by the fact that most museums collect such a wide range of objects that cost differences due to the nature of the collections tend to be masked. Again, further study at a more specific level within institutions may lead to a more precise statement of the importance of this variable.

Museum governance

The survey results indicated that in many areas of expenditure and policy the nature of museum governance is a significant variable. Information from the case studies has helped to place the interpretation of the findings into a more realistic framework.

The case studies have confirmed that independent museums generally place a lower priority on curatorial functions than do the national and university museums, with local authority museums occupying a median position. The differences in practice may not be as great as apparent differences in the allocation of financial resources. Evidence has been presented which shows that local authority and independent museums make extensive use of volunteers and employment training programmes to undertake curatorial and documentation projects. While these practices may narrow the gap, there are distinct differences in priorities, especially in the area of research. Research is recognized as a major core curatorial function at the national and university museums, but receives little attention at many of the independent museums.

Security costs also appear to vary with the factor of governance. This may be partially explained by the factor that the most valuable collections tend to be held in the national institutions. The priority given to collection security appears to be related to a perception of risk, with more resources being assigned to care for the most valuable things. Where the need is greater, the costs are likely to be higher. On the other hand, there is no evidence to suggest that local and independent museums are lacking an appropriate level of concern about security issues. The security function in galleries is often covered by staff who have other functions such as guides, educators or even cleaners. In addition, although insurance costs are a major cost item to many of the smaller museums, they are frequently considered to be part of administrative rather than security costs.

This last practice is symptomatic of difficulties in interpreting apparent variations in administrative costs. There is a considerable amount of variation in the way in which administrative costs are defined. In addition, in large organizations, managerial and administrative functions are widely delegated and thus diffused throughout the institution. Projections of administrative costs in these cases may well underestimate the actual costs of administration. On the other hand, the smaller museums have limited numbers of permanent staff who typically have little time left to allocate to curatorial duties after dealing with a wide range of administrative and public responsibilities. On balance, the survey results may exaggerate the differences between the museum categories, but it is likely that a part of the observed difference is real.

Cost differences for building occupancy, maintenance and repair reflect in large measure different practices in accounting for costs. It has been noted that the cost allocations for the national museums in past years did not reflect the full costs because buildings were cared for by the government's Property Services Agency (PSA). This is no longer the case and if revised figures were used for the survey, they would undoubtedly show national museum allocations for buildings to be much closer to those reported by the independent museums.

COST PROJECTIONS

This section notes the importance of perceiving collecting costs in the context of an 'opportunity cost' analysis, and provides a framework of cost categories for the projection of collecting costs.

Opportunity cost

If collections management is to be effective in controlling collection growth it is important that the implications of making a collection decision be fully explored before a commitment is made. It is in recognition of this that some museums have initiated the policy of requiring detailed justification of all acquisition decisions. In addition to costs, curators or keepers are also required to consider the availability of staff and space resources. These are also costs, although their value may be expressed only in terms of availability. If space is not available, it either needs to be created or a decision taken to say 'no'. Or, viewed in another way, if an artefact is acquired, it will consume staff and space resources that would otherwise be available for other purposes. There is, therefore, an opportunity cost for every decision. This cost is the value of resources that would have been released for other uses if a different decision had been made.

A procedure that assigns a cost or value to all factors to be considered in making collection decisions would be useful in comparing applications for the use of scarce resources. The sum of these costs constitutes the opportunity costs of a prospective decision. In making collection decisions, these costs need to be balanced against projected benefits of proposed or competing uses in order to arrive at a decision.

In order to ensure that the costs are comparable, it may be useful to consider future costs or obligations, which may be calculated as capitalized costs. This is realistic, as the resources which may be required to care for a collection could be used or invested in other ways now or in future.

In her paper on 'The cost of accepting objects', Dr Rachel Maines (1986) pointed out that many of the costs (and benefits?) relevant to museums 'resist quantification' in monetary terms. In some cases these qualitative considerations will be decisive. This does not, however, lessen the value of assigning a monetary cost whenever possible, even if it is essentially notional. A realistic projection of the total cost implications of collection decisions should contribute towards more informed decisions and a more rational allocation of resources.

A framework of costs

The cost categories which have been analysed in this paper should prove useful in establishing a framework for projecting the cost of managing and caring for prospective acquisitions. The cost categories to be considered are:

- *Initial cost of acquisition*
- purchase
- curatorial
- documentation
- conservation
- storage

- *Operating costs for management and care*
- curatorial functions for collections management
- documentation
- stock-taking
- research
- conservation
- security
- building maintenance and repair overload
- administrative overload

Initial cost of acquisition

In calculating the costs of acquisition, the actual cost should be expressed as a capital investment, regardless of the source of the funds used for purchase or to pay for other costs associated with the acquisition.

The costs to be included will be:

- *Purchase*. The purchase cost (if any) should be calculated to include related expenditures such as costs of removal, packing, appraisals, auction fees, or any other direct expenditures on the actual acquisition.
- *Curatorial*. The second category would include the curatorial costs associated with acquisition, including curatorial time spent in negotiating the acquisition, in carrying out background research and preparing documentation to support acquisition.
- *Documentation*. The third category of expenditure would be for the initial documentation including entry records and cataloguing. Estimates for these costs presented ranged as high as £10 per accession. Costs could be higher depending on the amount of detail to be recorded for each item and the amount of research required.
- *Conservation* or restoration costs should also be considered as part of the initial cost, regardless of whether any work is carried out immediately. The projection should include cost for condition assessment and preparation of condition report as well as any active intervention required to stabilize and preserve the accession. In the instance of artefacts which it is proposed to restore for display or demonstration, the cost to undertake this work should be projected as part of the display or activities costs rather than the acquisition cost.
- *Storage* cost is the final category which should be included here. There are several components to this. The projection should include an estimate of the cost to prepare collections for storage including staff and material costs. In addition, the projection should include a notional estimate of the capital cost for the space occupied by the collection in storage. Even when the object is to be placed on display this calculation should be based on the amount of space it would occupy if placed in store. The experience of the curator or keeper is the best guide to the estimate of space needed, although it is important that it should reflect the space needed for storage under proper conditions. Capital costs for renovation or new construction vary considerably and should be based on industry averages in the museum region.

In summary, a projection of the initial cost of acquisition should include the following cost elements:

- purchase cost (if any)
- curatorial costs of the acquisition
- immediate documentation costs
- conservation or restoration costs
- cost of providing adequate storage space

The total of these costs will be the initial acquisition cost. As these add to the value of the assets of the museum they may be regarded as a capital investment.

Operating costs for management and care

In order to project the full dimensions of the financial obligation being assumed when collections are acquired, it is also useful to consider the continuing costs for maintaining the collection.

The annual costs for managing and caring for collections represent an obligation which is accepted at the time of acquisition and may be considered to be part of the initial cost of acquisition for the purpose of accounting for the cost and comparing with other possible uses for the museum's resources. Some of the cost categories to be considered are:

- curatorial functions for collection management
- documentation
- stock-taking
- research
- conservation
- security
- building maintenance and repair overload
- administrative overload

Although it might be possible to prepare detailed projections of these costs it would be a tedious process and the results would be problematic. For planning purposes it is only necessary to know relative costs.

A reasonable approximation of operating costs may be calculated by applying the operating costs to the space occupied by artefacts on a pro rata basis.

The average operating cost per square metre is £178.40. For the purposes of projecting costs related to collection management and care, this should be multiplied by the percentage of the budget allocated to those functions. We have seen that on average they are about 67 per cent, which would yield a projected cost of about £120 per square metre.

Capitalized costs

To complete this calculation of cost obligations, the annual operating costs should be capitalized in order to make them comparable with the initial costs of acquisition, which represent a capital investment, as noted above. For the sake of illustration this would mean a capitalized operating cost of £1,200 for an artefact requiring 1 square metre of storage space.

This projection is not a very sensitive one, however, as size is the only independent variable in the equation. A more sensitive and realistic projection should make allowance for the variation of conservation and management needs of different materials, types of artefacts and intended uses. A simple way to introduce this consideration is to adopt a weighting system. Cost experiences provided to us in the case studies indicated that an appropriate range would go from 0.5 to 2. For example, sensitive materials requiring more expensive storage or care could be assigned a weighting factor up to 2 in recognition that costs to maintain them will be higher. Stable materials on the other hand could be given a weighting of 0.5 in recognition of the fact that they will cost less than the average accession to maintain.

The final calculation will be the addition of the capital cost and the capitalized operating cost to constitute a single measure of the obligation implicit in a prospective addition to the collections.

PRACTICAL APPLICATIONS

Practical applications of this study may be realized in three directions:

- A management framework for projecting collection costs.
- The need for standards development.
- The need for further study.

A management framework for projecting collection costs

Realistic accounting of the costs of looking after museum collections is an essential precondition for the development of effective systems for justifying, receiving and allocating resources. In this report we have demonstrated that the real costs of fulfilling the primary function of museums to collect and preserve are on average over two-thirds of their annual operating budgets. To this must be added the capital costs of acquisition and constructing facilities to house the collections.

We have discussed ways in which the projected costs of collection care and management can be calculated in order to establish a basis for comparative analysis and to assist in establishing priorities. The estimates of costs are based upon actual cost experience and include a capitalized projection of future operating costs. The estimate of costs will provide guidance for estimating the opportunity cost of collection decisions.

The proposed framework will provide an estimate of collection management and care costs at two levels, for individual artefacts or collections, and for the institution. Assessment of the values to be set against them will be based upon an examination of both qualitative and quantitative considerations. The cost figures will be concrete measures, but it is important to realize that they will provide standardized projections intended to assist the management process. The advantage of adopting a system to account for both the initial and future costs of collecting is to lay the ground for better-informed management decisions. When the full costs are known from the outset, decisions on acquisition will be more rational and informed.

The need for standards development

Estimates have to be made in the light of a recognized standard of excellence. Without such a standard, the projection of collection costs will inevitably be somewhat arbitrary, and may not reflect the true requirement for an individual artefact, or for an institution.

Contributors and contributions to the evolution of standards in several relevant fields in the UK include:

Collections management	• MGC Registration Scheme • Funding of training and research • Corporate planning
Documentation	• Minimum MGC registration standards • MDA
Security	• National Security Adviser • MGC Security Team
Conservation	• MGC Conservation Unit • Proposed Environmental Adviser
Storage	• Archaeological storage guidelines • Standards for archive storage

The example of the archaeological and archival standards suggests the potential for developing parallel standards for other collection materials. Specialist groups, working in co-operation with the MGC Conservation Unit, may be instrumental in evolving standards for each group of materials or collection category, which would be instrumental in projecting collection costs more precisely.

The MGC Registration Scheme is the logical next step towards the articulation of national standards which could be used as the basis for assessing performance. The scheme identifies and endorses basic museum functions within an acceptable constitutional framework, and incorporates many elements of the MA Code of Practice. However, it does not in itself constitute such a standard: it does not, for example, attempt to set minimum standards for conservation, environmental control or security. The opportunity to expand the scheme in its second phase (from 1992/93) may provide the opportunity to consider the development of such standards.

The need for further study

Like most such studies, this survey of the cost of collecting draws attention to the need for further study of more specific issues. In particular, three of the major cost variables identified here would profit from further study:

- *Condition of the collections*. A study aimed at developing a consistent way of measuring collection condition, and projecting conservation costs, could yield useful results.
- *Building type and condition*. It would be equally useful to investigate the effect of the use of various building types on collection costs. In particular, the collection care cost implications of utilizing a listed building versus a purpose-built structure would be a valuable focus for enquiry.
- *Type of collection*. As a step towards the generation of standards for collection care, it would be useful to follow this study with specific enquiries into costs of particular types of collection.

At the same time, it is crucial to remember that many of the most important costs and benefits to be accounted are incalculable. The collections are the basis for everything that museums do. As one of the directors expressed it, 'Without the collections there would be no museum.' In the final analysis, it is not possible to place a monetary value on the irreplaceable collections that are the foundation of the nation's museum service. However, a systematic study of the benefits of collecting might well provide a valuable parallel and balance to the present work.

Part 2
Acquisitions and protecting cultural property

5

Museums and the horrors of war
Manfred Lachs

The destruction of cultural property as a result of armed conflict is well recorded, but the Hague Convention for the Protection of Cultural Property in the Event of Armed Conflict, 1954 does not have the wide support of states. This extract, from Dr Manfred Lachs's presentation, given on the thirtieth anniversary of the Hague Convention, discusses the need for worldwide recognition of the universality of culture and calls for its protection through the support of instruments such as the Hague Convention.

THE DEFENCES OF CULTURE

While man's yearning for peace has been his innermost desire from time immemorial, his march through history has, as we all know, been accompanied by frequent armed struggle. Looking back over a period of thirty-five centuries, less than three hundred years have been free from wars. The search for wealth, plunder and domination, but also the goal of freedom and independence, have motivated man's resort to armed force. Little need be said of the destructive effect of wars on all continents or of the misery and death brought in their wake. They have become part of our lives, unfortunately, and are viewed as inescapable. Armies have become important parts of societies – war itself is considered an art and is so described by historians. Obviously it has been the arch-enemy of culture and civilization, particularly when ravaging whole countries, destroying men and what human labour and spirit has tried to build for centuries.

Hence the continuous efforts made throughout history to make war disappear from its pages; to make it only a part of the past. We have made some progress in this respect. We have outlawed war, but not very successfully. Even after the gigantic destruction caused by the Second World War we have witnessed so many armed struggles. While trying to abolish war we try to make it more humane, to limit its destructive possibilities. It is true that sceptics express serious doubts as to the value and effect of these efforts. To remind you only of Moltke's famous letter to Bluntschli and the Portalis memoire to the Academy of Toulouse. And the letter published in the London *Times* in 1869, in which a famous Cambridge professor said: 'To attempt to disarm war of its horrors is an idle dream and a dangerous delusion; let us labour at the more practical task of making it impossible.'

However this practical task has proved almost impossible. We must therefore make war more humane, a task initiated by great men like Dr Francis Lieber, Jean Gaspard Bluntschli and Antoine Pillet – followed by the adoption of a series of international instruments and the Convention for the Protection of Cultural Property in the Event of

Armed Conflict. For it is rightly claimed that there is 'nothing illogical in trying to eliminate war and to regulate its conduct'. Thus we must pursue our efforts to achieve the goal of a world without war – and meanwhile try to limit the ravages of reality whenever and wherever we have to face them.

The call for protection went beyond men in uniform, the wounded, prisoners of war and civilians, to objects requiring special attention. Have we made progress in this respect? I think we have, and the first inklings to this effect are to be found in the earlier work done at The Hague and Washington. But the Convention concluded thirty years ago under the auspices of Unesco, the thirtieth anniversary of which we are celebrating tonight, constitutes in this respect a very special event.

First, it reminded man that the culture of nations is the most precious jewel he possesses. Not only royal mausolea, not only mummies saved by history and accident; but the real cultural monuments: towers, castles and churches – from the stone tombs, the Stone-henge which had been built and rebuilt before the Mycenean civilization began in Greece; developed in the ages of the Gothic Renaissance, baroque, up to yesterday. Here as elsewhere the Eurocentric approach is outdated: we are bound to think in world-wide dimensions. It is through war and other careless actions that many treasures of culture on other continents were destroyed or few traces left. Whether or not these monuments bear testimony of what some historians describe as 'sun and light' or 'dusk and darkness', they reflect the history of nations.

This leads me to the second subject, namely history, and the Convention of 1954. History, need I stress, history is a very precious part of our lives. By condemning history, we condemn it to oblivion and make nations lose their identity. History, as Jules Michelet rightly claimed: 'Cette grande épopée nous est donnée sur les tombes, murmures des âges s'adressant au fond de chacun de nous, afin qu'il s'y reconnaisse et ce serait là, signe et critère de vérité historique.' What I have in mind is the eternal silence created by the destruction of culture. As Michelet continued: 'Adieu le passé, c'est aussi adieu la postérité.' Here is a second element which is so essential in presenting works of culture of the past.

The third is the recognition that the cultural heritage of every people taken together constitutes the cultural heritage of mankind as a whole. In protecting the past culture of others we protect our own, part of the whole. Here lies the great symbolic meaning of that achievement which was the Convention concluded thirty years ago. I think we have matured enough to realize the meaning of the words in that Convention: 'damage to cultural property belonging to any people whatsoever means damage to the cultural heritage of all mankind'.

Thus it is this Convention which, for the first time, uses the legal notion of common heritage of mankind in the domain of culture – embodied in so many forms. That great historian Jacob Burckhardt once claimed that culture and state were entirely different phenomena, and culture must not be submitted to power – he saw in their link an evil, an evil to be avoided. But obviously it is threatened. Who can protect culture if not the state? It is the power of the state which has to yield to culture, by protecting it. That is the great importance of the Convention of 1954 which extends the boundaries of culture into the domain of international relations, and brings the notion of the 'cultural heritage of all mankind' into the legal dictionary which, with the passage of time, has been enriched by other concepts of common heritage: outer space and the ocean floor. This, I think, is Unesco's great achievement on which I wish to congratulate it: it has made culture a legal notion.

Though a lawyer, so far I have spoken little of law, but it should not be surprising, because when you speak of culture you mean law. For law itself is a meaningful part of culture; it is called upon to defend it. For the real meaning of its task is to help history to recover and rescue what is or may be in danger. But there is much more to it: history and culture are closely interwoven with each other and their fate is linked with law.

The Convention is very explicit on the subject. It lays down, you will recall, the prohibition of direct hostilities against objects of culture. To breathe life into it – to make it what it should be – is Unesco's great task.

The protection of cultural property has become part of the generally accepted laws of warfare – whether it is international or not of an international character. These provisions should have become new chapters in military instructions and manuals of the laws of warfare distributed to members of the armed forces. Consequently respect for property becomes part of man's education. It is interesting to note how here, as in other areas, the functions and tasks of Unesco overlap. The Convention is not only an instrument binding states but its continuous operation implies teaching, so essential in shaping the minds of man and nations to reach beyond the subject, the destiny of the international community. Thus in all three spheres which I referred to, the Convention should penetrate the minds of hundreds of thousands, make them realize its importance; and Unesco's future work is essential for the fulfilment of this task.

6

Export licensing unit, 1993: UK export licensing system for works of art, antiques, collectors' items, etc.

Department of National Heritage

This guidance paper sets out the new arrangements for acquiring an export licence for the export of works of art and other objects from the United Kingdom. In particular, it describes the categories and financial limits, along with an explanation of the Waverley Criteria.

The Department of National Heritage outline the export controls as follows:

1 The Secretary of State for National Heritage is responsible for the operation of controls, on heritage grounds, on the export from the UK and the Isle of Man of works of art, antiques and collectors' items, but with the exception of those objects described in Annexe A.

2 Works of art over certain monetary limits require an individual licence, either European Community, (EC) or United Kingdom, (UK). Both forms are from the Department of National Heritage.

EC EXPORT LICENCE

3 An EC licence is necessary for the export out of the European Community of cultural goods controlled by EC Regulation (EEC No 3911/92, Official Journal No. L395 of 31/12/92). It applies to those goods valued at or above the relevant EC licence limit specified at Annexe B (Table 6.1).

UK EXPORT LICENCE

4 A UK licence is necessary for intra-Community trade of those cultural goods valued at or above the relevant UK licence limit as specified at Annexe B (Table 6.1). A UK licence is also required for exports out of the EC of those goods valued at or above the UK licence limit but below the EC licence limit specified in Annexe B (Table 6.1).

RECENT IMPORTS

5 An application for an individual export licence (either an EC or UK) will be referred by the Department of National Heritage to an Expert Adviser (a senior keeper or curator in one of our national museums and galleries), although objects imported within the last 50 years are normally granted a licence without such referral.

IMPORTS FROM OTHER EC MEMBER STATES

6 Where an object has come from another EC member state, either directly or via a non-EC country, exporters requiring an EC licence should satisfy themselves as far as they are able that the object was lawfully exported from the member state in question if the export took place on or after 1 January 1993. The exporter should include a declaration to that effect with the EC licence application, and provide any available supporting documentation. For example, in the case of an export from Germany, you would simply need to state that the item was not on Germany's list of objects prohibited from export.

7 In some cases the exporter might have the export licence or a Single Administrative Document. But in the majority of cases, a declaration should suffice, or, where the object has been acquired at an auction sale (where the seller would have given assurances to the company on the question of lawful export), refer to the catalogue of the sale in Box 18 of the EC licence application. In the very few cases where doubt exists, the Department of National Heritage would check with the member state of origin by fax requesting a prompt response.

REVIEWING COMMITTEE ON THE EXPORT OF WORKS OF ART

8 Where an application for either an EC or a UK licence is referred to an Expert Adviser who then objects to the export under the Waverley Criteria (Annexe C) the case is referred to the Reviewing Committee on the Export of Works of Art. This is a non-statutory advisory body whose members are appointed by the Secretary of State for National Heritage (a note on the Committee's history is attached at Annexe D).

9 When an export licence application is referred to the Reviewing Committee, the applicant and Expert Adviser are invited to make written submissions giving the reasons why the object does or does not satisfy one or more of the Waverley Criteria. A meeting of the Committee is convened at which, in addition to the seven permanent members of the Committee (who are all experts in one or more fields of art, antiques, etc.), three independent members, experts on the particular item under consideration, will be present. The applicant and Expert Adviser are invited to be present at this meeting to add to their statements and, having been provided in advance of the meeting with a copy of the other's submission, to make comments on the opposing case. The Committee then decides whether to recommend that an export licence be granted or that a decision on the licence application be deferred for a specified period (normally between two and six months) to enable an offer to purchase to be made at or above the fair market value as recommended to the Secretary of State by the Committee.

10 An owner is entirely free to accept or reject any offer made. However, where owners do not accept an offer, or make known their intention to refuse an offer, whether

from a public institution or a private source, the Secretary of State will take the existence of the offer into account in deciding on the application and normally a licence will be refused. If an offer has been made and accepted by the owner, then the export licence application lapses.

ANNEXE A

The Secretary of State for Trade and Industry will remain responsible for granting licences for certain antiques:

(a) Arms and military equipment manufactured or produced less than 100 years before the date of exportation; and
(b) regardless of age, all atomic energy-related items, nuclear equipment, certain other categories of industrial and electronic equipment and goods capable of being used for chemical, biological or nuclear weapon purposes.

ANNEXE B

Table 6.1 Values at or above which an export licence is required (from 1 April 1993)

	UK licence (£)	EC licence (£)
Any antique item not shown below, more than 50 years old	39,600	39,600
Archaeological material found in UK soil or UK territorial waters	Zero	Zero
Archaeological material from outside the UK*	39,600	Zero
Elements forming an integral part of artistic, historical or religious monuments, which have been dismembered, and where are:		
more than 50 years old but less than 100 years old	39,600	No EC licence required
more than 100 years old	39,600	Zero
Incunabula more than 50 years old	39,600	Zero
Manuscripts more than 50 years old, including maps and musical scores, singly or collections	Zero	Zero
Archives, and any elements thereof, of any kind, on any medium, which are more than 50 years old	Zero	Zero
Architectural, scientific and engineering drawings produced by hand, more than 50 years old	Zero	11,900
Arms and armour, more than 50 years old	6,000	39,600
Textiles (excluding carpets and tapestries)**	6,000	39,600
Mosaics (other than those falling in the archaeological or monument categories above), which are more than 50 years old	39,600	11,900

Drawings executed entirely by hand on any medium and in any material, more than 50 years old	39,600	11,900
Original engravings, prints, serigraphs and lithographs, and their respective plates, and original posters, more than 50 years old	39,600	11,900
Photographs, films and negatives thereof, which are more than 50 years old	6,000	11,900
Printed maps which are:		
more than 50 years old but less than 200 years old	39,600	No EC licence required
more than 200 years old	39,600	11,900
Original sculptures or statuary, and copies produced by the same process as the original, which are more than 50 years old (other than those which fall within the archaeological category)	39,600	39,600
Books which are:		
more than 50 years old but less than 100 years old	39,600	No EC licence required
more than 100 years old	39,600	39,600
Collections and specimens from zoological, botanical, mineralogical or anatomical collections	No UK licence required	39,600
Collections of historical, palaentological, ethnographic or numismatic interest	No UK licence required	39,600
Means of transport which are:		
more than 50 years old but less than 75 years old	39,600	No EC licence required
more than 75 years old	39,600	39,600
Portraits or likenesses which are more than 50 years old, of British Historical Persons**	6,000	119,000
Paintings in oil or tempera, which are more than 50 years old (excluding portraits of British Historical Persons)	119,000	119,000
Paintings in other media, which are more than 50 years old (excluding portraits of British Historical Persons)	39,600	119,000

Notes:

1   * Archaeological material from outside the UK. There is a discretion under the EC regulation which allows member states not to require EC export licences for objects of limited archaeological or scientific interest. Guidance on this can be obtained from the Department of National Heritage.

    ** If the object is a Portrait of a British Historical Person or a textile (excluding carpets and tapestries) for export within the EC and worth at or above the UK licence limit and below the EC licence limit, an application may be made to the Director of the National Portrait Gallery (in respect of portraits) or the Director of the Victoria & Albert Museum (in respect of textiles) for an export certificate.

2   A British Historical Person is someone listed in the *Dictionary of National Biography, Who's Who,* or *Who Was Who.*

3   EC member states: Belgium, Denmark, France, Germany, Greece, Ireland, Italy, Luxembourg, The Netherlands, Portugal, Spain, United Kingdom.

ANNEXE C: WAVERLEY CRITERIA

1 Is the object so closely connected with our history and national life that its departure would be a misfortune?
2 Is it of outstanding aesthetic importance?
3 Is it of outstanding significance for the study of some particular branch of art, learning or history?

ANNEXE D: REVIEWING COMMITTEE ON THE EXPORT OF WORKS OF ART

Background

1 In 1950, the Chancellor of the Exchequer appointed a committee under the Chairmanship of Lord Waverley:

   To consider and advise on the policy to be adopted by His Majesty's Government in controlling the export of works of art, books, manuscripts, armour and antiques and to recommend what arrangements should be made for the practical operation of policy.

2 In 1952, the Waverley Committee published its Report and in accordance with its recommendations, the Reviewing Committee on the Export of Works of Art was set up. This is an advisory body, with no statutory basis. Its terms of reference are:

   (a) To advise on the principles which should govern the control of export of works of art, antiques, etc., under the Import, Export and Customs Powers (Defence) Act, 1939.
   (b) To consider all cases where refusal of an export licence for a work of art or antique is suggested on grounds of national importance.
   (c) To advise in cases where a special Exchequer grant is needed towards the purchase of an object that would otherwise be exported.
   (d) To supervise the operation of the export control system generally.

7

Convention on the means of prohibiting and preventing the illicit import, export and transfer of ownership of cultural property

UNESCO

This Convention is considered to be the most important international instrument in the battle to protect cultural property as it has the greatest number of signatories to it, including the United States of America (one of the world's major art-importing countries), but not the UK, Japan or Switzerland.

Adopted by the General Conference at its sixteenth session, Paris, 14 November 1970

Having decided, at its fifteenth session, that this question should be made the subject of an international convention.
Adopts this Convention on the fourteenth day of November 1970.

The General Conference of the United Nations Educational, Scientific and Cultural Organization, meeting in Paris from 12 October to 14 November 1970, at its sixteenth session,

Recalling the importance of the provisions contained in the Declaration of the Principles of International Cultural Co-operation, adopted by the General Conference at its fourteenth session,

Considering that the interchange of cultural property among nations for scientific, cultural and educational purposes increases the knowledge of the civilization of man, enriches the cultural life of all peoples and inspires mutual respect and appreciation among nations,

Considering that cultural property constitutes one of the basic elements of civilization and national culture, and that its true value can be appreciated only in relation to the fullest possible information regarding its origin, history and traditional setting,

Considering that it is incumbent upon every state to protect the cultural property existing within its territory against the dangers of theft, clandestine excavation, and illicit export,

Considering that, to avert these dangers, it is essential for every state to become increasingly alive to the moral obligations to respect its own cultural heritage and that of all nations,

Considering that, as cultural institutions, museums, libraries and archives should ensure that their collections are built up in accordance with universally recognized moral principles,

Considering that the illicit import, export and transfer of ownership of cultural property is an obstacle to that understanding between nations which it is part of Unesco's mission to promote by recommending to interested states, international conventions to this end,

Considering that the protection of cultural heritage can be effective only if organized both nationally and internationally among states working in close co-operation,

Considering that the Unesco General Conference adopted a Recommendation to this effect in 1964,

Having before it further proposals on the means of prohibiting and preventing the illicit import, export and transfer of ownership of cultural property, a question which is on the agenda for the session as item 19.

ARTICLE 1

For the purposes of this Convention, the term 'cultural property' means property which, on religious or secular grounds, is specifically designated by each state as being of importance for archaeology, prehistory, history, literature, art or science and which belongs to the following categories:

(a) Rare collections and specimens of fauna, flora, minerals and anatomy, and objects of palaeontological interest.

(b) Property relating to history, including the history of science and technology and military and social history, to the life of national leaders, thinkers, scientists and artists and to events of national importance.

(c) Products of archaeological excavations (including regular and clandestine) or of archaeological discoveries.

(d) Elements of artistic or historical monuments or archaeological sites which have been dismembered.

(e) Antiquities more than one hundred years old, such as inscriptions, coins and engraved seals.

(f) Objects of ethnological interest.

(g) Property of artistic interest, such as:
  (i) Pictures, paintings and drawings produced entirely by hand on any support and in any material (excluding industrial designs and manufactured articles decorated by hand).
  (ii) Original works of statuary art and sculpture in any material.
  (iii) Original engravings, prints and lithographs.
  (iv) Original artistic assemblages and montages in any material.

(h) Rare manuscripts and incunabula, old books, documents and publications of special interest (historical, artistic, scientific, literary, etc.) singly or in collections.

(i) Postage, revenue and similar stamps, singly or in collections.

(j) Archives, including sound, photographic and cinematographic archives.

(k) Articles of furniture more than one hundred years old and old musical instruments.

ARTICLE 2

1 The states parties to this Convention recognize that the illicit import, export and transfer of ownership of cultural property is one of the main causes of the impoverishment of the cultural heritage of the countries of origin of such property and that international co-operation constitutes one of the most efficient means of protecting each country's cultural property against all the dangers resulting therefrom.

2 To this end, the states parties undertake to oppose such practices with the means at their disposal, and particularly by removing their causes, putting a stop to current practices, and by helping to make the necessary reparations.

ARTICLE 3

The import, export or transfer of ownership of cultural property effected contrary to the provisions adopted under this convention by the states parties thereto, shall be illicit.

ARTICLE 4

The states parties to this Convention recognize that for the purpose of the Convention property which belongs to the following categories forms part of the cultural heritage of each state:

(a) Cultural property created by the individual or collective genius of nationals of the state concerned, and cultural property of importance to the state concerned created within the territory of that state by foreign nationals or stateless persons resident within such territory.

(b) Cultural property found within the national territory.

(c) Cultural property acquired by archaeological, ethnological or natural science missions, with the consent of the competent authorities of the country of origin of such property.

(d) Cultural property which has been the subject of a freely agreed exchange.

(e) Cultural property received as a gift or purchased legally with the consent of the competent authorities of the country of origin of such property.

ARTICLE 5

To ensure the protection of their cultural property against illicit import, export and transfer of ownership, the states parties to this Convention undertake, as appropriate for each country, to set up within their territories one or more national services, where such services do not already exist, for the protection of the cultural heritage, with a qualified staff sufficient in number for the effective carrying out of the following functions:

(a) Contributing to the formation of draft laws and regulations designed to secure the protection of the cultural heritage and particularly prevention of the illicit import, export and transfer of ownership of important cultural property.

(b) Establishing and keeping up to date, on the basis of a national inventory of protected property, a list of important public and private cultural property whose export would constitute an appreciable impoverishment of the national cultural heritage.

(c) Promoting the development or the establishment of scientific and technical institutions (museums, libraries, archives, laboratories, workshops . . .) required to ensure the preservation and presentation of cultural property.

(d) Organizing the supervision of archaeological excavations, ensuring the preservation *in situ* of certain cultural property, and protecting certain areas reserved for future archaeological research.

(e) Establishing, for the benefit of those concerned (curators, collectors, antique dealers, etc.) rules in conformity with the ethical principles set forth in this Convention; and taking steps to ensure the observance of those rules.

(f) Taking educational measures to stimulate and develop respect for the cultural heritage of all states, and spreading knowledge of the provisions of this Convention.

(g) Seeing that appropriate publicity is given to the disappearance of any items of cultural property.

ARTICLE 6

The states parties to this Convention undertake:

(a) To introduce an appropriate certificate in which the exporting state would specify that the export of the cultural property in question is authorized. The certificate should accompany all items of cultural property exported in accordance with the regulations.

(b) To prohibit the exportation of cultural property from their territory unless accompanied by the above-mentioned export certificate.

(c) To publicize this prohibition by appropriate means, particularly among persons likely to export or import cultural property.

ARTICLE 7

The states parties to this Convention undertake:

(a) To take the necessary measures, consistent with national legislation, to prevent museums and similar institutions within their territories from acquiring cultural property originating in another state party which has been illegally exported after entry into force of this Convention, in the states concerned. Whenever possible, to inform a state of origin party to this Convention of an offer of such cultural property illegally removed from that state after the entry into force of this Convention in both states.

(b) (i) To prohibit the import of cultural property stolen from a museum or a religious or secular public monument or similar institution in another state party to this Convention after the entry into force of this Convention for the states concerned, provided that such property is documented as appertaining to the inventory of that institution.

(ii) At the request of the state party of origin, to take appropriate steps to recover and return any such cultural property imported after the entry into force of this Convention in both states concerned, provided, however, that the requesting state shall pay just compensation to an innocent purchaser or to a person who has valid title to that property. Requests for recovery and return shall be made through diplomatic offices. The requesting party shall furnish, at its expense, the documentation and other evidence necessary to establish its claim for recovery and return. The parties shall impose no customs duties or other charges upon cultural property returned pursuant to this Article. All expenses incident to the return and delivery of the cultural property shall be borne by the requesting party.

ARTICLE 8

The states parties to this Convention undertake to impose penalties or administrative sanctions on any person responsible for infringing the prohibitions referred to under Articles 6 (b) and 7 (b) above.

ARTICLE 9

Any state party to this Convention whose cultural patrimony is in jeopardy from pillage of archaeological or ethnological materials may call upon other states parties who are affected. The states parties to this Convention undertake, in these circumstances, to participate in a concerted international effort to determine and to carry out the necessary concrete measures, including the control of exports and imports and international commerce in the specific materials concerned. Pending agreement each state concerned shall take provisional measures to the extent feasible to prevent irremediable injury to the cultural heritage of the requesting state.

ARTICLE 10

The states parties to this Convention undertake:

(a) To restrict by education, information and vigilance, movement of cultural property illegally removed from any state party to this Convention and, as appropriate for each country, oblige antique dealers, subject to penal or administrative sanctions, to maintain a register recording the origin of each item of cultural property, names and addresses of the supplier, description and price of each item sold and to inform the purchaser of the cultural property of the export prohibition to which such property may be subject.

(b) To endeavour by educational means to create and develop in the public mind a realization of the value of cultural property and the threat to the cultural heritage created by theft, clandestine excavations and illicit exports.

ARTICLE 11

The export and transfer of ownership of cultural property under compulsion arising directly or indirectly from the occupation of a country by a foreign power shall be regarded as illicit.

ARTICLE 12

The states parties to this Convention shall respect the cultural heritage within the territories for the international relations of which they are responsible, and shall take all appropriate measures to prohibit and prevent the illicit import, export and transfer of ownership of cultural property in such territories.

ARTICLE 13

The states parties to this Convention also undertake, consistent with the laws of each state:

(a) To prevent by all appropriate means transfers of ownership of cultural property likely to promote the illicit import or export of such property.

(b) To ensure that their competent services co-operate in facilitating the earliest possible restitution of illicitly exported cultural property to its rightful owner.

(c) To admit actions for recovery of lost or stolen items of cultural property brought by or on behalf of the rightful owners.

(d) To recognize the indefeasible right of each state party to this Convention to classify and declare certain cultural property as inalienable which should therefore *ipso facto* not be exported, and to facilitate recovery of such property by the state concerned in cases where it has been exported.

ARTICLE 14

In order to prevent illicit export and to meet the obligations arising from the implementation of this Convention, each state party to the Convention should, as far as it is able, provide the national services responsible for the protection of its cultural heritage with an adequate budget and, if necessary, should set up a fund for this purpose.

ARTICLE 15

Nothing in this Convention shall prevent state parties thereto from concluding special agreements among themselves or from continuing to implement agreements already concluded regarding the restitution of cultural property removed, whatever the reason, from its territory of origin, before the entry into force of this Convention for the states concerned.

ARTICLE 16

The states parties to this Convention shall in their periodic reports submitted to the General Conference of the United Nations Educational, Scientific and Cultural Organization on dates and in a manner to be determined by it, give information on the legislative and administrative provisions which they have adopted and other action which they have taken for the application of this Convention, together with details of the experience acquired in this field.

ARTICLE 17

1 The states parties to this Convention may call on the technical assistance of the United Nations Educational, Scientific and Cultural Organization, particularly as regards:

    (a) Information and education.
    (b) Consultation and expert advice.
    (c) Co-ordination and good offices.

2 The United Nations Educational, Scientific and Cultural Organization may, on its own initiative, conduct research and publish studies on matters relevant to the illicit movement of cultural property.

3 To this end, the United Nations Educational, Scientific and Cultural Organization may also call on the co-operation of any competent non-governmental organization.

4 The United Nations Educational, Scientific and Cultural Organization may, on its own initiative, make proposals to states parties to this Convention for implementation.

5 At the request of at least two states parties to this Convention which are engaged in a dispute over its implementation, Unesco may extend its good offices to reach a settlement between them.

ARTICLE 18

This Convention is drawn up in English, French, Russian and Spanish, the four texts being equally authoritative.

ARTICLE 19

1 This Convention shall be subject to ratification or acceptance by states members of the United Nations Educational, Scientific and Cultural Organization in accordance with their respective constitutional procedures.
2 The instruments of ratification or acceptance shall be deposited with the Director-General of the United Nations Educational, Scientific and Cultural Organization.

ARTICLE 20

1 This Convention shall be open to accession by all states not members of the United Nations Educational, Scientific and Cultural Organization which are invited to accede to it by the executive board of the Organization.
2 Accession shall be effected by the deposit of an instrument of accession with the Director-General of the United Nations Educational, Scientific and Cultural Organization.

ARTICLE 21

This Convention shall enter into force three months after the date of the deposit of the third instrument of ratification, acceptance or accession, but only with respect to those states which have deposited their respective instruments on or before that date. It shall enter into force with respect to any other state three months after the deposit of its instrument of ratification, acceptance or accession.

ARTICLE 22

The states parties to this Convention recognize that the Convention is applicable not only to their metropolitan territories but also to all territories for the international relations of which they are responsible; they undertake to consult, if necessary, the governments or other competent authorities of these territories on or before ratification, acceptance or accession with a view to securing the application of the Convention to those territories, and to notify the Director-General of the United Nations Educational, Scientific and Cultural Organization of the territories to which it is applied, the notification to take effect three months after the date of its receipt.

ARTICLE 23

1 Each state party to this Convention may denounce the Convention on its own behalf or on behalf of any territory for whose international relations it is responsible.
2 The denunciation shall be notified by an instrument in writing, deposited with the Director-General of the United Nations Educational, Scientific and Cultural Organization.

3   The denunciation shall take effect twelve months after the receipt of the instrument of denunciation.

ARTICLE 24

The Director-General of the United Nations Educational, Scientific and Cultural Organization shall inform the states members of the Organization, the states not members of the Organization which are referred to in Article 20, as well as the United Nations, of the deposit of all the instruments of ratification, acceptance and accession provided for in Articles 19 and 20, and of the notifications and denunciations provided for in Articles 22 and 23 respectively.

ARTICLE 25

1   This Convention may be revised by the General Conference of the United Nations Educational, Scientific and Cultural Organization. Any such revision shall, however, bind only the states which shall become parties to the revising convention.
2   If the General Conference should adopt a new convention revising this Convention in whole or in part, then, unless the new convention otherwise provides, this Convention shall cease to be open to ratification, acceptance or accession, as from the date on which the new revising convention enters into force.

ARTICLE 26

In conformity with Article 102 of the Charter of the United Nations, this Convention shall be registered with the Secretariat of the United Nations at the request of the director-general of the United Nations Educational, Scientific and Cultural Organization.

Done in Paris this seventeenth day of November 1970, in two authentic copies bearing the signature of the President of the sixteenth session of the General Conference and of the Director-General of the United Nations Educational, Scientific and Cultural Organization, which shall be deposited in the archives of the United Nations Educational, Scientific and Cultural Organization, and certified true copies of which shall be delivered to all the states referred to in Articles 19 and 20 as well as to the United Nations.

The foregoing is the authentic text of the Convention duly adopted by the General Conference of the United Nations Educational, Scientific and Cultural Organization during its sixteenth session, which was held in Paris and declared closed the fourteenth day of November 1970.

In faith whereof we have appended our signatures this seventeenth day of November 1970.

The President of the General Conference
ATILIO DELL'ORO MAINI
The Director-General
RENE MAHEU

Certified copy
Paris,

Director, Office of International
Standards and Legal Affairs,
United Nations Educational,
Scientific and Cultural Organization

8

Law and diplomacy in cultural property matters
Anne McC. Sullivan

Including legal case studies of disputes over ownership of cultural property, this chapter discusses and explains the international legislation currently protecting cultural property.

Given in tribute and taken as plunder, objects of value and beauty have travelled the world throughout history. In our time, the art trade is heated by precarious financial markets, making art an attractive investment with ever-escalating value. Political instability, cultural vogue and the drive for profit all contribute to phenomenal activity in the international art market. A maelstrom of ownership theories, property laws and export/import policies now surrounds the material heritage of mankind. This article considers actions taken by Unesco, individual nations, museums and private parties as they confront the complicated questions relating to ownership and possession of works of art. Particular focus is given to recent cases in the United States, which herald a shift in sensibility favourable to the claims of other nations as they seek the retrieval of their cultural heritage from America.

The first section outlines the ethical and legal policies adopted by nations of the world concerning ownership of cultural property, and international protection efforts. At issue here are the opposing doctrines of 'cultural nationalism' and 'cultural internationalism'. Federal laws and treaties of the United States are then described, with particular emphasis on the Cultural Property Act of 1983 and its recent applications, illustrating both the legal remedies and limitations other countries encounter when seeking to reclaim their cultural patrimony here. Section III continues with case histories demonstrating a tradition of return based on extra-legal diplomacy and charity, historically the over-whelmingly frequent means of returning cultural property to countries of origin.

Sections IV and V review laws of jurisdictions in the United States involving questions of cultural property return; rules on statutes of limitation; key decisions in New York courts; and the remarkable case in federal court in Indianapolis deciding the ownership of Byzantine mosaics from the Panagia Kanakaria in Turkish-occupied Cyprus. This case is helpful to an understanding of judicial policy in the United States today, not simply because the mosaics were held to be the property of their country of origin, but due to the basis of the court's reasoning.

The evolving doctrine of 'due diligence', recently articulated in the mosaics case, enunciates a new degree of care by which the art trade may be judged in the US courts. As such, this doctrine also serves as a suggested guideline for daily transactions between sellers and buyers. 'Due diligence' in this context offers two emerging standards against which behaviour in art transactions is being measured. First, diligent investigation of provenance is recommended to buyers of art, especially antiquities, in the United States who wish to be assured of good title in a market where country of origin claims play an increasing role. And second, diligent follow-up is recommended to victims of stolen art. Individuals, institutions or governments who suffer cultural property losses should take diligent and timely steps to retrieve it, or they may not be entitled to the full protection of the law in US courts.

From antiquity, the vicissitudes of nations have had a dynamic impact on how and where art travels, and this is still emphatically true today. Generally, the law follows in time and reacts to these events, often coming too late to be of real benefit. But law which expresses timely values, applies careful reasoning and offers meaningful standards, such as the United States Cultural Property Act and the mosaics case, can be of significant help in regularizing transactions and making art market behaviour more predictable. These recent case and statutory laws of the United States are playing a critical role in bringing public policy considerations into the trade in objects which carry the history of the creative human spirit.

I ETHICAL AND LEGAL POLICIES

Who 'owns' cultural property which has been moved around the world and precisely which objects are at issue? Two doctrines based on opposing philosophies address these seemingly simple questions in entirely divergent ways: cultural nationalism and internationalism.

Cultural nationalism

Generally, the policy followed by a nation corresponds to its relative wealth and the degree to which its economy is ordered by the government. Cultural nationalism is the term applied to the policy of nations which place top priority on keeping their national cultural patrimony within their borders. This approach is generally followed by the 'developing world' and communist states including, among others, the former Soviet Union, China, Egypt, India, Nigeria, Zaire, Peru and Mexico. Many of these nations are rich in cultural property either known to exist or still undiscovered which is at risk of removal for import into more economically developed nations. Cultural nationalist arguments based on ethics, law and pragmatism support the view that the country where the object was made or found has the strongest claim to it. Three arguments supporting this approach are raised below.[1]

The first premise of cultural nationalism is moral, that objects surviving from the past are the national patrimony and form a constituent part of the national identity. Indigenous people are entitled to possess their cultural heritage, and each country has the overriding claim to its material history. This is a sympathetic position, but problems arise in identifying exactly which cultural properties should be protected from trade. Should everything ever produced in the past be kept within its country of origin? Perhaps not every object. Some countries protect specific monuments by itemizing them in national legislation. Such official documentation can be advantageous when seeking legal remedy, but certain circumstances are not helped by such listings. For example, it is not possible to describe items as yet undiscovered. And what about the definition of 'cultural property' – does it include palaeontological material for example? The specificity which makes such inventories and definitions effective in an individual case may result in a limited range of application.

Second, some nations bolster their claims with legal principles of property ownership. What is presumed here is that the material past can be 'owned' by a nation and that property laws are the best way of establishing ownership. This view often results in legislation declaring that a nation owns all cultural materials located within its territory. A number of countries make blanket declarations that all such property belongs to the government, or to the government on behalf of the people. This is a comprehensive policy because it avoids categories or descriptions. Also it simplifies matters by making clear that the government has standing to sue in legal proceedings.

One problem identified by this approach is that where penalties exist for private possession of cultural property, citizens may be reluctant to come forward with archaeological finds for fear of prosecution. It has been said that this policy may estrange people from their heritage,[2] and some governments try to avoid this problem by offering rewards for objects tendered. Another question raised by this approach is whether objects originally made or found within one nation now located in another are covered by such a law and whether they must be returned, and if so under what authority? Scope of jurisdiction and means of enforcement render distinct limitations for countries which seek the return of objects, and possession has most often been nine-tenths of the law.

The third argument advanced by cultural nationalists is that scholarly value and aesthetic integrity of monuments is impaired by the removal of objects. A loss to scholarship is suffered when objects are removed from excavations without the benefit of contextual study. And while it is not difficult to agree in general that this kind of loss should be avoided, questions still remain.

First, perhaps certain classes of object can be collected or exported without jeopardizing a scholarly understanding of them. And perhaps not all art is required for a nation to retain its cultural integrity. Arguably some objects can be traded in the interest of international co-operation and learning without irreparable patrimonial loss. This has led to the policy of preserving certain objects in 'representative collections' and allowing others, deemed not intrinsic, to be traded internationally.

Cultural internationalism

In contrast, the doctrine of cultural internationalism places the value of mankind's common heritage above the interests of individual nations or cultures, and espouses a freer international trade in art. This approach is generally followed by wealthy, industrialized nations with strong market economies including, among others, the United States, Australia, Canada, the United Kingdom, Switzerland, France and Germany. Cultural appreciation and investment appetites lead these buyers into a market where purchases are made for study, display, profit and rescue.

The time-honoured justification for cultural internationalism is that many objects would have been lost or inadequately conserved if they had not been 'rescued' by foreigners.[3] The merit of free art trade is said to be that it encourages the flow of objects to places where they are valued the most and conserved the best. The theory continues that those who rescue the property earn an ongoing claim to it. And over time, the treasures become adopted as part of the heritage of the rescuer nation and should remain so transplanted. For example, the rescue/adoption argument is the policy of the United Kingdom in the matter of the marble sculptures taken from the Parthenon by Lord Elgin.

But is this arguably paternalistic approach at all justified? It may be ethically preferable for objects to remain in their country of origin even if the best conservation methods are not available. Conservation-centred arguments suggest that countries of origin whose conservation capabilities improve have a renewed claim to recover objects. But who should decide which conservation methods are adequate or acceptable? And further, does the practice of rescue archaeology provide the shield of a continuing claim to the rescued property? A moderate approach would forgive past property 'adoptions' and be more protective prospectively on behalf of countries of origin by passing protective import legislation and entering bilateral agreements.

The second premise advanced by cultural internationalists is that many objects have value which contribute to the common culture of humanity. This idealistic view recognizes the growing closeness of the 'global village' and honours the philosophy of a united humanity, where human history and artefacts are appreciated across national and political boundaries. But who is qualified to say whether some or all cultural property falls into this category? Perhaps exhibitions and loans between nations are preferable to trade and permanent ownership. And who should be making these decisions: national governments, bilateral committees, private parties, Unesco? A great many questions surround the issues of how human culture can be both shared and conserved.

And last, some cultural internationalists argue that restrictions on sale and export actually encourage illegal activities such as site-looting and black-market trade. The argument is that, as enforcement steps up, outmanoeuvres will keep pace. This view justifies purchases made on the black market in the interests of protecting objects from continuing risk as they move around the world. The utilitarian approach of preferable ends justifying questionable means is called upon here, demonstrating that these arguments are at once philosophical and practical.

Part of the difficulty for law-makers is predicting human and market behaviour. Legal commentators stress the critical lack of empirical analysis on the effectiveness of various legal approaches when dealing with the many values which come into play in the international art trade.[4] Research has not been done on public opinion or on the effect of various types of laws. This is in part because of the secrecy which often surrounds art transactions. If public awareness of these issues develops, perhaps empirical studies will follow, giving governments guidance in formulating realistic controls on smuggling and in creating optimal conditions for study and appreciation of cultural treasures.

International law on cultural property: Unesco

With its Constitution in 1945, Unesco began to codify a global approach on cultural property matters. But the Constitution does not specify a policy on returns, and the history of United Nations General Assembly and Unesco resolutions reveals a struggle between cultural nationalism and internationalism roughly along the lines of the North–South dialogue. In 1970, Unesco adopted the Convention on the Means of Prohibiting and Preventing the Illicit Import, Export and Transfer of Ownership of Cultural Property.[5] In the Convention the two basic doctrines of cultural nationalism and internationalism rest on the ground of uneasy compromise with respect to which objects are covered and who bears costs. Legal questions including conflict of laws issues are raised in determining who does the enforcing, the country of origin, or the country with possession. Having decided that it has jurisdiction, a local court would also have to determine whether its law or that of a foreign jurisdiction applies.

As to the question of which objects are covered, the Convention speaks as of its date. It does not cover artefacts removed during earlier colonial or foreign rule, or objects traded illicitly before 1970. This grandfathering provision is a victory for art-importing nations and reflects a political division within Unesco. As an example of the lack of consensus on the issue of objects covered, Zaire proposed a resolution including a retro-active provision for the return of all artefacts lost as a result of colonial or foreign occupation.[6]

On the question of cost, issues include both the burden of paying for the recovery process and whether good-faith purchasers should be compensated for their loss. The Convention provides that the 'requesting State shall pay just compensation to an innocent purchaser or to a person who has valid title to that property . . . [a]ll expenses incident to the return and delivery of the cultural property shall be borne by the requesting party'.[7] This protection of good-faith purchasers is another victory for art-importing states. A number of developing states complained about being required to pay market prices to recover items they believe were wrongfully removed in the first instance, and some are not parties to the Convention for that reason.

Concerning enforcement and resolution of conflict of laws, the Convention provides that member nations agree to two principles. First, Article 7(b)(i) proposes import restrictions on cultural property that is stolen from a member nation which belongs to 'a museum, or a religious or secular public monument or similar institution . . . provided that such property is documented as appertaining to the inventory of that institution'. This requirement makes clear that the Convention does not extend to property owned by private individuals, neither does it protect property which a public institution has not documented in its inventory. If a curator or director of antiquities seeks protection under the Convention, carefully updated inventories should be kept.

Further, following such a loss, Article 5 requires state parties to '[s]ee that appropriate publicity is given to the disappearance of any items of cultural property'. What might be appropriate is not described, and the standard is an evolving one. Based on some of the cases reviewed below, it is advisable that reports be made to Interpol, the International Council of Museums (ICOM), and the International Foundation for Art Research (IFAR) and scholarly organizations specializing in the study of that type of object.

The second principle concerning enforcement is applied in Article 9 of the Convention which provides that a member state 'whose cultural patrimony is in jeopardy from pillage of archaeological or ethnological materials' may request another member state to impose import restrictions. This section provides Convention protection only for objects which fulfil the national patrimony requirement (how this is met is not described) *and* which are in jeopardy from pillage (neither is 'in jeopardy' defined). Only then can the requesting country apply to the importing country for restrictions pursuant to the Convention. With the ambiguities as well as other compromises and limitations, only 69 of the 161 member states of Unesco had ratified the Convention by February 1991 (see Appendix).

Protective measures taken by member states

The Convention proposed no model legislation, and countries have gone their own way in controlling art exports. Generally there are two types of national policy.[8] First is export control of particular types of items. The presumption here is towards free trade, by screening exports to retain only the most important objects while allowing a generally free trade. Canada, Japan and the United Kingdom have particularized export controls. The second approach is total export restriction, or embargo. Some Latin American and Mediterranean countries, the former Soviet Union and the People's

Republic of China have export embargoes. Most commonly, embargoes are supported by legislation declaring national ownership of cultural property, including objects still undiscovered. Egypt is one of the countries with such a blanket policy, as the accompanying illustration suggests.

Unidroit

Unidroit is an international organization with the objective of making uniform laws applicable to particular areas of international activity. To this end, Unidroit assembles experts on given subjects to draft treaties. The drafts are sent to subscribing governments for comments, following which an international conference of governments may be called for adoption of the treaty in question. Unidroit has its headquarters in Rome. In August 1990, Unidroit published a *Preliminary Draft Convention on Stolen or Illegally Exported Cultural Objects*, which has been sent to participating governments for consideration. The Draft Convention attempts to expand on the coverage of the Unesco Convention in part by affording protection to a broader category of objects. At issue for example is the possibility of coverage for objects in private collections, not merely those owned by a government, museum or religious institution, as well as coverage for thefts other than 'pillage of archaeological or ethnological materials'. A meeting is scheduled for later in 1991 which may focus international attention on the possibility of more uniformity of laws between nations on cultural property matters.

II LAWS AND TREATIES OF THE UNITED STATES FEDERAL GOVERNMENT

The United States Federal Government has provided several remedies for countries of origin seeking to retrieve cultural property from US shores. There is no overriding policy or uniform mechanism for returns. As a general proposition, the fact that an object has been illegally exported from its country of origin does not mean that its entry into the United States is illegal unless a treaty or specific legislation applies. The explanation for this rests in the US free-market philosophy that owning property is a right and that trade should be unrestricted. Any law which impairs this right is necessarily an exception, even to the point that the United States is in the extreme minority of nations with limited export restrictions on its own cultural property.

Cultural Property Act

The United States ratification of the Unesco Convention was not effective until enabling legislation was passed by Congress in 1983 in the form of the US Convention on Cultural Property Implementation Act.[9] The Act is the result of compromise and its application is intended for precise circumstances. It speaks as of its date, applying only to cultural property stolen after 12 April 1983. To be covered, the property in question must originate from a country which is not only a member of Unesco, but a party to the Convention (a 'Party State'). A party state seeking protection under the Act is required to submit a written request to the President of the United States which is received on his behalf by the Director of the US Information Agency (USIA). The specific investigation and decision-making functions are delegated to the Cultural Property Advisory Committee, an eleven-member group which has its administrative quarters at the USIA.[10] The Act allows import restrictions in certain situations for archaeological and ethnological material. Archaeological material is defined in Section

302 as objects 'of cultural significance; and at least 250 years old; and normally discovered as a result of scientific excavation, clandestine or accidental digging, or exploration on land or under water'. And ethnological material is defined in that section as objects 'of a tribal or nonindustrial society and important to the cultural heritage of a people because of its characteristics, comparative rarity or its contribution to the knowledge of the origins, development, or history of that people'.

Import restrictions on objects so qualifying as archaeological or ethnological may be allowed under either the general provisions of the Act, or more quickly under emergency provisions.

The general provisions of the Act operate as preconditions to negotiation of a bilateral or multilateral agreement. Under Section 303, a determination may be made by the President, or the Committee on his behalf, that:

(A) the cultural patrimony of the State Party is in jeopardy from the pillage of archaeological or ethnological materials of the State Party;

(B) the State Party has taken measures consistent with the Convention to protect its cultural patrimony;

(C) (i) the application of the import restrictions . . . with respect to the archaeological or ethnological material of the State Party, if applied in concert with similar restrictions implemented, or to be implemented within a reasonable period of time, by those nations (whether or not State Parties) individually having a significant import trade in such material, would be of substantial benefit in deterring a serious situation of pillage, and

(ii) remedies less drastic than the application of the restrictions are not available; and

(D) the application of the import restrictions . . . is consistent with the general interest of the international community in the interchange of cultural property among nations for scientific, cultural and educational purposes.
(US Convention on Cultural Property Implementation Act Section 303)

These requirements seek assurance that the material to be protected is important and at risk, and that the country of origin has done its best to provide its own protection before seeking this remedy. Finally, a showing must be made that US import restrictions will indeed operate as a deterrent to pillage and theft. These determinations are required to be made by the Committee within 150 days of submission of the request. If this is accomplished, import restrictions may be imposed *after* the negotiation of a bilateral or multilateral agreement in co-operation with the Secretary and officials of USIA. Currently, application of this provision is being considered in connection with a request by Canada for negotiation of a bilateral agreement.

More expeditious consideration is available under Section 304 of the Act. Archaeological or ethnological material of a Party State may be declared subject to emergency conditions if that material is:

(1) a newly discovered type of material which is of importance for the understanding of the history of mankind and is in jeopardy from pillage, dismantling, dispersal or fragmentation;

(2) identifiable as coming from any site recognized to be of high cultural significance if such site is in jeopardy from pillage, dismantling, dispersal, or fragmentation which is, or threatens to be, of crisis proportions; or

(3) a part of the remains of a particular culture or civilization, the record of which is in jeopardy from pillage, dismantling, dispersal, or fragmentation which is, or threatens to be, of crisis proportions;

and the application of the import restrictions . . . on a temporary basis would, in whole or in part, reduce the incentive for such pillage, dismantling, dispersal or fragmentation.

(US Convention on Cultural Property Implementation Act Section 304)

These determinations are required to be made by the Committee within 90 days of submission of a request. If this is accomplished import restrictions go into effect immediately after they are published in the *Federal Register* by the US Customs Commissioner. The Customs Service, under the authority of the Secretary of the Treasury, enforces these restrictions by seizing protected property. Under these circumstances, there is no requirement of a bilateral or multilateral agreement.

Four requests for import restrictions have been made under the emergency provisions of the Act. Three of the requests have been granted, covering specific categories of artefacts from El Salvador, Bolivia and Peru.[11] These matters are discussed below. An emergency request from Guatemala is under consideration as of this writing. The request of El Salvador concerned pre-Hispanic material from the archaeologically rich south-western corner of the country, a 66-square-mile area called the Cara Sucia Archaeological Region. This area contains evidence of three millennia of occupation, from 1500 BC to AD 1500, including some of the earliest known Mesoamerican pottery. Intensively looted in the 1980s, this region suffered a loss of irreplaceable burials, structures, ceramic and stone objects. Expert reports on the pillage and transfer of looted objects to the international market strengthened the Salvadoran request for restrictions. In particular, Salvadoran customs records showed that the US was a major importer: 30 per cent of the Salvadoran government's confiscations involved US citizens. These findings, plus a declaration of intent of the Salvadoran government to implement new and more comprehensive legislation to protect its cultural treasures, provided the basis of the Committee's recommendation in favour of temporary emergency import restrictions, which went into effect on 11 September 1987.[12]

Bolivia requested and received temporary emergency import restrictions for antique textiles from the Andean community of Coroma. The Committee's review of the request included interviews of anthropologists specializing in the study of Andean cultures as well as an evaluation of the US and international market in these textiles. The native Aymara culture, which predates the arrival of the Incas to the Andes, produced the textiles. Naturally dyed garments such as tunics, ponchos, capes, shawls and headdresses, the garments are woven from the very soft wool of the alpaca and vicuna and worn in special ceremonies. The simple designs, often of vertical stripes or bands, woven into the pieces record messages and codes of community events and concerns. Some of the textiles date from the fifteenth century and they continue to hold an important place in Coroma culture as symbols of humanity.[13]

Again the critical finding was made that the US market demand for these items was substantial. In this case, the loss of nearly half of Coroma's textile treasures was attributable to US trade. Bolivian middlemen have been prosecuted there and community elders have both taken steps against those involved in the trade and made pleas to US museums and collectors not to acquire the textiles. The Committee found that the record of the Aymara culture is in jeopardy as defined in Section 304(a)(3) of the Cultural Property Act, and that restrictions would reduce the incentive for illicit trade in these ancestral textiles. Import restrictions were imposed on 14 March 1989.

The most recent ban under the Act protects artefacts of another native South American culture, the Moche. The Moche people lived in the river valleys of northern Peru from approximately AD 100–700 Now called the Sipan Archaeological Region, the area covers approximately 35–40 square kilometres. The government of Peru sought restrictions to help curb the looting of the area, which worsened following the discovery in 1987 of the noblemen's tombs of Sipan, the richest intact tombs known in the western hemisphere. Gold, silver, copper and copper-plate objects of exquisite craftsmanship have been found, fuelling a lively illicit art trade in the US and other countries.

Emergency restrictions on material from Sipan went into effect under the Cultural Property Act on 7 May 1990. The lengthy descriptive list of protected items published in the *Federal Register* includes masks, crowns and flutes of gold, owl heads of gilded copper, silver sceptres, rattles and jewellery, ornamented ceramics and feathered ornaments. It is notable that the situation in Sipan met two separate criteria of an emergency condition under the Cultural Property Act, either one of which alone would have been sufficient for restrictions to be granted. In accordance with Section 304(a)(2) it was found that certain artefacts of Sipan, a region of high cultural significance, are in jeopardy from pillage and dispersal which is, or threatens to be, of crisis proportions. And in accordance with Section 304(a)(3), the artefacts are part of the remains of a culture, the Moche, the record of which is in jeopardy. Finally, as is required in all the emergency determinations, application of import restrictions on a temporary basis was held to reduce the incentive for pillage and illicit dispersal of the material.[14]

The importance of the Cultural Property Act and the restrictions which have been promulgated according to it are both symbolic and concrete. To date, the United States is the only major art-importing county to implement the 1970 Unesco Convention, sending a message of international co-operation and respect for material culture around the world. To this is added the fact-finding apparatus of the Act, which requires specific identification of cultural property loss, a corresponding market and a country of origin commitment to preservation before import restrictions can be granted. The advantage of this specificity is that dealers, museums, collectors and the public can know which types of items are likely to have been illicitly imported, possibly curbing demand for these treasures. By avoiding broad categories and vague descriptions, the procedures under the Cultural Property Act make import restrictions, once determined, more clearly understood and enforceable.

United States Customs Service

It is the United States Customs Service, operating under the aegis of the Secretary of the Treasury, which enforces import restrictions by seizing protected property. But as we have seen, objects can be 'protected' by nations on either the import or export side. Does this mean that the US Customs Service is obliged to enforce the export restrictions of other nations without a finding of US jurisdiction and resolution of conflict of laws questions? Generally settled legal principle answers no to this, but the landmark 1979 case *United States* v. *McClain* holds otherwise.[15]

In *McClain*, American citizens purchased Mexican artefacts which had been illegally excavated and smuggled into the United States. Upon attempting to sell the objects, the individuals were charged and convicted with criminal transport of stolen property. The convictions were upheld by the 5th Circuit Court of Appeals. And with the Supreme Court declining to hear further argument, *McClain* stands for the precarious concept that the US Customs Service may selectively enforce foreign export laws. Controversy over *McClain* contributed to the momentum for passage of the Cultural Property Act, as lawmakers sought a more comprehensive import and enforcement policy. But the Customs Service continues to promulgate directives concerning seizure of property without specific Congressional authorization and *McClain* is still on the books. A hydra-headed policy has resulted which includes not only the Cultural Property Act, the *McClain* case and Customs directives, but bilateral agreements as well.

Bilateral agreements

In addition to the 1970 Convention, Unesco has adopted a number of resolutions encouraging member countries to enter into bilateral agreements to agree upon the rules which will apply in specific two-country relationships. The United States has entered into two bilateral agreements. One is a treaty with Mexico implemented in 1972. The treaty takes a strong line against innocent purchasers by making no provision for their compensation. Any importer of pre-Columbian art from Mexico takes the risk that the property will be seized and returned to Mexico with no reparation for loss. Similar agreements have been entered into with Peru, Guatemala and Ecuador. In addition to these measures, the Pre-Columbian Monumental Sculpture and Murals Statute of 1972 authorizes the Customs Service to seize any architectural sculpture or mural or fragment from a pre-Columbian Indian culture entering the United States without a proper export licence. The export laws of thirteen Latin American nations are thereby enforceable by the US Customs Service within its discretion. This statute and the bilateral agreements have great value as precise import restrictions. The objects are tainted by illegal import and can be seized by the Customs Service whenever they are discovered.

Commentators have observed the disarmingly parallel traffic of antiquities and illegal drugs. Latin America, the Middle East and Asia render much of the ancient art which appears on the market and these regions also contain areas hospitable to coca, marijuana and opium poppy plants.[16] American diplomacy may have capitalized on this in some instances. For example, the treaty with Mexico was negotiated while the Nixon Administration exerted pressure for marijuana field spraying in Mexico.[17] So we see that cultural property protection may provide leverage on the playing field of international politics.

The range of remedies provided by the Congress and executive power of the United States with respect to different countries is varied, as the measures outlined above make abundantly clear. This complicates the situation of a foreign claimant country attempting to retrieve cultural property from the United States because no uniform policy prevails. As the examples in section III demonstrate, returns are often achieved outside of legal mechanisms. Some follow in the tide of political developments, and many are accomplished by discreet diplomacy and charitable gesture.

III CASE STUDIES

The Second World War brought profound change to the recent history of cultural property, and its consequences are still unfolding. Colonial rule declined, sharpening the call of cultural nationalism, as the UN and Unesco measures show. And nineteenth-century-style 'tribute' has been increasingly denounced, such as the taking of bronzes from Benin by a British naval expedition to punish the King of Benin for boycotting a meeting called in London.

Before and during the Second World War, the Nazis plundered hundreds of thousands of art objects, and the Allied victors made dramatic, ceremonial returns of many of the hoards. The Art Looting Investigation Unit of the US Office of Strategic Studies was one of the agencies to effect recovery of a great deal of art. But other objects escaped war destruction only to be lost or ignobly dispersed, and post-war politics further complicated matters. The US Army dropped one particular investigation in 1949 when the territory in question became part of East Germany. Last year, this case emerged as one of the greatest art thefts – and diplomatic retrievals – of the century.

Medieval treasures of the Lutheran Stiftskirche Domgemeinde, stowed in a mine-shaft for safe-keeping, came under the guard of the US Army's 87th Armored Field Division in April 1945 as the War drew to a close. First-lieutenant Joe T. Meador made at least two forays into the trove, according to fellow soldiers then battle-weary and disinterested. Meador mailed the packages to his home town of Whitewright in north central Texas farm country, whither he returned to run the family hardware business. On rare occasions the reclusive Meador displayed his astounding cache to neighbours and employees. After he died in 1980, Meador's heirs, brother Jack Meador and sister Jane Meador Cook 'inherited' the plunder and its loaded questions. In April 1990, a jewel-encrusted ninth-century manuscript containing the Four Gospels, originally from Quedlinburg, was procured for a negotiated US $3 million 'finder's fee' by the West German Cultural Foundation of the States. The trail led an investigator to Whitewright, into safety deposit boxes under the names of Joe Meador's siblings. More objects from the church treasury were revealed there, including additional manuscripts, gold, silver and ivory reliquaries, and rock crystal flasks.

Political events contributed to a resolution of the tangle. The unification of Germany allowed the West with its financial and diplomatic strength to co-operate on behalf of the church without stepping on ownership claims of the eclipsed East German state. Lawyers for the church won an order from a Federal Court in Texas prohibiting the Meador heirs from removing the objects from the bank vault. As investigations by the Internal Revenue Service, the Federal Bureau of Investigation and the Department of Justice commenced, settlement talks took place. The final agreement required the return of the objects in exchange for US$2.75 million, including a downward adjustment of the payment for the ninth-century manuscript initially retrieved. A remarkable feature of the deal is a provision that the Germans have no wish for the Federal government to take action against the Meador heirs. The German government agreed to so inform the appropriate United States agencies. Criticized as misguided diplomacy, ransom and extortion by some, the Quedlinburg settlement stands as the highest-paid return in a lengthy tradition of pragmatic compromises outside the court-room, often in the wake of felicitous political circumstances.

In 1971 Iceland welcomed the return of two of the most valuable manuscripts of its medieval past, the Flateyjarbok and Codex Regius. These manuscripts were returned by Denmark, which had removed them 250 years earlier during colonial occupation. Public debate over these manuscripts had continued for well over twenty-five years. Interestingly, Iceland never brought a legal action against Denmark, either nationally or internationally. Instead, the political will of the Danish Parliament was urged by an appeal to 'natural justice'.[18]

Demonstrating the phenomenon that a precise geographical area can be particularly at risk of cultural loss, two statues of Sivapuram Nataraja have been subjects of inter-national disputes. Both are twelfth-century idols from the Tamil Nadu in India, where theft of statues has been a serious problem. Upon consecration, these images are considered sacred beings with specific rights and powers. One such Siva was dug up from a temple precinct and passed through a chain of buyers until it was purchased by a Canadian oil company for its chairman, a collector. The statue was shipped to the United Kingdom for conservation and the British police ultimately seized it. The oil company sued the police, as did the state of Tamil Nadu. The police interpleaded between the two plaintiffs to protect themselves between the competing claims.[19]

Finding a proper plaintiff in this case posed a substantial problem. Hindu law bestows legal capacity upon a consecrated idol, giving such a statue the power to sue and be sued. But the courts of England would not recognize a god as having standing to sue. The plaintiff would be 'at best, Almighty God or, at worst, a piece of stone'.[20] Nor was the government of India allowed as a plaintiff because no provision of Indian law enabled it to assert title to cultural property. Ultimately, the temple was allowed as the plaintiff and the statue was restored to the temple, even though under Indian law the temple would have no standing. This case demonstrates the diversity of principles and beliefs regarding property ownership and the incongruities which arise when two nations with distinct traditions turn to legal remedies for the return of cultural artefacts. Legal assumptions and traditions may have to be compromised for a solution to be found, even when the court-room has been reached.

In the second Sivapuram Nataraja case, the statue had been removed from a temple for restoration and held for several years by a collector in Bombay. A copy was substituted for the temple. The original was sent to the United States under a false export certificate and purchased by Norton Simon in 1972 for US$1 million. It was the featured object in an exhibit at the Metropolitan Musem of Art in 1973. The exhibition was cancelled when the government of India applied diplomatic pressure on the museum. India filed suit to recover the statue but a settlement was reached before trial: the Siva would be returned to India after a ten-year period, which it was in 1986. The Nataraja pair of cases compels recognition of the art market reality that whole regions often suffer pillage and looting, and suggests that the United States Cultural Property Act is responsive to this by specifically providing for relief on a regional basis.

A recent case involving a museum as a party concerned a Khmer dynasty lintel entitled *The Birth of Brahma with Reclining Vishnu on a Makara*. In 1988 the lintel was returned to Thailand having been on display at the Art Institute of Chicago since 1967. The Unesco Convention offered no remedy when the Thai government requested its return, in part because Thailand declined to be a party to the Convention. The Thai position is that, as a relatively poor nation, it would receive no justice from a plan obliging payment of compensation at market prices, which is required by the Convention. Negotiations are stalemated although an offer has come from the Cheney Foundation to obtain another Thai sculpture for the Art Institute. Once again a solution may spring from an ethical position outside the letter of the law.

In summation, international agreements such as the Unesco Convention do contribute to an international climate of sympathy on cultural property questions, but simply have not offered solutions in most cases. But where legislation, treaties and diplomacy may have failed, courts may offer a forum for a recovery attempt. Section IV reviews judicial decisions of the US courts, followed by an analysis of the Cypriot mosaics case.

IV DOCTRINES APPLIED IN US COURTS

Civil rather than criminal law operates most often in this sphere, with the exception of the anomaly of *McClain*. Litigation in return cases generally hinges upon superiority of title rather than prosecution for theft, which most often has taken place earlier in a chain of transactions. These actions are in replevin.[21] Replevin cases often turn on the question of 'due diligence'. Due diligence is a measure of prudence as is properly to be expected from a reasonable person under the particular circumstances. It is not measured by any absolute standard, but depends on the relative facts of the case. But there is scant law as to what meets a due diligence test, and the Unesco Convention does not give an indication of what a country is expected to do in order to be diligent in avoiding the import of wrongfully exported cultural property, or in pursuing its recovery once it has been stolen. Whatever due diligence is, it is required by US courts in two situations in art transactions.[22] The first is a buyer's inquiry into suspicious circumstances surrounding a purchase. This means that a purchaser should do whatever a reasonable and cautious buyer would do to be a good-faith purchaser and avoid buying stolen property,[23] or else title to the object will be impaired. The second is a victim's search for stolen property. A victim is advised to do whatever a reasonable, injured owner would do to find and recover the art, or the claim will be barred either by a statute of limitations,[24] or by the common law principle of laches.[25]

Statutes of limitations

In jurisdictions of the United States a thief cannot convey good title. Not even a good-faith purchaser who has been diligent can obtain good title to an object purchased from a thief. But a good-faith purchaser can have the opportunity of cleansing title. The passage of time works to the advantage of a good-faith purchaser, if circumstances allow and the applicable statute of limitations has passed, or, failing that, laches would apply to estop an adversary claimant. A critical question for victims of art theft and for purchasers is when the applicable statute of limitations begins to run. This can be a difficult determination in complex fact situations. Jurisdictions differ widely as to what event triggers the running of the statutory clock and the length of the running period. The usefulness of due diligence for a victim of theft is that if diligence is practised, the clock may not start ticking until the object is located (or should have been located), or the holder of the object is identified (or should have been identified). Diligence therefore can postpone the starting of the clock and allow a victim time to bring a claim within the statutory period. The hard-line rule which is favourable to thieves is that the clock starts to run from the time of the theft. This allows thieves to garage their thefts until the statute has run and title is purified. Switzerland has a five-year-from-time-of-theft rule, which enhances its role as the transaction nexus of the art world, with an estimated annual art turnover of US$2 billion. And Japan has laws disadvantageous to original owners, including a two-year statute of limitations beyond which a theft victim cannot bring a claim for stolen property.[26]

New York cases

New York courts follow the 'demand and refusal rule', whereby the clock begins to run only after a demand has been made by the plaintiff for return of the object and refused by the holder of the object.[27] In its simple form, this rule is favourable to victims; if they are diligent, the clock may not run against them until they become aware of the location of a stolen object and request its return. And a recent judicial limitation suggests that what constitutes diligence for individual theft victims in New York may simply be a reasonableness test undertaken as a court balances equities between the claimants.

In *DeWeerth* v. *Baldinger* the plaintiff DeWeerth had lost a painting by Claude Monet which had been stored in a house in Germany where American armed forces were billeted during the Second World War.[28] It was purchased in good faith by Baldinger in 1957 and then exhibited by him in a New York gallery in 1981, when DeWeerth became aware of its location. The United States Court of Appeals for the Second Circuit, applying the substantive law of New York, refused to return the painting to DeWeerth, holding she did not try hard enough to recover the painting. The court took judicial notice of the plaintiff's sophistication and remarked that she had not been sufficiently diligent. DeWeerth had failed to take advantage of several mechanisms set up specifically to locate art lost during the Second World War including a programme initiated by the allied forces and a US State Department programme. She had not searched purposefully or continuously, had not used the resources available to her and so failed to halt the running of the statute of limitations clock in favour of Baldinger, a good-faith purchaser. *DeWeerth* has caused concern in New York by suggesting that a precisely crafted diligence standard might become the rule.

The most recent New York matter on point, however, gives far greater protection to theft victims by restating the demand and refusal rule and by casting doubt on due diligence as a common standard to be uniformly applied. In *Guggenheim* v. *Lubell*,[29] the defendant Lubell purchased a Claude Monet gouache study for the painting *Le Marchand de Bestiaux* in good faith from a dealer in 1967. Nearly twenty years later, the Guggenheim Museum informed Lubell that it owned the painting, which had been stolen from it, and demanded its return. The Guggenheim admitted it had performed no diligence other than searching its premises in the course of a routine ten-year inventory, when the painting was noted as missing. Its whereabouts had been accidentally discovered by a former Guggenheim employee working at an auction house. After the demand for return, good-faith purchaser Lubell refused to surrender the painting, claiming that the statute of limitations had long since passed. At issue was whether the museum had failed to be diligent by not taking earlier steps to retrieve the painting.

The trial court found in accordance with *DeWeerth* that the plaintiff had practised insufficient diligence, having 'done nothing for 20 years except search its premises'. But this holding was reversed by the Appellate Division and then affirmed and clarified by the state's highest court, the Court of Appeals, in February 1991. The court approved of arguments that the museum had reason to refrain from publicizing its loss: that doing so might drive the stolen work further underground and could reveal security weaknesses. 'All owners of stolen property should not be expected to behave in the same way,' said the court, observing the lack of usefulness of a strict due diligence standard. This decision is an interim victory for the Guggenheim, and implies new assurance for loss victims by declining to apply a rigid principle.

At the time of this writing, two matters with national patrimony and due diligence issues are pending in New York. The Government of Turkey seeks the return of over 200 art objects from the Metropolitan Museum of Art, known as the Lydian Hoard, in a trial scheduled to begin in Federal District Court sitting in the Southern District of New York. Ancient gold, silver and bronze objects, dating from the sixth to the fifth centuries BC, are included among the treasures, which the Metropolitan Museum assembled by gift and purchase in 1966. Claiming the artefacts are the fruit of illegal excavation and smuggling, the Turkish government first requested their return in 1970 and a suit was filed in 1977. In 1990, the museum failed to have the suit dismissed on grounds of unreasonable delay by the Turkish authorities. The case raises questions of national ownership of cultural property and retrieval of pillaged objects, which the Turks claim, and proof of status as a good-faith purchaser and laches, which the museum claims.

The second matter concerns the fate of the Sevso Treasure, a collection of fourteen pieces of fourth-century Roman silver ornamented with scenes from classical mythology and daily life. It had been consigned for sale to Sotheby's by the Marquess of Northampton, one of Britain's richer men. In May 1990, a preliminary injunction was granted requiring the trove to remain in New York for adjudication of ownership.[30] Sotheby's admitted the possibility that the silver had been smuggled out of its country of origin, probably Lebanon, and estimated its pre-sale value at approximately US$70,000,000. The hoped-for sale had been planned to take place in Switzerland, but the silver was brought to New York on a promotional tour to generate interest in a private sale. There it rests pending claims of both Lebanon and former Yugoslavia, which has successfully intervened alleging that the treasure originated there years before its discovery in Lebanon.

In declaring New York jurisdiction in this case, the court remarked on the failure of Sotheby's to produce the Lebanese export licences it claims to possess, and the lack of information offered as to the identity of the seller, or the circumstances of Lord Northampton's assemblage of the astounding collection. New York has been adjudicated the best forum for this litigation in part because the court said 'it is clear that the illegal marketing of artifacts from a country's cultural and historical heritage will not only cause irreparable loss and harm, but that a balancing of the equities must favor the country attempting to retain its heritage'. Such language sends a signal to foreign governments that they may find success in reclaiming their past in the United States. And with due diligence on the wane in New York, a balancing of equities may be undertaken where provenance should be an area of careful inquiry by buyers, and victims should bring timely and conscientious claims.

Indiana courts follow the more commonly applied 'discovery' rule. The clock starts to run from the time the victim knew or should have known of the whereabouts of the property. And it is this rule which applied in the case of the Cypriot mosaics.

V THE CASE OF THE AUTOCEPHALOUS GREEK-ORTHODOX CHURCH OF CYPRUS AND THE REPUBLIC OF CYPRUS V. GOLDBERG AND FELDMAN, FINE ARTS, INC.[31]

Background

Cyprus lies approximately 40 miles south of Turkey and has a rich ancient history owing to its key location in the seaways of the eastern Mediterranean. The Church of Panagia Kanakaria stands in open country on a road approaching the village of Lythrankomi on the southward slope of the Carpas peninsula. An extensive monograph on this church and its decoration was published in 1977.[32] The church was originally a timber-roofed, three-aisle basilica, built about AD 500, shortly after which the mosaic composition on the central apse was executed. Careful preservation kept the mosaic fairly well intact through several destructions of the church. Most importantly, a treaty in 688 between Justinian II and Abd el-Malik neutralized the island and kept it beyond effective Byzantine imperial jurisdiction. This prevented enforcement of iconoclast edicts and to this we owe the survival of the Kanakaria mosaic composition, which until the late 1970s was 'one of the few surviving in the Byzantine sphere in pristine condition (as far as it is preserved) . . . of prime importance as a close reflection of the art of Constantinople'.[33] The cultural value of the mosaic is also reflected in Cypriot law. Chapter 31 of the Laws of Cyprus, the 'Antiquities Law', was enacted in 1935 to protect properties against destruction or unauthorized export of any government-designated antiquity. The Panagia Kanakaria is on the government list as protected, although its title vests in the Autocephalous Church of Cyprus.

The human figures in the mosaic composition are a little less than life-size. The Theotokos is enthroned, holding Christ depicted as an adolescent, not the customary infant, on her lap. Archangels rendered from an oblique view approach the central image. The head of Christ faces front, but the draped figure has swinging curves and oblique accents, making it one of the most classicizing of the Byzantine mosaics which have survived.[34] The enclosure of the central group in a mandorla points to an early date involving the theological debate concerning the nature of the Incarnation which took place under the influence of Constantinople. It is the only mosaic example of the Theotokos to survive Iconoclasm. The apse itself was framed with a border of medallions of busts of the twelve apostles.

The population of Cyprus is approximately 80 per cent Greek Christian, the remainder being Islamic Turks. Turkey invaded Cyprus in 1974, conquering the northern third of the country and setting up a regime known as the Turkish Republic of Northern Cyprus. This so-called republic is recognized by no country in the world except for Turkey. It is for this reason that such deep political passions are aroused by the case. The Turkish regime has been repeatedly criticized for its allowance or encouragement of destruction of ancient sites within the occupied zone.[35] Before the trial opened, the Turkish Cypriot government tried to claim the mosaics. Their motion was denied on the ground that the Turkish Cypriot government is not recognized by the United States. This is important because it shows the willingness of US courts to include the circumstances of war and occupation among the facts to be taken into account when cultural property claims are at stake.[36]

After the Turkish invasion, the church of Panagia Kanakaria was used for worship until 1976 when Turkish occupation troops forced villagers to move to the Greek section of the island. According to testimony at trial, fragments of the mosaic composition were chiseled from the ceiling of the church and secretly transported to Munich between 1976 and 1979.

In terms of background Peg Goldberg has been said to have an unlikely one for an antiquities dealer. Educated at Indiana University and Christian Theological Seminary, she worked in health services and social work, and was the first woman elected a county commissioner in Indiana. She switched careers in 1981 and started selling nineteenth- and twentieth-century art.[37] In June 1988, she travelled to Amsterdam in pursuit of a Modigliani for a client, accompanied by the flamboyant Robert Fitzgerald. He is a self-proclaimed adventurer and art dealer who has done business under four aliases. Exotic jungle birds and cats, shrunken human heads from Amazon Indians feature in his deals, as well as a ship salvage off the coast of Nicaragua made possible through his friendship with the former dictator General Anastasio Somoza. Fitzgerald's reputation added spice to the proceedings and contributed to the disapproving tone of the court's decision.

In Amsterdam, Fitzgerald introduced Goldberg to his friend Michel van Rijn. The court took judicial notice of van Rijn's reputation as well. In 1985 he was convicted *in absentia* by a French court for forging the signature of Marc Chagall on some lithographs he was trying to sell. Van Rijn and Fitzgerald as a team are being sued in the United Kingdom in a much-publicized matter to determine ownership of a modello claimed to have been used by Michelangelo in creating his statue of the David.

Over lunch at the Amsterdam Mariott Hotel, van Rijn fascinated Goldberg with the availability of the Kanakaria mosaics. He told her that they were owned by Aydin Dikman, the former 'official archaeologist' for Turkish Cyprus, who found them in an 'extinct church' which was being used as a pen for livestock.[38] Dikman was ill, needed money, and here was the chance to make a remarkable art deal. The three flew to Geneva where Dikman (or someone claiming to be him) displayed portions of the mosaic composition and, as Goldberg said, 'I fell in love with them'.[39] But she did not have enough money to make the purchase without the help of her friend Nick Frenzel of Merchants National Bank, via whom speedy approval for a loan of US$1,224,000 was arranged.[40] Meanwhile, Fitzgerald had assured her that the resale would be around US$5–6 million. Before closing the sale, Goldberg asked Dikman for documentation of the mosaics. He showed her customs and shipping documents, including an export licence from the so-called Turkish Republic of Northern Cyprus. That government has come forward and said that the document is a fake. The other documents presented at trial fail to mention Dikman or the mosaics.

This was not the first time Dikman had done a Kanakaria deal. He has been identified as the missing link in the purchase of frescoes from the Panagia Kanakaria by the Menil Foundation in 1983. This was a complicated deal between Dikman, the Foundation and the Department of Antiquities of Cyprus, with the help of several middlemen. In the end, the Menil Collection paid Dikman for the goods and agreed to keep the items on loan for fifteen years before returning them to Cyprus. The Department of Antiquities was never given the identity of Dikman as the source, although Dikman was known in the press as being involved in smuggling from Turkish-occupied Cyprus.[41] Goldberg has testified that she made many calls from her Geneva hotel in the three-day period in which the transaction was consummated. She claims she called Unesco, customs officials in West Germany and the Turkish Republic of Cyprus and IFAR. But her only documentation for the calls was a rolodex card on which she had written 'IFAR – OK' and 'Unesco – no treaties'. None of these calls could be confirmed by the alleged recipients or by Goldberg's records. In fact, there is very little documentation of the transaction. The bill of sale does not name or identify Dikman as the seller. It does give an express warranty as to title and gives assurances as to legality of 'shipment' (not 'export') from point of sale, that is, from Switzerland. But the document is silent as to which country's law applies, and it is not a viable warranty under the laws of Cyprus or the United States. Goldberg flew the mosaic pieces to Indianapolis, going through customs at John F. Kennedy Airport in New York. The customs declaration shows how little description is required on art coming into the United States, and there is no duty required on works of art imported into this country.

Back in Indiana, Goldberg went about getting the mosaic fragments restored by a man named Myron Vorax, a conservator at the Children's Museum in Indianapolis, who has admitted that he had no experience in the restoration of mosaics. He began work without even a photograph to guide him. It seems Goldberg had not even by now obtained a copy of the Megaw and Hawkins monograph. Vorax proceeded to reset loose tiles, reinforce the plaster backings and paint in large damaged areas to simulate a tile pattern. Vorax never dreamed such legal complications would arise. 'I feel like the man who took the bullet out of John Wilkes Booth', he said.[42]

In December 1988, antiquities prices hit a peak with the sale of a Cycladic head at Sotheby's for US$2 million. Goldberg was marketing the mosaics and her asking price to the Getty Museum in Malibu, California, was US$20 million. Dr Marion True, the Getty's Curator of Antiquities, declined the offer and notified Cypriot officials. They asked Goldberg to return the works. She refused and the Cypriot church and government brought the case to federal court in Indiana.

The decision of the court

The choice of law question was first addressed in order to decide whether the substantive law of Indiana or Switzerland applied. The court held that while Switzerland was the site of the taking of possession of the mosaics, there were not significant contacts with Switzerland to bring its law into play. Rather, Indiana law should apply because Indiana was the domicile of the buyer and the principal place of her business, the financing was provided by an Indiana bank, and the mosaics were in Indiana at the time the claim was filed. The mosaics were ruled stolen; not even a good-faith purchaser can obtain title from a thief under Indiana law. Goldberg simply did not have title regardless of how diligent she might have been. No good title from a thief is the general rule in the United States and this case strongly upheld that principle, even though it never identified the thief. The case was quite simple under Indiana law once the theft was proved.

A dramatic demonstration of proof was made on the question of whether the mosaics were stolen. The plaintiffs called as a witness the Reverend Pavlos Maheriotis, who was chosen by the Archbishop to represent the Autocephalous Church. Father Maheriotis carried a staff topped by a double-headed gold eagle and testified appealingly that the church had not been abandoned, but relinquished under force. He said: '[T]he church wants the mosaics back because they are our spiritual treasures. They were once put upon the wall and they were sanctified through the prayers and through the holy liturgy and they are part of our Christian life.'[43]

On the statute of limitations question, the court applied the 'discovery' rule, which is favourable to victims. The clock does not begin to run until the plaintiff knows, or is on reasonable notice of, the identity of the possessor of the object. The trigger event was held to be Cyprus's learning of Goldberg's possession of the mosaics. This event was recognized in spite of several arguments raised by the defence that the clock should have started running either: first, in 1979 when the Director of Antiquities was informed by a tourist that the mosaics were missing from the church; second, in 1982 when a newspaper article appeared in Cyprus mentioning the stolen mosaics and when, separately, the arrest of Dikman took place in Kyrenia for an unrelated art theft; or third, in 1984 when the Menil Foundation purchased Cypriot frescoes from Dikman. But intermediaries had assured Cyprus in 1984 that their source (Dikman) had no more objects. And the court rejected any of these three dates as a discovery event. The clock ran only when Cyprus knew of the possessor and, moreover, according to the court, a reasonable victim could not have been expected to have discovered the thief earlier because the mosaics were fraudulently concealed.

Under Indiana law, a result in favour of the plaintiffs was made without difficulty once the theft was proved. Despite this, the court nevertheless performed an extremely careful analysis of whether the defendant would have been a good-faith purchaser under Swiss law. Good faith on the part of a buyer is presumed under Swiss law. But the plaintiffs brought due diligence considerations into play and successfully rebutted this presumption.

On the question of the buyer's diligence, the defence brought New York art dealer Andre Emmerich to testify concerning the practice in the trade, in an effort to show that Goldberg's efforts to allay her suspicion were no less than those of the average dealer. Emmerich testified that Goldberg's inquiries met the highest professional standards: 'she left no stone unturned'.[44] And that the haste of the sale was not uncommon: 'business

. . . is, if you take too long, the deal goes elsewhere'.[45] When asked if it would have been prudent for Goldberg to check with the Cyprus Church: 'to require Goldberg to check with the Church of Cyprus before [buying the mosaics] is like requiring a dealer to check with the Vatican [before buying] every madonna or saint'.[46]

For their part, the plaintiffs introduced Gary Vikan, a curator at The Walters Art Gallery in Baltimore, who called the circumstances:

> highly, highly, highly suspicious . . . [as for Dikman] . . . He is a Turk from the region and the objects are Christian. That you are going to wonder about. The one thing that really strikes me about this as being strange is that he is an archaeologist. This is a good thing, I guess, but when in the world did archaeologists get in the business of selling antiquities? I mean, this is bizarre.[47]

Asked what a prudent person would have done in these circumstances, Vikan replied: 'Walk. . . . Get out, turn your back, go away. . . . All the red flags are up, all the red lights are on, all the sirens are blaring.'[48] And in fact the court agreed with that view. Goldberg as a purchaser failed to meet a due diligence standard in a dubious transaction environment and thereby was not entitled to protection for her title for at least six reasons:

1 She knew the mosaics came from an occupied area.
2 The objects were unique and important.
3 There was a disparity between the selling price and the appraised value, and it was substantial.
4 The reputation of the seller was unknown.
5 The suspect reputations of several of the cast of characters acting as middlemen were known to her.
6 And the transaction was carried out in haste (one week from the day Goldberg learned of the availability of the mosaics).

On the other side of the due diligence equation, the continuing diligence of the theft victim, the court noted with great favour the measures taken by Cyprus, even though they were not necessary for the decision. Upon learning in 1979 that the mosaics were missing, the Republic contacted Unesco, ICOM and the Council of Europe. Dr Vassos Karageorghis, Director of Antiquities, also spoke to individuals at various museums, including the British Museum, the Louvre, Dumbarton Oaks, and to the auction houses Christie's and Sotheby's. The Cypriot Embassy in Washington sent press releases to several hundred people, including journalists, members of congress, scholars and archaeologists. As a result of these efforts Cyprus has recovered some antiquities, including the frescoes and mosaics from the Menil Foundation, as well as those in this case.

VI CONCLUDING OBSERVATIONS

This case breaks no legal ground on the merits. In key respects, it is a blueprint for the successful national patrimony case. Its importance lies in the demonstration of a new sensitivity to the value of the material past, the fragility of human heritage and ancient artefacts in the face of a vigorous market. Public opinion, museum ethics and international and national regulations have begun to change. As Gary Vikan said:

> the world before 1970 was quite a different place in terms of trading in antiquities. With the Unesco Convention there began a sea change . . . by that I mean a gradual transformation. At the beginning the wind is coming from one way and blowing

back, at the end, it is coming from the other way. You cannot tell the minute at which it is no longer blowing in that direction. A gradual significant transformation.[49]

The spirit of this change was felt in the Court of Appeals' resounding affirmation of the District Court's determination that the mosaics must be returned to Cyprus. Observing that war's destruction imperils the monuments of humanity, the court quoted Lord Byron's poem 'The Siege of Corinth':

> Out upon Time! who for ever will leave
> But enough of the past and the future to grieve
> O'er that which hath been, and o'er that which must be:
> What we have seen, our sons shall see;
> Remnants of things that have pass'd away
> Fragments of stone, rear'd by creatures of clay!

Profit from plunder is reaped by 'only the lowest scoundrels' and 'blackguards', said the court, referring to those unnamed parties who pulled the mosaic fragments from the church, smuggled and sold them. Peg Goldberg was chastened for failing to make a more careful examination of the shady circumstances of the sale. The court recommended that, in cases such as these, dealers would be wise to pursue an inquiry, possibly including: a formal search by IFAR; a check for authenticity made and documented by disinterested experts; a search into the background and title claim of the seller; insurance protection; and a contingency sales contract. A good-faith purchaser allaying suspicion in this way might prevail over an original owner, even where a faulty chain of title includes theft or fraud.

And from the mosaics trial, victims of cultural property loss can learn that textbook-perfect diligence includes continuous notice in writing, with photographs, to: the local police and Interpol; ICOM; IFAR; major newspapers, art and archaeological periodicals in world art capitals; scholars in the particular area of art in question; dealers, museums and other collectors having an interest in the type of object concerned.[50]

A public policy awakening in favour of hearing cultural property claims seems to have been urged by the Kanakaria case, at least in the United States. May judicial refinement, effective national legislation and international co-operation continue to provide reasonable and meaningful solutions to disputes arising in a market where greed and investment objectives have often overwhelmed the means of nations to protect their cultural patrimony.

ACKNOWLEDGEMENTS

I wish to express my gratitude to Joan Breton Connelly, Assistant Professor of Fine Arts at New York University, for bringing the significance of the Cypriot mosaics case to my attention. The International Foundation for Art Research and Stephen K. Urice kindly made research material available. Special thanks are given to Professor Norbert S. Baer of the Conservation Center of the Institute of Fine Arts for his encouragement and generous assistance.

NOTES

1 Warren, K. 'A philosophical perspective on the ethics and resolution of cultural property issues', pp. 8–11 in Messenger (1989).

2 Bothmer (1981), pp. 122–3.

3 Warren (1989), note 1, p. 3.

4 Nafziger (1983), pp. 323–32.

5 1970 Convention on the Means of Prohibiting and Preventing the Illicit Import, Export and Transfer of Ownership of Cultural Property, 14 November 1970. See 'Legal references' and Appendix to this article.

6 Thomason (1990), pp. 47–96.

7 1970 Convention, note 5, art. 7(b)(ii).

8 Bator (1983), pp. 37–41.

9 US Convention on Cultural Property Implementation Act, 1983. See 'Legal references' and Appendix to this article.

10 The Act requires that the Cultural Property Advisory Committee members reflect a range of interest groups, including archaeologists, art dealers, museum administrators and representatives of the general public.

11 United States Information Agency, 'Curbing illicit trade in cultural property', May 1990 update.

12 Hingston, A. 'US implementation of the Unesco Cultural Property Convention', in Messenger (1989), pp. 129–47.

13 United States Information Agency (1990), p. 11.

14 Hingston (1989), note 12.

15 *United States* v. *McClain*, Court of Appeals, 5th Circuit, 1979, Vol. 593 *Federal Reporter* (2nd Series), p. 658, cert. denied, vol. 444 *US Reports*, p. 918.

16 Meyer (1983), p. 12.

17 Stille (1988), p. 1.

18 Greenfield (1989), p. 45.

19 Interpleader arises when a disinterested stakeholder from whom several parties claim property asks the competing claimants to litigate the matter among themselves, without embroiling the stakeholder (*Black's Law Dictionary*, 1979, 5th edn).

20 Greenfield (1989), note 18, p. 185.

21 Replevin is the principle which allows a party with superior title to recover the property *in specie* from one who has wrongfully taken it or has inferior title (*Black's Law Dictionary*).

22 Due diligence is the measure of prudence to be expected from a reasonable person under the particular circumstances, not measured by any absolute standard, but depending on the facts of the case (*Black's Law Dictionary*).

23 A good-faith purchaser is one who buys without notice of circumstances which would put a person of ordinary prudence on inquiry as to the title of the seller (*Black's Law Dictionary*).

24 A statute of limitations prescribes a time limit within which a given cause of action may be brought. Such a statute declares that no suit shall be maintained on a given cause of action unless brought within a specific time after the right accrued. It is a precise cut-off period beyond which a claim is stale (*Black's Law Dictionary*).

25 Laches is a common law principle based on the maxim that equity aids the vigilant and not those who slumber on their rights. Laches is applied when there has been a neglect to assert a claim which, taken together with the lapse of time and other circumstances, operates as a bar to bringing a claim. Laches may come into play if a statute of limitations fails or cannot be aptly applied (*Black's Law Dictionary*).

26 Lowenthal (1990).

27 The period under the applicable statute of limitations in these cases is three years in New York.

28 *DeWeerth* v. *Baldinger*, United States Court of Appeals, 2nd Circuit, 1987, Vol. 836 *Federal Reporter* (2nd Series), p.103. United States Supreme Court, certiori denied, vol. 486 *US Reports*, p. 1056.

29 *Guggenheim Foundation* v. *Lubell*, 1989.

30 *Republic of Lebanon* v. *Sotheby's*, 1990.

31 Federal District Court, Southern District, Indiana 1989.

32 Megaw and Hawkins (1977).

33 Ibid., p. 145.

34 Ibid., p. 98.

35 In 1989 the Press and Information Office in Nicosia published a 75-page booklet entitled *Flagellum Dei: The Destruction of the Cultural Heritage in the Turkish Occupied Part of Cyprus*, replete with news stories concerning cultural losses following the invasion.

36 Pinkerton (1990), pp. 1–29.

37 Lowenthal (1989b).

38 *Cyprus* v. *Goldberg*, Trial transcript, p. 456.

39 Ibid., p. 447.

40 The bank questioned the propriety of this loan after the trial, and Frenzel repaid it from his own pocket, the *Wall Street Journal*, 23 April 1990.
41 Mannheimer and Gelarden (1989).
42 The *Indianapolis Star*, 9 April 1989. Further, a claim for damages done by substandard conservation work was filed by the plaintiff's lawyers.
43 *Cyprus* v. *Goldberg*, note 38, Trial transcript, p. 119.
44 ibid., Deposition of Emmerich, p. 34.
45 Ibid., p. 62.
46 Ibid., p. 74.
47 Ibid., Trial transcript, pp. 347–8.
48 Ibid., p. 353.
49 Ibid., p. 367.
50 Pinkerton (1990), p. 28.

REFERENCES

Art and antiquities

Anon (1989) 'Cyprus looks for justice in US Court', *Indianapolis Star*, 26 May.

Anon (1989) 'UN campaign to combat the illicit international trade in religious and cultural artifacts, *United Nations Observer and International Report* 11 (December): 1.

Bator, P. M.. (1983) *The International Trade in Art*, Chicago: Chicago University Press.

Black, H. C. (1979) *Black's Law Dictionary*, fifth edn, St Paul: West Publishing.

Bone, J. (1989) 'Cyprus wins return of stolen mosaics', *The Times* (London) 5 August.

Bothmer, B. V. (1981) 'The care of antiquities, Egypt's proud patrimony', *Actes de la table ronde organisée à l'occasion du centenaire de l'IFAO*, Christophe Grimal (ed.), LXXXVIII: 8–12 janvier.

Fitzpatrick, J. F. (1983) 'A wayward course: the lawless customs policy toward cultural property', *New York University Journal of International Law and Policy* 15: 857–94.

Gelarden, R. J. and Mannheimer, S. (1989) 'Mosaics sale lucrative for dealer: middleman came out $675,000 richer', *Indianapolis Star*, 3 June.

Greenfield, J. (1989) *The Return of Cultural Treasures*, Cambridge: Cambridge University Press.

Honan, W. H. (1989a) 'Trial to decide owner of mosaics begins', *The New York Times*, 31 May.

—— (1989b) 'Details of profits in mosaics trial', *The New York Times*, 3 June.

—— (1989c) 'Deciding how diligent art collectors have to be', *The New York Times*, 4 June.

—— (1990a) 'A trove of medieval art turns up in Texas', *The New York Times*, 14 June.

—— (1990b) 'Germans send lawyers to Texas for stolen art', *The New York Times*, 15 June.

—— (1990c) 'Second missing manuscript turns up in German hands', *The New York Times*, 16 June.

—— (1990d) 'Those in art case may settle it themselves', *The New York Times*, 9 July.

—— (1990e) 'IRS inquiry delays talks on stolen artworks', *The New York Times*, 19 July.

—— (1990f) 'Judge clears way for trial over Turkish art at Met', *The New York Times*, 20 July.

—— (1991a) 'Looted treasures returning to Germany', *The New York Times*, 8 January.

—— (1991b) 'Deal on stolen German art meets with mixed reaction', *The New York Times*, 9 January.

—— (1991c) 'Stolen treasure: three stories', *The New York Times*, 30 June.

Kilman, S. (1990) 'Merchants National finds artful way to settle a bad debt', *Wall Street Journal*, 20 April.

Lewis, J. A. (1990) 'On the trial of stolen treasures: the historian & the Quedlinburg Cache', *Washington Post*, 11 July.

Lowenthal, C. (1989a) 'Lazy theft victims may lose their claim', *Wall Street Journal*, 16 May.

—— (1989b) 'Custody battle over Byzantine mosaics', *Wall Street Journal*, 28 July.

—— (1990) 'The Japanese connection', *Wall Street Journal*, 13 March.

Mannheimer, S. (1989) 'Mosaics possession a knotty legal hassle', *Indianapolis Star*, 9 April.

Mannheimer, S. and Gelarden, R. J. (1989) 'Mystery man's name appears in another art deal gone sour', *Indianapolis Star*, 30 May.

McAlee, J. R. (1983) 'The McClain Case, Customs and Congress', *New York University Journal of International Law and Policy* 15: 813–38.

Megaw, A. S. H. and Hawkins, E. J. W. (1977) *The Church at the Panagia Kanakaria at Lythrankomi in Cyprus – Its Mosaics and Frescoes*, Washington, D.C.: Dumbarton Oaks.

Merryman, J. H. (1983) 'International art law: from cultural nationalism to a common cultural heritage', *New York University Journal of International Law and Policy* 15: 757–63.

—— (1985) 'American law and international trade in art', Laline, P. (ed.) *International Sales of Works of Art*, General Workshop, 11–13 April.

Merryman, J. H. and Elsen, A. (1980) *Law, Ethics and the Visual Arts*, Philadelphia: Pennsylvania University Press.

Messenger, P. M. (ed.) (1989) *The Ethics of Collecting Cultural Property: Whose Culture? Whose Property?*, Albuquerque: University of New Mexico Press.

Meyer, K. E. (1974) *The Plundered Past*, London: Hamish Hamilton.

—— (1983) 'The other illicit traffic', *The New York Times*, 8 June.

Nafziger, J. A. R. (1983) 'Comments on the relevance of law and culture to cultural property law', *Syracuse Journal of International Law and Commerce* 10: 323–32.

Norman, G. and Keys, D. (1990a) 'Sale of Roman treasure could fetch £100m', *Independent*, 9 February.

—— (1990b) 'History of a great treasure emerges from the shadows', *Independent*, 7 March.

Pinkerton, L. F. (1990) 'Due diligence in fine art transactions', *Case Western Reserve Journal of International Law* 22: 1–29.

Press and Information Office, Republic of Cyprus (1989) *Flagellum Dei: The Destruction of the Cultural Heritage of the Turkish Occupied Part of Cyprus*, Nicosia: Press and Information Office.

Schneider, E. C. (1982) 'Plunder or excavation? Observations and suggestions on the regulation of ownership and trade in the evidence of cultural patrimony', *Syracuse Journal of International Law and Commerce* 9: 1–19.

Stille, A. (1988) 'Was this statue stolen?', *National Law Journal*, 14 November.

Thomason, D. N. (1990) 'Rolling back history: the United Nations General Assembly and the right to cultural property', *Case Western Reserve Journal of International Law* 22: 47–96.

United States Information Agency (1990) 'Curbing illicit trade in cultural property: US assistance under the Convention on Cultural Property Implementation Act', updated, May 1990.

Wilkes, D. (1988) 'Bangkok: breaking tradition', *ArtNews* 87: 51.

Legal

Autocephalous Greek Orthodox Church of Cyprus and the Republic of Cyprus v. *Goldberg and Feldman Fine Arts Inc. and Peg Goldberg*, Federal District Court, Southern District, Indiana 1989. Vol. 717 Federal Supplement, p. 1,374; United States Court of Appeals, 7th Circuit, 24 October 1990, affirmed docket no. 89–2809.

Cyprus v. *Goldberg*, Trial transcript, vols I–VI.

DeWeerth v. *Baldinger*, United States Court of Appeals, 2nd Circuit, 1987. Vol. 836 Federal Reporter, 2nd series, p. 103; United States Supreme Court, cert. denied, vol. 486, US Reports, p. 1056.

Federal District Court, Southern District, Indiana, 1989, Vol. 717 Federal Supplement, p. 1374; United States Court of Appeals, 7th Circuit, 24 October 1990, affirmed, docket no. 89–2809.

Guggenheim Foundation v. *Lubell*, New York Supreme Court, *New York Law Journal*, 15 February 1989. New York Appellate Division, appeal dismissed 1989, no. M-2303. New York Court of Appeals, affirmed, *New York Law Journal*, 14 February 1991.

1970 Convention on the Means of Prohibiting and Preventing the Illicit Import, Export and Transfer of Ownership of Cultural Property, 16th session, 14 November, UNESCO 27 UST 3 TIAS No. 8226, 823 UNTS 231.

Republic of Lebanon v. *Sotheby's*, New York Supreme Court, *New York Law Journal*, 9 May 1990.

United States v. *McClain*, Court of Appeals, 5th Circuit, 1979, Vol. 593 *Federal Reporter* (2nd series), p. 658; cert. denied, vol. 444 *US Reports*, p. 918.

US Convention on Cultural Property Implementation Act, title III, Public Law 1983, 97–446, as amended.

APPENDIX

Unesco Convention on the Means of Prohibiting and Preventing the Illicit Import, Export and Transfer of Ownership of Cultural Property 14 November 1970, Paris, Assembled by the Cultural Property Advisory Committee, USIA

Table 8.1 List of states having deposited an instrument of ratification, acceptance or accession as of February 1991 (Total = 69)

States	Date of deposit of ratification (R) acceptance (Ac) or accession (A) (Day/month/year)	Date of entry into force (Day/month/year)
Algeria	24. 6.1974 (R)	24. 9.1974
Argentina	11. 1.1973 (R)	11. 4.1973
Australia	30.10.1989 (Ac)	30. 1.1990
Bangladesh	9.12.1987 (R)	9. 3.1988
Belize	26. 1.1990 (R)	26. 4.1990
Bolivia	4.10.1976 (R)	4. 1.1977
Burkina Faso	7. 4.1987 (R)	7. 7.1987
Brazil	16. 2.1973 (R)	16. 5.1973
Bulgaria	15. 9.1971 (R)	24. 4.1972
Byelorussian SSR	28. 4.1988 (R)	28. 7.1988
Cameroon	24. 5.1972 (R)	24. 8.1972
Canada	28. 3.1978 (Ac)	28. 6.1978
Central African Republic	1. 2.1972 (R)	1. 5.1972
Colombia	24. 5.1988 (Ac)	24. 8.1988
Côte d'Ivoire	30.10.1990 (R)	30. 1.1991
Cuba	30. 1.1980 (R)	30. 4.1980
Cyprus	19.10.1979 (R)	19. 1.1980
Czechoslovakia	14. 2.1977 (Ac)	14. 5.1977
Democratic Kampuchea	26. 9.1972 (R)	26.12.1972
Democratic People's Republic of Korea	13. 5.1983 (R)	13. 8.1983
Dominican Republic	7. 3.1973 (R)	7. 6.1973
Ecuador	24. 3.1971 (Ac)	24. 4.1972
Egypt	5. 4.1973 (Ac)	5. 7.1973
El Salvador	20. 2.1978 (R)	20. 5.1978
Greece	5. 6.1981 (R)	5. 9.1981
Guatemala	14. 1.1985 (R)•	14. 4.1985
Guinea	18. 3.1979 (R)	18. 6.1979
Honduras	19. 3.1979 (R)	19. 6.1979
Hungary	23.10.1978 (R)	23. 1.1979
India	24. 1.1977 (R)	24. 4.1977
Iran	27. 1.1975 (Ac)	27. 4.1975
Iraq	12. 2.1973 (Ac)	2. 5.1973
Italy	2.10.1978 (R)	2. 1.1979
Jordan	15. 3.1974 (R)	15. 6.1974

Kuwait	22. 6.1972	(Ac)	22. 9.1972
Madagascar	21. 6.1989	(R)	21. 9.1989
Mali	6. 4.1987	(R)	6. 7.1987
Mauritania	27. 4.1977	(R)	27. 7.1977
Mauritius	27. 2.1978	(Ac)	27. 5.1978
Mexico	4.10.1972	(Ac)	4. 1.1973
Nepal	23. 6.1976	(R)	23. 9.1976
Nicaragua	19. 4.1977	(R)	19. 7.1977
Niger	16.10.1972	(R)	16. 1.1973
Nigeria	24. 1.1972	(R)	24. 4.1972
Oman	2. 6.1978	(Ac)	2. 9.1978
Pakistan	30. 4.1981	(R)	30. 7.1981
Panama	13. 8.1973	(Ac)	13.11.1973
People's Republic of China	28.11.1989	(Ac)	28. 2.1990
Peru	24.10.1979	(Ac)	24. 1.1980
Poland	31. 1.1974	(R)	30. 4.1974
Portugal	9.12.1985	(R)	9. 3.1986
Qatar	20. 4.1977	(Ac)	20. 7.1977
Republic of Korea	14. 2.1983	(Ac)	14. 5.1983
Saudi Arabia	8. 9.1976	(Ac)	8.12.1976
Socialist People's Libyan Arab Jamahiriya	9. 1.1973	(R)	9. 4.1973
Senegal	9.12.1984	(R)	9. 3.1985
Spain	10. 1.1986	(R)	10. 4.1986
Sri Lanka	7. 4.1981	(Ac)	7. 7.1981
Syrian Arab Republic	21. 2.1975	(Ac)	21. 5.1975
Tunisia	10. 3.1975	(R)	10. 6.1975
Turkey	21. 4.1981	(R)	21. 7.1981
Ukrainian SSR	28. 4.1988	(R)	28. 7.1988
United Republic of Tanzania	2. 8.1977	(R)	2.11.1977
United States of America	2. 9.1983	(Ac)	2.12.1983
Uruguay	9. 8.1977	(R)	9.11.1977
Union of Soviet Socialist Republics	28. 4.1988	(R)	28. 7.1988
Yugoslavia	3.10.1972	(R)	3. 1.1973
Zaire	23. 9.1974	(R)	23.12.1974
Zambia	21. 6.1985	(R)	21. 9.1985

9

Collecting for the twenty-first century

J. Kenyon

This extract outlines some of the main findings from a survey of the collecting habits of museums in the Yorkshire and Humberside region. The conclusions could be applied to many museums in the UK.

Methods of acquisition

Most of the material entering industrial and social history collections in the region is donated. In subject areas which are widely seen as collectable, for example, (certain) ceramics, furniture, militaria, coinage and silver, donations are less likely. In these cases, purchase is more frequently the only way to acquire suitable examples for the collection.

A number of the museums surveyed in detail do not have a specific budget for the purchase of objects. In those museums that do, their purchase fund is frequently seen as insufficient and not reflecting current prices. This has severely limited acquiring relevant material in some cases. Social history museums continue to rely on MGC Purchase Funds administered through the Victoria & Albert Museum.

In industrial museums, again, most material is donated. If material is purchased it is usually relatively inexpensive. The cost of actually moving the objects acquired to the museum can cause problems. In some cases, this has involved hiring low loaders, cranes or other handling equipment. The MGC PRISM Fund (Preservation of Industrial and Scientific Material) administered by the Science Museum, is of benefit in this area.

Museums which need to hire vehicles or equipment in order to handle or move objects in the collection should take account of this. Museums must consider the *cost* of collecting, even where items are donated. (See the *Cost of Collecting* and *The Road to Wigan Pier?*)

Dependent upon their size and nature, museums should seek to establish a purchase fund. The purchase fund should realistically reflect the current market prices of the type of items which the museum wishes to acquire.

SUBJECT AREAS OF NEGLECT AND DUPLICATION WITHIN THE REGION

Definition

Museum collections are built up with the aim of producing a 'comprehensive' or 'representative' three-dimensional record of the area they serve. The results do not always correspond with the intentions, for reasons examined later in this chapter. This can lead to a lack of usable material on one hand, and too much of another type on the other.

Areas of neglect are defined as those where museum collections are weak, where there are omissions, either within individual museums or throughout the region as a whole.

Areas of duplication are defined as those where the individual museum or the region has a large number of identical or similar objects.

The duplication of mass-produced material throughout the region's museums needs to be examined with reference to the provenance of those objects and the way in which many of them tell the story of a particular area. Their use in other museum functions like education and reminiscence work must also be considered. Distinctions need to be made between duplication within collections and duplication between museums.

Classification and analysis

The Social History and Industrial Classification (SHIC), as published in 1983, was used for listing collections. Items were classified under one heading only. No cross-referencing was applied.

The way in which information is analysed is inevitably influenced by the structure of the classification. For instance, the level of breakdown is far more detailed in some sections than others. For example, in SHIC Section 2, Domestic and Family Life, Heating 2.31, has 12 sub-headings compared with none under Textile Crafts and Hobbies, 2.83.

Two pieces of data have been excluded from the analysis. Otherwise the overall picture of collections across the region would have been severely distorted. The data in question are:

- 90,000 transport records, held by the Museum of Army Transport, listed under SHIC Code 1.81, War and Defence category (E).
- 501,909 photographs recently collected by a West Yorkshire Museum, listed under SHIC code 2.865, Still Image Production, category (P). These have yet to be sorted by that museum.

All other items under Still Image Production which are not photographs are included in the analysis. This applies to objects such as cameras and accessories, processing equipment, projectors and transfer and hand-painted lantern slides.

This report does not examine areas of neglect and duplication in great detail. The following findings aim to give an overall picture of the situation in these areas, illustrated by specific examples. The reasons why neglect and duplication have occurred in the past are relevant to future planning and are dealt with below.

Why neglect and duplication have occurred

A number of factors have produced areas of neglect and duplication within collections in the region. The main ones are dealt with below. A particular object or subject area may be neglected or duplicated for one or a combination of these reasons.

Lack of policy

In the absence of overall aims and objectives and specifically of a collecting policy the growth of many collections has been unplanned and unstructured. The choice of material has very largely been dictated by the interests and specialisms of curators, collecting fashions and what has been offered by the public.

Poor documentation

Poor documentation in the past has meant that many museums do not actually know what they have in their collections. Objects have been acquired by curators unaware that there are already examples in the collection. Alternatively, items have been rejected when staff have presumed that they must already be represented in the collections, perhaps due to their commonplace nature. Sensible policies for future collecting can only be compiled based on the knowledge of what existing collections contain.

Lack of selectivity

A number of museums have suffered from curatorial inability to say 'no'. This has in some cases been from an unwillingness to upset or offend donors, in other cases the desire to accept anything which is not already in the collection. Compounded by the lack of a policy to guide decisions, this has resulted in duplication and collecting of unsuitable material. In some cases items have been acquired which are damaged or incomplete, poor examples, exact duplicates of existing material or differing to only a minor extent. Some items completely outside the museum's subject area have been collected. Smaller items such as razors and spectacles have been less likely to be rejected as they do not pose an obvious storage problem.

Passive collecting

Passive collecting as the main method of acquisition has inevitably produced imbalance in collections. The material offered, although important, has traditionally reflected the donor's perception of what museums collect. This is usually anything old, valuable, special or rare. This includes items relating to people's own lives which they considered important and, therefore, treasured. Hence the number of wedding dresses, christening robes, and biscuit tins from royal events throughout the region's collections. This also means that collections have reflected the types of people who visit them and offer material rather than those who do not.

Availability of material

The collections in the region consist of items which for varying reasons have survived. This may be by chance or intention. Some have survived because they were so widespread, others because they are particularly robust. Certain objects have been saved intentionally because they continued to be useful, or perhaps were valued or treasured for sentimental or aesthetic reasons.

Some subject areas are neglected in museum collections because relevant objects did not survive. They may have been considered ordinary or of little use or value in the past and thrown away. Other items were used until they wore out. For example, working-class clothing passed down until it ended life as a rag rug, a duster or floor cloth.

In some cases relevant objects to illustrate particular activities are few or may not have existed. For example, objects relating to spoken tradition, dancing and games such as hopscotch.

In some service industries and support services within industries it may be hard to identify relevant material to collect. The objects available may be of such a general nature that they give no indication of the specific work involved, for example, general office machinery.

10

Hambledon Cricket Club Account Book: one of six offers the government accepts in lieu of tax (press release)

Department of National Heritage

The Acceptance in Lieu Scheme is an important source of items for museums and galleries in the United Kingdom. This press release discusses the acceptance of six important items and gives an indication of the range of objects accepted into the scheme. It also provides additional information about the terms and conditions of the scheme.

Six items, including paintings by Reynolds and Van Dyck and the Hambledon Cricket Club Account Book, have been accepted by the government in lieu of inheritance tax, David Mellor, Secretary of State for National Heritage, announced today.

Answering a written parliamentary question from David Wilshire, MP for Spelthorne, Mr Mellor said:

> Since my announcement on 3 June at column 570, I am pleased to inform the House of the acceptance of a further six offers: a painting, *Up and Out*, by Richard Hamilton in lieu of £7,000; Hambledon Cricket Club Account Book in lieu of £39,120; two paintings, *John Frederick Sackville, 3rd Duke of Dorset* by Sir Joshua Reynolds and *Lady Frances Cranfield* by Sir Anthony Van Dyck, in lieu of £404,544; two busts by Rysbrack in lieu of £418,920; a painting, *Lady Charlotte Bonham-Carter*, by Peter Greenham in lieu of £8,500; and land known as Nolands Farm in lieu of £57,920.

> The paintings *Up and Out* and *Lady Charlotte Bonham-Carter* have been allocated to the Tate Gallery. The two paintings by Reynolds and Van Dyck, *John Frederick Sackville, 3rd Duke of Dorset* and *Lady Frances Cranfield*, are to remain at Knole House, and the Rysbrack busts are to remain at Hagley Hall. Nolands Farm has been allocated to the National Trust. No decision has yet been taken on the allocation of the Hambledon Cricket Club Account Book.

NOTES FOR EDITORS

The painting *Up and Out* by Richard Hamilton. Richard Hamilton is one of the most important figures in British contemporary art. *Up and Out* is an analysis of the stages of movement through a door and is a distinctive example of the artist's intermediate stage of development. The acceptance of this picture coincides with a major retrospective of his work at the Tate Gallery starting on 17 June.

Hambledon Cricket Club Account Book. Hambledon Cricket Club, Hampshire, was formed in 1750 and has been described as 'the birthplace of first-class cricket'. The book contains minutes from 1772–96 and records of the earliest 'professional' players of cricket. It also documents the decline of Hambledon and the emergence of the Marylebone Cricket Club as the centre of English cricket.

The two busts by Michael Rysbrack are of Sir Peter Paul Rubens and Sir Anthony Van Dyck and will stay at Hagley Hall near Stourbridge, Worcestershire. The busts have been a integral part of the elaborate decoration of the entrance hall (White Hall) at Hagley since 1760. The White Hall is rococo ensemble, which includes a carved stone chimney piece, fine plasterwork on the ceiling, copies of celebrated classical statues, four busts of Roman emperors and, opposite the chimney piece, the Rysbrack busts.

John Frederick Sackville, 3rd Duke of Dorset by Sir Joshua Reynolds and *Lady Frances Cranfield* by Sir Anthony Van Dyck. The full-length Reynolds portrait was commissioned by the Duke of Dorset himself in 1769 and since has been an important part of the decoration of Knole House. The Duke was a patron of Reynolds and there are other commissions in the house. The painting also forms part of an almost unbroken line of Sackville family portraits. The Van Dyck is an earlier portrait dating from the 1630s. It is also a full-length study and the subject is Lady Cranfield, one of the Duchesses of Dorset.

Lady Charlotte Bonham-Carter by Peter Greenham. Peter Greenham, Keeper of the Royal Academy Schools until his recent retirement, is one of the outstanding contemporary British painters of commissioned portraits. The sitter, Lady Bonham-Carter, was a prominent feature of artistic society. The dress she is wearing in the portrait, made by Fortuny, became almost as famous as its owner as it was the garment Lady Bonham-Carter always chose to wear at art functions.

Nolands Farm is situated near Yatesbury and Calne in Wiltshire. It comprises 109.04 acres of downland along the north-east slope of Cherhill Down and is made up of 80 per cent permanent pasture. It also borders land already belonging to the National Trust, containing the Iron Age Oldbury Castle and the Wiltshire White Horse.

Under the terms of the National Heritage Act, 1980, the responsibility for the re-imbursement of the Commissioners of Inland Revenue of the net cost of heritage property accepted in lieu of tax passed to the Office of Arts and Libraries and the Department of Environment. Parliamentary approval is being sought for this function to be carried out by the Department of National Heritage.

The Inland Revenue Commissioners accept property in lieu of Inheritance Tax with the consent of the ministers concerned.

The annual basic provision on the joint votes is £2 million. However, as announced in July 1985, sums for accepting large and important items may be drawn on the Public Expenditure Reserve.

Public access to all of these items accepted in lieu is available. This includes those at Knole House and Hagley Hall, which are open to the public.

The Museums and Galleries Commission advises the Secretary of State on the allocation of works of art accepted by the Commissioners of Inland Revenue in satisfaction of Inheritance Tax. Institutions interested in applying to house the unallocated offer announced today should contact the Capital Taxes Officer at the Museums and Galleries Commission for further details (071 233 4200).

11

Acceptance in lieu
Museums and Galleries Commission

This chapter reproduces a leaflet – produced by the Museums and Galleries Commission, which runs the Acceptance In Lieu Scheme – which describes the terms and conditions of the scheme and its benefits to the museums community.

> *In this World nothing can
> be said to be certain,
> except death and taxes.*
>
> *(Benjamin Franklin)*

Works of art, and other kinds of heritage items including land and buildings, can be accepted by the Inland Revenue in lieu of inheritance taxes. Anyone liable for inheritance tax can offer an item in whole or part settlement of that liability. This is known as 'Acceptance in Lieu' (AIL).

THE OFFER AND ITS ACCEPTANCE

AIL is not restricted to paintings. Other items may be accepted in lieu. Whatever is offered, it must be 'pre-eminent' of its kind, of particular historical or local significance, or a 'pre-eminent' addition to the collection to which it is allocated.

An offer in lieu of tax should be made in writing to the Capital Taxes Office (CTO). Detailed information, including a valuation, description and at least three photographs, must be supplied.

If the CTO is satisfied that the offer can proceed, it is referred to the Museums and Galleries Commission (MGC). Offers of buildings or land are referred to the Department of the Environment (DOE).

The Heritage Ministers decide, with advice from the MGC, whether items may be accepted in lieu. If the Ministers agree that the object may be accepted in lieu, the CTO issues the legal paperwork which provides the formal evidence of the offer and its acceptance by the Inland Revenue.

ALLOCATION OF THE OBJECT

The AIL object is not retained by the Revenue but is allocated to a public institution.

The MGC's advice to Ministers on allocation of the object takes account of the following:

(a) If the offer is conditional upon allocation to a specific institution, allocation will be made to the institution if the Heritage Ministers agree that the condition is appropriate.

(b) If an offer is unconditional, institutions are asked to make an application for allocation. The MGC considers all applications and, taking into account any wishes which have been expressed, makes a recommendation to the Minister for the Arts. If he accepts that recommendation, permanent allocation of the object follows. Pending permanent allocation, the item is temporarily allocated to an appropriate institution, usually a national institution in London.

(c) Items can be offered because of their *historical association* with a historic building which is in public ownership of, for example, the National Trust or a local authority. Such items will be transferred to the owner of the building so that they can remain in, or return to, their historic setting.

(d) Items which are pre-eminent in the context of a historic house in private ownership can remain *in situ* but ownership is transferred to a publicly funded museum or gallery.

THE BENEFITS OF AIL

(a) No tax is payable on the disposal of the item; its market value is reduced to take account of 75 per cent of the inheritance tax which would otherwise have been payable, and this reduced value (known as the 'special price') is the amount of tax which is settled by the offer in lieu. If the tax liability is less than the 'special price', an offer in lieu can be made, but it must be made conditional upon allocation to a named institution and the balance of the special price (i.e. the amount by which the special price exceeds the actual tax liability) must be paid by the recipient institution to the offerer.

(b) Interest on the amount of tax settled by the offer is remitted from the date of the offer providing the value of the item is not increased while the offer is being processed.

(c) There is a reduction in the amount of tax payable on the estate.

(d) Items are saved for the nation without the need to call on the resources of funding bodies such as the National Art Collections Fund, the National Heritage Memorial Fund, etc.

(e) Public institutions acquire items without having to purchase them.

FURTHER INFORMATION

If you would like to know more about Acceptance in Lieu and how you may benefit, please contact:

Heather Wilson, Museums and Galleries Commission
16 Queen Anne's Gate, London SW1H 9AA
Telephone 071 233 4200

General information on the taxation of heritage objects and sales by Private Treaty may also be obtained from Heather Wilson.

USEFUL ADDRESSES

The Office of Arts and Libraries
Horse Guards Road, London SW1P 3AL
Telephone 071 270 5846

Capital Taxes Office
Inland Revenue, Rockley Road, London W14 0DF
Telephone 071 603 4622

THE MUSEUMS AND GALLERIES COMMISSION

Founded in 1931, the Museums and Galleries Commission, which received its royal charter in 1987, promotes the interests of museums and galleries throughout the UK. It funds the seven Area Museum Councils in England and the Museum Documentation Association, and provides capital, purchase and other grants to assist local museum developments. It also administers the Government Indemnity Scheme covering loans for exhibitions. The MGC's Museums Security Adviser monitors the security systems in museums throughout the UK. In 1987 the MGC set up The Conservation Unit as a forum for information, advice, planning and support relating to conservation of the cultural heritage. The Conservation Unit maintains a register of conservators and restorers to provide an authoritative guide to the professional expertise available.

We see the great
everlasting things that matter
for a nation

(Lloyd George, 1914)

12

Legislation relating to the acquisition and disposal of museum collections in the United Kingdom

Geoffrey Lewis and Anne Fahy

These notes set out the main legislation relating to the acquisition and disposal of museum collections in all types of museums in the UK.

This note draws attention to the main legislation in the United Kingdom relating to museums and the heritage as it affects the acquisition and disposal of collections. It does not, however, include tax legislation, which is the subject of a separate note. Nor does it cover the general law of property, trust or succession. Legal advice should always be sought if in doubt about matters relating to the acquisition and disposal of collections.

GENERAL LEGISLATION

There is no general legislation in the United Kingdom regarding the responsibilities of museum governing bodies towards their collections. Such information may be included in the enabling statutes of individual museums, and where this is so details are given later in this note. There are, however, laws of general application in certain situations. These include:

European Convention on the Protection of the Archaeological Heritage

This Council of Europe convention was ratified by the United Kingdom in 1973. In doing so the government has undertaken to delimit and protect sites and areas of archaeological interest (as in the above statutes), to prohibit and restrain illicit excavations and ensure that they are conducted by qualified persons, and that the results are controlled and conserved. It also requires museums to avoid acquiring material from illicit excavations or material obtained unlawfully from official excavations.

Protection of Wrecks Act, 1973

This allows the Secretary of State for Trade to designate an area round an unclaimed wreck in or on the sea bed which is considered to be of archaeological, historical or artistic interest. Unauthorized exploration within such a designated area is an offence. All unclaimed wrecks in territorial waters and finds from them are the property of the

Crown under the Merchant Shipping Act, 1894 and must be reported to the Department of Trade.

Ancient Monuments and Archaeological Areas Act, 1979

Under this statute sites and monuments of national importance may be scheduled and any disturbance of such a site requires the prior authority of the Secretary of State for the Environment (in England and Wales) or the Secretary of State for Scotland. A monument or site in territorial waters may also be scheduled under this Act. It also permits the designation of archaeological areas (mainly historic town centres) for short periods to allow excavation to take place in advance of development. Temporary authorized removal of finds resulting from excavation is permitted for study and treatment but they remain the property of the owner of the site unless otherwise determined by the owner or if the law of Treasure Trove applies. Unauthorized use of a metal detector on a site protected under the Act is an offence.

Wildlife and Countryside Act, 1981

All birds, their nests and eggs are protected under this statute and, with the exception of certain game birds, it is an offence to hold such material unless authorized. It was established during the passing of the Act that museums with collections of birds' eggs prior to the enforcement of the Act could testify by affidavit if challenged. The Act establishes a register of all authorized persons selling or trading in dead birds and this is held by the Department of the Environment. The Act also protects a number of animals and plants which are listed in Schedules. The Secretary of State has the power to revise the schedule; the most recent revision is The Wildlife and Countryside Act, 1981 (Variation of Schedule) Order 1988.

Endangered Species (Import and Export) Act, 1976

This Act requires that a licence be obtained to import certain species. Certain museums have been granted Open Individual Licences which permit them to exchange scientific material with overseas museums. This legislation is administered by the Department of the Environment.

The Firearms Acts (Firearms Act, 1968, Firearms (Amendment) Bill, 1988)

The Firearms Acts control the ownership and use of firearms. Museums with collections of firearms and ammunition must be in possession of the appropriate licences for their collections. Collections which include shotguns and other firearms should possess either a Shotgun Certificate (for shotguns), a Firearms Certificate, or a Museums Firearms Licence. The Museum Firearms Licence is an alternative to the Shotgun Certificate and the Firearms Certificate and unlike them, it licenses the institution rather than named individuals.

Import, Export and Customs Powers (Defence) Act, 1939

Although the United Kingdom has not ratified the 1970 Unesco Convention, Section 1 of this Act enables the Department of Trade to make orders prohibiting or regulating imports into, or exports from, this country. Current Export of Goods Control Orders require that a licence is obtained for any item which is over fifty years of age and which has a value in excess of £35,000 apart from pictures, where the limit is £100,000, and portraits, certain textiles, and arms and armour where the limit is £6,000. A licence is required for all manuscripts and archaeological material.

Such items are examined by an expert adviser and if considered of national importance are referred to the Reviewing Committee on the Export of Works of Art who consider the case on the following grounds (known as the Waverley Criteria):

1   Is the object so closely connected with our history and national life that its departure would be a misfortune?
2   Is it of outstanding aesthetic importance?
3   Is it of outstanding significance for the study of some particular branch of art, learning or history?

Before refusing an export licence on such grounds, the Committee also takes into account whether a purchaser might be found to ensure its retention in this country.

Note that the Open General Export Limits are changed normally on an annual basis.

Treasure Trove

The principle of Treasure Trove dates back to Anglo-Saxon common law. In England and Wales it relates to items of gold or silver found in the ground or a structure which are adjudged to have been deposited with the intent of recovery, the owner or his heir now being unknown. Strangely it is for a Coroner's Court to determine whether or not such material was deposited with the intention of recovery, and this is reiterated in the Coroner's Act 1988. Accordingly such finds must be reported immediately to the Police or the Coroner. If the Coroner's Court determines that the find is Treasure Trove, it is forfeited to the Crown, the finder receiving a reward equivalent to the full market value. If otherwise, the finder is permitted to retain his discovery. All other types of discovery from the ground remain the property of the owner of the land in which they were found.

Bona vacantia

In Scotland ownerless objects, bona vacantia, belong to the Crown under common law and everything considered to be of archaeological or historic significance may be claimed by the Crown, whether or not the items are of gold or silver. Discoveries must be reported to the Procurator Fiscal (or the Sheriff of the Region concerned) who will conduct an enquiry and advise the Queen's and Lord Treasurer's Remembrancer as to whether they should be retained. In such a case the full market value is paid to the finder.

STATUTES RELATING TO SPECIFIC MUSEUMS AND GALLERIES

Public museums and art galleries may be deemed not to have the power to dispose of items in their collection without the authority of the Charity Commissioners, or the appropriate Secretary of State in the case of public sector institutions, unless power to sell has been given under the terms of the original gift or bequest, or specific powers have been conferred by Statute, Royal Charter or similar instrument.

The issues were discussed fully in the Report of the Committee of Enquiry into the Sale of Works of Art by Public Bodies, 1964 from which the following (paras 30–1) is an extract:

The basic principle upon which the law rests is that when private persons give property for public purposes the Crown undertakes to see that it is devoted to the purposes intended by the donor, and to no others. When a work of art is given to a museum or gallery for general exhibition, the public thereby acquires rights in the object concerned and these rights cannot be set aside. The authorities of the museum or gallery are not the owners of such an object in the ordinary sense of the word: they are merely responsible, under the authority of the Courts, for carrying out the intentions of the donor. They cannot sell the object unless authorised to do so by the Courts, or by the Charity Commissioners or the Minister of Education on behalf of the Courts, because they have themselves nothing to sell. If they attempt a sale in breach of trust, it is the function of the Attorney General to enforce the trust and protect the rights of the public in the object by taking proceedings in the Chancery Division.

These general principles must be taken in conjunction with the following specific points:

(a) Where a work of art is given to a charitable institution, one of whose principal purposes is the exhibition of such objects to the public, a natural presumption arises that it has been given for this purpose; and unless this presumption is displaced by evidence to the contrary it cannot be sold without special authority;

(b) If a work of art is part of the general property of an exhibiting institution such as a museum or gallery, as is the case when it has been bought out of general funds, it cannot be sold unless the governing instrument of the institution (which may be for example a Statute, a Royal Charter or a Scheme of the Charity Commissioners) clearly permits such a course.

(Cottesloe 1964: 30–1)

The legislation relating to acquisition and disposal in different museums and galleries varies considerably as the following comments and extracts show.

ENGLAND AND WALES

British Museum Act, 1963

This statute relates to both the British Museum and the Natural History Museum. It provides that the trustees keep the objects within the authorized repositories of the museum except where temporary removal is necessary for purposes connected with the administration of the museum or the care of its collections, and to make the objects available to the public. The trustees shall not dispose of items in the collection except under provisions in Sections 5 and 9 of the Act, which read as follows:

Section 5:

1 The Trustees of the British Museum may sell, exchange, give away or otherwise dispose of any object vested in them and comprised in their collections if:

(a) the object is a duplicate of another such object, or

(b) the object appears to the Trustees to have been made not earlier than the year 1850, and substantially consists of printed matter on which a copy made by photography or a process akin to photography is held by the Trustees, or

(c) in the opinion of the Trustees the object is unfit to be retained in the collections of the Museum and can be disposed of without detriment to the interests of students provided that where an object has become vested in the Trustees by virtue of a gift or bequest the powers conferred by this subsection shall not be exercisable as respects that object in a manner inconsistent with any condition attached to the gift or bequest.

2 The Trustees may destroy or otherwise dispose of any object vested in them and comprised in their collections if satisfied that it has become useless for the purposes of the Museum by reason of damage, physical deterioration, or infestation by destructive organisms.

3 Money accruing to the Trustees by virtue of an exercise of the powers conferred by this section or section 6 of the Museums and Galleries Act 1992 shall be laid out by them in the purchase of objects to be added to the collections of the Museum.

Section 9:

1 Any movable property vested in the Trustees of [the British Museum or the Natural History Museum] may be transferred by them to the Trustees of the other Museum.

Museums and Galleries Act, 1992

The Act received Royal Assent in March 1992 and provided for the establishment of incorporated boards of trustees of the National Gallery, Tate Gallery, National Portrait Gallery and Wallace Collection. The Act specifies the general functions of the trustees to maintain, exhibit, grant access to collections and to promote public understanding and enjoyment of their collections. The Act replaced the National Gallery Act, 1856, and the National Gallery and Tate Gallery Act, 1954.

The Act broadly follows the arrangements set out in the National Heritage Act, 1983, which deals *inter alia* with the Victoria & Albert Museum and the Science Museum.

The Act also formalized the change in name from the Natural History Museum (BM) to the Natural History Museum.

The Act also permits the boards of trustees to:

1 Form companies (for example, to produce and publish books, films or other informative material; produce replicas or reproductions of works; the provision of catering).

2 Empower the National Gallery, Tate Gallery and National Portrait Gallery to acquire works of art and related documents for their collections and to transfer objects to certain other collections, but otherwise prohibits the disposal of objects other than under limited powers accorded to the Tate Gallery and National Portrait Gallery and limited transfer between certain museums and galleries. Any disposals from the Wallace Collection remain prohibited.

3 Empower the National Gallery, Tate Gallery and National Portrait Gallery, subject to constraints, to lend and borrow objects.

4 Enable specified museums, galleries and libraries to transfer objects from their collections to any other specified institution subject to any trust or condition.

5 Provide for certain gifts of works of art to the nation to be vested in specified museums, galleries or libraries.

6 Enable government to transfer land to certain museums, galleries and libraries notwithstanding any restrictions or prohibitions to the contrary.

7   Provide for the payment of grant-in-aid to certain museums, galleries and other bodies.

In terms of powers of disposal, Section 6 of the Act states:

> Any body for the time being specified in Part 1 of Schedule 5 to this Act may, by way of sale, gift or exchange, transfer an object the property in which is vested in them and which is comprised in their collection, if the transfer is to any other body for the time being specified in either Part of that Schedule.

Schedule 5

Part I

Transfers to and from certain collections:

The Board of Trustees of the Armouries
The British Library Board
The Trustees of the British Museum
The Trustees of the Imperial War Museum
The Board of Governors of the Museum of London
The Board of Trustees of the National Gallery
The Board of Trustees of the National Galleries of Scotland
The Board of Trustees of the National Library of Scotland
The Trustees of the National Maritime Museum
The Board of Trustees of the National Museums and Galleries on Merseyside
The Board of Trustees of the National Museums of Scotland
The Board of Trustees of the National Portrait Gallery
The Trustees of the Natural History Museum
The Board of Trustees of the Science Museum
The Board of Trustees of the Tate Gallery
The Board of Trustees of the Victoria & Albert Museum

Part II

Transferees only:

The Court of Governors of the National Library of Wales
The Council of the National Museums of Wales
The Trustees of the Ulster Museum
The Trustees of the Ulster Folk and Transport Museum

Imperial War Museum Act, 1920
National Maritime Museum Act, 1934

Both Acts permit the trustees of these museums to exchange, sell or otherwise dispose of any duplicate objects and, with the consent of the Secretary of State, to so dispose of objects no longer required for museum purposes. With the consent of the Secretary of State any monies received from the sale of objects may be used to buy additional objects.

Museum of London Acts, 1965 and 1986

Similar provisions apply to the Governors of the Museum of London except that such a decision requires not less than a two-thirds majority.

National Heritage Act, 1983
The Merseyside Museums and Galleries Order, 1986

These two pieces of legislation are very similarly drafted. The first provides the governing instrument for the Victoria & Albert Museum, the Science Museum and the Armouries, while the other is concerned with the National Museums and Galleries on Merseyside. Subject to the purposes of the legislation the boards of these museums may acquire (whether by purchase, exchange or gift) any objects which in their opinion it is desirable to add to their collections.

The boards of these museums may not dispose of an object vested in them and comprising part of their collections unless:

(a) the disposal is by way of sale, exchange or gift of an object which is a duplicate of another object;

(b) the disposal is by way of sale, exchange or gift of an object which in the board's opinion is unsuitable for retention in their collections and can be disposed of without detriment to the interests of students or other members of the public;

(c) the disposal is by way of sale or gift made to, or exchange made with, institutions mentioned in Schedule 5, Part I of the Museums and Galleries Act, 1992;

(d) the disposal (by whatever means, including destruction) is of an object which the appropriate board is satisfied has become useless for the purposes of its collections by reason of damage, physical deterioration or infestation by destructive organisms. For this purpose any trust or condition (express or implied) prohibiting or restricting the disposal of the object may be overridden.

Money accruing to the boards as a result of disposal mentioned above shall be applied to the acquisition of objects to be added to the appropriate museum collection.

The boards of the museums may accept loans, depending on the terms of the loan, for exhibition, study and research purposes.

With regard to outward loans, these may be made from the collections and the boards are required to give special consideration to requests for public exhibition purposes but to have regard to the interests of students and other persons visiting the museum's collections, the suitability of the prospective borrower, the purpose of the loan, the physical condition and rarity of the object and any risks to which it might be exposed. Except in the Merseyside Order where items are subject to a condition, consent has first to be obtained from the donors, etc., unless twenty-five years have elapsed since they were vested in the relevant board in which case such a condition is normally considered void.

Public Libraries and Museums Act, 1964

This enabling legislation provides general powers to certain local authorities in England and Wales to provide and maintain museums and galleries and do all such things as may be necessary or expedient for this. The Act provides specific provision for the accumulation of a purchase fund but there is no explicit reference to the disposal of collections. However, Schedule 2 of the Act states that the proceeds of the sale of any object may be paid into the cumulative art fund, provided no trust terms prevent this.

LOCAL ACTS

Sometimes local Acts of Parliament give additional powers to the local authorities concerned and this may affect the acquisition and disposal policies of their museums.

The following are extracts from such Acts:

Greater Manchester Act, 1981

Section 149:

(2) The art gallery and all works or other objects of art therein shall be held upon trust by Manchester Council for the benefit of the citizens of Manchester and shall at all times be kept in fit and proper order.

(3) Notwithstanding anything in subsection (2) above, the Manchester Council may from time to time sell or exchange any works or other objects of art for the time being acquired by them for the art gallery but the money arising from any such sale shall be applied in the purchase of other works or other objects of art and for no other purpose and any such works or objects received in exchange shall take the place for all purposes of the works or objects given in exchange:

Provided that where any work or object has become vested in the Manchester Council by virtue of a gift or bequest –

(a) the Manchester Council shall, if reasonably practicable, consult with the donor or with the personal representatives or trustees of the donor before exercising the powers of this subsection; and

(b) the powers conferred by this subsection shall not, during a period of twenty-one years commencing on the date on which it became vested, be exercisable as respects that work or object in any manner inconsistent with any condition attached to the gift or bequest, except with the consent of the donor or the personal representatives or trustees of the donor.

(4) The Manchester Council may from time to time accept by way of gift or bequest any works or other objects of art which they consider to be desirable acquisitions and all such works or objects shall belong to and form part of the art gallery.

(5) The Manchester Council shall continue to administer the fund established under section 14 of the Manchester Corporation Act 1882 and they shall devote the same at their discretion to the purchase of works or other objects of art to be held in trust for the benefit of the citizens of Manchester and all such works or objects shall belong to and form part of the art gallery.

(6) Admission of the public to the art gallery shall be free of charge on such days of the week as the Manchester Council may determine and the Council shall determine the terms and conditions of admission of the public on other days.

It should be noted (5) above that the Manchester City Council have had powers to accumulate funds for purchases since 1882 and this facility is preserved.

County of Lancashire Act, 1984

This Act, although promoted by the county council, also applies to all district councils in Lancashire:

Section 58:

(1) A district council may lend, exchange or otherwise part with possession (but not ownership) of any specimen, work of art or book vested in them which in

the opinion of the authority is not required for exhibition or use in any museum, art gallery, library or other building of the authority.

(2) A district council may make arrangements by way of loan, exchange or gift with any person being the owner of any museum, art gallery or library for the transfer to that person of any specimen, work of art, or book vested in the authority which in the opinion of the council is more suitable for exhibition or use in the museum, art gallery or library of that person than in a museum, art gallery, library or other building of the council.

(3) Where any object has become vested in the district council by virtue of a gift or bequest –

(a) the district council shall, if reasonably practicable, consult with a donor or with the personal representatives or trustees of the donor before exercising the powers of this section; and

(b) the powers conferred by this section shall not, during a period of 35 years commencing on the date on which it became vested, be exercisable as respects that object in any manner inconsistent with any condition attached to the gift or bequest except with the consent of the donor or the personal representatives or trustees of the donor.

(4) Any moneys received by a district council in the exercise of the powers of this section shall be applied by them in the purchase of specimens, works of art or books.

SCOTLAND

National Galleries of Scotland Act, 1906
National Heritage (Scotland) Act, 1985, Part III

Three institutions are administered by one board of trustees: the National Gallery of Scotland; the Scottish Portrait Gallery; the Scottish National Gallery of Modern Art. When the board of trustees was established all property transferred was to be held in trust by the board. Under the terms of Statutory Instruments of 1949 and 1951, however, they acquired restricted powers of disposal in certain collections for material no longer required, provided that this was not inconsistent with the terms of a bequest. Under the terms of the Museums and Galleries Act, 1992, the trustees are permitted to dispose of objects from the collections by sale, gift or exchange, or transfer to those institutions contained in Part I of Schedule 5 of the Act.

National Heritage (Scotland) Act, 1985

The powers of acquisition and disposal of objects given to the board of trustees of the Royal Museums of Scotland under this Act are virtually identical to those given in the National Heritage Act, 1983 (see above). This Act was also amended by the Museums and Galleries Act, 1992, in the same way as the National Galleries of Scotland Act, 1906, above.

Education (Scotland) Act, 1980

An education authority in Scotland may provide and maintain museums within its area and under section 27(1) of the Act have the power:

(a) To acquire any objects which, in their opinion, it is desirable to include in a collection contained in a museum maintained by them under this section.

(b) To lend any object vested in them and comprised in any such collection, on such terms and conditions as they see fit, to any person or any purpose.

(c) Unless subject to any trust or contrary condition, to transfer any object vested in them and comprised in any such collection to the governing body of a museum maintained by a person other than the education authority, for the purpose of being included in a collection contained in that museum.

(d) Unless subject to any trust or contrary condition, to sell, exchange, give away or otherwise dispose of any object vested in them and comprised in a collection contained in a museum maintained by them under this section, if for any reason that object is not, in their opinion, required for retention in any such collection.

Public Libraries Consolidation (Scotland) Act, 1887

This legislation permits a library authority, or a museum and art gallery authority under this Act, to purchase specimens of art and science and other such articles and things as may be necessary in the exercise of this function and also to sell or exchange any works of art, or other property of which there may be duplicates provided that money or property received from such a transaction shall be applied for the purpose of the Act.

NORTHERN IRELAND

Museums (Northern Ireland) Order, 1981

This order, issued under powers given in the Northern Ireland Act, 1974, covers both the two national museums and any museums and art galleries provided by the district councils.

a) The Ulster Museum and

The Ulster Folk and Transport Museum

Although there are separate boards of trustees for the two museums, their powers of acquisition and disposal are the same. Section 5(1) of the Order permits the Trustees, *inter alia*, to:

1 Incur expenditure on the purchase of any object which, in their opinion, it is desirable to acquire.

2 Accept gifts or bequests of money or objects or other property and execute any lawful trust having objects similar to the objects of the trustees or incidental or conducive to the attainment or furtherance of any object to the trustees.

3 Exchange, sell or otherwise dispose of any movable property which is no longer required for the purposes of the museum, unless that is inconsistent with any conditions attaching to the property subject to which the property was vested in them, and on any such exchange may give or receive money for equality of exchange.

4 Except where the terms upon which the property is held expressly provide to the contrary, lend any movable property for the time being vested in the trustees for a period not exceeding one year and, with the approval of the Department of Education for Northern Ireland, for any longer period.

5 Destroy any movable property vested in the trustees which is useless or of no value to the museum.

(b) District council museums and art galleries

No guidance is given in the Order regarding the acquisition or disposal of collections although a district council may make bylaws for the preservation of property vested in it, or in its custody for museums and art gallery purposes.

REFERENCE

Cottesloe, Lord (1964) *Report of the Committee of Enquiry into the Sale of Works of Art by Public Bodies*, London: HMSO.

13

The Bowes Museum Canaletto Appeal

G. Stansfield[1]

Museums often embark upon high-profile fund-raising campaigns to acquire objects for their collections. Sometimes the campaigns are successful and other times they are not; much depends upon the careful planning and co-ordination of the campaign. These notes provide a case study of how one museum successfully raised the funds to purchase two pictures by Canaletto, and it contains many useful hints for other museums considering trying to raise cash for objects in such a way.

BACKGROUND

1 Pictures had been on loan to the Bowes Museum for ten years and they were known to be among the most popular exhibits.
2 Owner approached museum concerning sale. He offered private treaty sale and up to nine months to raise the money.
3 It was decided to attempt to purchase the paintings because of 1. Also the owner wanted the paintings to stay in the North East.
4 An open market price of £400,000 was agreed and the owner obtained the private treaty price from the Capital Taxes Office.

FINANCIAL STRATEGY

5 A list was prepared of the possible sources of funds and the amount they might provide. It was clear from this that a public appeal would have to be launched to raise the shortfall.
6 Tentative enquiries were made by letter, telephone and personal approach to the Victoria & Albert Museum, the National Art Collections Fund, the National Heritage Memorial Fund, Friends of the Bowes Museum, Assistant Director of Education (the museum's senior officer). Initial responses were sufficient to encourage the museum to proceed although NHMF expressed doubt as to whether they would be able to give a grant.
7 Museum committee was asked in private session whether it could make an extra grant. This they agreed to do, so that the museum was committed to contribute £40,000 (10 per cent of total).

ROLE OF THE FRIENDS OF THE MUSEUM

8 The Friends were asked to run the appeal because:

(a) They are a charity.
(b) They could provide volunteers.
(c) They could provide a network of influential contacts.
(d) They could underwrite the expenses of the appeal.
(e) They could act quickly.

(The Friends' resources are an investment of £50,000 bringing an annual income of £5,000 per annum).

PUBLICITY

9 It was decided to produce a good quality leaflet with colour illustrations and with text that anticipated possible questions. The colour separations for the leaflet were also used to produce postcards which were sold at 50p with a special stamp thanking donors. Information sheets were prepared on:

(a) The museum and its normal finances.
(b) The Friends and their finances.
(c) How business could help.

Information packs were prepared to include all the above and the museum's publicity leaflet.

10 Letters were drafted to send to charities and to local industry. All were signed individually by the president of the Friends and were sent with an information pack.
11 A circular letter was sent to Friends regarding donations, events, volunteer help.
12 The pictures were rehung in a prominent position with information boards including a column indicating the level of donations, with space for press cuttings, news items, posters, etc. A donations box was provided and later an information desk.

PRESS LAUNCH OF APPEAL

13 In response to approaches to the *Darlington and Stockton Times*, the paper offered to sponsor the appeal with weekly articles and a fund-raising advertising supplement. (This was seen to be a vital component in the success of the Appeal.)
14 Personal calls were made to major newspapers asking for press cover on the day of launching with some success. Both TV stations visited the museum. Local press made good use of press releases and photographs. Full information and many photographs were circulated locally and nationally. At the launch of the appeal it was also possible to announce an NACF grant of £40,000.

MAJOR GRANTS AND RESEARCH

15 The public appeal was in fact for only 25 per cent of the price (£100,000). Grant applications to major funding bodies were made by the curator. This required back-up art historical information for which research was required. Research continued alongside fund-raising and generated articles for local magazines and lectures.

HELP FROM THE PRESS

16 The *Darlington and Stockton Times* kept progress of the appeal before the public through stories relating to individual donations. Local societies volunteered fund raising efforts. News items included photographs of cheques being presented, VIP visits to the museum, weekly progress with the appeal. The time expended on this aspect of the appeal was enormous.

APPEAL OFFICE AND INFORMATION DESK

17 Located in the staff tea-room, two permanent staff helped supervise on a daily basis with a rota of volunteers from the Friends. Indices were compiled, circulars sent out, donors thanked and contributions noted. Also dealt with telephone calls and publicity.

Later an information desk was located in the gallery where volunteers answered enquiries and sold raffle tickets.

Three indices were compiled:

(a) Appropriate charities (drawn from the *Directory of Grant-making Trusts*).
(b) Local and national businesses (drawn from *The Times* top 1,000 companies and local directories).
(c) Private donors.

Note: The indices are of long-term value to the museum.

ROYAL VISIT

18 HM Queen Elizabeth the Queen Mother is Patron of the Friends. A visit had been planned for some time but took place during the appeal (actually on the day of the birth of Prince William). As a result the museum received national TV coverage.

JUNIOR FRIENDS

19 The Junior Friends set out to raise a mile of 2ps. In the end they raised a quarter of a mile (£300). One child raised £100.

PUBLICITY IN LONDON

20 It was felt that the reluctance of arts writers to travel to Barnard Castle could only be overcome by taking the pictures to London. Eventually Agnew agreed to show the paintings and allowed the museum to hold a press view and evening reception for potential donors. This was particularly useful for members of trusts. Agnew also put their publicity firm at the museum's disposal at no charge.

MID-TERM CRISIS

21 It had been hoped that the V&A might agree to fund the purchase of one picture in each of two succeeding financial years. In fact they offered £100,000 (less than had been anticipated) and passed the responsibility to the NHMF. Eventually in spite of their earlier lack of enthusiasm, NHMF agreed to back the appeal but on condition that this should not be made known generally. The research and public support were major factors in influencing NHMF.

FINAL WEEKS

22 Because many Trusts meet only infrequently, the larger grants were not confirmed until the final weeks. The more grants that were announced, the more donations were received. By the deadline the appeal had raised £84,000 of the £100,000. In the event the balance of the appeal was met by NHMF.

SUMMARY OF RESPONSES

23 (a) Industry. Total £4,463. Timing was bad because the appeal came during the worst of the recession.
    (b) Local response was active and enthusiastic. Total raised £7,885. However, this was of vital importance in attracting trust donations.
    (c) Trusts provided a total of £56,885.

TIMETABLE

24 It needed five months to sound out potential donors and helpers and to prepare the appeal literature. Trusts need up to six months to meet and answer appeals. Nine months is the minimum to organize a truly public appeal.

EFFECTS ON NORMAL MUSEUM WORK

25 Normal office work was totally interrupted. Museum work was slightly neglected and forward planning much affected. The strain was tremendous.

LONG-TERM BENEFITS

26 The experience would be valuable if the situation arose again and the indices would be useful. Relations with local press were improved. The appeal helped to improve the local status of the museum.

NOTE

1 Drawn from extensive notes generously provided by Mrs E. Conran, Curator, The Bowes Museum.

14

Preservation of Industrial and Scientific Material (PRISM) Grant Fund

Museums and Galleries Commission/Science Museum

The PRISM Fund provides funds towards the acquisition and conservation of items important in the history of technology and science. It is open to local authority and university museums, and museums with registered charity status in England and Wales (Scotland has its own fund administered by the National Museums of Scotland). Eligible museums must also have achieved registered status (see the MGC National Registration Scheme). This chapter reproduces a leaflet that provides information about the organization and scope of the PRISM Fund.

Preservation of Industrial and Scientific Material (PRISM) Grant Fund

Administered on behalf of the Museums and Galleries Commission (MGC) by the Science Museum.

GUIDELINES FOR APPLICANTS

Purpose of the Fund

The Fund was established in 1973 to further the preservation, in the public domain, of items or collections important for the history and development of science and technology in all their aspects. Grants are available from the Fund towards the costs of acquisition and conservation of such material.

The Fund's scope extends to England and Wales, and a parallel fund for the purchase of objects relating to the arts, literature and history is administered by the Victoria & Albert Museum. A corresponding scheme for both purposes is administered in Scotland by the National Museums of Scotland, Chambers Street, Edinburgh EH1 1JF.

Who is eligible to apply?

- MGC Registered museums.
- At the fund manager's discretion, applications may also be accepted from charitable organizations engaged in the preservation of scientific, technological and industrial artefacts or monuments, although they may not be eligible for registration

The material for which grant-in-aid is sought must be established in the public domain, and there must be a long-term intention to hold and maintain it. This material must not be treated by the applicant organization as disposable assets, nor used as a collateral for loans.

Note: Should an applicant organization cease to fulfil PRISM Grant Fund eligibility criteria the MGC will be entitled to reclaim any grants made.

The following are *not eligible* to apply:

• Private individuals.
• Society- or company-run museums without charitable status.
• Nationally funded institutions

All new applicants will be required to furnish proof of their eligibility.

Charitable bodies not registered with the MGC must supply:

• A copy of their constitution, memorandum and articles of association, trust deed or other governing instrument.
• A copy of the charity commissioner's filing slip.
• A copy of the most recent audited accounts (where applicable)

All new applicants must provide copies of their current collecting and disposals policies.

What material is eligible for grant-aid?

Any movable object or group of objects illustrating the history of any branch of technology or science (including natural history).

Archives and manuscript material with a significant technological, scientific or industrial content, *but excluding* books acquired for library or reference purposes.

An objective of the Fund is to assist projects in conformity with a national pattern which avoids unnecessary duplication but encourages regional specialities. Applicants must be able to demonstrate that the proposed acquisition or conservation project complies with a previously declared collecting policy which has been discussed/agreed with other museums or bodies which collect in a similar subject/geographical area.

Eligible costs

• Purchase price. Buyer's premium at auction may be considered for grant-aid. Items from a sale catalogue must have been personally inspected by the applicant *before* an application is made.
• The costs of dismantling, transport and re-erection.
• The conservation of material either on acquisition or from existing collections. Priority will be given to items of more than local significance. Costs may include the use of specialist contractors, tool hire, materials and consumable items.

Note: Gross costs of less that £500 will not normally be considered for grant-in-aid.

Applications must be submitted *before* the object has been acquired, or project commenced. Applicants must *not* enter into any undertaking with vendor or contractor prior to making an application, other than the gathering of quotations where appropriate. If there is any urgency an application may be made by fax to 071 938 9736.

Ineligible costs

The costs of the following cannot be reimbursed by the Fund:

- Any project where the object is not/will not be wholly owned by the applicant.
- Items of capital equipment including tools and plant, showcases and display materials, lighting and environmental control equipment.
- Direct labour costs, i.e. wages of staff on museum complement, and the notional value of volunteer or sponsored labour and materials.
- Apparatus for providing motive power to working objects, and items required for compliance with safety legislation for the continuing operation of an object.
- Maintenance and repair costs of operating objects.
- Costs of repairing objects accidentally damaged.
- Any costs paid *before* an application is submitted

Submitting an application

Applicants should:

- Complete an application form, available from the fund manager (see details at end of pamphlet),
- Include any documentation required as proof of eligibility if applying for the first time.
- Present a clear case for the significance of the object in a local or national context, and demonstrate how the object complies with the applicant institution's collection policy.
- Provide good quality photographs; at least two different views showing the object/condition of the object. Where appropriate, drawings should be included.
- In the case of conservation applications, applicants must provide:

    (a) A full specification of the work proposed.
    (b) Evidence that appropriate conservations skills are available.
    (c) A detailed statement by the conservator/contractor of how it is intended this work will be carried out.
    (d) Evidence that a realistic timetable for conservation work has been drawn up.
    (e) Detailed costings. In particular materials and labour elements *must* be shown separately

Applications are sent to expert referees (usually senior staff in a national museum) for assessment. In some cases an inspection of the material by the fund manager or referees may be necessary.

How much grant-aid is available?

- The maximum grant that can be awarded is 50 per cent of the eligible costs (exclusive of VAT where reclaimable), subject to funds being available. Where the referee considers the costs to be excessive, support will be limited to 50 per cent of what is considered a fair price.
- Grants are limited to £15,000 on any one item; £20,000 if the item is considered of exceptional significance.
- Aggregated grants to any institution are limited to a total of £20,000 in any one year.
- At least 25 per cent of the remaining eligible costs must be raised locally (not normally including sponsorship 'in kind').

- 25 per cent *may* be found from other nationally administered grant-aiding bodies (except below).
- The total amount of grant-aid from MGC sources, including the PRISM Grant Fund and Area Museum Councils, may not exceed 50 per cent of the total eligible cost of the project. Where AMCs are being used as conservation contractors, PRISM grant-aid will be calculated to take account of any AMC discount rate

Claiming the grant

- When an offer of a grant is made a Declaration Form is enclosed with the formal letter.
- The object or conservation work should be fully paid for and the object in the custody of the applicant institution. In the case of conservation projects extending over more than twelve months the grant may, by prior arrangement, be claimed in instalments.
- The applicant must complete the Declaration Form, noting carefully the undertaking not to dispose of, mortgage, charge or otherwise surrender their rights over grant-aided objects without prior approval from the MGC. They must also notify the MGC if the object is damaged, lost or stolen and undertake (1) in the event of loss or irreparable damage to the objects, there shall be repaid to the Museums and Galleries Commission the full amount of grant aid or a proportion of any compensation or insurance settlement commensurate with the grant-aid, (2) that if the disposal of grant-aided objects by sale is permitted, a proportion equal to the percentage of the original grant (or the original sum, whichever is greater) will be paid to the MGC from any monies received.
- The applicant should then return the Declaration Form together with receipts or other proofs of payment to the fund manager. Where payment is made in a foreign currency, the exchange rate operative at the time of the transaction must be quoted.

Note:

- Grants left unclaimed for twelve months after qualifying payment has been made will be revoked without further warning except in the case of a conservation grant being paid in instalments.
- Applicants must notify the fund manager if any acquisition bid fails for any reason, or a conservation project has to be postponed or cancelled. Failure to do so may prejudice future grant applications.

Standards of care and access

Applicants should refer to the MGC *Care of Collections Standards*. Those for both archaeology and biology collections are currently available; standards for geological and industrial collections are in course of preparation. Please contact the information officer at the MGC for further details.

Generally:

- Items should be housed on a permanent basis in secure, environmentally suitable conditions.
- Long-term loans of grant-aided material to other institutions require prior approval from the fund manager. Any costs incurred are ineligible for grant-aid.
- MGC representatives may visit the institution to inspect grant-aided objects. Applicants are expected to co-operate with arrangements for such visits.

- Evidence that storage or display conditions are below a standard acceptable to the MGC and its representatives will prejudice further grant applications.
- Where applicants have problems housing exhibits adequately they must contact the MGC so that help and advice may be given before serious deterioration can begin.
- Other restrictions over grant-aided material may be applied according to circumstances.
- The MGC expect objects purchased or conserved with Fund assistance to be displayed so that there is no bar to access by disabled people. We suggest that you read *Guidelines on Disability for Museums and Galleries in the United Kingdom* published by the MGC, and consult with your local AMC and disability groups

Acknowledgement of grant-aid

Successful applicants should formally acknowledge grant-aid from the Fund using the following form of words:

> This [object] was purchased/transported/conserved/restored [delete as applicable] with assistance from the Preservation of Industrial and Scientific Material (PRISM) Grant Fund, administered on behalf of the Museums and Galleries Commission by the Science Museum.

This acknowledgement should normally be included in display labels or captions, but where there is a difficulty please contact the fund manager to discuss the matter.

Artwork will be available from the PRISM Grant Fund for a logo which may also be used to identify grant-aided material.

Mention of the role of the Fund should be made in any publicity concerning a grant-aided object.

A list of grants awarded by the PRISM Grant Fund will be published in the MGC's annual report and the MGC and Science Museum reserve the right to publish photographs or illustrations sent in support of grant applications. Confidentiality of details of negotiations by grant applicants will be respected by the Fund's officers.

Further details

Application forms and further details are available from:

> The Manager, PRISM Grant Fund
> The Science Museum, South Kensington,
> London SW7 2DD
> Telephone: 071 938 8005
> Fax: 071 938 9736

15

The Science Museum Fund

John Robinson

This chapter describes in more detail the working of the PRISM Fund and provides examples of objects the Fund has assisted museums in purchasing.

One of the less well-known activities of the Science Museum is its stewardship of the Grant-in-Aid Fund. Established in 1973, the Fund assists non-national museums throughout England and Wales with up to 50 per cent of the costs of buying, moving or conserving items of local historical significance – something that would otherwise be beyond their means. Although the money to pay grants from the Fund is channelled through the Museums and Galleries Commission (MGC), it is at the Science Museum that individual applications are considered and referred to whichever curator has specialist expertise in the relevant area. Staff from other national museums are sometimes consulted for their opinion on grant applications. Applicants also have the opportunity to benefit from advice on the repair and conservation of the objects that they propose to acquire with the help of their grant. If for any reason a grant cannot be offered, the Science Museum is frequently able to lend an item from its own collections to help a provincial museum complete its displays. Having accepted from the MGC the delegated role of administering the Grant-in-Aid scheme in this way, the Science Museum has been able to widen its responsibility for pastoral advice and support to smaller museums with science and technology collections throughout the country.

British engineering has always been strongly export-oriented, and museums in this country frequently have to look overseas for examples of particular engineering milestones, originally produced in Britain but no longer to be found within our own shores. For example, a rare Hornsby steam traction engine, built in Grantham in 1892 and one of only two known to have survived, was acquired by a local Rotary Club in Tasmania and offered as a gift to the Museum of Lincolnshire Life on condition that all costs of shipment and restoration would be met in Lincoln. Our fund has undertaken to meet half of these costs. Similarly, an early nineteenth-century beam engine used for many years to drive the fire-clay plant at the Coalbrookdale Company's Lightmoor brickworks was collected from Shropshire in 1929 and taken to the technology museum then being established in Dearborn, near Detroit, by Henry Ford (whose interest in the British engineering industry was evidently greater than our own at that time). In recent years, the Henry Ford Museum has rationalized its collections, giving the Ironbridge Gorge Museum the opportunity to repatriate this historic beam engine which had worked in the Ironbridge area for nearly a century. We have offered to provide half the costs of shipping the engine – together with an historic wrought-iron balloon boiler – back from Detroit. Also in 1988, a grant of £10,000 allowed the British Motor Industry Heritage Trust to bring back to Britain a Daimler DE36 landaulette. One of a pair delivered to George VI in 1949, it had subsequently been shipped to Australia for use at Government House in Brisbane. It is now on display among other historic Jaguar and Daimler cars at Syon Park.

Speed of response to a grant application can sometimes be crucial if an item is not to be lost. For example, natural erosion of the banks of the River Usk in South Wales progressively revealed the remains of a wooden boat buried in the mud, and its survival immediately excited the interest of the Glamorgan–Gwent Archaeological Trust and the Newport Museum. Prolonged and torrential rain later in October 1987 unexpectedly washed the boat out of the bank and deposited it some distance downstream. Local archaeologists had by then spent enough time surveying and recording the boat to be able to confirm its historic interest as a rare survivor of early nineteenth-century South Wales canal transport. Thanks to the Science Museum's promise of a grant towards costs, the boat's remains were successfully recovered for preservation at Newport Museum.

Another example of the need for urgent recovery action because of natural exposure – and a reminder that the scope of the Fund regularly includes natural history material – was the very large fossil ichthyosaur skeleton excavated early in 1987 from a sea-cliff at Charmouth near Lyme Regis. This remarkable find of a marine reptile some 180 million years old proved to represent a new taxon: museums and wealthy collectors in West Germany, Japan and elsewhere showed a strong interest in acquiring the 7.7 metre skeleton. However, a grant of £10,000 from the Science Museum – together with substantial help from the National Heritage Memorial Fund and the proceeds of a public appeal – secured the future of this important find in Bristol City Museum, where it has formed the centrepiece of a special 'Sea Dragon' exhibition.

A humble wrought-iron gate found lying in long grass near the Willsbridge Mill head-quarters of the Avon Wildlife Trust was recognized by London industrial archaeologist Malcolm Tucker as a relic of Thomas Pearsall (1758–1825), patentee of a new method of constructing roofs, doors and other components made from wrought iron. (Tucker's grandfather had founded and operated the water-driven ironworks at Willsbridge.) A series of large roofs built according to Pearsall's patent at London's West India Docks partly collapsed in 1813, and his system was not widely adopted. The discovery of the gate close to where it would have been made provided an interesting link with a pioneering period in structural engineering, and a modest grant from the Science Museum made it possible to conserve it against further decay and exhibit it at the Willsbridge Mill Visitor Centre.

A similar story comes from South Wales. A wrought-iron coal-tram used underground at the Tredegar colliery ceased to be used more than a century ago, but remained in a disused level of the mine until ground movements threatened the collapse of the old galleries, when it had to be recovered by a specialist mines rescue team. A grant towards expenses secured this early nineteenth-century transport relic for the Big Pit Mining Museum at Blaenavon.

Proper recording and documentation are an important adjunct to any preservation or restoration scheme, since the evidence brought to light in the course of overhauling a historic machine or clearing an industrial site will be lost forever unless there is a systematic procedure of photography, drawing, measuring and note-taking. For example, an abandoned timber-framed windmill in the Sussex village of Lowfield Heath was under threat from the progressive expansion of Gatwick Airport; this pre-1750 building stood within only a few hundred yards of the airport boundary. So in 1985 a trust was set up by local residents to save the rapidly deteriorating structure and remove it to a place of safety. Measured drawings and extensive photographs were prepared as the structure was carefully dismantled and the surviving machinery delicately lifted out by crane during the summer of 1987. With hindsight, this initiative came just in time: the hurricane of the following October would certainly have damaged the windmill beyond repair had it not already been re-erected at a new site close to Gatwick Zoo where it will again be accessible to visitors.

In the case of the village wheelwright's and carriage shop at Brompton Regis in the Brendon Hills, a family enterprise extending over 134 years was due to end with the retirement of the three grandsons of John How, the founder and original occupant. When staff from the Somerset County Museum were invited to collect material from this remarkable rural time-capsule, they realized the importance of extending their recording activity beyond just documenting the hardware destined for their museum store; they therefore amplified this with tape-recorded reminiscences from the How brothers, all of whose working lives had been devoted to meeting the carpentry and engineering needs of this isolated Somerset village. In their enthusiasm to measure and document the artefacts that are to come into their collections, curators frequently overlook the elusive evidence that can be provided in this way by those who worked the machinery or used the tools. Without a record of those skills, the tools and implements of dead men and women will eventually themselves become lifeless in a museum.

The sum provided by the Government to operate the Fund each year has been increased only once in sixteen years – when it went up by £18,000 to £168,000 in April 1983. Since the rate at which we are authorized to offer grant-aid never exceeds 50 per cent of eligible costs, there is an inbuilt guarantee that matching finance must be found from local resources by the applicants themselves. However, in the case of many preservation projects initiated by volunteers, a grant of 50 per cent towards, say, materials for new components or transport of a large and heavy item, will represent only a tiny proportion of the total input.

The very success of these local initiatives has meant that the rate at which unexpected 'finds' are coming to light has slowed down. Rarely now do we hear of an unrecorded Bugatti discovered at the back of a barn, and the compilation of local inventories of industrial monuments provides a clearer overview, from a national angle, of just what survives from earlier eras. Consequently, the Science Museum is looking towards reducing the proportion of its limited resources devoted to *acquisition* grants. The need to support *conservation* projects, however, will continue to grow.

We have always maintained regular liaison with parallel grant-giving bodies such as the Historic Buildings and Monuments Commission and, since 1980, the National Heritage Memorial Fund. We are now considering the possibility of a closer partnership with these and other publicly funded aid agencies in order to provide more effective support for the regular upkeep of those industrial sites or collections that cannot expect to achieve self-sufficiency from visitor revenue alone. Many such sites find themselves tempted to diversify their attractions, and hence dilute their archaeological integrity, in their efforts to balance the books. There is a clear need for comparatively modest sums in grant aid to help relieve nationally important sites in this predicament of the pressure to compromise their historical authenticity. Such support would have to be administered selectively, but could help to secure the continuing excellence of a whole portfolio of industrial monuments which might otherwise be driven by financial pressures into the sort of mediocrity that the Museums and Galleries Commission – by example as much as by financial support – exists to dispel.

16

Victoria & Albert Museum 1992 Purchase Grant Fund
Museums and Galleries Commission

The MGC/V&A Purchase Grant Fund provides assistance for local authority and university museums, art galleries, libraries and record offices in England and Wales to purchase objects relating to the arts and literature and history (a similar fund is operated in Scotland by the National Museums of Scotland). MGC registered status is a basic requirement for eligibility for funds. This chapter provides information about the regulations and scope of the Fund.

PURPOSE OF THE FUND

The Fund, which has been in existence since 1881, contributes towards the purchase of objects relating to the arts, literature and history by local and university museums, art galleries, libraries and record offices in England and Wales. It is administered by the Victoria & Albert Museum on behalf of the Museums and Galleries Commission (MGC).

A parallel fund to assist in the acquisition of objects relating to the natural sciences and technology is administered by the Science Museum, London. Similar funds for both purposes are administered for institutions in Scotland by the National Museums of Scotland, Edinburgh.

WHO IS ELIGIBLE TO APPLY?

Museums and galleries, record offices and specialist libraries which exist for the benefit of the public, provided that they:

(a) Maintain a permanent collection housed in suitable conditions.
(b) Have an acceptable constitution and financial basis.
(c) Are staffed by suitably qualified personnel.
(d) Provide an appropriate range of visitor services including regular public access.

Registration under the MGC scheme for museums and galleries is the basic criterion for application to the Fund. Those institutions not covered by the scheme, such as libraries and record offices, will be investigated independently by the Purchase Grant Fund Office.

Applications cannot be accepted from nationally funded institutions or Friends organizations.

WHAT IS ELIGIBLE FOR GRANT-AID?

Any museum item or collection relating to the arts, literature or history priced at £750 and over. These might include archaeological, ethnographical and printed material, rare books, objects illustrating social and popular culture as well as the fine and decorative arts.

Manuscripts, including estate maps, writers' manuscripts, documents and letters with good historical content and archival photographs, priced at £350 and over.

Ineligible – artificial grouping of items individually priced at less than £750 (or £350 in the case of archival material), circulating exhibition services or loan schemes, reproductions, facsimiles, current publications, museum or library equipment, conservation costs, delivery charges, framing or valuation charges, value added tax.

HOW MUCH GRANT-AID IS AVAILABLE?

The maximum grant that can be awarded is 50 per cent of the purchase price (exclusive of VAT) subject to funds being available.

In order to qualify for a maximum 50 per cent grant at least 25 per cent of the cost must be found from locally raised sources, such as the applicant's own purchase vote, special appeals, contributions by Friends organizations, private donations from individual benefactors or local industry.

The remaining 25 per cent can be sought from other nationally administered grant-aiding bodies such as the Beecroft Bequest, Friends of the National Libraries, National Art Collections Fund, National Heritage Memorial Fund, Pilgrim Trust, etc. Please consult the Purchase Grant Fund Office if in doubt as to the exact nature of any potential fund source.

ARE GRANTS OF LESS THAN 50 PER CENT EVER GIVEN?

Although the maximum subvention is set at 50 per cent the Purchase Grant Fund may offer less if funds are short, if an applicant is able to contribute a higher percentage of the cost, or if the object in question is considered to be overpriced.

Grant-aid may only be given at the maximum rate of 2:1 local money. Should less than 25 per cent be available from local sources or if more than 25 per cent of the price is obtained from other national sources, the purchase will no longer qualify for a full 50 per cent grant and the Fund's contribution will be reduced accordingly.

In the case of auction sales grant-aid will be limited to 50 per cent of the previously agreed level of support or 50 per cent of the actual price paid, whichever is the lower. If the lot is acquired at a figure below our minimum level of support (i.e. £750, or £350 in the case of archival material) it will no longer qualify for grant-aid.

THE FUND'S CONTINUING INTEREST IN ITEMS ACQUIRED WITH GRANT-AID

Even when the grant has been paid and our files are closed, the Purchase Grant Fund retains an interest in the items it has helped acquire.

Housing objects – items must be housed on a permanent basis by the applicant institution in secure and environmentally controlled conditions. While the Fund places no restrictions on the temporary loan of grant-aided material, venues should be able to provide conditions comparable or superior to the applicant's own. The Purchase Grant Fund cannot contribute towards the purchase of items specifically acquired for circulating exhibition services or regular loan schemes.

Selling objects – in signing the grant claim form (Form B) an institution undertakes not to dispose of the item in question without prior approval. Those intending to sell objects for revenue purposes will seriously prejudice their chances of receiving grant-aid in the future. Museums should abide by the MGC registration guidelines with regard to the disposal of collections; libraries and record offices would be expected to consult the Royal Commission on Historical Manuscripts. In the event of an object being sold the Purchase Grant Fund is entitled to reclaim 50 per cent of the sale price (or a proportion of the sale price equal to the original percentage of grant aid).

Loss or damage to objects – the Purchase Grant Fund Office must be notified if an item acquired with grant aid is damaged or stolen. In the event of a total loss the Purchase Grant Fund is entitled to reclaim 50 per cent of any insurance payment (or a proportion of the payment equal to the original percentage of grant-aid).

Publicity – the Purchase Grant Fund aims to stimulate a wider public interest both in the work of the Fund and in the important collections which it assists through talks, journals and the press. The assistance of the MGC/V&A Purchase Grant Fund must be acknowledged in all publicity connected with the purchase and in all display information.

HOW TO APPLY FOR GRANT-AID

1 Making application

(a) Contact the Purchase Grant Fund Office by telephone or letter to obtain an application form (Form A). The eligibility of any *new applicants* to the Fund will need to be established at this stage.

(b) Only items which have not yet been bought are eligible for consideration. They must remain unbought until the result of the grant application is known.

(c) Form A should be returned completed with a full supporting statement. At least two sets of good photographs of the item are essential. These are not returnable and should be submitted on the understanding that they may be used by the Purchase Grant Fund in articles and for publicity purposes. Photographs are not normally necessary in the case of manuscripts and documents when a detailed description and photocopies are usually sufficient. Failure to supply all the necessary information will delay grant consideration.

(d) Items put forward for consideration must already have been seen and verified by a representative of the applicant institution and not merely chosen from a catalogue. Applicants are also expected to have checked the possible interest of other relevant institutions in accordance with their declared collecting policy.

(e) It is not usually necessary for the item to be brought to the Fund for assessment as good photographs should be supplied with each application. However, our expert advisers may need to examine the object more closely and it is the responsibility of the applicant to make it available for inspection.

(f) A museum discount (usually 10 per cent) should be sought wherever possible.

Applicants should also be aware of the price advantages attached to private treaty sales (further details are available from the Capital Taxes Officer at the MGC).

2 Auction sales

(a) In the case of urgent auction sales it is important to discuss the matter by telephone in the first instance. Normally five working days' notice is required.
(b) If the auction house is out of London good supporting photographs, in addition to two photocopies of the catalogue entry, must be supplied (except in the case of manuscripts and documents – see 1(c) above).
(c) A grant offer will be made by telephone before the sale. A bidding level ceiling will be agreed by the Purchase Grant Fund Office and grant-aid will be limited to 50 per cent of that amount, or 50 per cent of the actual price paid, whichever is the lower. Should the lot be acquired at a figure below our minimum level of support (i.e. £750, or £350 in the case of archival material) it will no longer qualify for grant-aid.
(d) In the event of a successful outcome the applicant will receive written confirmation of the exact level of grant-aid together with the grant claim form.

3 Offer and payment of grants

(a) An offer is made by letter stating the exact level of grant-aid and enclosing the grant claim form (Form B). The one exception is in the case of auction sale applications when the grant offer will have been made by telephone before the sale takes place. The object must not be bought until a formal offer of grant-aid is made.
(b) The applicant is now free to conclude the transaction with the vendor. Form B should be returned together with a copy of the receipted invoice once the object has been safely received by the applicant institution. Our grant is a reimbursement.
(c) Form B should be completed and signed by the officer with financial responsibility for museum purchases.

Further information sheets on institution eligibility, housing and loan of grant-aided objects, care of archival material and composition of trust deeds are available from:

> MGC/V&A Purchase Grant Fund
> Victoria & Albert Museum, London SW7 2RL.
> Telephone 071 938 8510

Part 3
De-accessioning and disposal

17

Disposals from museum collections: a note on legal considerations in England and Wales

Adrian Babbidge

The legal situation relating to museum disposals in England and Wales is extremely complex and uncertain. This chapter discusses the existing legislation relating to museum disposals and the future of the legal status of disposals.

Twenty years ago the legal issues which obfuscate disposals from museum collections were described as 'a muddy corner of the law through which some may attempt to drive a coach and horses'.[1] Today the water is no clearer and the postillions are more inclined to make a splash. It may be timely, therefore, to examine how English law bears on what can be one of the most controversial of museum issues.

The laws of Scotland and Northern Ireland differ, of course, from those of England and Wales, and this paper does not consider their situation. Nor can it be prescriptive. Only Acts of Parliament and Statutory Instruments have the force of law; the courts alone can interpret the law authoritatively. The views expressed herein are not those of a lawyer, but of a practising museum worker. They are no more than personal opinions. Proposed disposals from museum collections should be subject to legal advice specific to each circumstance.

STATUTORY CONTROL

A limited number of museums have disposals policies regulated by Act of Parliament. Such legislation is usually specific to institutions, and identifies whether, when and how disposals may be undertaken. Many British nationally funded museums function under Public Acts; a few Private Acts, usually promoted by local councils, provide a framework for a number of local authority museums. There are also a number of idiosyncrasies: disposals from the London Transport Museum, for example, are governed by the Historical Relics Scheme prescribed by the Transport Act, 1962.

Only the National Gallery and Tate Gallery are expressly forbidden from disposing of items in their collections. Although the National Gallery Act, 1856, enabled trustees to dispose in certain circumstances, a campaign during its revision as the National Gallery & Tate Gallery Act, 1954, led to the rescission of those permissive powers, and barred disposals from the collections of both institutions, other than by transfer to other specified nationally funded museums where they might be more appropriately held. The schedule listing those institutions has been adopted by subsequent Acts to enable transfers between national museums.

The earliest of the Public Acts still in force – the Imperial War Museum Act, 1920 – is in many ways a prototype for those which followed. It permits its trustees to exchange, sell or otherwise dispose of duplicate items and, with the ministerial consent, other objects no longer required for museum purposes. With similar consent, income from such disposals can be used to purchase to enhance the collections. These criteria were adopted without substantive variation in the National Maritime Museum Act, 1934.

The British Museum Act, 1963, which governs both the British Museum and the Natural History Museum, is more specific. It allows exchange, gift or other disposal of duplicates, printed material after 1850 of which there is a photographic record, and material useless due to damage, physical deterioration or infestation. There is also a more general permission for the trustees to dispose of items which, in their opinion, are 'unfit to be retained and when disposal would not be to the detriment of students', but only when such action would not be inconsistent with the conditions of a gift or bequest.

The National Heritage Act, 1983, under which the Victoria & Albert Museum, Science Museum and Royal Armouries are regulated, and the Merseyside Museums & Galleries Order (1986), are similar to the British Museum Act except that they allow for specific trusts or conditions to be overriden where damage, deterioration or infestation makes them useless. This legislation, as with the British Museum Act, requires income from disposals to be applied to purchase of objects for the collections.

The Museum of London Acts, 1965 and 1986, permit exchange, sale or other disposals of duplicates, or objects no longer required for museum purposes; income derived is to be applied to purchases for the collection. Exceptionally, disposal under the Museum of London Act requires a two-thirds majority of the Museum's board.

None of these Acts includes controls over disposal which are as rigorous as those embodied in the Museums and Galleries Commission's *Guidelines for a Registration Scheme for Museums in the United Kingdom* (1988). Some museums have, however, introduced their own internal systems or standing orders to reinforce the legislative requirements. The Museum of London, for example, requires an external assessor to report on a proposed disposal; transfer to other museums is the preferred option, and only if that is not appropriate does the item go to sale by public auction.

Other relevant legislation may be found in Private ('Local') Acts, intended to extend the range of its sponsor's powers beyond those conferred by public legislation. A local authority may sponsor such an Act for its own purposes, or several authorities may work together in promoting such legislation for their mutual benefit. Occasionally such Acts – which tend to be *omnium gatherum* of miscellaneous powers – include museum provisions, and some of these concern disposal from collections. For example, Section 149 of the Greater Manchester Act, 1981 allows, *inter alia*, disposal of items in the City Council's art galleries for any reason, but requires the proceeds of any such action to be applied to the acquisition of other works. In the case of gifts or bequests, the governing body is required, if practicable, to consult with donors, or their personal representatives or trustees – who have a right of veto for 21 years following the gift or bequest – before exercising their power of disposal. Similarly, Section 58 of the County of Lancashire Act, 1984, which applies to district councils in Lancashire, restricts disposals to loan, exchange or gift to other museums, subject to consultation with donors or their personal representatives where appropriate, with a 35-year right of veto over such action from the date of gift or bequest. The section also includes the requirement for any income received in this way to be applied to the 'purchase of specimens, works of art, or books'.

THE COTTESLOE REPORT

Although a few fortunate museums have disposals regulated by Public or Private Acts, the majority of museums in England and Wales – whether governed by local authorities, independent trustees or universities – have to look to the common law for guidance. For the past 30 years the opinion given in the *Report of the Committee of Enquiry into the Sale of Works of Art by Public Bodies* (1964) has been widely regarded as authoritative in this respect. The Committee, chaired by Viscount Cottesloe, asserted the following:

> The basic principle upon which the law rests is that when private persons give property for public purposes the Crown undertakes to see that it is devoted to the purposes intended by the donor, and to no others. When a work of art is given to a museum or gallery for general exhibition, the public thereby acquires rights in the object concerned and these rights cannot be set aside. The authorities of the museum or gallery are not the owners of such an object in the ordinary sense of the word: they are merely responsible, under the authority of the courts, for carrying out the intentions of the donor. They cannot sell the object unless authorized to do so by the courts, or by the Charity Commissioners or the Minister of Education on behalf of the courts, because they themselves have nothing to sell. If they attempt a sale in breach of trust, it is the function of the Attorney-General to enforce the trust and protect the rights of the public in the object by taking proceedings in the Chancery Division.

It should be noted that administrative change during the intervening years has rendered the reference to the Minister of Education obsolete, since the Education Act, 1973 removed powers of suspension over educational trusts from the Secretary of State for Education and Science, and consolidated them with those of the Charity Commission. The Commission thence became the only administrative body with regulatory powers over charities. There has been no other specific legislative change which might modify the advice given.

This guidance has subsequently been embodied in the Museums Association's *Code of Practice for Museum Authorities* (1977) and its several revisions, and in the Museums and Galleries Commission's *Guidelines* for museum registration. As the only authoritative word on the subject, the Cottesloe opinion has gained a common acceptance amongst museum workers. It has not, however, been tested in the courts. It rests, fundamentally, on the belief that by the act of making a gift to a museum, a donor is creating a charitable trust.

THE CHARITABLE TRUST

A charitable trust is a legal relationship created when a person places assets for the public benefit under the control of trustees. Although there are similarities between charitable and other types of trust, only a charitable trust can be perpetual, and thereby provide the long-term security implied in the Cottesloe opinion. What constitutes such a trust is a matter for the courts, or for the Charity Commission, which acts for the courts in these matters. The law on which their decisions are taken is based on an Elizabethan statute as interpreted in subsequent court decisions.[2] It is the same foundation as that on which many independent museums are built, whether as unincorporated associations or trusts, or as companies limited by guarantee. However, charitable trusts can be created as much by gifts to local authorities and chartered bodies as to independent museums

To constitute a charitable trust, a gift must meet a number of criteria. The intention of the gift must be certain; it must fall wholly and exclusively within the general criteria of what is charitable; and it must be for the public benefit. Case-law that donations to existing museums can be charitable gifts is long-standing, and goes back to 1826;[3] subsequent judgments have held that gifts of objects of art to form a museum open to the public are valid charitable gifts, as being of public utility or benefit.[4] The general principle that gifts to museums have the potential for charitable status is clear. However, in practice, this status has to be proved for each individual gift.

There are a number of issues which need to be considered in establishing charitable status. There needs to be a benefit to the general public, which implies access and availability. Indeed, the Cottesloe opinion limits its definition of 'protected' items to those 'given to a museum or gallery for general exhibition'. What about those items held in reserve collections, or infrequently exhibited, for whatever reason? The quality of the item may also be an issue, as suggested in the judgment of Lord Justice Harman in *Re Pinion*:[5]

> where a museum is concerned and the utility of the gift is brought into question it is, in my opinion, essential to know at least something of the quality of the proposed exhibits in order to judge whether they will be conducive to the education of the public. . . . Here it is suggested that education in the fine arts is the object . . . there is a strong body of evidence here that as a means of education this collection is worthless. . . . there is a haphazard assembly . . . of furniture and objects of so-called 'art' about which expert opinion is unanimous that nothing beyond the third-rate is to be found. It was said that this is a matter of taste . . . but here I agree with the judge that there is an accepted canon of taste on which the Courts must rely, for it has itself no judicial knowledge of such matters, and the unanimous verdict of the experts is as I have stated . . . I can conceive of no useful object to be served in foisting upon the public this mass of junk. It has neither public utility or educative value

The evidence required to prove a charitable trust – whether by Agreement, the will which makes a bequest, correspondence, council minutes or the like – must be strong and specifically identify the nature of the gift. Complete and exact contemporary documentation is essential. Whatever the evidence, it should clearly indicate the form and charitable intent of the gift, and its nature must be such that it is capable of being accepted and used as intended; there must also be a certainty that at the time of acquisition it would be used for those purposes and no other. There is no doubt that the standard forms and documentation systems used in British museums do not by themselves have the potential to prove any such trust.

ENFORCEMENT OF CHARITABLE TRUSTS

Intended disposal in such cases would require sanction by the courts or by the Charity Commission. If such permission is not sought, then action may be taken through the Attorney-General, who usually acts on the information of the Charity Commission, though he can act independently of it. Proceedings would commence with a summons in the Chancery Division of the High Court. The Attorney-General would come to court as an Officer of the Crown informing the judge, as another Officer of the Crown, of the breach of trust or neglect of duty which requires remedy. The court would hear the evidence and, if satisfied that the action taken or proposed was against the public interest, could order an injunction for its restitution or prohibition of disposal.

Although the Attorney is the only party who can conduct such actions, it is possible for a private citizen or a body corporate, or group thereof, to initiate proceedings as (a) relator(s). A relator need have no personal interest in the matter and the only qualifications are that they have not been disqualified from bringing actions for the usual reasons, and not be indigent; a written authority to so act, endorsed by a solicitor, is lodged at the District Registry. Although the carriage for the action, the relator has no status in determining its progress. Thus, for example, if part way through the proceedings the Attorney wishes to discontinue, the relator cannot prevent this. However, a relator is liable for costs, and indeed is normally introduced to relieve the Attorney of such liability.

SPECIAL ISSUES FOR INDEPENDENT MUSEUMS

Independent museums are often registered charities. Their establishment has invariably demanded the establishment of a trust fund, either by way of an initial endowment or, if a company, by the guarantee of its members. The primary duty of its trustees is to maintain that fund to meet those objects specified in its governing instrument. Where museum collections are part of the trust fund, the trustees are required by law to seek the consent of the Charity Commission for any disposal. The duty of the Commission, however, is not to superintend good curatorial practice and help preserve collections, but to maintain the value of the trust fund. Trustees also have a duty in the case of a disposal of assets to undertake that task in a manner which brings the most benefit.[6] These requirements mean that disposal other than by open sale to the highest bidder – notwithstanding that the most appropriate curatorial solution might be by transfer to another museum – could be a breach of trust.

Some trust deeds have addressed this problem by separating museum collections from the trust fund in their governing instrument, but this might remove oversight of disposals from the commission.[7] Nor does it resolve the issue as to whether disposal should always be by sale to the highest bidder, with the possibility of any contrary action being subject to challenge in the courts.

A more considerable problem arises on a charity being wound up. Where there are funds available to meet all outstanding debts then the transfer of collections to a like institution may be effected, subject to the Charity Commission's consent. However, where funds are insufficient to meet all debts there is a charge on the collection to the extent required to meet those liabilities. The general rule is that the interests of creditors are the first priority, of its charitable objects second, and of its employees third. Although charity trustees have an obligation to prevent any charge falling on its trust fund, and thereby are responsible for underwriting any shortfall, this is often incapable of implementation. In this case the collections would be at risk of liquidation to meet the museum's debts.

SPECIAL ISSUES FOR LOCAL AUTHORITY MUSEUMS

The basis for the operation of local authorities has seen substantial change in recent years. From the time of the Municipal Corporations Acts of the 1830s, local authorities, whilst not charitable corporations in themselves, were seen as trustees of the property they held for public purposes and for the benefit of their ratepayers. As such they were accountable to the courts in the same way as charity trustees. This characteristic of local government has diminished in recent years, with local councils assuming a quasi-trading role, with greater freedom to buy and sell. Whilst past disposals of public assets would have required Treasury consent, later delegated to appropriate ministers acting on behalf of the Crown, such consents are no longer routinely required.

Since the legislative basis for local authority museums – the Public Libraries & Museums Act, 1964 – was enacted at a time when there was tighter regulation of property disposals by central government, it is perhaps not surprising that it does not consider this matter. The Act (s 12) simply enjoins a local authority 'to provide and maintain museums ... within its administrative area or elsewhere, in England and Wales ... and do all such things as may be necessary or expedient in connection with the maintenance or provision thereof'. The only mention of disposals (s 15, Schedule 2) is in a model management scheme for the cumulative purchase funds enabled by this enactment. It includes a requirement that proceeds from disposal by sale are to be applied as income to such funds. Perhaps of greater significance, the Act fails to identify the legal status of gifts to museums. In the absence of museum-specific requirements, the general legislation concerning gifts to local authorities must be examined.

Both the Education Act, 1944 and Local Government Act, 1972 make reference to the status of gifts received by local authorities. Section 85 of the former says:

> a local education authority shall have power, and any such authority or former authority shall be deemed always to have had power, to accept, hold and administer any property upon trust for purposes connected with education

and Section 139 of the latter:

> Subject to the provisions of this section [local authorities] may accept, hold and administer –
>
> (a) for the purpose of discharging any of their functions, gifts of property, whether real or personal, made for that purpose
>
> or
>
> (b) for the benefit of the inhabitants of their area or some part of it, gifts made for that purpose
>
> and may execute any work (including works of maintenance or improvement) incidental or consequential on the exercise of powers conferred by that section

Although gifts made in these ways constitute trusts, they are unlikely to be charitable. Both the Local Acts referred to before, Greater Manchester and Lancashire, with their 21- and 35-year powers of veto over disposal to donors, suggest that, since they are not perpetual, they cannot be charitable. Case-law shows the difficulty of creating charitable trusts with the local authority as trustee. The judgment in *Re Endacott* (1960) decided that the nature of a local authority's activities is not so clearly defined as being of a charitable character as to impose a charitable limitation on the words of a gift to that authority, as the statutory power of the council is not confined to charitable purposes.[8] It is probable, therefore, that without the most specific terms of gift, donations to local authorities are not charitable and fall outside the scope of the Cottesloe opinion.

THE FUTURE

The legal status of museum collections is not clear. The years since the Cottesloe opinion in 1964 have seen changes – particularly in terms of the nature of local authorities – which have cascaded to erode the foundations of trusteeship on which public museum collections have depended. Future trends will probably exacerbate the situation. The position of independent museums is no more satisfactory. Recent reports have recommended that the Charity Commission relax its regulation of charities including those over disposal of property.[9] Past controls, such as they were, will disappear to enable charity trustees to do what they believe to be best for their organizations. The likelihood of intervention by the Attorney-General in any case concerning museum disposals, given evidential and other requirements to prove charitable status, seems remote.

The only positive note is the Museums and Galleries Commission's Registration Scheme which, although voluntary, does provide a potential financial sanction (withdrawal of eligibility for its and Area Museum Council grant schemes) for those which transgress its disposals code. Taken with public opinion, these could be powerful deterrents to unsound disposals. Recent events – notably the sale of museum collections by Derbyshire County Council – have shown, however, that in certain circumstances these deterrents can be ineffective.

Full legislative control over disposals from museum collections is unlikely to be promoted by the government. However, there needs to be some formal – and binding – reaffirmation of the Cottesloe opinion if public confidence in the custodial role of museums is to be sustained. The Museums and Galleries Commission's recently published report on local authorities and museums suggests that a government circular issued jointly by the Department of the Environment and territorial departments might be useful.[10] Without the sanction of the courts, however, any such directive could only be a paper tiger, and in any case would have only limited influence on disposals from museums subject to the oversight of the Charity Commission. Whether by legislation, creation of precedent by an action in the courts or by judicial review, the matter must be addressed and resolved if public confidence is to be sustained.

NOTES

1 Jacob, J. (1971–2) 'The sale of museum objects: the principles involved, and an account of some cases in point', *Museums Journal* 71: 112–15.
2 The Charitable Uses Act, 1601, as classified by Lord Macnaghten in *Commissioners for Special Purposes of Income Tax* v. *Pemsel* [1891] AC 531 HL, and other judgments.
3 *British Museum Trustees* v. *White* (1826) 2 Sim & St, 594.
4 *Re Holbourne, Coates* v. *Mckillop* (1885) 53 LT 212; *Re Spence, Barclays Bank* v. *Stockton on Tees Corporation* [1937] 3 All ER 684.
5 *Westminster Bank Ltd* v. *Pinion* [1964] 1 All ER 890 CA.
6 For example, in *Buttle* v. *Saunders* [1950] 2 All ER 193.
7 Including the draft Deed in Adrian Babbidge, *Charitable Status for Museums*, AIM Guideline 3 (revised edition 1989).
8 *Corpe* v. *Endacott* [1959] 3 All Er 562.
9 Home Office (1987) *Efficiency Scrutiny of the Supervision of Charities*; Home Office (1989) *Charities: A Framework for the Future*, London: HMSO.
10 Museums and Galleries Commission, (1991) *Local Authorities and Museums – a Report of a Working Party*, London: Museums and Galleries Commission.

18

Infamous de-accessions

Iain Robertson

De-accessioning and disposal is one of the most contentious areas in museums, with those who are in favour and those who are vehemently opposed. Iain Robertson highlights cases of de-accessioning that have taken place in the distant and recent past.

Most museums and galleries in the United Kingdom cling steadfastly to their two core functions of preservation and study, entering the market-place only as a last resort and then by a side door. As a result, when a de-accessioning does take place little consideration is given to current market values or to which items can best be dispensed with. Cases of disposal, although rare, are accompanied by outcries from the press, followed by further legal and administrative controls and apologetic responses from museum curators and directors. More often than not the motives behind disposal are inglorious, rather than an underlying desire to rationalize the collection. Rarely have the proceeds from sales been used to upgrade the exhibits or seriously tackle the problem of overfilled store-rooms; in fact, profits from these surreptitious deals normally go towards maintenance costs. Only occasionally does the interest from the capital sum go towards setting up a purchase fund.

The de-accessioning of Tahitian and Oceanic material from Leeds City Museum in 1952 was a mismanaged affair of no financial benefit to the museum. It succeeded, simply, in splitting up the unique and valuable collection of items gathered together by George Bennet in the 1820s. The museum's present director, Peter Brears, spoke of the narrow-minded interests of his forerunner David Owen, who had no interest in the uncatalogued collection lying in the museum's vaults. A dealer and private collector, K. Webster, had misrepresented himself to the museum as an emissary from the New Zealand government, falsely claiming that the collection was destined for the Dominions Museum, New Zealand. Barbara Woroncow (director of Yorkshire and Humberside Museums Council) adds that Webster was allowed 'unsupervised access to the material', and that 'everything that was really good – hundreds of items, African and American material – all went in one job lot'. In exchange, Leeds received ten medieval items.

In the museum's defence, however, it has to be said that it was in a state of disarray, following the severe bombing it sustained during the war, which may perhaps have accounted for the absence of records for the ethnographic collection. Many items ended up in Webster's private collection, although, ironically, these finally arrived at their supposed destination, the Dominions Museum, as part of the Webster Bequest. The fate of many of the items is uncertain, however, it is clear that a large part of the collection appeared in the James Hooper sale of the mid-1970s and according to Woroncow, at least two drums from the Austral Islands in Polynesia (valued at £500,000 each) have found a place in the Metropolitan Museum via the Rockerfeller Bequest.

More recently, in April 1985, staff at the University of Newcastle took it upon themselves to sell the George Brown Collection, also of ethnographic material, to the university of Osaka for £50,000, despite interest from the National Museum of Papua New Guinea (surely its rightful home) and the British Museum. According to Professor Fowler, keeper of Newcastle University Museum of Antiquities, the collection, originally intended as a teaching aid for the university's department of anthropology, had fallen into disuse, after the closure of the department in a round of government cuts. The objects then lay dormant in the storerooms of the Hancock Museum, Newcastle, which never formally accessioned them. University charters may disallow de-accessioning but these statutes are easily overturned, if necessary by amendments from the board of governors. The interest from the sale's capital sum went towards the foundation of a research fund. Professor Fowler believes that: 'The George Brown affair prompted the Museums and Galleries Commission to set up their registration scheme of which, happily, we were one of the first institutions to be accepted.'

A further incident concerning ethnographical material, which surely provides ammunition for those who maintain that British museums and galleries take a high-handed and inflexible stance over cultural restitution, is that of the reluctant return of the Proconsul Africanus, a two million-year-old skull, by the then British Museum (Natural History) to Kenya. The skull, excavated on Rusinga Island in 1947 by Mary and Louis Leakey, was placed on long-term loan in the Natural History Museum where it remained on display until 1949. The chief secretary of Kenya confirmed in a letter written in 1948 that the object was eventually to be returned. However, when Richard Leakey, by then director of the national museums of Kenya, was satisfied that the National Museum of Nairobi was able to receive the skull, the British Museum (Natural History) claimed that it had been a gift not a loan, and that it had been accessioned by them in 1975. In 1982 a copy of the chief secretary's letter came to light, but it still took several months for the board of trustees to return the skull.

The Whitworth Art Gallery in Manchester, taken over by Manchester University in 1958, responded to over forty years of financial shortfalls by selling the James H. Abbott collection of stamps between 17 and 20 June 1968 at H. R. Harmer Limited, international stamp auctioneers, for £49,229. The interest from this sum went towards a purchase fund. Once again the items were not catalogued or displayed, yet it was undoubtedly a very important, if isolated, collection. As a philatelist, Abbott was ahead of his time. He became known as the 'Father of the Manchester School', a group of expert philatelists who pioneered the study of overprints and surcharges.

The Whitworth's current policy on disposals is watertight, according to recent acting director Jennifer Harris. The New Collections Policy of 23 February 1989 states: 'The university accepts the principle that there is a strong presumption against the disposal of any items in the gallery's collection. This would only be done in circumstances (not easily envisaged) where disposal was clearly to the benefit of the gallery and its regional and national public.'

Works of art realize even greater prices at auction. The Dulwich Picture Gallery sold Domenchino's *Adoration of the Shepherds* to the National Gallery of Scotland for £100,000 in 1971 and with the proceeds they bought a much-needed burglar alarm system. In view of the gallery's numerous 'unintentional de-accessions' – eight Rubens and Rembrandt paintings stolen in 1966 with one Rembrandt recovered but stolen again three times – the sale of the Domenchino might be seen as a calculated sacrifice. The ultimate decision lay with outside authorities: Margaret Thatcher, then minister of education, gave final consent for the sale.

Local authority collections are particularly at risk. In 1978 the London Borough of Southwark sold a collection of paintings at Christie's for £20,000. The works were seriously undervalued and the profits from the sale, instead of going towards helping the struggling arts groups within the department of leisure and recreation, were absorbed into the borough council budget. Under Section 15 of the Public Libraries and Museums Act, 1964, a local authority is allowed to establish a fund for the purchase of objects. There is, however, no reference to the use of monies from disposals in either that act or the Local Government Act, 1972. The Museums Association has said, however that any monies received from de-accessioning should be applied solely for the purchase of additions to the museums' collections.

In the late 1950s and early 1960s, the Lady Lever Art Gallery and the Royal Academy both found themselves in situations where survival depended on the sale of a part of their collection. In two auctions at Sotheby's, on 6 June 1958 and 17 March 1961, the Liverpool gallery de-accessioned valuable furniture and paintings by Fantin Latour, Richard Wilson, Millais and Pre-Raphaelite artists, all for knock-down prices. Julian Treuherz (keeper of art galleries, National Museums and Galleries on Merseyside) explained that the Lady Lever sale was made while the gallery was still a private concern under the first Lord Leverhulme, who had provided most of the museum's exhibits at the institution's foundation in 1922, whereas Merseyside County Council did not take over until 1978. Similarly the Royal Academy, another independent, self-financing organization, sold Leonardo's *The Virgin and Child with St Anne and St John the Baptist* to the nation for only £800,000, in July 1962, accepting substantially less than it might reasonably expect to achieve at auction.

Very few de-accessionary restrictions can be applied to private sector institutions and in the event of imminent bankruptcy, trustees are free to raise large sums through sales for operational costs. The situation with charitable trusts regarding de-accessioning is complex and wholly dependent on the nature of the particular trust deed. The Academy, for example, is legally entitled to dispose of any of its assets to further the objects of its foundation. In the case of the cartoon, there were no records of acquisition and the proceeds could be put to any use. Nevertheless, the authorities were spurred into action by the Royal Academy sale and a report was carried out, chaired by Lord Cottesloe, enquiring into 'the sale of works of art by public and semi-public bodies' in 1964. It was decided that: 'When a work of art is given to a museum or gallery for general exhibition, the public thereby acquires rights in the object concerned and these rights cannot be set aside.' That is, the museum and gallery authorities were no longer owners of their collections, but merely guardians responsible for carrying out the donors' wishes. Under recommendation *xi*, it was decided that the report's 'integral conditions should be treated as a whole and the extraction of individual items of value prevented whenever possible'.

More recently, an OAL consultation paper of August 1988 entitled *Powers of Disposal from Museum and Gallery Collections* acknowledges in a section entitled 'Effects on bequests and gifts' that any new legislation should include 'appropriate safeguards'. The report maintains that each collection should be individually assessed with disposal requiring the unanimous consent of trustees and directors or a two-thirds majority. The MGC believes that objects should be offered to other British museums and galleries in Britain before going into the open market.

There is a limit to the value of items that may be legally exported from these shores of £16,000, but it has not been made clear whether this applies to individual items or the entire collection. Inevitably, this loophole has been profitably exploited. The latest report of the reviewing committee on the export of works of art announced that £523,860,474 worth of art of national importance had been exported after reference to expert advisers.

University, local authority and private collections have been the principal offenders in de-accessioning. The various museums and galleries contacted about this issue took great pains to point out the fruitlessness of de-accessions, however, with assurances that such situations would be unlikely to occur again. But the greatest tragedy is surely not so much that the objects were de-accessioned, but that lack of outside financial support meant that impoverished institutions were forced to relinquish parts of their collection and that the amounts realized were often insubstantial and greatly under-valued. Selling a selection of modern master paintings to acquire Velázquez's *Juan de Pareya* for $5,544,000 as the Metropolitan did in 1972 is one thing, de-accessioning a Domenchino to update a burglar alarm system is quite another.

19

Attitudes to disposal from museum collections

Geoffrey Lewis

Starting from the perspective that there are different attitudes towards cultural property in different countries, which are enshrined in their legislation, Geoffrey Lewis goes on to look at how attitudes towards disposal differ between states. In particular, the differences between the United States and Europe are discussed, along with professional attitudes towards disposal.

For a paper comparing attitudes to disposals from museum collections, the starting-point would normally be an assessment of attitudes towards museum collecting itself.[1] Examination of professional opinion and legal statements in governing legislation and elsewhere, however, reveals a surprising diversity of opinion. Further, there is at times a mismatch between the legislative perception of museums and their collections and actual practice: this can occur inconsistently within countries and there are certainly major variations between countries. From this it can be anticipated that a similar diversity of attitude exists towards disposal both between and within countries.

Before coming to the issues relating to the acquisition and disposal of museum collections, therefore, a brief examination of the notion of cultural property is desirable. This is the material of museum collections but it has its own independent legislation. How then have attitudes towards cultural property developed and what is their current standing? For the purposes of this article the term cultural property, following normal international practice, is taken to include material from the arts, humanities and sciences.[2]

THE NOTION OF CULTURAL PROPERTY

Historical

The notion of the special nature of cultural property is of considerable antiquity. By the early nineteenth century it had already taken on a familiar form: for example, when the British Parliament considered the purchase of the Earl of Elgin's collection of marbles from the Parthenon, such issues as the propriety of ambassadorial collecting and the significance of a nation's cultural heritage were considered in the House of Commons (1816) debate. The restitution of the works of art which had been removed during the Napoleonic Wars, following the decision of the Congress of Vienna in 1815, is well known and another clear recognition of the special nature of cultural property at this time.

Much of the international recognition of the significance of cultural property occurs in legislation relating to its protection in the case of armed conflict. Thus, the Lieber Code, developed in 1863 for use during the American Civil War, allowed the appropriation of all public property by the victorious forces but required that works of art, libraries, collections, etc., should be protected and their eventual ownership determined by peace treaty. The Hague Convention, 1907, stated that 'the property of institutions dedicated to educators, the arts and sciences, even when State property, shall be treated as private property'. The Hague Convention of 1954,[3] currently in force, introduces a clear international aspect: 'cultural property belonging to any person whatsoever shall be recognized as the cultural heritage of all mankind'. This is emphasized elsewhere in the Convention by suggesting that it is the 'international responsibility of all nations to protect their own and other people's heritage'.

In the twenty years from 1960 no fewer than twelve Conventions or Recommendations were passed by the Unesco General Conferences on the importance of cultural property; some of the reasons for this have been discussed elsewhere (Lewis 1988). There has been similar activity at a regional level under the aegis of the Council of Europe, commencing with the European Cultural Convention, 1954, from which developed, in due course, conventions on the archaeological and architectural heritage, with the most recent, in 1985, covering offences concerned with cultural property. For that matter the Treaty of Rome – concerned as it is with establishing a common market and therefore the free flow of trade within the European communities – has a specific clause in it to allow restrictions on the movement of art objects with a view to protecting national treasures of an artistic, historic or archaeological value.[4]

Contemporary legal attitudes to cultural property

At an international level, attention must be drawn particularly to the Unesco Convention of 1970 which today continues to provide an important statement on the international attitude towards cultural property.[5] It is interesting, from a European standpoint, to compare the region's approach to this Unesco legislation with that of the European Convention on the archaeological heritage, passed by the Council of Europe in 1969.[6] Both are concerned with counteracting illicit transfers between countries as a safeguard to the heritage of the country of origin and particularly the scientific integrity of the material. Sixteen European States,[7] including the United Kingdom, have ratified the legislation on the archaeological heritage, but only five member states of the Council of Europe have endorsed Unesco's 1970 Convention.[8] Britain is not among them.

North America

The notion of cultural property as applied to the United States heritage is not recognized in export law in that country. Indeed there are no restrictions, other than for archaeological material, on the export of cultural property. It should, however, be noted that the United States does have cultural property legislation in relation to the import of heritage material from other nations.[9] In this aspect it ratifies the 1970 Unesco Convention on illicit trafficking. As Malaro (1985) points out, however, it was not the intention of the US Congress in enacting this legislation to control museum acquisition policies, and it was left to museums to conform voluntarily to the standards set in the legislation; many have done so.

Canada passed cultural property protective legislation in 1975;[10] in doing so it ratified the 1970 Unesco Convention and was one of the first industrialized nations to do so. In drawing this up certain assumptions were followed:

- that important aspects of the Canadian heritage should be kept in the country;
- that those owning such material should not be penalized simply because they wished to sell it abroad or otherwise export it;
- that the system of control should be voluntary, but actively supported by the relevant private, commercial and custodial communities;
- that because of the voluntary nature of legal compliance, substantial incentives for those affected by it had to be provided;
- the importation of cultural property into Canada should be in such a way as to respect the laws of other countries

(Cameron 1980)

This legislation can be regarded as closer in spirit to the Unesco 1970 Convention than that for the USA.

Europe

Apart from England and the Republic of Ireland, civil law systems prevail in the countries of western Europe under which public property is normally regarded as inalienable in the law of the public domain. Thus, the inclusion of public museums within the terms of public domain legislation provides very strong protection for state museum collections. This is the position in France,[11] where the principle has been extended to local government and other public bodies,[12] thus preventing disposal also from the collections held by these museums. This means that only material in private museums and collections does not have this protection, although important works in private hands are classified,[13] preventing export. Powers to declassify inalienable material in France have never been extended to cultural goods.

Similar principles apply in Italy,[14] Spain and Switzerland. In Spain the legislation, with its concept of inalienability, has been developed to include all archaeological discoveries,[15] as well as the property of the Royal Crown.[16] Cultural property in the possession of religious institutions also is closely controlled and may be transferred only to the state, other public bodies or to other religious institutions.[17] Different circumstances prevail in Belgium where ecclesiastical material is considered part of the public domain together with certain monuments, edifices and their contents. However, other cultural property, such as that in public museums, is not classified in this way in Belgium.[18]

Specific cultural property legislation applies in a number of European countries, whether or not they operate under a civil code. The form of this legislation varies considerably. It can relate to the whole artistic, historic and scientific heritage or only to a narrow subject area within one of these fields; it may be concerned with all heritage material or only with specified material of excellence within it; it may relate to named material only. In addition, different principles may be applied to different types of owner or be invoked only in a certain set of circumstances, such as export or death.

A number of European countries have general, cultural property legislation which protects the artistic and historic heritage and in some cases extends to the natural sciences. In the case of Greece, however, the legislation is specific and protects the excavated archaeological heritage and works of art made prior to 1830.[19] In Sweden and the United Kingdom, legal protection of cultural property applies only in the event of export. Treasure Trove, a common law inheritance in England, may contribute protection in certain cases but it is not, of course, cultural property legislation. Taxation relief in respect of the transfer of heritage material to the public sector in the United Kingdom (Lewis 1990) may also be regarded as a protective measure where a museum is the beneficiary.

174

Those countries with general protective legislation will normally classify the material concerned, and this presupposes some form of listing or registration. The arrangements for designating cultural property are normally organized at a national level, but in Germany and Switzerland this is the responsibility of the Länder and Cantons respectively, while in Belgium the matter of cultural objects may be dealt with at Community level.[20] The administration of the schemes falls under a variety of government offices and not necessarily the government department which has responsibility for museums.

Other countries

Cultural property legislation in many countries reveals the harsh truth that a scarce commodity or a denuded heritage will concentrate the mind in this matter. The impetus for, and subsequent ratifications of, the 1970 Unesco Convention on illicit trafficking came mainly from the non-industrialized countries. In Africa, the Arab world and, to a considerable extent, Asia and Latin America, cultural property legislation claims all such material to the state and may prohibit its disposal and export or at least require government approval before any transfer can take place (e.g. Algeria, Angola, Jordan, Kenya). Sometimes the law will allow for pre-emption by the state concerned (e.g. Israel, Kuwait, Libya, Nicaragua, to name a few countries that take this view). There can be no doubt of the special character of cultural property and, with few exceptions, notably the United States of America, countries go to considerable lengths to protect this aspect of their heritage. This is the material that museums collect, and the question now is whether these concepts are reflected in the museum legislation.

LEGAL ATTITUDES TO MUSEUM COLLECTIONS

In view of the extensive legislation covering cultural property, it might be expected that the primacy of the collection and its protection would be to the fore in museum and related legislation. In fact this is by no means always the case. Museum enabling legislation, where it exists, is often more concerned with the utilization of the collection. This may be perfectly acceptable where there is separate strong legislation protecting cultural property, but otherwise it fails to address that tension between preservation and use which is so prominent in museum work. As a result, considerable variations of emphasis on objectives occur which may substantially affect attitudes both to collection and disposal.

United States

The majority of United States museums are outside the public sector, operating as non-profit organizations, and can often be classified as charitable corporations. There is no law governing the museums of the United States *per se* and therefore no Federal or State requirement on such institutions other than those that apply to all such bodies. The legal position of the United States' non-profit organization is that it has powers to dispose of its assets – collections being viewed as realizable assets – unless its charter specifically limits this. The approach to de-accessioning amongst the country's museums results, therefore, from local determination by the museums' own governing bodies.

In expressing an American viewpoint, therefore, Marie Malaro (1985) states that collecting is a 'combination of intelligent selection and thoughtful pruning'. In this she follows closely the ruling in the Wilstach Estate case where despite requirements by will for the collection of Mrs Wilstach 'to be preserved . . . taken care of . . . kept in good order . . . kept together', it was determined that as the collection had been provided 'as a nucleus or foundation of an Art Gallery for the use and enjoyment of the people', buying and selling was a necessary power to exercise this properly.[21] This is of course only one case but the precedent could be developed, for example, in the case of a collection given for educational purposes. This could reduce a museum collection to little more than an educational resource centre whose holdings should change at the whim and fancy of educational fashion.

Another factor appears to have affected United States' attitudes. A number of its museums developed initially out of the desire to diffuse knowledge and refine public taste rather than to house an existing collection. This brings different requirements from, for example, the responsibility of a scholarly collection in a museum's formative years. In the latter case its significance and permanence as an archive is likely to be emphasized, although there is a variety of approaches in the different disciplines, as Marie Malaro (1985) points out. These differences, of course, relate to purpose. Art collections tend to be made to be viewed. The finds from a scientifically conducted archaeological excavation, however, may never be shown but are no less important as a historical document. For zoological and botanical material, of course, the same may well apply in addition to its significance as a taxonomic or habitat archive.

Europe

In Europe there is a strong presumption against disposal, in contrast to the circumstances and practice in the United States.[22] This is no doubt influenced partly by the Roman legal tradition where public domain legislation prevents disposal from museum collections in certain countries. However, the general tenor of national museum legislation, where it exists, is against transfers from collections and then, if this occurs, only between museums. The trustees of the national museums in Britain, *inter alia*, are required to care for, preserve and add to the objects in their collections; they are empowered to dispose of items only if they are duplicates, are unsuitable to be retained in the collection (having regard to student usage) or have become unsuitable by reason of damage or deterioration. A very restrictive definition of the word 'duplicate' is applied. The National Gallery, however, has been prevented by Statute from disposing of any of its collections since 1954. The transfer of items between certain national museums is authorized under the same legislation.[23]

The legal position of the non-national museums of Europe is less clear, although the same principles appear customarily to be followed in the public sector. Where transfers occur, they will be only on the decision of the governing board of the museum; a gift with conditions may require higher authorization.

In some cases, museums do not have separate legal identity from the government that established them or authorized their existence. Other countries, however, appear to be giving their national museums greater autonomy. In Spain, the Prado now has separate legal identity with stronger powers than other museums in Spain;[24] these prevent the sale or exchange of works of art from its collection. The Centro de Arte Reina Sofia in Madrid has similar status.

This is also the case in the United Kingdom, and greater autonomy and powers have been given to a number of the national museums over the last ten years: the Victoria & Albert Museum, the National Museum of Science and Industry (the Science Museum), the Royal Armouries and the Royal Museums of Scotland are all now governed by Statute.[25, 26] In comparison, recent museum legislation in Britain gives a clearer statement of the museum function and therefore of the duties of trustees. However, there is still considerable imprecision in much of the extant legislation regarding the full objectives of a museum. They have no legal mandate, *per se*, to ensure the collection and protection of the nation's movable cultural property. This is not peculiar to the United Kingdom.[27] In Austria and France, for example, the notion of a 'museum' – which, as in the United Kingdom, may be a private or public-sector institution – does not find expression in museum legislation.[28]

It might be argued that recent national museum legislation in Britain under National Heritage Acts implies that they are the repository for the nation's cultural heritage.[29] However, this concept normally comes into its own only where the museum legislation is integral with that for the protection of an aspect of the cultural heritage. This is the case in Poland and also in Greece where all excavated archaeological material and works of art made prior to 1830 are protected.[30,31]

However, there is some evidence of changing attitudes in certain countries of Europe. In Britain the government department concerned with museums, the Office of Arts and Libraries, undertook in 1989 a study on the disposal of museum collections,[32] although the outcome of this has still to be announced. In February 1991 the Audit Commission (1991) reported on its 'value for money study' of local government museums and galleries in England and Wales and recommended that government should clarify the law regarding the disposal of museum collections.[33] In Sweden a new policy was introduced in the State Budget for 1990–91 which announced that items 'useless and not required for the activities of the museum' may be sold.[34] The National Swiss Museum has authority to sell works of art from its collection, provided two similar works remain, or if they are surplus to requirements.[35] However, the constitutions of a number of Swiss private museums prohibit sales from their collections.

Other countries

As already noted above, a number of the national museums in African and Middle Eastern states operate under antiquities legislation and serve as the national repository for archaeological material. Perhaps one of the most comprehensive of these is in Nigeria.[36] Here the National Commission for Museums and Monuments has responsibilities for the control of all antiquities, ethnology, science and technology, as well as natural history material within the country, and provides national museums in most of the component states. This service provides a national repository for the country's cultural property. The National Museum in Wellington, New Zealand, also has a specific mandate to act as a national repository for New Zealand material generally.[37]

PROFESSIONAL ATTITUDES

Illicit trade (moral and legal considerations apart) suppresses information to the detriment of scholarship and the understanding of the specimen. The International Council of Museums (1970) issued a statement on the ethics of acquisition at the time of the 1970 Unesco Convention but this has now been superseded by a much fuller statement in its *Code of Professional Ethics* (ICOM 1990). This code suggests *inter alia* that each museum authority should: publish, and regularly review, its collecting policy; ensure that it acquires valid title to all acquisitions; respect wildlife protection and conservation legislation in collecting for the natural sciences; and refuse to purchase material illicitly removed from archaeological sites. There is a general presumption of the permanence of museum collections, that in the event of disposal other museums should have first refusal and that any moneys resulting from a sale should be used solely to supplement the collections. In the event of a request for the return of cultural property to its country of origin, dialogue based on scientific and professional principles should be initiated between the parties.

Ethical codes and guidelines on museum collections have been drawn up in a number of countries and they generally emphasize the permanent nature of museums and their collections. In addition, some museums have their own statements; an example is that of the Royal Ontario Museum in Toronto.[38] This code states that collections will maintain their significance only as long as the individual objects retain their physical integrity, authenticity and usefulness for public and research purposes. Selective disposals are considered acceptable where objects no longer have one or more of these attributes. In making this statement the code also states that the museum fully recognizes its role as guardian of public property.

In the absence of ratification of the 1970 Unesco Convention by the governments of some of the major nations in Europe, the museum profession has paid particular attention to codifying its position in the matter. In the United Kingdom, for example, the British Museum, the Museums Association and other national bodies issued a statement as early as 1972 clarifying their position in the matter;[39] this statement is endorsed in subsequent policy statements by the Museums Association, including its Code of Conduct for Museum Curators.[40]

SOME CONCLUSIONS

The extent and nature of the international legislation on cultural property provides a clear indication of its international and national importance. The notions which have been associated with it over the last two centuries help to identify its special significance. It is a special class of property, and society considers that it needs to be protected. Further, although it may be publicly owned, it is to be treated separately from public property. It is viewed, simultaneously, as the 'cultural heritage of all mankind' and also as a means of promoting national identity. The latter has a particular bearing on disposal, the issues concerning the prohibition of illicit transfers of cultural property and, for that matter, on requests from nations for the return or restitution of material.

At the same time this body of international legislation also recognizes the scientific value of the material – including the site or context from which it may be derived and that much of it is the primary evidence contributing information and understanding to different disciplines. Its contributions to knowledge and its ability to promote cultural understanding together make it an important medium for exhibition, education and entertainment. Because of these factors there has to be close control on transfers of ownership of important cultural property internationally, regionally and nationally.

At the operational level among the nations of Europe, there appears to be strong support for the protection of the archaeological heritage which is paralleled by that for the natural heritage. This is not reflected, however, in recognition of the broader protection of cultural property which could be offered through ratifying the 1970 Unesco Convention. The national legislation in Europe, with the possible exception of Switzerland and Sweden, does provide some protection but is diverse in character and varying in the protection it affords. Those countries operating with public domain legislation provide stronger protection – inalienability – to cultural property in national collections. Some countries may provide supplementary legislation to meet particular requirements. There are, however, certain disadvantages, one of which is the generality of a code for public property and the lack of flexibility that this brings when the special requirements of cultural property, such as temporary export for exhibition purposes, have to be met.

Legislation governing the administration of museums and their collections is normally subsidiary to national laws governing cultural property. These national provisions are, however, fragmented and unclear, particularly among the industrialized nations. A key problem appears to be the failure to link the notion of a nation's heritage with museum collections. As a result the emphasis may centre on collection utilization rather than protection, and at worst may see the collection only as an exploitable resource. There is a case for model legislation to be drawn up by representatives of all interested parties which takes a comprehensive view of the museum function.

That model should give pre-eminence to the character of museum collections as a part of the nation's heritage, but it must recognize the need for collection control with rational decision-making both in the collection and disposal of specimens. The policy for this should be based on informed opinion from all interests represented in museum collections. Criteria to achieve this need to be established, but in the United Kingdom some important first indicators are available in the guidelines for the registration of museums. It would be necessary, however, to go much further than these, including the establishment of more specific criteria in relation to different types of collection. The matter is urgent and professional initiative should be encouraged rather than leaving the matter to uninformed legislators.

ACKNOWLEDGEMENTS

I would particularly acknowledge my gratitude to Marie Malaro whose paper stimulated thought in new directions, which is reflected here,[41] and to the Museums Association for inviting me to contribute to its seminar on this topic. Certain of the information in this paper was gathered by the organizers of the Third Symposium on the International Art Trade and Law, held in Amsterdam in June 1990 and analysed and presented there by the author (Lewis 1991). This opportunity is also gratefully acknowledged.

NOTES

1 The substance of this paper was given at the Museums Association seminar 'Disposals from Museum Collections' at the Museum of London, 18 February 1991, and was in part a commentary on a paper by Marie C. Malaro prepared for the seminar but in the event not delivered (published in *Museum Management and Curatorship* 10(3), September 1991: 273–9).

2 See, for example, the definition in the Unesco Convention on the means of prohibiting and preventing the illicit import, export and transfer of ownership of cultural property, 1970. The term 'cultural property' is the subject of some dissatisfaction because of the connotation of commercial exploitability. O'Keefe and Prott (1989) prefer the term 'cultural heritage'.

3 Unesco (1954) *Final Act of the Intergovernmental Conference on the Protection of Cultural Property in the Event of Armed Conflict*, The Hague: Unesco.

4 European Communities (1957) *Treaty of Rome*: Article 36.

5 Unesco: Convention on the means of prohibiting and preventing the illicit import, export and transfer of ownership of cultural property, 1970.

6 Council of Europe: European Convention on the protection of the archaeological heritage, 1969.

7 Austria, Belgium, Denmark, France, Germany, Greece, Italy, Liechtenstein, Luxembourg, Malta,

Portugal, Spain, Sweden, Switzerland and the United Kingdom.
8 Cyprus, Greece, Italy, Portugal and Spain.
9 United States, *Convention on Cultural Property Implementation Act, 1983*
10 Canada, *Cultural Property Export and Import Act 1975.*
11 France: Code on the Public Domain, article 52.
12 France: Law 88–13 of January 1988, article 13.1.
13 France: Law of 31 December 1913.
14 Italy: Royal Decree 363 of 30 January 1913 and Law 1089/39 of I June 1939.
15 Spain: Law on Historical Patrimony 1985, article 44.
16 Spain: Law on National Patrimony 1982, article 6.2.
17 Spain: Law on Historical Patrimony 1985, article 28.2.
18 Belgium: La Cour de Cassation, 11 November 1886: pas, 1886, 1, p.410.
19 Greece: Antiquities Law: 5351 of 1932.
20 Belgium: Flemish Decree of 17 November 1982.
21 Court advice given to the Trustees of the W. P. Wilstach collection in 1954. The collection was donated originally to the City of Philadelphia.
22 See Malaro (1985, 1991) and Weil (1990), for example.
23 United Kingdom: National Gallery and Tate Gallery Act, 1954.
24 Spain: Royal Decree 1432/1985.
25 United Kingdom: National Heritage Act, 1983.
26 United Kingdom: National Heritage (Scotland) Act, 1985.
27 United Kingdom: Inheritance Tax Act, 1984, Schedule 3 describes a museum – in the specialized context of taxation relief – as 'any institution which exists wholly or mainly for the purpose of preserving for the public benefit a collection of scientific, historic or artistic interest'.
28 Austria: Federal Law of 1 July 1981 on the organization of research. This describes the tasks of museums as: collecting, safeguarding, presenting to the public and inventorying art objects, undertaking research and advising other museums (Bundesgesetzblatt, 1989: 663).
29 United Kingdom: National Heritage Act, 1983; National Heritage (Scotland) Act, 1985, for example.
30 Poland: Law on the Protection of Cultural Property and on Museums, 15 February 1962, Article 46.
31 Greece: Antiquities Law: 5351 of 1932.
32 United Kingdom: 'Powers of Disposal from Museum and Gallery Collections: a consultative paper', issued by the Office of Arts and Libraries, August 1988 (typewritten report).
33 United Kingdom: Audit Commission (1991) *The Road To Wigan Pier?: Managing Local Authority Museums and Galleries*, London: HMSO.
34 Sweden: State Budget, 1990–91.
35 Switzerland: Federal Law of 27 June 1890: The Swiss National Museum.
36 Nigeria: Decree 77 of 28 September 1979: The National Commission for Museums and Monuments Decree 1979.
37 New Zealand: National Art Gallery, Museum and War Memorial Act 1972, Section 11.
38 Royal Ontario Museum *Statement of Principles and Policies on Ethics and Conduct* (ROM, Toronto, 1982).
39 The statement included the following: 'That it is and will continue to be the practice of museums and galleries in the United Kingdom that they do not and will not knowingly acquire any antiquities or other cultural material which they have reason to believe has been exported in contravention of the current laws of the country of origin.'
40 See also Malaro (1991) for the new Code of Ethics adopted in the USA.
41 Malaro, M. (1991) 'Deaccessioning: the American perspective', *Museum Management and Curatorship* 10(3).

REFERENCES

Audit Commission (1991) *The Road to Wigan Pier?: Managing Local Authority Museums and Art Galleries*, London: HMSO.
Byrne-Sutton, Q. (1988) *Le trafic international des biens culturels sous l'angle de leur revendication par l'Etat d'origine*, Zurich: Schulthess Polygraphischer Verlag.
Cameron, D. (1980) *An Introduction to the Cultural Property Export and Import Act*, Arts and Culture Branch, Department of Communications, Government of Canada.
Garcia Fernandez, J. (1987) *Legislación sobre Patrimonio Histórico*, Madrid: Editorial Tecnos.
House of Commons (1816) 'Report from the Select Committee appointed to inquire into the expediency

of purchasing the Collection mentioned in the Earl of Elgin's Petition to the House . . .', *Parliamentary Papers*, III: 49.

International Council of Museums (1970) *Ethics of Acquisition*, Paris: ICOM.

—— (1990) *Statutes [&] Code of Professional Ethics*, Paris: ICOM.

Knapp, B. (1990) 'Restrictions on importation and exportation in the art trade', in Lalive, P. (ed.) *International Sales of Works of Art*, Vol. 2, Paris: ICC Publishing.

Lewis, G. (1981) 'The return of cultural property', *Journal of the Royal Society of Arts* 129: 435–43.

—— (1988) 'Museums: international and national self-regulation', in Lalive, P. (ed.) *International Sales of Works of Art*, Paris: ICC and University of Geneva.

—— (1990) 'Heritage giving through taxation in the United Kingdom', in Lalive, P. (ed.) *International Sales of Works of Art*, Vol. 2, Paris: ICC Publishing; Deventer: Kluwer.

—— (1991) 'International issues concerning museum collections', in Briat, M. and Freedberg, J. A. (eds) *International Sales of Works of Art*, Vol. 3, Paris: ICC Publishing; Deventer: Kluwer.

Lundbaek, M. (1985) 'Organization of museums in Denmark and the 1984 Museum Act', *International Journal of Museum Management and Curatorship* 4: 21–7.

Lyster, S. (1985) *International Wildlife Law*, Cambridge: Grotius.

Malaro, M. (1985) *A Legal Primer on Managing Museum Collections*, Washington, D.C.: Smithsonian Institution Press.

—— (1991) 'Deaccessioning: the American perspective', *Museum Management and Curatorship* 10(3): 273–9.

Merryman, J. H. and Elsen, A. E. (1987) *Law, Ethics and the Visual Arts*, Vols 1 and 2 (2nd edn), Pittsburgh: University of Pennsylvania Press.

O'Keefe, P. J. and Prott, L. V. (1984) *Law and the Cultural Heritage*, Vol. 1: *Discovery and Excavation*, London: Professional Books/Butterworth.

—— (1989) *Law and the Cultural Heritage*, Vol. 3: *Movement*, London: Butterworth.

Unesco (1958) *A Guide to the Operation of the Agreement on the Importation of Educational, Scientific and Cultural Material*, Paris: Unesco.

—— (1984) *The Protection of Movable Cultural Property, Compendium of Legislative Texts*, I & II, Paris: Unesco.

Weil, S. E. (1990) *Rethinking the Museum and other Meditations*, Washington, D.C.: Smithsonian Institution Press.

Williams, S. A. (1978) *The International and National Protection of Movable Cultural Property*, Dobbs Ferry, NY: Oceana.

20

Scottish sense

Robert Clark

The law relating to disposal in Scotland is different to that of England and Wales. This chapter sets out the differences and the clearer legal situation that resides in Scotland.

In his chapter, Adrian Babbidge outlines the law affecting disposals from museum collections in England and Wales. However, things are very different in Scotland. This is largely because of its distinctive legal system, which is founded upon the concept of legal principles rather than upon precedent, or 'judge-made' law. In Scotland each case is tested against broad principles on which all parties agree.

Local government museums run by district and islands councils are covered by the Local Government (Scotland) Act, 1973, as amended by the Local Government and Planning (Scotland) Act, 1982; regional councils may run museums under the Education (Scotland) Act, 1980. This legislation does not specifically place restrictions upon the right of a local authority to dispose of items from its museum collections. The opinion of the Scottish Office's solicitors, given to the Scottish Museum Federation a few years ago in response to a specific case, was that in the absence of specific legislation to the contrary, a council is free to treat its museum collections in the same way as the rest of its moveable property: it has the freedom to retain or dispose, as it sees fit.

However, this general right of disposal is overridden where different laws apply. Where a local authority has taken over a museum previously run by another body, the collections sometimes continue to be held under the terms of a trust, or may be subject to a reversion clause forbidding disposal. Further, as in England and Wales, the terms of a gift might prohibit or restrict disposal, and would be enforceable in court so long as the terms had been set out in a properly drafted deed.

The same legal principles apply to other bodies running museums in Scotland, such as universities, regiments, companies or societies, which can do anything they want that is not forbidden by law.

PROTECTING TRUSTS

The main difference in Scotland comes with museums run by trusts. The Trust (Scotland) Act, 1925, is the only legislation normally cited by name, with general principles enshrined in older legislation and common law. It is generally held that the trustees of a trust only have authority to do those things which their deed of declaration of trust authorizes, though there are often powers provided allowing the administrative provisions of the deed to be varied by the trustees. Ultimately, should a body of trustees seek to exceed their powers, their actions would be void in law. The final sanction lies with the lord advocate, who can take proceedings to ensure that the terms of a trust are obeyed and to remove and replace trustees. In contrast to everyone else running museums, trustees can only dispose of items from their collections if they have specific powers to do so. In fact, older trusts are often legally quite free to dispose of their museum collections: this is because the 1925 legislation, which was obviously not drafted with museums in mind, does not require trustees to differentiate between their general assets and any museum collections, which are deemed to be 'assets' – unless the deed says something different.

This is, in fact, the key to the whole issue. In general, you can – within reason – put just about anything you want into a trust deed, in confidence that the law will uphold the deed against the desire of the trustees to do something different: the presumption is that a trustee acts as a free agent in signing the deed, and thereby agrees to be bound by it. Furthermore, museum trusts should be charitable bodies. The Charity Commission has no jurisdiction in Scotland, where the only arm of the state with formal responsibility for ascertaining whether or not an organization is charitable is the branch of the Inland Revenue responsible for ascertaining whether bodies are charitable for tax purposes. Unlike the Charity Commission, Scotland's Inland Revenue Claims Branch has no supervisory or regulatory role, and, once its narrow area of concern is satisfied, is able to 'recognize as charitable' a range of different bodies, with a large variety of different constitutions.

The results of this are worth spelling out: south of the border, the Charity Commission cannot recognize a distinction between a museum trust's collections and its money. Indeed, they consider museum collections to be just another part of a charitable trust's assets, which it must be free to dispose of without legal restriction, to finance its educational objectives – the only aspects of a museum which they are able to recognize as charitable. In Scotland, since there is nothing in the Income and Corporation Taxes Act, 1988 (a piece of legislation which in fact applies equally in England, Wales and Scotland) to indicate that the preservation of museum collections is not (for tax purposes) a legitimate charitable objective, the Inland Revenue is happy for a museum trust to define its objectives in such a way. It allows it to retain collections as a distinct entity, subject to strict safeguards written into the museum's deed.

Over the past year, since the museum registration scheme was extended to Scotland, the Scottish Museums Council has begun to turn this situation to advantage. When the legal enforceability of a deed of declaration of trust is combined with the opportunities arising from the Inland Revenue's non-restrictive approach to the drafting of such deeds, the result is a powerful weapon in defence of museum collections. In liaison with the Association of Independent Museums, a model deed has been drafted that incorporates simple powers and safeguards for sensible and ethical disposals from a museum's collections, based on the provisions of the museum Registration Scheme's Guideline 18. Several museums have used the model to establish themselves as trusts, or in updating trust deeds, and many more are at the drafting stage.

Through this work, the Scottish Museums Council has sought to turn to advantage Scotland's distinctive legal system for the greater security of museum collections. However, museums should view the question of disposals from the collections as an integral part of the development planning process, and with no less concern than they have for new acquisitions. Those who have the confidence to collect should also have the courage to dispose, and good planning means that adequate mechanisms should exist and procedures be laid down before any specific disposal question arises.

The moral and practical issues surrounding the problem of disposals from museum collections has recently been opened out to more debate than ever before. The Museums and Galleries Commission Local Authorities and Museums report (1991) called for the legal status of museum collections to be properly defined, while in *The Road To Wigan Pier?* (1991) the Audit Commission called for rationalization of collections and the disposal of 'unwanted objects'. This may be an extreme view, but museum staff should not seek to justify an opposition to all disposals on point of principle, for in these changing times such a position increasingly becomes untenable. From time to time, both for the good of the material and the museum, individual objects or whole collections need to be transferred between institutions; while an open mind must always be kept when duplicate specimens become available. Finally, many museums still need to do much sorting and weeding out to rationalize the effects of enthusiastic but ill-advised collecting, perhaps by an MSC scheme, or in a museum's formative years. In all these cases, a full and detailed disposal policy provides the means to prevent our successors from being left with the operational and financial consequences of our, and our predecessors', mistakes.

NOTE

Thanks to Alan McWilliam WS of Biggart, Baillie & Gifford WS, Edinburgh, who have been advising the Scottish Museums Council on legal matters relating to museum registration.

REFERENCES

Audit Commission (1991) *The Road To Wigan Pier?: Managing Local Authority Museums and Art Galleries*, London: HMSO.

Museums and Galleries Commission (1991) *Local Authorities and Museums – a Report of a Working Party 1991*, London: HMSO.

Scottish Museums Council (1990a) *Specimen Deed of Declaration of Trust for use in Scotland*, Edinburgh: Scottish Museums Council.

—— (1990b) *Collecting and Disposal Policies for Museums*, Edinburgh: Scottish Museums Council.

Part 4
Documentation

21

Why museum computer projects fail

Lenore Sarasan

Although this article is now rather old, it still contains so much common sense about museum documentation and why automation projects can fail that it is still worth reading.

During the 1970s, museums experienced a dramatic shift in their attitude toward collection documentation. For decades, record-keeping took a back seat to collecting and preserving objects and came to be viewed as a task of secondary importance. The organization of the filing system was left largely to the discretion of the first registrar of an institution, who in many instances paid little attention to what techniques were used at other museums or may have given little thought to creating a comprehensive system.

When modifications were made to the original system, they often were not designed to rationalize or enhance it, but instead reflected the personal interests and tastes of the current curator in charge of the collection. The result was that no two museums had systems that were alike. This problem was further aggravated by constraints on the time and personnel needed to keep the files current and in order. Rather than functioning as a coherent, interrelated system of information, collection documentation at many museums devolved into a series of disjointed, poorly integrated files and ledger books.

Though major problems existed within these information files, they functioned adequately because they were supported by a strong framework of oral tradition. In many museums, information about the collection was maintained through the collective memory of curators and support staff rather than the files. Without oral tradition, many collection information systems would have failed even to fulfil the two basic functions of museum documentation – to lead the user to the specimen in a reasonable period of time, and to interrelate all the information sources so that a user might easily find all the information recorded about a particular object. This *status quo* began to change for many museums during the 1960s and 1970s, however, as the older generation of curators and support staff retired, and museum personnel in general became more transient. With the departure of long-time staff members went rationales for file organizations, the whereabouts of artefacts and a considerable amount of unrecorded history about specimens. Little, if any, written information existed about the cataloguing procedures and documentation systems they had followed.

Concurrently, information needs increased dramatically as public attention became focused on cultural heritage and ecological concerns, and as primitive art and antiquities

187

became valuable collectibles. Questionable accessioning and de-accessioning practices in some museums gained adverse national publicity, and suddenly there was pressure – from administrators, government officials, insurance brokers and curators – to do something about the state of affairs. After decades of neglect, record keeping came to be the object of much concern as it became painfully apparent that far too many museums could not easily ascertain what they had, what they were supposed to have or where it all was.

The pressure to 'do something' about the state of collection documentation together with major recent innovations in data processing led many museums to undertake computerization projects with the hope that by automating specimen records, documentation would be brought under control. Today, several hundred individual computer projects exist in North American museums, and it is apparent that in the haste of some institutions to 'do something' they have not necessarily done it well.

COMPUTER PROJECTS: A BRIEF HISTORY

For more than fifteen years, museums in the United States have struggled to apply computer technology to the problems of collection management. These efforts have resulted in a unique pot-pourri of projects – several disjointed 'national' plans and a few hundred individual efforts. An early attempt at a nationwide approach to museum computerization was made at the University of Oklahoma in 1965. A software system called GIPSY was used to automate the consolidated records of ethnographic collections held in Oklahoma museums. This project was to serve as the pilot for an inventory of the estimated one million ethnological objects held in museums throughout the United States. Although expanded to museums in Missouri, the project never attained its goal of a national inventory and was abandoned.

In the late 1960s, a group of New York museums formed the Museum Computer Network (MCN) to serve as a forum for discussing the information problems common to museums. The GRIPHOS system, developed during the late 1960s and early 1970s to satisfy the specific information needs of museums, was adopted by a number of the museums belonging to the MCN group as what was then believed to be the beginning of a national museum network. Although GRIPHOS is still recommended by the MCN for use in museums, fewer museums use it now than did in the 1970s.

In the early 1970s, the Smithsonian Institution began developing the SELGEM system to replace an earlier information system, SIIR. Like GRIPHOS, SELGEM was designed with the special needs of museums in mind, but unlike GRIPHOS, it was written in COBOL, a programming language that was available not only on IBM equipment but on other computers as well.

SELGEM was envisioned as possibly developing into a nationwide system. As SELGEM was distributed to more and more museums, dissatisfaction arose as the implementation of the system did not meet the expectations of users and museum staffs felt more and more that it was being forced upon them. Though considerable use of SELGEM continues, it was not established as a national system and by the late 1970s most efforts at such promotion ceased.

After the first wave of enthusiasm for computers in museums passed, economic reality had to be faced. Individual museums participating in the SELGEM and GRIPHOS projects found they were investing a considerable amount of money and effort with few tangible results. As disillusionment set in amidst a growing controversy over national schemes, individuals began developing 'home-grown' systems to meet internal needs.

By the mid-1970s, computerization had become rampant. Dozens of individual departments in various museums put together their own computerization projects, but there was little communication between projects and minimal sharing of ideas and approaches. At times, several unco-ordinated projects using separate equipment and separate programmes existed within a single institution.

By the late 1970s, hundreds of separate projects existed in American museums. Most of these were bogged down in the data entry stage for a variety of reasons, including vague project goals and attempts to enter too much information about each specimen. A few museums had completed their input phase only to discover that the data file they had built could not be searched or sorted in the manner in which they had expected. So much energy had been expended in trying to get the information into the computer that little attention had been paid to how to get it out once it was in. It came as a shock to many that retrieval considerations should have preceded the start of data entry.

As the decade ended, a few bright efforts glimmered on the horizon. Yet little communication existed, and no centralized clearing house had been established to co-ordinate these activities or even to gain an overview of what was going on across the country. By 1981, *naiveté* concerning the use of computers was still widespread, even among people running projects. By and large, the experiences and methodologies that have been developed over the years in individual projects are not being shared with the museums that are just beginning projects. The problems that characterized museum computer projects a decade ago continue to characterize them now.

THE ASC STUDY

In 1979, the Association of Systematics Collections (ASC) undertook a study funded by the National Museum Act to analyse and evaluate the recurring problems museums face when trying to apply computer technology to the problems of collection management. It was hoped that a hard look at the existing situation could help museums avoid costly errors in the future.

METHODOLOGY

To achieve the broadest possible understanding of the methods that had been used to computerize museum records, projects were examined in a variety of disciplines and a variety of museum environments. The study first identified computer projects through a mail survey and media campaign; then gathered information about these projects through a short mail questionnaire; then conducted visits to selected sites. At the same time, it compiled an extensive bibliography; surveyed software systems used in museums; and surveyed projects outside the United States.

The initial mail survey was sent to approximately 8,000 individuals representing more than 8,000 zoos, aquariums, herbariums, planetariums, art, history, science, natural history and children's museums. More than 1,200 of these institutions responded to the mail survey, and 320 indicated that they were involved in applying computer technology to collection management activities. A brief questionnaire was sent to these 30 museums requesting information on the discipline, nature and progress of the software systems being used. Information was received on more than 300 individual projects. Information gathered from these responses and from site visits to more than sixty individual projects, was used to form the analysis that follows.

FINDINGS

On the positive side, the extensive computerization of museum collection documentation in the United States has both generated an awareness of the data processing potential in museums and led to significant innovations in data entry and inventory methods. On the negative side, most of this activity has not been accompanied by the careful preparation and ongoing attention needed to bring a project to fruition.

The kinds of problems that characterized attempts to computerize museums a decade ago continue to characterize them now. The major difference is that years ago there were only a few dozen projects, whereas now there are a few hundred. Though there have been significant achievements in the field, the following discussion addresses the prevailing circumstances responsible for the overall poor achievement level of most projects.

Museum personnel often do not understand the *significant* distinctions between programmers, systems programmers, systems analysts, systems designers and computer operators. They tend to apply the term 'programmer' to anyone affiliated with computers. Without knowing what level of computer specialist is needed in a particular situation, the wrong type of person may be hired for a job, or an unwary person may be hired as a programmer without realizing that he or she is expected to fill all the functions of the aforementioned positions. A second-rate programmer often costs more in the long run than hiring a skilled person in the first place. Hiring errors may be compounded by the reluctance of many museums to dismiss someone who has been hired.

Budgets. As non-profit entities, museums have formidable constraints on their budgets. Without the help of grants, most computerization efforts could not be undertaken, but there are also limitations on the amount of funding that may be reasonably requested. In museums, an unanticipated cost, even of a relatively minor nature, cannot easily be absorbed. This may cause major delays or even halt the project.

Time and decision-making. When working in museums, one frequently has the sensation that time passes more slowly and less decisively than in the outside world. Indeed, it is the timeless, academic atmosphere of museums that attracts many people to a museum career. However, in many museums the leisurely pace frequently infects the decision-making processes, prolonging and delaying even the most routine administrative decisions. In projects where maintenance contracts on an in-house mini-computer may run over $10,000 annually and where an idle programmer may be paid at the rate of $24,000 per year, timely decisions can mean the life or death of a project.

Human factors. Many museums are lucky if they have an electric typewriter. The lack of familiarity with technology is much greater in museums than in the commercial world where computers, word processors and optical scanners have become standard fare. If computers are to be introduced successfully into the relatively non-technical environment of museums, the psychological impact on staff members cannot be ignored. The introduction of computers may pose a threat to many administrators, curators and support staff. The negative impact on a computer project that can result from this disruption should not be underestimated.

MANAGING THE PROJECT

Project initiation. Ideally, any computer project should start with the preparation of a detailed *written* plan of implementation, which is developed by: analysing the existing manual filing system; defining problems; establishing project goals; determining steps needed to achieve those goals; determining a realistic time frame for the project; determining costs; evaluating whether the project is worth doing, given projected time and costs. While these processes precede the start of most computer projects in business, few museum staffers are familiar with these steps or their importance and they are seldom followed.

Our analysis indicates that the most frequent problems museums face when applying computers to collection management activities can be traced to three factors: poor project management; a serious lack of understanding the principles and functions of documentation; and a serious lack of understanding the use of computers. The effects of these factors are compounded by several elements common to the larger museum environment.

THE MUSEUM ENVIRONMENT

Salaries. Particularly in the area of technology, museum salaries cannot compete with those offered in the private sector. For skilled systems designers and programmers, the difference can run to tens of thousands of dollars. Although there are other rewards and incentives that museums offer to curatorial and support personnel, at the present there is very little in the museum environment to attract the typical systems-level programmer, who may easily earn from $15 to $50 per hour in industry.

Project manager. The approach used to manage the daily operation of a project frequently compounds any problems that may have existed at its outset. The project manager generally did not initiate the project; it was either put into motion by a superior or was part of the duties of the position that the project manager assumed. Thus, the project manager may have to cope with problems inherent in the initial design of the project and may not even be particularly interested in automation.

The amount of work involved in managing a computer project is usually vastly underestimated by the project's originator. Most project managers have other full-time responsibilities and simply cannot devote sufficient time to a computer project to control it adequately. The project manager may realize that problems are occurring but does not have enough time to investigate or resolve them.

Most seriously, the project manager usually lacks technical competence in data processing and may not even be conversant in the terminology of computers. Very few managers bother to take an introductory course on data processing or read an introductory book on the subject. Unprepared and unequipped to handle the demands of the job, he frequently comes to function merely as a supervisor for data entry operators.

The people responsible for initiating a computer project and for running it must be familiar with technical matters so that they will be able to ask the computer professional the correct questions and understand the answers. Further, they must know enough about collection documentation and the existing manual system to set reasonable goals and enough about computers to reach those goals. In most museums, however, there is little realization that problems even exist. Projects just keep chugging along without direction, inputting data – for years.

COLLECTION DOCUMENTATION

The recent attention focused on record-keeping procedures has not given rise to much discussion of a theoretical nature about the elements of documentation, documentation systems, or the closely related topics of data entry and information retrieval. While computerization efforts in Canada, England and many other countries generally have been preceded by, or have been developed in conjunction with, major efforts to define documentation and its functions, few computerization efforts in the United States have been accompanied by such research. In American museums, data entry frequently starts without an understanding of the manual documentation system and with little thought of what will comprise the automated documentation system. Numerous museums have found themselves with masses of computerized data that are substantially unusable for data retrieval purposes. This realization is generally made *after* data entry has been completed. Some museums have been forced literally to start over while others have spent huge amounts of time and money in attempts (often only partially successful) to reorganize the computerized data into a usable form.

The elements of documentation. A precise vocabulary defining the elements of documentation has been developed by the library and information science communities and is applicable to both manual and automated systems. Museums should use this vocabulary in all discussions of documentation and record keeping to avoid the confusion that may result in serious errors.

A *data element* is the smallest unit of information to which reference is made. The information in one data element does not overlap the information in another. 'Year of accession' and 'number of specimens' are examples of data elements.

A *data field* is a specified area within a *record* where a particular kind of data are recorded. Data fields are usually given names, like 'material of composition' and 'genus', for ease of reference. Whether a data field contains only a single data element, related but different data elements, or several examples of the same data element depends on the information retrieval system used.

A *record* is a series of related data fields. All the data fields pertaining to a particular specimen, whether recorded on a catalogue card or stored in a computer, comprise a record. A *data file* is a set of records that is treated as a unit. Accession books and card catalogues are examples of files.

Syntax control is a constraint placed on the form of data to make it more precise and consistent, such as always recording a proper name with the last name first, or always using upper case to record data.

An *information retrieval system* is a method of extracting information from a data file. In a manual system, a person is the information retrieval system. In an automated system, data may be retrieved in a variety of ways.

In a manual system, data elements, data fields and syntax control do not need to be strictly controlled because a human brain serves as the processing device for information retrieval. When a system is automated, a machine, which cannot think, does the processing. Therefore, stringent control must be exercised over the form in which the data are entered. While a person can easily discern which part of the following dates is the year – 22/11/80; May 24, 1948; 2 June 1915; eighteenth of April '75 – a computer cannot.

Not recognizing the need for a rigorous approach to automated documentation, many museums mistake the catch-all 'categories' on catalogue cards as basic data units. This leads to substantial problems, since these 'categories' are not precisely defined and often contain several data fields or several data elements, recorded differently from card to card. Incredibly, there is a prevailing misconception among project managers that a computer is smart enough to know a state from a country, for instance, or an object name from a material, and that it will place all of them in a consistent order automatically or with little programming.

Documentation systems. The components of a system of documentation are usually separate files interrelated through a set of references called pointers, which may be implied or explicit, for example, 'see collector's card'. The collector's card, in turn, should contain a reference back to the catalogue file. To function efficiently, the pointers and the files themselves must be complete; the information in all the files referring to the same items must be consistently recorded. When data are changed, all references to it must also be changed. The expediencies of time have adversely affected the consistent updating of data and the completeness of pointers in the manual documentation files of museums. As a consequence, information searches are frequently incomplete or incorrect.

A common belief exists that by automating a manual system, an organization and structure that it has lacked in its manual form will appear. This simply is not true. When disjointed, poorly interrelated manual systems are computerized without restructuring, the result is disjointed, poorly interrelated automated systems replete with all the problems of the manual systems. This does not mean that the data in the original system have to be in perfect form before they are entered – the computer can be a powerful tool for upgrading the quality and consistency of data, though museums seldom use it as such. It does mean, however, that data fields should be defined and very close attention must be paid to how things are going into the computer.

Data entry. The data entry stage is where the majority of projects get stuck. There are three primary reasons for this: too much data are entered per specimen; inefficient methods are used to enter the data; or insufficient quality control is imposed on the data as they are entered.

To prevent these problems, several steps should precede the data entry stage:

- A list of data fields should be compiled – both those data fields contained in the existing documentation and others that would be desirable. For instance, storage location might appear on the list even if it were not presently recorded. (An example data fields list: accession number, catalogue number, object name, materials of composition, mode of acquisition, storage location, etc.).
- A short, working definition should be assigned to each data field in the list to eliminate any ambiguities of meaning.
- The need for syntax control should be determined for each data field. Within one file, for instance, material of composition may appear in both adjectival form (wooden boat) and noun form (wood boat) and in both generic (wood) and specific (oak, ebony) form. A determination might be made that all terms for materials will be entered in the noun form and that generic terms will be provided if only a specific term appears.
- A inventory of existing documentation sources should be taken. For each separate file, information should be recorded on its purpose, physical description, physical location, number of entries, how the source is ordered and the data fields it contains.
- A determination should be made of which documentation file is the most accurate source of each data field.
- A determination should be made of which data fields are needed to fulfil the goals of the computer project. If the primary goal of the project is a physical inventory, then catalogue number, object name and storage location may suffice. If future storage needs are also being determined, then object condition, measurements and

material may need to be added. If only six data fields are needed to fulfil the goals of the project, *only* six should be entered, *not* twenty-five because someone decides that 'if we're going to go through the catalogues anyway, we might as well capture everything'.

- A determination should be made of which documentation source is the best for the configuration of data fields satisfying the needs of the project. If one particular source is of high enough quality for all or most of the data fields selected, data may be entered directly from this source. If not, a decision might be made to use data collection sheets (flimsies) and compile the data from various sources onto this form. The time needed to collect the data on to the sheets must be determined through a carefully planned test phase, not guesswork.
- A determination must be made of which data fields need vocabulary control.
- In order to set an accurate time frame for data entry, a determination must be made of the average number of characters per data field and the average number of times the field appears. These figures are usually determined by taking a literal character count of the contents of all data fields on every hundredth or five-hundredth catalogue card or catalogue entry.
- Based on realistic estimates of data entry time, a determination must be made of which is the optimal data entry device and approach. If it will take 8,000 hours of data entry time to input the necessary data fields, then paper tape may not be the way to go. On the other hand, if only 300 hours of data entry time are needed, it probably is not worth it to have a sophisticated data entry computer programme devised that would reduce the data entry time by half.

These ten steps constitute a systems analysis of the existing manual system and are useful whether computerization is undertaken or not. Even on a large collection of over 250,000 objects this analysis should take only about one or two weeks.

Once data entry begins, the project manager must monitor it regularly to make sure data are meeting the standards that have been set. Errors should be recorded on special 'data correction' sheets, and only one person should be responsible for error correction. The corrections should be double-checked by a second person. Dates of correction should be recorded along with any overall edits or changes in syntax control that might prove advisable as data entry proceeds and the eccentricities of the manual system become more apparent. When quality control is not imposed during the data entry stage, more time is spent correcting data than entering it.

Information retrieval. Information retrieval problems arise in museum projects for two major reasons: first, museums generally do not recognize the integral relationship between data retrieval and data entry and therefore put off data retrieval considerations until after their projects are well underway; second, project initiators and managers are ignorant of the substantial differences between data retrieval strategies and the impact these differences have on many aspects of the project plan.

A variety of methods are available to retrieve data from a database, ranging from in-house developed sequential, tape-oriented, batch systems (such as SELGEM or GRIPHOS) to sophisticated commercial products supporting complex interactive querying and report writing (such as INQUIRE or SPIRES). Museum people are not aware that there are numerous approaches to database management, and that the system used directly affects the form in which data are entered into the computer. The choice of a system may have other serious repercussions on a project as well. Sometimes there are limitations on the number of records that can be entered into a database, or a system may work for a few thousand records but breaks down when applied to a hundred thousand records.

The choice of system also directly affects the kinds of questions that can be asked of the database.

Ignorance of the essential distinctions between systems can ruin a project. Yet museums launch into data entry with the attitude that 'we don't know what we will be using to retrieve data but we wanted to get started on data entry right away'. The concept of entering data in a 'generalized' form so it will be compatible with any retrieval system is largely a myth. The retrieval system used will almost always make a major difference to the way data are entered.

USING COMPUTERS

Most museums are not using computers efficiently. Many try to use them to perform functions at which humans excel, while using people to perform tasks for which computers are designed. To illustrate this point, here are three common approaches to problems encountered in museum projects.

Example 1. A museum is computerizing its 15,000 anthropological specimen records. It decides to send the records to a keypunch company for data entry. The records, though, have been done in several different styles and are inconsistent. For example, sometimes state or province appears before country, sometimes after; in some instances, not all levels of geographical data are present. The keypunch operators cannot be expected to filter the data as they are entered, so they key the data just as they appear in the geography category on each card. The project manager plans to change the order of the geographical data once it is entered into the computer because 'once it's in the computer we can do anything with it'. She has consulted a programmer at a nearby university and was told: 'Sure, we can do that.' The project manager was not experienced enough in dealing with programmers to realize that the programmer did not mean, 'Yes, the computer is now fully equipped to do just that without cost to you', but rather, 'Yes, with unlimited funds and time, anything is possible.'

The computer, which cannot even tell that 'S' and 's' are the same letter, has been asked to do the impossible task of recognizing different hierarchical levels of worldwide geographical terms. The project manager has made a serious error and, most likely, all the geographical data will have to be re-entered at a later time.

Example 2. A history museum is entering information on its 50,000 objects into a computer. The project manager, who is also a curator with other full-time duties, must proof the computer listings of the entries after they are entered to check for typographical errors and consistent use of terminology. The curator finds he is spending all his evenings laboriously proofing oversized, clumsy printouts, and in fact is spending more time proofing than the data entry operator is spending inputting the data. It is especially difficult for him to determine if object names are being consistently entered since he must find previous entries for comparison each time he has a question on correct form.

A better approach would have been to write a short programme to construct vocabulary lists. A vocabulary list is an alphabetical listing of all the terms within a particular data field, often accompanied by the number of times they appear in the file. With a vocabulary list, the curator's time would have been greatly reduced, since typographical errors would have been easy to find and inconsistencies in terminology and spelling readily apparent.

For instance, a vocabulary list for object names might contain the following series of terms:

bakset	2
basket	22
basketry	6
baskets	17
baskett	1

The number of actual words the curator must read is dramatically reduced by this simple time-saving device. In addition, it can provide invaluable profiles of the composition and depth of a collection.

SUMMING UP

During the 1970s, collection managers and administrators became increasingly aware that the manual systems that had been used to access information about specimens and to physically locate objects within collections were rapidly breaking down. The growing awareness of responsibility for objects placed in the public trust and the greater information needs generated by researchers, environmental protection agencies, insurance brokers and others encouraged museums to look to computerization as a solution to their problems. And, indeed, computer technology does offer a viable solution to the kinds of collection management problems that museums have – inventory and information control over large bodies of objects and data. Though at least 400 individual collection management projects using computers are now underway in American museums, only a handful have been successful in using computers effectively.

A sharp contrast exists between the operation of data processing projects in the profit sector and in museums. Few museums follow the careful analysis and procedures that have been established in industry. In most museum projects, no feasibility study is performed, costs and time schedules are not adequately gauged, and project managers are woefully unequipped to cope with the ongoing details of a project. Poor planning and management coupled with a lack of understanding of collection documentation characterize most efforts. Although museums by and large appear to be satisfied with the progress of their work, if measured by data processing standards, most projects would not be judged successes due to their low productivity levels and poor operating procedures.

Museums are not trying to put a man on the moon or operate an early warning missile site. Museums are, by and large, only trying to use the computer for a rather mundane task – high-speed searching of large quantities of data. The main requisite for success in this endeavour is to put data into the computer in an orderly fashion so that they may be extracted in an orderly fashion. This simple principle has not been followed in most projects.

The problems museums are experiencing lie not in computer hardware and software but rather are inherent in the procedures used to initiate and manage projects. Without determining what they want to do or exactly how to do it, museums rush into computerization with a *naiveté* that is startling. Unless the factors of poor planning and poor management are overcome, museums will not realize the potential benefits of computers, benefits they can ill afford to lose.

Museums have an obligation not only to preserve objects but to make those objects and the information pertaining to them accessible. If museums are to achieve the potential of computers, they must begin a serious attempt to overcome the obstacles that have thus far kept them from using the technology effectively. Proper analyses of existing systems must precede computerization efforts, and project initiators and managers must be willing to acquire sufficient knowledge about computers to use them effectively. If project personnel are not willing to make this investment, they should seriously reconsider becoming involved in costly projects that hold little possibility of success.

REFERENCES

Dudley, D. H., Wilkinson, I. B., *et al.* (1979) *Museum Registration Methods*, 3rd edn, Washington, D.C.: American Association of Museums.

Fong, E. (1978) *Database Management Systems – An Overview*, Washington, D.C.: National Bureau of Standards.

Heaps, H. S. (1978) *Information Retrieval: Computational and Theoretical Aspects*, New York: Academic Press.

Lancaster, F. W. (1972) *Vocabulary Control for Information Retrieval*, Washington, D. C.: Information Resources Press.

—— (1979) *Information Retrieval Systems: Characteristics, Testing and Evaluation*, 2nd edn, New York: John Wiley & Sons.

Porter, K. (1976) *Computers Made Really Simple*, New York: Thomas Y. Crowell.

Reibel, D. B. (1978) *Registration Methods for the Small Museum: A Guide for Historical Collections*, Nashville, TN: American Association for State and Local History.

Roberts, D. A. and Light, R. B. (1980) 'Museum documentation: progress in documentation', *Journal of Documenation* 36(1): 42–84.

22

Museum information systems: the case for computerization

Pnina Wentz

This chapter discusses the nature of museum documentation systems and presents an argument for computerization. Once automation is considered, the need for standardization in terminology becomes essential and Wentz clearly describes the reasons why terminology control is required. A number of case studies from UK museums are presented along with a consideration of image systems, though this is now rather out of date.

INTRODUCTION

Many activities undertaken by museums are associated with registration and documentation procedures. They result in information held in various files and catalogues, such as inventory files, acquisition registers, object catalogues, etc. Traditionally the typical approach has been to maintain a register of acquisitions as a tool for inventory control, and card indexes or catalogues which have been compiled to document the collection.

Manual systems for creating and maintaining museum records and catalogues have considerable limitations and problems:

(a) Records and catalogues are usually compiled and maintained separately by the individual museum departments. As a result it is not possible to have an overview of the entire collection and to relate records of different departments.

(b) Individual departments may have their own procedures for documentation activities. As a result there may be no consistency in methods of recording information between departments.

(c) In larger and older systems procedures for recording information may have changed over a period of time. Past records may be incomplete and inconsistent with later practice.

(d) Compiling detailed records manually is a time-consuming and labour-intensive task which includes a considerable proportion of repetitive clerical routines.

(e) Manual recording systems tend to remain static as they are difficult to maintain and update. They are inflexible tools which do not respond to changing user needs.

(f) In a manual system the number of access points for searching and retrieval is necessarily limited.

The accountability pressure on museums to adopt more efficient methods for stocktaking and inventory control was often the starting-point for the development of new recording systems, at a time of increasing awareness of the potential of computers as a powerful tool of data processing and management.

The wide range of potential computer applications in museums include:

Administrative management:

> Pre-acquisitioning
> Acquisitioning
> Accessioning
> Inventory control
> Loans
> Exhibition planning/management etc.

Object documentation:

> Cataloguing
> Subject description/subject access systems
> Image access systems

Conservation management:

> Administrative aspects
> Recording condition before treatment
> Recording techniques and materials used
> Monitoring effectiveness of treatment

Dissemination:

> Publications
> Production of catalogues
> Public access to museum databases

Library/archive applications

PLANNING FOR COMPUTERIZATION

Many aspects of these activities share a pool of common data which can be approached in different ways by different users of the system. Thus, a desirable approach to computerization of museum information is to create an integrated system which is capable of supporting a whole range of museum activities while sharing relevant data and maintaining their interrelationships. However, many museums may not need all components and may not be able to devote sufficient resources to develop a wide range of applications simultaneously. Nevertheless, it is important to identify the overall objectives of computerization and the functional requirements of the system as a whole in the early planning stages of an automation project.

Abell-Seddon lists a number of desirable objectives and benefits to be gained from a computerized system:[1]

1 Combine existing documentary sources into a unified information system relating all aspects of the collection.
2 Provide access to information by reference to any expression contained in existing documentary sources and by any combination of such expressions.
3 Improve and standardize methods of recording and documentation.
4 Facilitate amendments and updates.
5 Improve, both in terms of speed and quality, response to inquiries and requests for information from museum staff, researchers/scholars and the general public. It is desirable to identify different levels of access and their information needs.

Database development can be viewed as a number of processes. The first process, before any computerized system is implemented, involves an analysis of each component of the existing manual system. Data analysis and modelling provide an overall conceptual view of the database and are independent of any specific implementation. Within this conceptual overview it is possible to determine priorities according to available resources and select specific subsets of actual implementation. It is important to choose a flexible system, capable of growing and incorporating all the required components as and when required.

It may be argued that confining the analysis to components of an existing manual system may be too restrictive, in particular when the existing system is not adequate. Keepers, curators and other museum professionals may be unaware of the full range of possibilities and potential of computerized systems. Consequently, they may formulate needs and requirements in terms of manual systems rather than exploit the full capabilities of computers as tools of data processing and management. It is therefore necessary to acquire an understanding of the principles and requirements of computerized information systems, data entry and information retrieval.

CHARACTERISTICS OF SOFTWARE

Database Management System (DBMS) software offers facilities to overcome many of the limitations of manual files. A DBMS can be defined as 'an organized collection of related sets of data, managed in such a way to enable the user . . . to view the complete collection or a logical subset as a single unit . . . to facilitate shared access to data and maintain the reliability, security and integrity of the database by controlling access and supervising updates'.[2]

The main characteristics of DBMS are:

- *Data independence*. The 'separation of structural information about the data from the programs which manipulate and use the data'.[3] Changes in the application programmes do not necessarily require changes to data and vice versa.
- *Integrity*. The facility 'to ensure that the database is internally consistent and valid'.[4] Designed to protect against invalid updates and to control a multi-user environment, in which many users may access the system at the same time.
- *Security*. Ensuring that access is restricted only to authorized individuals through passwords and authorization.
- *Recovery*. The facility to ensure recovery of data after a system failure.
- *Data dictionary*. Provides a formal description of the data structures to ensure consistency of use throughout the system.
- *Access to the database*. Databases may be accessed on different levels by different types of users. It is possible to distinguish between facilities intended for *ad hoc* queries by end-users, and applications where regular manipulation of data are required, such as creation and deletion of records, modifying data, etc.

End-user access may include 'user-friendly' features such as menus, and formatted screens for users to enter queries in appropriate fields, following a given example (query-by-example). A number of systems may provide formal query languages, such as SQL, which offers a structured syntax for processing queries in a systematic way. Another important feature is the facility to formulate queries using relational algebra (set operations, known as Boolean operators, union, intersection and difference) to express combinations of selection criteria. The ability to process queries in natural language, though desirable, is restricted by the facilities of the data dictionary. True natural language processing requires a sophisticated scheme of knowledge representation, not yet available in commercial DBMS packages. Research in this field is taking place in the domains of artificial intelligence and machine translation.

Many applications using DBMS software were developed for business and commercial environments. It is therefore essential to examine such packages carefully to assess their suitability for handling museum data. The software has to support variable length fields, structured and free-text fields and repeatable fields. It must be possible to handle a complex network of interrelationships between entities. Full indexing and retrieval facilities on various types of fields have to be incorporated.[5]

STANDARDS AND STANDARDIZATION

An essential requirement of any computerized information system is consistency in handling data. This can be achieved through the development of standards for description of the structure and content of records. A data standard incorporates a definition of all the data categories which could appear in a comprehensive museum record and the relationships between the categories. For example, the British Museum data standard results from the amalgamation of the requirements of ten departments, with each department using its own subset selected from the master (Jones and Allden 1988). This approach has the advantage of facilitating sharing of data between different departments but it requires central system development.

Data standards may be developed internally to meet the requirements of a specific institution, or it may be possible to use existing, published standards. Published standards are available for activities with a tradition of co-operation such as library cataloguing, which is based largely on formal characteristics of items. In contrast, museum cataloguing incorporates substantial scholarly interpretation of unique items and it may be argued that the diversity of museum collections and the unique nature of many museum objects, present considerable problems for standardization.

The Museum Documentation Association has developed and published a data standard to support its manual and computer systems. The main advantage of using an agreed standard is that it enables sharing and exchange of information between museums. A working group on the Reconciliation of Standards was formed at the recent meeting of CIDOC (the International Documentation Committee of ICOM), to act as forum for discussion of existing data standards prepared by different museums, and to develop a draft international standard. However, any system must allow for the extension or revision of the data standard to incorporate new or changed categories, as it is not always possible to anticipate future requirements.

TERMINOLOGY CONTROL

The diversity of museum collections has been reflected in the diversity and richness of the vocabulary used to describe museum objects. Information has been presented using a variety of methods; records of objects acquired at different periods may employ different terminology; records may be incomplete and may contain different levels of detail. This is bound to lead to inconsistencies in the description of objects and searching may become inefficient. Computerization encourages the development of standards for vocabulary control to ensure consistency in the description and retrieval of the content of museum records and to enable sharing and exchange of museum information. Thesauri and authority lists are tools for terminology control which may be developed mainly for computerized information systems.

Thesauri guide the users in the selection of appropriate terms by:

- Providing definitions and scope notes to clarify meaning and usage of terms within the context of the specific system.
- Providing references to a preferred term from a range of possible alternative synonymous terms.
- Indicating broader or narrower terms to enable hierarchical searching.
- Indicating other relevant related terms.
- Providing guidelines on standardization of form of terms (e.g. singular or plural, noun or process or action)

Authority lists provide guidance on the preferred form for recording names of individuals, institutions and places, where a number of alternatives may exist.

Most existing systems of vocabulary control were developed mainly for records of texts, while in a museum context a controlled vocabulary is needed for creating verbal representations of objects, specimens and images. Consequently some existing methods of vocabulary control may be regarded as too rigid for museum applications. For example, designating a term as a 'preferred term' implies a rejection of some alternative terms. A museum information system may require using a variety of approaches for different parts of the collection or for different aspects of the description of an object. Consequently, it may be preferable to allow for some 'synonyms' to coexist (e.g. current term and archaic term, different ways of expressing time concepts), provided clear scope notes are made and the information is recorded in the specifically designated fields.

In documentary databases the controlled vocabulary is frequently just one of the sources for subject retrieval. A record in a documentary database is likely to include additional fields useful for subject access, such as titles and in particular abstracts.[6] Abstracts are a rich source of subject information written in natural language. They complement the terms selected from the thesaurus for describing the content of the document. A similar approach in designing records for a museum information system would be to include free-text fields to record relevant detail in a descriptive language, in addition to the fields designated for controlled vocabulary. In searching, controlled vocabulary and free-text search techniques used together can achieve an optimal result.

Specific aspects of museum terminology likely to require some form of terminology control are:

- Geographical information.
- People/institution names.
- Object names.
- Materials and techniques.
- Time concepts/dates.
- Subject access to content of images

Geographical information

Geographical information presents a number of problems for databases which are multidisciplinary in scope and cover a wide range of periods and places. There is a need to provide for the geographical, historical, political, religious, anthropological and archaeological dimensions. Place names and political boundaries may change over time; some places no longer exist; the same place may have more than one contemporary name, perhaps reflecting a different cultural/political/linguistic tradition. Place names may occur in different roles, e.g. place of origin, place of exhibition, whilst foreign names present problems of spelling and transliteration. Geographical information may be recorded and retrieved on different hierarchical levels (e.g. continent, region, country, province, place, locality, site). If a place name is entered on one level only (e.g. Paris), it should be possible to locate the record in response to requests using broader or narrower terms (e.g. France or Montmartre).

Personal and institution names

A person may have more than one name or change a name or use pseudonyms. Furthermore a single individual may feature in different roles, e.g. artist/maker and owner/collector, and a proper name may be entered in different forms, with all the familiar problems of spelling and transliteration of foreign names. Similar problems occur with names of institutions, but with the added complication that traditionally institutions have been recorded on a geographical basis, thereby adding the problems of geographical information.

Object names

Terms used as names of objects may have changed their meaning over time, whilst terms may have more than one meaning (homographs) and several terms may exist to describe a single object (synonyms). Traditionally, museum objects were recorded under their common names without references to their membership of a broader category.[7] This makes it impossible to relate items belonging to the same category at different levels of specificity. As with geographical information, object names need to be related hierarchically to make it possible to locate relevant records in response to requests using broader or narrower terms. Hierarchical organization requires clear principles of classification – in geographical classification the principle is self-evident (whole/part). In classification of objects it is possible to use a number of principles (e.g. based on function of objects, or on morphology or on social context).

Dates

There are several methods to express concepts of time. They may be linked with geographical, religious or cultural/political concepts, such as Jewish or Christian or Moslem dating systems, culture/period (dynasties, etc.), archaeological dating systems, styles in art. More than one method may be used in any one record.

Subject access to content of images

The subject content of images is distinct from the physical description of the objects carrying the images (e.g. paintings, photographs, illuminated manuscripts). As well as providing a description of an object, it is necessary to describe the content and the meaning of the images it contains.

A controlled vocabulary may be used to select the terms required to describe the objects, places, people, etc., represented in an image. However, most controlled vocabularies do not provide facilities for indicating the relationships between terms, which would be essential for an adequate verbal description of images. Relying on keywords or classification codes alone, results in fragmented visual information, omitting the relationships between the various components of the image. For example, it is not sufficient to use the terms 'child' and 'tree' to describe the subject of an image; it is necessary to indicate whether the child is 'under', 'in front of', 'behind' or 'on' the tree. Using terms without the relational prepositions is inadequate for visual description. A solution could be to add a free-text field for description in natural language.

It is useful to distinguish two levels in the description of images, in particular for records of fine art objects. A descriptive level which consists of recording the primary subject matter, images of objects, places, people, conditions and actions. The second level, iconographic analysis, reflects a knowledge of a specific culture and its symbols, used in the interpretation of the primary images. Iconographic description requires specialized tools for terminology control and subject experts for indexing.[8]

The foregoing discussion highlights one of the most complex aspects of museum information, and some of the difficulties arise from the need to provide verbal descriptions of the content of visual images, so that they can be incorporated into records in a database. The availability of systems which provide direct access to the image itself, such as systems incorporating videodisks and digital disks for image storage, may reduce considerably the dependence on verbal descriptions of images (see below).

LANGUAGE/SCRIPT

Many museums are likely to require facilities for recording materials in several languages and scripts. Considerable difficulties may arise with regards to computer processing of character sets and computerized information retrieval.

Computer processing of character sets

The first decision required is whether to use the original scripts or transliterate. However, transliteration practice may not be standardized, and it may not be possible to process the character sets of the required languages, whilst there may be problems in designing keyboard layout for multiscript processing. It is also necessary to decide whether to inter-mix or separate different scripts used in the same record and how to handle bi-directional situations, i.e. a mixture of right-to-left (e.g. Hebrew/Arabic) and left-to-right scripts. A number of software packages for Hebrew and multilingual word processing are available in Israel and the United States. They require some hardware modification or a graphics card to display and print the characters. There is no standardized character set and not all products have complete character sets for either Hebrew or Roman script. Some systems offer multilingual facilities including Roman, Hebrew, Arabic, Cyrillic and Greek characters.

Information retrieval

Linguistic features fundamentally affect information retrieval. The grammar and orthography present special problems in Hebrew, not encountered in English. The inflected character of the language creates numerous forms of nouns and verbs in declension and conjugation. There is a need to recognize prefixes, infixes and suffixes in many forms, such as prepositions which become prefixed particles. Vocalization and diacritical marks provide the sounds in traditional Hebrew. In modern Hebrew certain letters were designated to indicate the vowels but they are not used consistently. This results in coexistence of several systems of spelling, creating potentially numerous synonyms and homographs.

AUTOMATED SYSTEMS IN SOME UK MUSEUMS

A number of large, national museums are developing computerized systems, independently. In some museums this may be a second generation of computing, as various projects and experiments in using computers for museum applications have been carried out since the 1960s. On the other hand, small and medium-size non-national museums are less likely to have sufficient resources for independent system development. Many of these museums have used the facilities offered by the Museum Documentation Association which was set up in 1977 to develop systems for museum documentation and act as an advisory and training agency. The MDA designed a number of computer applications, developed a formal data standard and various recording forms, cards and registers for manual data entry. For many museums the only opportunity to introduce computerization at moderate cost is by using the MDA system and its support services.

With limited resources the priorities are often to create a collection management tool and a retrospective inventory first, by selecting a number of key fields for rapid data entry from a potentially very detailed record structure and planning for completion of records at a later stage.

A recent survey of commercial software systems used in United Kingdom museums (excluding software developed in-house) identified eight museum-specific packages,[9] of which five were in actual use,[10] and five general-purpose packages which have been used for museum applications.

THE BRITISH MUSEUM[11]

The primary objective of computerization within the British Museum has been to 'produce a full inventory plus object locations as auditing aids for safeguarding the collections' (Jones and Allden 1988). Since 1979, a number of computerized projects had been set up in different departments. However, the need for a museum-wide collection management system could not be met by the individual projects, and in 1987 it was decided to develop a new computer system. A study of operational requirements for a new system was carried out with the aim of identifying 'essential' and 'desirable' features, both from the end-user viewpoint and technical operational requirements. It was recognized that the collection management function could be enhanced to provide a valuable research tool by providing a comprehensive record structure, with each department using its own subset selected from the master record.

The major requirements were identified as follows:

1 Powerful data entry features to be able to input a very large number of records rapidly and accurately. The provision should include validation facilities and allow the creation and maintenance of thesauri and authority lists.
2 The system should incorporate user-friendly features such as menu-driven access and natural language query language, to enable curatorial staff without previous computing experience to use the system effectively.

3 It should be possible to transfer the existing computer records, produced in earlier projects, to the new system.

4 The system must be able to support up to seventy terminals and have sufficient disk storage for 2m records immediately and 5m in the long-term in a multi-user environment.

5 The software has to support a complex record structure with variable-length fields, structured and free-text fields, repeatable fields, and repeatable groups of fields.

6 Comprehensive search facilities on various types of fields have to be supported, such as keywords or free-text searching, range and numerical searching, embedded string searching, etc.

7 The system must be expandable to incorporate further applications.

The system which was chosen was:

Prime computers (UK) hardware
16 MB Prime 9955 Mark II
Three disk drives with 2.3 GB Storage tape-unit
Dot-matrix and laser printers
25 VDUs and ten PCs

using:

INFORMATION Database Management System
PRIMEWORD word processing package

in conjunction with:

Ampersand Systems Ltd
&PACE (applications generator)
&MAGUS (a specialized application package for museums)

&MAGUS (museum and gallery users system) is a set of software tools specifically designed for collection management and documentation in museums. It is being developed specifically for the British Museum and was recently introduced in the National Army Museum. The system is entirely menu-driven, and data entry is through formatted screens which can be split over a number of pages of input. All data fields are variable length and are repeatable. Descriptive text fields are available as small display windows taking only a small amount of screen space when not in use, but may be expanded to full screen size to allow for text entry using word-processing facilities. Data validation is available during data entry either by reference to lists of allowable values for any data field, or through thesauri developed for particular data fields. &MAGUS also incorporates an Inquiry Language enabling a number of selection criteria to be linked by Boolean operators, as well as range-searching facilities. Data fields with associated thesaurus may use the thesaural relationships to retrieve the relevant broader or narrower or related terms.[12]

In preparation for the new system a museum-wide global record structure was developed. Each department will be able to select a subset of fields from the global structure according to their individual needs. In addition, a number of working parties were formed to develop thesauri in specific fields relating to the new record structure. The priority subject areas for thesaurus development are: geography/place names; object names; materials; techniques. As well as providing a system for effective collection management, the new system has considerable potential as a research tool. The retrieval facilities of the system enable comprehensive searches to be conducted in response to complex scholarly enquiries.

NATIONAL MUSEUM OF SCIENCE AND INDUSTRY: SCIENCE MUSEUM[13]

The Science Museum has had a central online database for its collection records since 1982, using the general-purpose software Adlib on a Prime minicomputer. The main features of the system are:

- A data dictionary allows any number of fields to be defined. Although each field is given a nominal length, the data length is not limited because a single data element can be extended into several repeats of the field. Empty fields or empty parts of fields do not take up disk storage space. Fields may be grouped.
- Data entry is through formatted screens, which can be designed and modified as necessary. Various output formats may be designed.
- The software supports an online thesaurus which can be browsed during data entry or searching.
- An authority file validates terms on input and can automatically replace non-preferred forms by preferred forms.
- The database may be subdivided hierarchically into several levels of 'datasets' which use subsets from the data dictionary and can be merged together when required. Thus, it is possible to introduce different levels of access: curators have full access to amend records created in their own departments but may search across the whole database.
- All new acquisitions are entered directly on the computer system. Retrospective records were created from existing record cards and it is intended that they will be edited and enhanced when resources become available

The Science Museum is using Adlib both for the museum's objects database and the library records.

VICTORIA & ALBERT MUSEUM[14]

The Victoria & Albert Museum is at the stage of preparation for museum-wide computerization. A detailed systems analysis for collection management within the museum was carried out and an 'entity-relationship model has been constructed to describe the manner of a given object's entry to or exit from the museum . . . its physical location, any processes carried out on it and a brief catalogue description of the object' (Miles 1988: 163). The model serves as an overall framework which can be broken down into a number of groups such as inventory, finding lists, loan administration and basic cataloguing. The groups will be tested by setting up pilot projects within the framework, using a relational database management system.

The emphasis throughout the system development is on constructing an integrated, large shared database to enable users to link between records originating from different departments (e.g. between conservation records and object records). It is intended to create a 'core record', including fields essential for collection management purposes, to enable rapid data entry in the first instance, with the potential of expanding the record at a later date. The museum is currently considering a suitable database management software system for implementation.

MODES[15]

MODES (museum object data entry system) is a software package developed by the Museum Documentation Association (MDA). MODES is implemented on IBM-PC compatible machines using MS-DOS and is therefore potentially affordable for small museums. In addition the MDA provides training and support services and a commitment to continuous system development.

MODES is provided with an application which supports object documentation and consists of:

- A data structure called OBJECT representing the MDA object data standard and recording conventions.
- Layout specification to provide outputs such as catalogues, labels or index cards.
- Templates for item recording structure

Templates are formatted screens for convenient data entry and twenty templates are provided with MODES, whilst users may modify or create additional templates. Records are divided into fields which are organized hierarchically on four levels. Each record contains only the fields for which information is available and there is no limit on field size. Information can be carried forward from record to record by declaring 'constants' to store repeated fields and data.

MODES can be used in three ways: (a) supporting an existing manual system; (b) as a computerized data-entry system with simple retrieval capabilities; and (c) as a front-end to another software package.

The third option can transform MODES from a modest package, supporting up to a 4-megabyte file size only on a single-user machine, into a much more powerful tool which can be implemented on machines capable of supporting a multi-user system. It is possible to use MODES for data entry and record maintenance, and output the records to a disk file in a format that can be read by other software packages.

A limitation of MODES is that 'it is not a collection management system. It does not support dynamic links between files'.[16] As it is not a relational database, data stored in different files (e.g. an inventory file and a conservation file) cannot be shared and may have to be repeated. Another limitation is that MODES is designed as a data entry system and it does not provide adequate retrieval facilities. To overcome these limitations, another package, TINmus/ir, is designed to be complementary to the MODES data entry package. TINmus/ir is an application of the TINman relational database system, developed jointly by the MDA and IME Ltd.[17] Records are created and amended using MODES and then loaded into a TINmus/ir database which holds information in separate files (e.g. objects, people, locations, events, dates, etc.). The files are linked to show appropriate relationships. Retrieving information using TINmus/ir can be done either by selecting an option from a menu or by using query-by-form (QBF) technique which consists of filling in query forms on the screen. The QBF facility supports Boolean logic within each field.

THE IMPACT OF IMAGE MANAGEMENT TECHNOLOGY

Today it is not possible to conclude without some observations on the impact of optical laserdisks on museum information systems. The ability to provide images, text and sound on one medium, together with the facility to link the laserdisk equipment with computers, offers an integrated system across a variety of media.

Alsford and Granger (1987) discuss a number of advantages for museums, as multimedia institutions with vast amounts of visual and textual information:

- Increasing access to the collection with minimal risks in terms of conservation and security.
- Increasing access to the content of the collection, by bringing visual and textual information together.
- Providing a tool to support research and exhibition planning.
- Providing a public access system to support exhibitions and educational activities.
- Enabling the sharing of information resources via dissemination of disk-based collection information.

Images may be stored on videodisks or optical laserdisks. The data on optical disks are 'represented digitally, as on magnetic storage media. Whether they represent text, numbers, images or sound, the digital bits and bytes are computer data subject to the same processing and transmission as if they were stored on magnetic disks' (Chenhall and Vance 1988).

Optical laserdisks provide very large storage capacity and they have been used to store large amounts of textual information. However, as Hamber and Saunders (1987: 29) note, 'one of the fundamental problems facing electronic digital image storing is the enormous "space" required compared with text storage'. The quality of the images depends on the methods of photography and on the quality of the monitor used for display.[18] Current projects (such as the Musée d'Orsay and the Dutch Open University projects) suffer a number of limitations, but it may be argued that the technology has reached a stage where it can provide an image management system as a reference tool. The integration of images with textual records is bound to have considerable impact on the design of museum databases and on access to museum information. However, substantial further progress is required before such systems can be considered as finished products which may substitute for the original images.

NOTES

1 Abell-Seddon (1988): 167–70.
2 Oxborrow (1986): 3.
3 Ibid: 7.
4 Ibid.: 179
5 The discussion and examples below clarify these requirements.
6 A growing number of databases provide full texts.
7 For a full discussion see Abell-Seddon (1988), Chapter 1.
8 For a detailed discussion of the different levels of interpretation of images and the implications for subject access to images, see Markey (1983, 1988) and Shatford (1986).
9 Neri (1988).
10 &MAGUS, MODES, MUSCAT, MASTERPIECE, TINMUS (used in conjunction with MODES).
11 Report based on a discussion with Dawn Abercromby of the Collection Data Management Section, The British Museum, on 23 November 1988, and on Jones and Allden (1988), and Ampersand Systems Ltd (1988).
12 For a full description of the system see Ampersand Systems Ltd (1988).
13 Report based on a presentation by Dr Leonard Will at the Museum Computer Group, on 7 October 1988 and on Will (1982).
14 Report based on a discussion with Gwyn Miles, Deputy Keeper of Conservation, Victoria & Albert Museum, on 30 November 1988, and on Miles (1988).
15 Report based on a training course conducted by Jennifer Hirsh of the MDA on 6 December 1988 and on Museum Documentation Association (1988).
16 Museum Documentation Association (1988).
17 For a fuller discussion of TINmus/ir see Light (1988).
18 For a fuller discussion see Hamber and Saunders (1987).

REFERENCES

Abell-Seddon, B. (1988) *Museum Catalogues: A Foundation for Computer Processing*, London: Bingley.

Alsford, S. and Granger, F. (1987) 'Image automation in museums: the Canadian Museum of Civilisation's optical disc project', *International Journal of Museum Management and Curatorship* 6: 187–200.

Ampersand Systems Ltd (1988) *&MAGUS: Museum and Art Gallery Users' System*, Bristol: Ampersand Systems.

Chenhall, R. G. and Vance, D. (1988) *Museum Collections and Today's Computers*, New York: Greenwood Press.

Hamber, A. (1987) 'The Musée d'Orsay video disc system', *CHArt Newsletter* 6: 11–18.

Hamber, A. and Saunders, D. (1987) 'Electronic digital imaging of paintings: a permanent archive and a visual resource', *CHArt Newsletter* 5: 19–36.

Jones, L. and Allden, A. (19880 'Information retrieval: how the British Museum computerized its collection', *Government Computing*: 17–20.

Light, R. B. (1988) *TINmus/ir: A Brief Description*, Cambridge: MDA (unpublished).

Light, R. B., Roberts, D. A. and Stewart, J. D. (eds) (1986) *Museum Documentation Systems: Developments and Applications*, London: Butterworth.

Markey, K. (1983) 'Computer-assisted construction of a thematic catalog of primary and secondary subject matter', *Visual Resources* 3: 16–49.

——(1988) 'Access to iconographical research collections', *Library Trends* 37: 154–74.

Miles, G. (1988) 'Conservation and collection management: integration or isolation', *International Journal of Museum Management and Curatorship* 7: 159–63.

Museum Documentation Association (1988) *Museum Object Data Entry System: MODES manual*, Cambridge: MDA.

Neri, J. M. (1988) 'Museum application software survey responses', *MDA Information* 12: 2–8.

Oxborrow, E. (1986) *Databases and Database Systems: Concepts and Issues*, Bromley, Kent: Chartwell-Bratt.

Roberts, A. D. (1985) *Planning the Documentation of Museum Collections*, Cambridge: MDA.

Sarasan, L. (1984) 'Visual content access: an approach to the automated retrieval of visual information', in Corti, L. (ed.) (1984) *Second International Conference on Automatic Processing of Art History Data and Documents*: 389–406. Papers, Pisa, Italy.

Shatford, S. (1986) 'Analyzing the subject of a picture: a theoretical approach', *Cataloging & Classification Quarterly* 6: 39–62.

Will, L. (1982) 'Computerisation of museum records at the Science Museum', *MDA Information* 6: 36–9.

23

Cataloguing collections – erratic starts and eventual success: a case study

Paul E. Rivard and Steven Miller

This case study presents an honest account of the experiences of the Maine State Museum in achieving a fully catalogued, automated documentation system. It includes three basic lessons for museum curators.

Collection documentation experiences at the Maine State Museum illustrate both appropriate and inappropriate ways to manage this essential responsibility. They tell of failure and success, lethargy and enthusiasm, abrogation and accomplishment. They illustrate dependence on administrative support, staff commitment, technology and respect for the museum's purposes. The contrasts we describe reflect a period when critics of United States museums advocated agendas far removed from museological reality. Unfortunately, these were embraced by the Maine State Museum.

Though its roots go back to 1836, the museum was established by the state legislature in 1965. Its new building opened to the public in 1971. Early collections record-keeping, with few acquisitions on hand, was unencumbered by long-standing protocols and the inertia they can induce — enviable in a beginning documentation effort. Computers looming on the horizon to handle information made the picture even rosier with promise of filling the vast need all museums have for amassing data and dispensing information.

Early years at Maine State Museum were contemporaneous with beginning efforts in applying computers to museum operations. The museum opened a year before the Museum Computer Network was formed; both shared the same developmental nursery and were attended by many of the same nursemaids. The museum was among the major institutional sponsors of the network, and a museum staff member served on its board for many years. Interest at the museum in supporting computer applications should have been beneficial. Starting out fresh, standardized nomenclature could be used; a logical and obvious database could be established; collections could be documented as they arrived; traditional practices did not interfere with new methods being developed; card catalogues were thought unnecessary, since everything would be done by computer and done better. The dream never came true.

Responsible registration was established and practised: collections were processed in an orderly manner; standard forms were used for accession, gift receipts, and source and locater files. Because this paper work was well managed, the museum was slow to document collections further. Card catalogues or similar research tools were not created. Since collections were few and registration reasonably thorough, the deficiency was not immediately felt.

The promise of computerization invigorated the staff initially, but only in theory. In reality, the museum embarked on a journey with data visionaries that actually repressed collection documentation. Endless discussions led to confusion, frustration, or down-right boredom that was overcome only recently by those seriously interested in computerizing collection records. In the early 1970s, collections went undocumented while the museum waited for technological 'pie in the sky by and by'.

Other factors also mitigated against collections documentation. Museums were attacked nationally in the 1960s as elitist, culturally myopic and irrelevant. Echoes of these charges must have rung in administrators' ears at the new Maine State Museum, for the central role collections play in a museum was ignored. Management was so intent on avoiding the pitfalls of 'old-fashioned' museums that no curatorial positions were established and no curators hired. Employment grew quickly to 26 members, and not one had the job title or responsibilities of a curator. Collections were viewed only as convenient illustrations for abstract, didactic, thematic exhibit scripts. Under these circumstances, it is not hard to understand why so little attention was given to collection documentation.

Inexperience was another contributing factor. Many staff members were working in a museum for the first time; others had attended graduate school or served as museum volunteers but had not worked long or intensively with collections. Some even assumed leadership roles on a regional and national level, professing a knowledge about cataloguing techniques, though never having done such work. Lack of curatorial insight clearly contributed to minimal assembly of information at the Maine State Museum. It may also explain why recorded data were often unreliable and identifications conjectural or based on hearsay. Even the use of a dictionary would have improved some of the inaccurate identifications.

Collection documentation also suffered because exhibits were in trouble. Six years after opening in 1971, the museum had completed no major exhibits. Understandably, there were repercussions. The director resigned as a crisis developed, placing the very survival of the museum in jeopardy. No one at the time noted or criticized the sorry state of collection documentation, though it was a flaw stemming from and revealing a policy that put collections last in operational priority.

Restoring public confidence, the new administration's principal task, set the agenda for most of the following decade. Clearing up the exhibit bottleneck came first; improving collection management was close behind. Critical changes were instituted. 'Research' positions were replaced by 'curatorial' ones. The same staff remained but with job descriptions spelling out responsibilities to assemble and study collections, develop sound research and make results available to the public.

Administrative and staff priorities from 1977 to 1987 stressed exhibits, collection growth, and resolving long-standing problems with collection records. Major exhibits were constructed throughout the museum, and collections increased ten-fold. Public respect was restored. Attendance increased over 400 per cent.

The new administration, shocked by the status of collections and their documentation, became quickly dismayed over delays caused by talk of computers. An order to compile a traditional card catalogue met with vehement resistance. This was a waste of time, it was urged, in the face of a computer age waiting round the corner. To diffuse this argument, computerization was made a separate issue. When (or if) it happened, it happened. Meantime, it was hoped, building a card catalogue would focus attention on collections. Sponsorship-level membership in the Museum Computer Network was cancelled, and work began with typewriters and index cards. The first catalogue card was created in 1979. But the golden opportunity of starting fresh was lost. The museum was then twelve years behind in cataloguing collections.

Progress with the card catalogue was promising at first. The newly defined curators quickly finished worksheets and cards for collections they knew best, holdings requiring little study. But the pace soon slackened. Pressure in exhibit building, the top institutional concern, was a convenient excuse used to postpone cataloguing. Furthermore, the pace of collecting had expanded rapidly. Collection documentation soon fell even further behind.

While computerizing collection data had been set aside because of bad prior experiences, prospects were beginning to look up. The 1960s mainframe was replaced by the PC with capacities few people had dreamed of. Thoughts about computerizing crept back into Maine State Museum discussions — from a different quarter this time.

Two staff groups apart from the central registration office kept good data: archaeology and conservation. Their records were excellent; they couldn't afford to leave excavated artefacts or those treated by conservators undocumented while awaiting a new technology. Encouraged by their own accomplishments, conservators and archaeologists were eager and successful converts to the PC's promise. With personal hardware, they pioneered what became the museum's collection-documentation computer programme. Because their data were already comprehensive and reliable, computerizing was relatively easy, demonstrating that large databases and collections as complex as those of archaeology could be handled.

Specifications for computer management of collections information were developed by the chief conservator and an archaeologist working under contract. Their efforts drew the museum back to considering computers. The first PC was provided to the registrar in 1986; others for curators and support staff followed. The registrar, an early and consistent advocate of computers, was assigned to apply the programme to serve registration needs. Rather than wait for the ultimate museum computer package to be handed us, we created our own. In time, approximately 2,400 catalogue cards were produced. But an overwhelming backlog had accumulated. Forty thousand artefacts still awaited attention.

Flaws first ascribed to computer programmes hampered productivity. Administrative review found that queries could not be initiated by accession number or date of origin! At first thought to be a computer problem, it turned out not to be. Records sometimes lacked dates or stated them in different ways, and artefacts were not always completely identified by accession numbers. The programme was quite capable of handling the entry categories, but no effort had been made to clarify entries during the cataloguing work. The real problem was 'junk in, junk out' or, perhaps more to the point, 'nothing in, nothing out'.

While these developments unfolded, a major turning point came from outside the museum. Several staff members were independently serving as trustees of a nearby museum operated by the City of Augusta. They suggested providing it with software and training oversight to see whether other Maine institutions might benefit from the State Museum's new collection computer programme. This was agreed to, and a college student with minimal computer experience (and none with museum collections) implemented the project in the summer of 1987. A computer catalogue was to be created for about 2,500 items in the city museum's collection. Not all Maine State Museum staff members had confidence that the student would get very far!

Six weeks later, State Museum administrators were invited to check on the city museum project. To their surprise, data for the entire collection were in the computer, everything was running well, and 'glitches' regularly plaguing the State Museum staff had been easily dealt with. Most surprising was the printer, which was busy tapping out a string of catalogue cards! In just a month and a half, the city museum had outdistanced all the computer work at Maine State Museum (which had yet to print its first card from the computer) and had done so with the State Museum's own programme!

The contrast in the city museum's achievement was embarrassing and revealing. Problems with collection documentation did not stem from poorly allocated resources, skewed priorities or troubling technology. The problem was in personnel attitude, pure and simple.

A new epoch in collection documentation at the State Museum began in 1987. More has been accomplished since than in the previous twenty years. The museum hired the student from the city museum project. She was employed every vacation period and summer recess for the next two years. The curator of decorative arts, the museum's best cataloguer, was promoted to chief curator and took charge of an aggressive record-keeping programme, assisted by other newly-hired curatorial and registration staff members. The computer programme for collection documentation was streamlined, simplified and made more practical. Large amounts of machine 'memory' were recovered by removing sub-programmes – devised to foster speed and cross-compilations – that turned out to be poorly designed and unnecessary in application. The inability to search by accession number or date of origin was soon corrected.

Just as we entered this productive phase, near catastrophe threatened to shut it down again. A principal off-site storage facility was found to be an asbestos hazard. Museum staff members volunteered to be trained and certified in asbestos abatement practices. They then cleaned and moved four floors of artefacts and specimens to new storage. In the process, we inventoried 40,000 objects as they were packed and moved, photographed 8,000 artefacts for catalogue purposes, and found more than 1,000 lacking accession numbers. Despite this enormous and unexpected burden (or perhaps because of it) collection documentation continued unabated.

Today, all Maine State Museum collection records are computerized, and a separate card catalogue contains photographs of virtually everything the museum owns. Information is skeletal in some cases because of meagre records from the past, but new acquisitions are documented as fully as possible. The museum identifies objects properly; ascertains age, where utilized, how, and by whom; and includes other information of possible interest. The museum acquired 3,050 objects in 1989; all are now documented in 'soft' and 'hard' copy.

After years of frustrating and embarrassing failure, the Maine State Museum is confident about its collection documentation. In giving advice on cataloguing now, the staff speaks from experience. Procedures, systems and computer programmes are made available to other museums, without charge. A collections accessioning and cataloguing work-book targeted for small museums and historical societies and an instruction manual with formatted diskette for COLMGR, the museum's own collection-managment programme, are also available without charge.

There are three important lessons in the saga of how the Maine State Museum handled collection documentation. First, be cautious about waiting until promising new technology is ready. Second, worthwhile documentation (including databases) is a consequence of quality work, not materials and equipment. Third, never assume that computers are smarter or more productive than their operators.

Part 5
Research

24

Foreign Ethnographic Collections Research Programme

Elizabeth Kwasnik

Collections research projects of this nature are extremely important in spreading aware-ness about the range of museum collections, enhancing individual in-house knowledge and expertise of objects and encouraging wider research into collections. The Foreign Ethnographic Collections Research Programme is a good example of such a project and the paper included outlines the aims and organization of the programme.

Readers who have been avidly following the progress reports which appear regularly in this magazine (yes, there are a few, believe it or not!) are asked to bear with us.

In 1990/91 the Scottish Museums Council was awarded a substantial grant from the Economic and Social Research Council (ESRC) to undertake a two-year research programme, the main objectives of which are:

- To establish the location of foreign ethnographic material in museums, universities, research institutes and private collections in Scotland.
- To encourage and co-ordinate the recording of information about foreign ethno-graphic collections by in-house museum staff.
- To record collections or organize recording by other specialists in cases where no professional staff are available to undertake the work.
- To establish a computerized database for the recorded information and to publish the findings of the survey.

The Council is working closely with the National Museums of Scotland and the University of Glasgow on this programme. The long-term purpose, in addition to the objectives listed above, is to assist in the improvement of the quality of care and use of ethnographic collections in museums and other collections through recording their existence.

'FOREIGN WHAT MATERIAL?'

'Ethnographic' material is often referred to as 'material culture' or 'tribal art'. The range of objects is extremely large and includes everyday items such as carved spoons, stools, weapons, tools and toys. It also includes more elaborate items such as ceremonial masks, ceramics, costume and sculpture. Relevance to the programme is determined not so much by what the item is, but where it comes from.

This programme is concerned with items originating from and made by the indigenous peoples of Africa, Oceania (e.g. Australia, New Zealand, Papua New Guinea and what used to be known as the South Sea Islands), Indonesia (e.g. Bali, Java), Asia, China, Japan, North America and Central and South America.

These collections reflect the history, both good and bad, of Empire and Commonwealth and the travels of Scots and residents of Scotland to all parts of the world, especially in the nineteenth century.

Some collections have been developed in a systematic way, documented by scholars, while others have resulted from occasional donations to museums from family or business travels and are not quite so well documented, sometimes not recorded at all. Within these collections are some items that are rare or unique.

In recent years the general public as well as the museum community have had their interest in ethnographical material awakened for a variety of reasons. Resources are being sought for education programmes more suited to a multicultural society. Concern for the preservation of world heritage has focused attention on ethnographic collections.

The data collected by the programme will be entered on to a national database managed by the National Museums of Scotland. The database will provide an invaluable research tool for bona fide researchers by indicating, in one centralized database, where material of relevance to their work may be found in Scotland.

To date some 12,000 records have been entered, representing some 14,000 individual objects. Inputting is continuing, so these figures are still growing.

DO YOU HAVE A PRIVATE COLLECTION OF ETHNOGRAPHIC MATERIAL?

Most of the information collected to date has come from collections in the public sector. However, there are still a number of collections in private hands which have yet to be approached with a view to inclusion. This is a particularly important area and every encouragement is offered to private individuals who have material which falls within the scope of this important survey. If you or your family have material which you think may be of relevance, please do get in touch with me as soon as possible. All communications will be held in the strictest confidence and no data will be entered into the database, or stored in any other retrievable form, without the express permission of the owner. This programme presents a rare opportunity for owners to have their collection documented, perhaps for the first time, and to have access to specialist advice on their collections at no cost to themselves.

The continuing support of museum colleagues and private owners is extremely encouraging and the feedback we receive from them is very helpful.

25

Scholarship and the public

Neil MacGregor

Museums have a responsibility to make information about their collections available. One means of doing this is through the production of scholarly publications that provide the basis for more popular and perhaps more accessible publications for the general public. Yet museum research and scholarship have appeared to be under threat since the mid-1980s and have suffered as museums attempt to become more user-friendly, open and accessible. Research of the collections, however, underpins all activities within the museum, and this chapter by the Director of the National Gallery, London, states the position of the Trustees of the National Gallery towards scholarship, drawing upon some of the arguments and points of concern in this area.

I should like to begin rather indecorously by disagreeing with one of the last questioners. You, Madam, said you were a customer of the national museums. I want to disagree very much; you are not a customer, you are an owner. I think it is essential to put the whole of this discussion into the context of what *we* are doing with *your* museums. I want to come back to that later on, but perhaps I may be excused for challenging you right away.

As Director of the National Gallery I must say that I feel at a certain disadvantage hearing my colleagues both at home and abroad talk with such lucidity about the aims of their institutions. When Wolf-Dieter Dube talks about the edict of William I of Prussia that established the rights and the duties of those who would carry out scholarly work, when Michel Laclotte talks about the series of *lois cadres* which lay down the basis on which French museums operate, I think wistfully of the rather confused Treasury Minutes of 1824, clearly an accident forced on a no less confused government because the Austrians had unexpectedly repaid part of their war debt, through which the British government bought the Angerstein Collection under the mistaken belief that they were setting up a new department of the British Museum. It was nearly a decade before that confusion was resolved, and it is really only accident that we are not all run by David Wilson!

But the accident, as happens not infrequently in England, produced something rather special. David Wilson, in his admirable book, *British Museum, Purpose and Politics*, says, in a striking phrase, that the British Museum is a 'back-street museum'. I do not think he means that in a Soho sense, but he does mean that it is not on a great public thoroughfare. And by contrast – and this time very consciously and very deliberately – the National Gallery was set up in the busiest, most polluted area of London. It was set up on the recommendation of Peel that it should be in the very gangway of London, right in the middle, so that as many people as possible should be able to get to it, so that the public should be able to enjoy *their* pictures. The question of public accessibility has been central to the existence of the National Gallery from the moment it was rather inadvertently created.

It has been observed – I think with reference to the Arian Heresy – that all great controversies depend on both sides sharing one false premise. And in the case of today's controversy – the controversy alluded to by Neil Cossons, that there is a choice that museums have to make between scholarship and popularity – I think this is entirely true, because I feel that polarity is non-existent.

The Trustees of the National Gallery addressed this problem in this year's *Annual Report*, published four months ago. Talking of the exhibition of Italian fourteenth century painting they wrote:

> The Exhibition demonstrated incontrovertibly that scholarship and public access are not, as has sometimes been asserted, alternatives between which museums and galleries must choose. Rather it is scholarship which adds a new dimension to accessibility. In consequence, we believe it is essential that scholarship remain a major priority if we are to serve the ever larger public we expect in the next few years.

And as a result of that they approved the appointment of several new curators.

I think it is worth dwelling for a moment on that – that scholarship is a way of making our collection accessible – and I am conscious that our collection is, of course, different from many of the other collections that are being discussed. We are a small collection of paintings and I would not want for a moment to undervalue the aesthetic response and the aesthetic enjoyment which many of the public – most of the public, I hope – get from those pictures. But it raises a wider question than that, because the access that we want to offer is a full one, a rich one, and I think that is a difficult matter.

I want to begin by suggesting that it is very important that we should not underestimate our public. The great success of the Open University since the 1960s has demonstrated the very widespread thirst among the general public for serious information and serious scholarship. The most recent development that I know of in this field, the pioneering Ford Project, which Ford of Great Britain have set up for their employees' development scheme, providing free education during worktime, has produced a startling take-up for the strictly and severely academic subjects. I think we can then assume that we do have a public which wants to be seriously addressed and – we should not be ashamed to say it – a public which needs to be seriously addressed if a public collection is to be properly explored.

The great enterprise of exploring the past through the physical remnants of the past is one that few of us would embark on single-handed. We have tried, especially this year in the National Gallery, to take a very particular approach to presenting scholarship to our public as a way of allowing the public to discover and to possess their collection. We have organized three separate exhibitions. The first was the Trecento Exhibition, *Art in the Making*, which was a physical examination of panel painting in fourteenth-century Italy. I think it is fair to say that it was a work of pioneering scholarship. The catalogue was a highly scientific publication and, in many areas, it broke new ground. It was among the most successful exhibitions that the Gallery has ever put on. Over 160,000 people came to look at pictures which, I think we would all agree, are among the most difficult in the National Gallery collection. They are pictures which, because of the subject-matter, because of the style, are extremely inaccessible. And yet a certain kind of scientific approach clearly allowed a great deal of interest, a great deal of enjoyment. In that area I think one can say that scholarship helped the public reach part of the collection that other approaches did not. And I can say with confidence, because we have been monitoring it, that since that exhibition the public time spent in the Early Italian rooms has remained materially higher.

The second exhibition of the year was, in a different way, about museum-based scholarship. It was an attribution exercise on the two versions of the Caspar David Friedrich landscape, of which we bought the one we believed to be the original. The aim was, again quite simply, to present to the public all the information available to the curator-scholar before having to make a decision – the drawings that are relevant, comparative paintings – and to leave the public themselves to come to the conclusion, to make the decisions themselves.

The third exhibition was a smaller exhibition of two paintings by Goya which we brought from the Prado, the intention being to put them beside the Velázquez *Rokeby Venus*, demonstrating in physical terms the thesis put forward in an article in the *Burlington Magazine* which proved that they had for a time hung together and that Goya's paintings were, in a direct sense, a response to Velázquez.

All three exhibitions were great popular successes. All three exhibitions, I think, demonstrate a particular phenomenon. We hear a great deal at the moment of the trickle-down effect of wealth, but I think we can say with confidence that the trickle-down effect of scholarship is very, very fast and very, very effective. All these exhibitions could happily have appeared in the *Burlington Magazine*, and all of them contrived to bring in a new public and to bring them back.

I should like to stress that the scholarship for these exhibitions was not conceived as scholarship for an exhibition. It was scholarship related intrinsically to the purpose of the National Gallery, and which was then presented to the public. It is important to stress that, because I think I would disagree with Wolf-Dieter Dube that 'research is the museum'. Our research has to be accountable to the public, and I think it is part of a greater purpose. Our purpose in our scholarship must be better to conserve the collections and, above all, better to allow the public to enjoy and to understand. I think the notion of curatorial scholarly accountability in museums is a very important one. We have tried regularly at the Gallery to have curators lecture to the public, explaining why they hang in a particular way; explaining how else the picture could be hung; explaining to the public what it is that they have been working at.

But if museums are not *for* scholarship – and I do not think they are – then what are they for? In this country they were set up very consciously on the model of private collections or cabinets, places of study. Gentleman scholars did of course emerge, but gentleman owners had their private collections of antiquities, of paintings, of natural history, in order themselves to form their own judgement, to refine their own taste and to understand better their place in the whole scheme of things, both natural and man-made – and that was the eighteenth-century ideal of private collections, based on the belief that possession of the past enables you to take possession of the future.

I believe our job in the National Gallery – and the function of scholarship in the National Gallery – is to enable the public to move around the past with confidence. They need the confidence that there are fixed points, individual objects which have been identified, dated, established; and various routes around those fixed points which they can follow and from which, if they like, pursue others. The process is, in a general sense, one of education, but I think in a sense it is not one of learning. If I could parody a famous Enlightenment *mot*, the great Goethe comment that in reading Winckelmann we do not learn anything, we become something, I think that the point for the public of museums is not that the public should learn something but that they should become something. What should they become? Heirs to the past, heirs to the collections which they own, deciding for themselves what they are going to do with it, what it means for them now and what it may mean for them in the future.

Most, I think, will want to use the collections personally, in locating themselves in the natural world, in examining their own or others' behaviour, in pondering the fate of individuals in society. These people need to be able to find the fixed points and the routes that the scholars have provided. But ultimately the exploration, the taking possession, has to be a personal one. There can be no doubt that we have to move on our own through the collections. We have ultimately to make our own decisions. I think that the role, then, of the scholars or the curators is not to put themselves between the public and the objects, not in any very elaborate sense to explain the objects, but to exhort the visitor to a direct experience, to an unmediated vision.

We hope, when the Sainsbury Wing opens, that we will offer to the public for the first time ever a possibility to explore the entire collection through interactive video. [The Sainsbury Wing opened in June 1991]. A great deal of scholarly input has already taken place. The entire collection has been put on to an image-retrieval system. Various kinds of information, various kinds of approach, will be available for the individual to choose from. But it will – and I think it is right that it will – be hard work, and this is where I would most disagree with what Neil was saying earlier. Neil Cossons suggested that the threat to scholarship, if there is one – and I do firmly believe there is one – comes not from change imposed by the government but from the reluctance of curators to take part constructively in that change. I believe that the threat to scholarship comes from an assumption that the enterprise of exploring the past is, or can be, an easy one. It is related, I think, to the much-aired notion of short attention span, of a society which, in the memorable title of a recent book, is amusing itself to death. Investigating the past is not a venture to be entered into lightly or wantonly. Although I believe it to be an enjoyable venture, it is one that requires a great deal of very hard work by every person who takes part.

The belief that it could be easy, the belief that it could be packaged, amusing, money-making, is not, of course, a new one. It is not a product of unprecedented financial stringency. Nor is it a product of a more sophisticated awareness of what our public wants. It is a misunderstanding of the nature of the endeavour which, as one would imagine, has already been well documented in the past; documented, I think perhaps best of all, and strikingly parodied in the 1860s, very shortly after the South Kensington museums were set up, by George Eliot in the first draft of her novel *Felix Holt*. It is a novel of quite alarming contemporaneity. There is a great deal of deploring the recent disappearance of the pound note: Treeby Magna, a fledgling spa in Loamshire, decides that it has to raise its visitor profile, to be more customer friendly, and it decides in terms that would be extremely familiar to us today to indulge in a little private health provision, to promote itself as a spa – and to set up a museum. George Eliot writes:

> An excellent guidebook and descriptive cards, surmounted by vignettes, were printed, and Treeby Magna became conscious of certain facts in its own history of which it had previously been in contented ignorance. Its castle, among the most remarkable of English ruins, had had every traditional honour that could belong to an English castle. Plantagenets had held wassail in it. The Houses of York and Lancaster had contended for it. And only the dullest mind could remain unthrilled

by the probable conjecture that the cruel tyrant, Richard III, had slept in it. . . .
Several articles in rusty iron dug up in the vicinity were deposited in a small
pavilion near the Pump Room, and with a larger number of mugs, baskets and
pincushions inscribed as 'Presents from Treeby' formed a museum. In short, every
inducement was offered to visitors who combined gout . . . with a passion for
antiquarian hypothesis, a general decay of the vital processes with a tendency to
purchase superfluous small wares and make inexpensive presents.

You will be pleased to know that the museum of Treeby Magna failed instantly. Thank
you.

26

Collections research: local, national and international perspectives

Alexander Fenton

This wide-ranging chapter discusses the place of research within the museum and the need for well thought out and developed research policies within museums. It then goes on to look at different approaches to co-ordinating research on a national level and international level.

Since collections are basic to the existence of museums and galleries, it follows that without them museums could not exist. Existence is one thing, however, and purposeful use another. Everyone knows the usual ways of using collections. We conserve them, store them, display them, and write about them, but in general we do not really apply the concept of collections research which illuminates the objects, and give perspectives which, on the one hand, can guide us towards selectivity rather than random in-gathering and, on the other hand, open up new paths of knowledge.

Collections research has often been regarded as something a curator did if he found time. It was thought to be a luxury in which smaller museums could not indulge ('unless one can call on a really big staff, provincial galleries are not for research', said one curator (Ogborn 1978)), although times are changing as trained professionals increase in numbers and spread more into general-purpose, smaller museums. It has been stated, with some degree of truth, that the major museums had the concentrations of subject-related expertise that allowed real research to proceed, and the supporting range of services that both helped staff research, and could be offered to the scholarly world (see Longworth 1987). Indeed, some museums, like the British Museum (Natural History), amount to research institutions in themselves, in this case devoted to a single coherent discipline, taxonomy (Greenaway 1983).

All the same, the large museums are not perfect. A well-based research policy is not something that can be worked out casually and few large museums have tackled the subject. They have taken research for granted, without establishing a policy and firm programme, though some do at least pay lip service to a research policy. The British Museum Act, 1963, for example, observed that a 'substantial research effort is needed to sustain the essential purpose of any great museum'. A recent policy statement from Nordiska Museet, Stockholm, emphasized that research was the nerve-centre of the museum's work and should be coupled to all its basic tasks. The National Museums of Canada put the undertaking or sponsoring of relevant forms of research second only to the collection, classification, preservation and display of objects in its list of purposes. Nevertheless, attempts to work out specific research policies have nowhere been made.

That there is a need for collections research policies within which research outlets in the form of well-labelled displays, publications and the like, can be promulgated with greater accuracy, economy and efficiency, in line with a museum's overall broad policy, is beyond question, especially in view of the present-day place of museums in the world of learning. A large museum with important collections forms a link with university expertise, with archaeologists and historians involved with artefacts, with geologists and natural historians. It also is or should be a transmitter and mediator of knowledge and expertise to other museums and museum staff, in fulfilment of an important pastoral role which relates to them and to 'heritage' in general, as part of a broad educational thrust. It has potential for making directly a strong impact on the educational system, not just through facilities like handling collections, teachers' aids and the taking of classes, but also at national curriculum development level. Because a large museum's range of professional expertise constitutes a kind of 'mini-university', there is an opportunity to take initiatives to fill gaps in the processes of research that institutes of higher learning are increasingly forced to ignore, especially in relation to the collections that give museums a unique cultural and educational role.

DEFINING MUSEUM-BASED RESEARCH

Museum-based research is not, in practice, different from other kinds of research except in its collection-based, three-dimensional emphases (which document-oriented historians sometimes find hard to grasp). There is no such thing as abstract research; nor is research something rare and special.

In many respects research is a process, building on the curator's personal interests and training, a constant reasoned accumulation of knowledge in the course of experience, a transformation of raw data in archives, computers and notebooks into vehicles of thought about the collections and their significance in terms of the development of the physical world and of humanity in general. It moves from the amassing of data through sorting and analysis to interpretation and understanding, the last sometimes flowing from a kind of inspiration, but it is inspiration for which step-by-step processes have prepared the ground.

A number of views about research have been put forward. One writer sought to distinguish between research and connoisseurship, which he regarded as 'the mature judgement of the nature origins, relationships and significance of a wide range of objects of some common character' (Greenaway 1984). Another writer thought it imprecise to apply the term 'research' both to collecting and ordering of data as well as to sorting it into meaningful conclusions, often to test hypotheses (Davies 1984). There have been attempts to distinguish between research on collections for academic use and research done to help the interested but non-specialist visitor (Farr 1984). But the fact remains that research is a multi-level concept with many facets at each level. The co-ordination of these levels, within individual museums, between local and national museums, with other centres of learning, and internationally, is more important than any long-winded discussion about the niceties of the concept of research. And we should not think that research is anyone's special prerogative. We all do it as soon as we start to go beyond the mechanics of compiling lists.

RESEARCH POLICY AND PERSPECTIVES

An attempt to work out a research policy with good perspectives in a large institution with a set of departments that covers all of human, natural and inanimate history from the beginning of time and for much of the world is not a simple matter. It must take account of collections built up over long periods, in some cases over two centuries; of departmental structures and of profiles of staff expertise; and of lines of development in the shorter or longer term. Fashions in research must be acknowledged also, and outside pressures may for a time dictate (or inhibit) research directions. There will be a strong bearing on the 'essential purpose' and general policy of the museum, and on the 'heritage' as represented in its own collections and in the collections and archives of other museums and bodies with related interests. Research may lead to a transcending of traditional bounds and point to an increasingly missionary role in education and in the community. It should contribute substantially to museological studies at practical and theoretical levels also, as part of the infrastructure of museum work within a country.

To be fully effective, research based on such criteria will stand on well-organized collections, archives and support facilities, including automation of documentation; on staff selected for skills in developing points of strength and identifying and filling gaps; and implicit in the whole must be the means of implementation for the benefit of the public and of specialists alike.

For a smoothly and purposefully working institution, the broad policy and research policy with its accompanying programme will march hand in hand. Research can provide a basic means of guiding museums into meaningfully functional development. It is at the centre of a two-way process or multi-channel set of processes in a major museum. Management, through the provision of finance, space, staff and facilities related to the collections and to the activities of 'partners' with like interests, develops and facilitates a research programme leading to displays, publications, teaching and the like. Out of this programme should come, through analysis of feedback, fresh ideas and possibilities for management to take into account, fresh knowledge of gaps in collections that can then be filled or – even more importantly in view of the high cost of storage space – knowledge that allows for greater selectivity in collection.[1] Fig. 27.1 provides in digested form a sample of what is appropriate to the work of a 'research museum', a major museum with a wide range of collections and facilities.

But what of the wider perspectives, particularly the relationships between national and general-purpose local museums that comprise the majority of the museums in most countries?

In this context, the Museums Association is in Britain playing an increasing role. Its *Corporate Plan* includes a research programme that lays emphasis on four strands: 'museum statistics and trends, social statistics and trends which impact on museums; case studies of excellent museum practice; and facilitating the development of collections surveys' (Museums Association 1988–92). This is not collections research directly, but the kind of data produced by such activity could help to give shape to museum research policies, and to facilitate collections research. The *Manual of Curatorship* is itself relevant in this context, as will be other elements of the Association's future publication plans, such as the manuals for Social History Curators, Heritage Management and Biological Curators.

Perspectives flowing from such effort will inevitably open up discussion about national collecting policies. This should not simply relate to who collects what and where, nor to the rising standards in non-national museums, including professional expertise and research capabilities (see Schadla-Hall 1987), but should take fully into account the pressures of the present time (tight budgets, limited specialist staff numbers, overflowing storage, etc.) and consider how a basically more economic approach can be achieved by

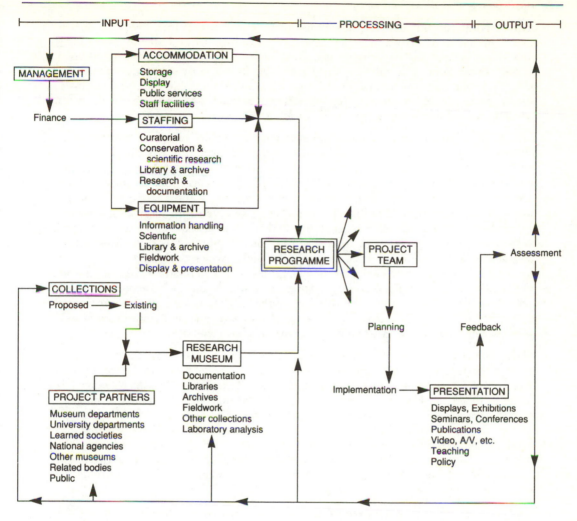

Fig. 26.1 Flow diagram for collections research

striving for an overview of the totality of our collections, which may be construed as the 'national heritage'. Within such a broad overview there will, of course, be different levels (district and region as well as 'national' units) but, somehow or other, the effort to see the heritage as a whole should be made, and tasks identified in the light of research-based knowledge. Economic considerations are not the prime factor, however, but rather the effort to harness and control the enormous educational potential of museum collections, through co-ordinated approaches.

COMMON GOALS: SAMDOK, SHIC, INTERPRETATION

This point can be exemplified by two approaches, one period-based and the other subject-based: SAMDOK and SHIC. SAMDOK is the more significant example, at least in its Swedish practice. The word is an acronym from Swedish *samtids dokumentation*, 'contemporary documentation', though we must remember that to a Swede 'documentation' implies a full process covering fieldwork, recording, acquisition and cataloguing, and is not simply the paperwork associated with collected objects. SAMDOK is a concept that relates to the modern world, stemming from a sense of social responsibility in collecting that seeks to find the identity of modern communities and transmit it for the future. It depends heavily on research as a prelude to the selection of items for presentation, acknowledging that blind collection is a poor investment.

SAMDOK, in Sweden, is a voluntary organization that enables co-operation between all cultural historical museums. It was formed with the support of the Swedish government in 1977. It sees the country's museums as an overall resource, for which responsibility must be divided. Participating museums work in 'pools' each accepting responsibility for specific areas of research and collection. The approach is valid enough for modern, mass-produced, centrally distributed material that has little or no specific local significance. It is, perhaps, less easy to apply for earlier material that does have such local significance, but the principle of approach, based on collaboration between museums of all levels of status, is an important one, as is the way in which the system uses research into social and economic characteristics as a means of avoiding *ad hoc* acquisition. One point should be stressed again: investment in research can lead to economies based on reasoned selection of items. It is a feature of the SAMDOK approach in Scandinavia that it has led to a fundamental questioning of museum roles and functions and to a reassessment of what they are about, and of the what and why of object collection.[2]

SHIC (Social History and Industrial Classification) is related in some degree; in some ways it represents the equivalent British way of going about things. It grew out of the work of the Group for Regional Studies in Museums (founded 1971), which changed its name to the Social History Curator's Group (SHCG) in 1982. The aim is to improve standards in social history curating – and, after all, social history collections are common to almost every museum in the country – through publication, seminars, training and campaigning. One whole issue of the *Museums Journal* was devoted to seventeen articles relating to the SHCG in 1985. These show much concern for the concept of twentieth-century collecting, and mark the anxiety that social history curators are feeling about the role of museums in the modern world.[3]

Inevitably, this quite strong movement is reflected in research orientations. There is what many would describe as a marked move to the left, an effort to explore topics such as the working life of working men, labour history in general, ethnic minorities, women's history, and the like. The group called Women, Heritage and Museums (WHAM) came into existence after a conference under that heading in 1984,[4] as a subgroup of the SHCG.

These activities mark nearly two decades of enthusiasm for social history in modern terms, partly in reaction to, but also flowing out of, the 'folk-life' tradition. They include entirely laudable efforts to integrate museums more closely with their communities (especially urban industrial) and much research has been directed accordingly to record areas of life such as housing, food and drink (including fast foods), education, religion, women's lives, sport and leisure, health, crime, death, etc.; (see O'Neill 1987; Jenkinson 1987), i.e., to a great degree, all the things with which local authorities are concerned.

Such work is building up useful archives of data for the future, but the major research tool to come out of the work of the SHCG is the SHIC, covering the primary areas of community life, domestic and family life, personal life and working life. This subject classification was said to be in use in over 350 museums and in twenty-two countries by 1987 (SHIC Working Party 1983); the implications for comparative research are great. SHIC, of course, complements the work of the Museum Documentation Association (MDA), whose remit is as wide as the range of items held anywhere by museums and galleries.[5]

These means of, and guides to, the accumulation of data on collections over a wide field are complemented by specific projects like Natural Science Collections Research, carried out from 1982 as a joint exercise between the Scottish Museums Council and the National Museums of Scotland. This followed similar activity in England where the North West Collections Research Unit (formed 1977) led to the publication of a Register of Natural Science Collections in North West England in 1981. The Scottish work is now in print also; it covers 3,338 collections and was built up as a database managed by the Manchester Museum Computer Cataloguing Unit (Ambrose and Stace 1984). Such projects, exemplifying co-operation between national and local museums and area councils, set important patterns for the topic-by-topic accumulation of research data to a level that can eventually constitute a national overview.

The twentieth-century-collecting issue with its accompanying aspects of labour history, urban history, industrial/working life history, women's emancipation history and the like has been one strong force in research approaches. Another has been the rise of interpretation, which has sparked off much thinking and led to much publication. In its original essence, the science of interpretation came to this country in the 1960s from the USA. It grew out of the perceived need in National Parks to explain to visitors what they saw around them, whether it related to past, present or future, and implicit in it also was the fostering of understanding and awareness that would encourage visitors to be more caring and conservation-conscious. It was site-specific to a large extent, with a main concern for the things of nature and for the effects on these of our activities.[6] Those who led in translating the concept of interpretation from the National Parks of the USA to Britain maintained a comparable approach (notably Aldrige (1975)).

However, a shift in emphasis quickly appeared. Thinking began to embrace not only the natural environment but also the 'built' environment and the human-made heritage in general. This often amounted to little more than the application of interpretive media and facilities to the elucidation of these matters.[7]

However, the important point for us is that the movement had a substantial effect on museums. In some cases it made them more outward looking, as in the case of the guided walks which Cardiff and other museums have seen as good ways of linking collections (especially geological) with the environment (Sharpe and Howe 1982). It also made museums begin to rethink their presentations of objects in galleries, most obviously in the case of interpretive displays of geological and natural history specimens, recreating, as it were, site interpretation indoors. But there is in reality a great difference between site interpretation, where all the objects and data relate to that site, and general museum collections, however strongly grouped thematically, that have been removed from their original context. Though the concept of interpretation has been taken up by museums, and has been much discussed in the pages of the *Museums Journal*, the main thrust of the movement has been through countryside bodies, including a number of mainly independent countryside museums which have sought to weld artefacts, sites, buildings, archives and oral history into a single, integrated interpretation strategy (Stansfield 1983: 47, 50). Such interpretation is, of course, heavily dependent on detailed research and the search for interrelationships.

Site interpretation is directional or manipulative, to the extent that it aims at modifying human behaviour towards conservationist ends through the progression: interpretation

→ understanding → appreciation → protection. The interpretation of objects within a museum context – and in this case it might be preferable to stick to the word 'explanation' – normally aims at education in the broadest sense, with no essential propagandist intention beyond the enhancement of knowledge,[8] though the various technical devices of site interpretation might well be employed to sharpen up communication and achieve readier assimilation of fresh knowledge. Thus, David Wright's discussion in the *Museums Journal* of interpretation in museums of general technology, even with his analyses of nominal, functional and contextual levels of interpretation, is basically an examination of device-aided explanation organized in logical sequences (Wright 1983).

There has been a flood of writing on interpretation (Barclay 1983), and it has undoubtedly given museum folk new perspectives, both in the integration of research data and in the technical presentation of information, but museum work still remains different, with a potential level of wide comparative exploration that site interpretation will normally lack or is not suitable for.

MATERIAL CULTURE

Museum collections are about objects and specimens. With regard to natural history and geology, research is a tight ship sailing through seas of disciplined international codes of practice and precision of nomenclature. Stress is laid on a dispassionate study of specimens for what they have to say in their own right. Accumulated data in the form of taxonomic lists and classifications gain wider scientific value because they are compiled under conditions of particular control. Artefact research may also have elements of science in that it can take advantage of laboratory techniques such as thermo-luminescence, X-ray fluorescence, neutron activation, dye and chemical analysis, and so on. To such scientific analysis can be added relevant factors like the historical setting in time, place and social milieu. Nevertheless, an element of subjective interpretation is often unavoidable and, though the aim is to reduce the subjective element, research into historical and aesthetic objects remains an art to a greater degree than a science.

It has been said that there is as yet no real theoretical basis for the study of material culture (Paine 1985). Perhaps museum people have a habit of looking too narrowly at their own artefact collections. The fact is that a substantial body of theory exists. Geologists and natural historians are obliged by the nature of their discipline to work internationally. Those concerned with artefacts must learn to do so also. As the SAMDOK 'movement' shows, the British museum world is not immune to outside influences, but we must learn to be more outward looking still.

America is often a rich source of inspiration. Schlereth's thought-provoking *Material Culture Studies in America* reviews the history of material culture studies in America from 1876 onwards, and examines theory, method and practice (Schlereth 1982). There is also Stocking's *Objects and Others. Essays on Museums and Material Culture*, which is more patchy and discursive but, nevertheless, shows that people in the USA are thinking about collections in museums. Britain is catching up, however, as a recent publication on material culture shows (Pearce 1989).

In Europe there is an enormous literature on the subject, though often in languages other than English. The journal *Ethnologia Europaea* is much concerned with theoretical bases. There are innumerable books on specific aspects of material culture often including theoretical introductions, and some take broad approaches to the subject, like D. W. H.

Schwarz's *Sachgüter und Lebensformen. Einführung in die Materielle Kulturgeschichte des Mittelalters und der Neuzeit* (Schwarz 1970).

There is no shortage of material. The real question is, what are we to make of it, how are we to use it, in looking afresh at our own collections? Few of us have consistent research policies in relation to our collections, at least of artefacts, and we tend to be blown about by winds of fashion like the twentieth-century collecting concept and the interpretation concept. But, in the end, we have to come down to the hard bit, and face ourselves with the meaning of our collecting activities in terms of our locality, region and nation, and with questions of co-ordinating activity on aspects of the 'national heritage' between museums of different levels of capability. If we can honestly try to do this, and in so doing begin to understand what characterizes one area rather than another, and how the life and culture of one area affects and is affected by that of others, close at hand or far away, then perhaps we can also begin to wield our collections more positively in adding our respective bits to the elucidation of the story of humanity, the begetter of the artefacts we curate.

NOTES

1 See *SHCG News* (1984) 7 (5), which comments specifically on research and documentation as a means of selection in the collecting of countryside material, but the comment is generally valid.

2 Much has been written about SAMDOK in Britain, though it has not caught on here as it has in the countries of Scandinavia, perhaps because we still have to learn to apply the full 'documentation' technique. There is also some confusion with the concept of 'twentieth-century collecting', which is in itself not clear, referring on the one hand to art objects and on the other to the paraphernalia of working life, whether domestic or in the workplace. See, for example, Cedrenius (1987); Kavanagh (1983, 1987); Rosander (1977); and Shaw (1987).

3 See, for example, *GRSM Newsletter* (1971–81); *Museums Journal* 85 (1) and Davies (1985).

4 *Women, Heritage and Museums*, report of the conference, 7–8 April 1984, Woolton Hall, Fallowfield, Manchester.

5 See Roberts *et al.* (1980) and several articles marking Information Technology Year in *Museums* (1982), 82 (2); also Stewart (1983); Stone (1984); and Roberts (1984).

6 Among the 'bibles' of interpretation in the primary sense are Tilden (1957) and Brown (1971).

7 See Pennyfather (1975) and Percival (1979). For a review of the development of the concept and its relationship to statutory government provision through a variety of Acts and countryside bodies see Stansfield (1983).

8 Though a modern view, entirely valid provided it is not one-sided, is that 'Museums . . . share with other educational and cultural institutions a responsibility for the forming of historical consciousness' (*SHCG News* (Winter 1985–6) 10 (4), in a comment on a seminar on labour history in museums).

REFERENCES

Aldridge, D. (1975) *Principles of Countryside Interpretation and Interpretive Planning*, Edinburgh: HMSO.

Ambrose, T. and Stace, H. (1984) 'National science collections research in Scotland', *Museums Journal*, 83 (4): 230–3.

Barclay, D. (1983) *Interpretation of the Environment, A Bibliography*, Dunfermline: Carnegie United Kingdom Trust.

Brown, W. E. (1971) *Islands of Hope. Parks and Recreation in Environmental Crisis*, Washington, D.C.: National Recreation and Park Association.

Cedrenius, G. (1987) 'Collecting today for today and tomorrow', in *Recording Society Today*, Edinburgh: Scottish Museums Council.

Davies, D. G. (1984) 'Research: archaeological collections', in Thompson, J. M. A. (ed.) *Manual of Curatorship*, London: Museums Association/Butterworth.

Davies, S. (1985), 'Social History Curators' Group', *Museums* 85 (3): 153–5.

Farr, D. (1984) 'Research: fine art collections', in Thompson, J. M. A. (ed.) *Manual of Curatorship*, London: Museums Association/Butterworth.

Greenaway, F. (1983) 'National Museums', *Museums Journal* 83 (1): 8.

—— (1984) 'Research: science collections', in Thompson, J. M. A. (ed.) *Manual of Curatorship*, London: Museums Association/Butterworth.

Jenkinson, P. (1987) 'A taste of change – contempory documentation in inner city Birmingham', *Recording Society Today*, Edinburgh: Scottish Museums Council.

Kavanagh, G. (1983) 'SAMDOK in Sweden: some observations and impressions', *Museums Journal* 83 (1): 85–8.

—— (1987) 'Recording society today', *Recording Society Today*, Edinburgh: Scottish Museums Council.

Longworth, I. (1987) 'The British Museum: a case study', *Museums Journal* 87 (2): 93.

Meiners, U. (1990) 'Research into the history of material culture. Between interpretation and statistics', *Ethnologia Europaea*, XX (1): 15–34.

Mohrmann, R. E. (1987) 'Anmerkungen zur Geschichte der Dinge. Die Form der Zeit' als Instrument der Periodisierung', in Wiegelmann, G. (ed.), *Wandel der Alltagskultur seit dem Mittelalter (Beiträge zur Volkskultur in Nordwestdeutschland 55)*: 103–16

Museums Association (1988–92) *Museums Association Corporate Plan 1988–92* (typescript) 8: 15–16, London: Museums Association.

Ogborn, E. A. (1978) 'Researching your collections – fine art', *Museum Assistants Group Transactions* 15: 7.

O'Neill, M. (1987) 'Recording modern Springburn', *Recording Society Today*, Edinburgh: Scottish Museums Council.

Paine, C. (1985) 'Report on SHCG Weekend, D. Hopkin', *SHCG News* 9: 4.

Pearce, S. M. (ed.) (1989) *Museum Studies in Material Culture*, London: Leicester University Press.

Pennyfather, K. (1975) *Interpretive Media and Facilities*, Edinburgh: HMSO.

Percival, A. (1979) *Understanding our Surroundings. A Manual of Urban Interpretation*, London: Civil Trust.

Roberts, D. A. (1984) 'The development of computer-based documentation', in Thompson, J. M. A. (ed.) *Manual of Curatorship*, London: Museums Association/Butterworth.

Roberts, D. A., Light, R. B. and Stewart, J. D. (1980) 'The Museum Documentation Association', *Museums Journal* 80(2): 81–5.

Rosander, G. (ed.) (1977) *Slutrapport rorande Samtids Dokumentation genom foremålsinsamling vid kulturhistoriska museer*, Stockholm: Nordiska Museet.

Schadla-Hall, T. (1987) 'Regional and national collections of archaeology', *Museums Journal* 87 (2): 90.

Schlereth, T. H. (1982) *Material Culture Studies in America*, Nashville, TN: The American Association for State and Local History.

Schwarz, D. W. H. (1970) *Sachgüter und Lebensformen. Einführung in die Materielle Kulturgeschichte des Mittelalters und der Neuzeit*, Berlin.

Sharpe, T. and Howe, S. R. (1982) 'Family expeditions – the museum outdoors', *Museums Journal* 82 (3): 143–7.

Shaw, J. (1987)'Recording society today, a postscript', *Recording Society Today*, Edinburgh: Scottish Museums Council.

SHIC Working Party (1983) *Social History and Industrial Classification. A Subject Classification for Museum Collections*; Vol. I: *The Classification*; Vol. II: *Index*, Sheffield: The Centre for English Cultural Tradition and Language.

Stansfield, G. (1983) 'Heritage and interpretation', *Museums Journal* 83 (1): 47–51.

Stewart, J. (1983) 'Museum documentation in Britain – a review of some recent developments', *Museums Journal* 83 (1): 61–2.

Stocking, G. W. Jun. (1985) *Objects and Others. Essays on Museums and Material Culture, History of Anthropology*, Vol. III, Madison, WI: University of Wisconsin Press.

Stone, S. M. (1984) 'Documenting collections', in Thompson, J. M. A. (ed.) *Manual of Curatorship*, London: Museums Association/Butterworth.

Tilden, F. (1957) *Interpreting our Heritage*, revised edn, Chapel Hill, NC: University of North Carolina Press.

Wright, D. W. (1983) 'Idealised structures in museums of general technology', *Museums Journal* 83 (2/3): 111–19.

Part 6
Security

27

Security is everybody's business
Museums and Galleries Commission

The Museums Security Adviser is based at the Museums and Galleries Commission, and has the brief to advise museums on security matters. The Adviser is particularly involved in assessing security provision at venues which have applied for the Government Indemnity Scheme and advising the national museums about the security of loan venues. These guidance notes provide a checklist for museum security.

THE NEED

Recent offences committed in this country and abroad indicate that criminals are very active in stealing works of art regardless of the fact that they may be identifiable by their uniqueness or value.

There is a well-established market for such items and the current world increase in prices of artworks makes them a very attractive proposition to a certain class of criminal. There is no indication that this type of offence will reduce.

THE THREAT

This can be defined as follows:

(a) The theft of exhibits during the time a museum or gallery is open to the public or closed; by an intruder breaking into the premises; by an authorized visitor or by a dishonest member of staff.
(b) The theft of exhibits whilst they are being transported from one venue to another.
(c) Damage to exhibits by wilful mutilation.
(d) Damage to exhibits by fire, either deliberate or accidental.

MUSEUM SECURITY

This is based on certain fundamental principles:

(a) Good physical protection to the shell of the building.
(b) A modern, well-maintained intruder detector alarm.
(c) A smoke/heat fire detection system.
(d) Efficient and well-disciplined warding and general staff.
(e) An effective internal security system.

SURVEY

1 *Perimeter* – Look for:

    (a) Protection by wall, fencing or electronics.
    (b) Security lighting at night.
    (c) Patrolled at night by guards, dogs or police.
    (d) Adjacent to other buildings.
    (e) Cars parked close to the main building.

2 *Shell*

    (a) All openings not used to be bricked up or permanently secured.
    (b) Windows, particularly on the ground floor, to be protected by bars, grilles, shutters or similar physical means.
    (c) Doors to be of substantial material and fitted with good quality security locks (BS3621).
    (d) Building provided with a modern efficient intruder alarm system terminating at a police station or central control station, monitored twenty-four hours.
    (e) Accessibility from adjacent buildings, by soil pipes, emergency escapes, temporary scaffolding, ladders, etc. to be catered for.

INTRUDER DETECTOR SYSTEM

This should never be the primary means of defence but always supportive of a strong physical shell. Remember that an alarm system does not 'protect' a building, it merely indicates that someone is trying to, or has succeeded in, gaining entry.

Museum staff should be made to realize that criminals are aware that, unless premises are properly protected, they can in some situations gain entry, steal a valuable item of artwork and make good their escape before the arrival of the police.

FIRE DETECTOR SYSTEM

Fire is the most serious hazard in any museum or gallery and those areas containing pictures, books, manuscripts, tapestries and other combustible material, must have a smoke ionization or similar detector system, which is monitored twenty-four hours.

INTERNAL SECURITY

(a) Internal doors should be of good quality material fitted with security locks.
(b) Trap protection should be provided to important or vulnerable areas.
(c) Galleries or stores containing high-value exhibits should be covered by passive infra red, microwave or other volumetric devices.
(d) The public and non-public areas should be physically separated by suited keyed doors, or some means of access control.

Public area

(a) The admission of the public should be regulated and their hand luggage searched in certain emergency conditions.

(b) All galleries and exhibition areas must be provided with a good standard of invigilation. Usually this means one man to one room and in cases where loans from the national collections or government indemnities are concerned, it would be insisted upon.

(c) If this coverage cannot be maintained, then galleries or exhibition areas must be closed off to the public.

(d) Pictures should be fixed to the walls by means of mirror plates and security screws (non-return).

(e) Pictures of particular rarity or value should be separately alarmed.

(f) Small pictures should never be exhibited near to doors, windows or fire escapes.

(g) Display cases should be of modern design (metal) and have well fitting, good quality locks.

(h) Display cases should be environmentally sound, fixed to the ground and be so located as to be capable of good surveillance.

(i) Cases containing gold or silver articles, or items of particular value, should be separately alarmed.

(j) Table displays should be secured by wire, nylon cord, wax or similar means or be provided with a local audible alarm. They should always be subjected to constant surveillance.

(k) A regulated 'sweeping up' operation should be practised at closing time each day to prevent anyone secreting themselves on the premises.

Non-public areas

(a) Curatorial and office staff should have a separate entrance if possible and their admission and departure regulated.

(b) A rigid, well-controlled key discipline should be practised.

(c) Keys to all display cases and exhibits must be subject to such discipline.

(d) There should be a proper system of accounting for any exhibit removed from display for any reason.

(e) There should be a well-kept accession register.

(f) There should be a well established means of cataloguing and stock-checking.

(g) The passage of goods in and out of the building should be supervised.

(h) Workmen should not be allowed uncontrolled access to the building.

OTHER POINTS TO CONSIDER

(a) There should be a contingency plan for any emergency, fire, theft, bomb incident or threat, etc.

(b) There should be regular practice drills to ensure staff know their responsibilities in such emergencies.

(c) There must be close liaison between senior members of the museum staff and the CPO.

(d) Security is not static. It must be constantly reviewed and upgraded.

(e) Encourage *all* members of staff to become security-conscious and to bring to notice any defects they identify which could jeopardize the collection.

(f) Ensure that *all* visitors to storage and other vulnerable areas are checked before being admitted. Allow unchaperoned access only to accredited persons in exceptional circumstances.

(g) Remember the visiting public will be affected by the example set by your staff – make sure it's a good one.

(h) Never become complacent – remember you'll never get the system absolutely right – so keep working on it.

(i) Expect the unexpected. Whilst you may not have catered for this, ensure that your system is flexible to cope.

If you want any advice on planning a security system, types of locks, fitting of windows, security grilles, steel roller shutters or other specifications contact:

Museums Security Adviser
Museums and Galleries Commission
16 Queen Anne's Gate
London
SW1H 9AA

Tel: 071 233 4200
Fax: 071 233 3686

28

Museum and gallery security
Museums and Galleries Commission

This chapter presents the Museums Security Adviser's policy for museum security.

1 The security policy

Successive holders of the post of Museums Security Adviser have devised and revised the current policy promulgated by the Museums and Galleries Commission. It provides a common standard for use in buildings housing collections which need to be protected from theft and damage and a level of security to be reached by those institutions wishing to take advantage of the government indemnity scheme administered by the Commission. The policy has five essential factors dealing with physical defences, intruder and fire alarm systems, invigilation and internal security arrangements.

(a) Physical defences

It is recommended that the shell of the building must be of substantial construction. In general, but not always, brick, concrete or stone buildings will provide the necessary resistance to forcible attack allowing time for an alarm system to initiate a response. The openings in the buildings such as doors, windows and rooflights must be reduced to the minimum necessary and those remaining strengthened to deter and delay entry.

(b) Intruder alarm systems

An intruder alarm system designed to initiate a signal upon a forcible attack being mounted against the security perimeter of the protected area should be installed. It is important that the system be constantly monitored and current police policy is to refuse to accept alarm terminations in police stations. Efficient and secure communication with an alarm company's central monitoring station can be established by telephone line and consequently the police alerted to problems within a very short period. It is recommended that a constantly monitored line be used so that interference or breakdown initiates an alarm signal. Reliance cannot be placed on a system which depends simply upon a bell or siren on an external wall to initiate a response.

(c) Fire detector systems

It is recommended that an automatic fire detector system be installed as it is important that an early indication of fire is given to the responding force. There are a number of systems available based on the detection of heat or smoke which will provide a signal by telephone line to the fire brigade or alarm company's central station as well as causing a local alarm to initiate an evacuation.

(d) Invigilation

Many exhibits cannot be physically protected if they are to be viewed as the artist intended. Furthermore, many institutions provide access to collections for researchers and students and the possibility of theft or damage cannot be ignored. Security attendants must therefore be employed and be given the duty to ensure that fundamental rules of security are followed to prevent theft, fire and damage.

(e) Internal security arrangements

These arrangements must, of course, be designed to suit the nature and use of the building. Clear and unambiguous policies and instructions should be devised to cover such matters as key security, supervision of contractors, access to non-public parts of the building, identification of accredited researchers, reception and collection of deliveries, searching and closing of the building and emergency procedures in the case of theft, vandalism, fire, flood or bomb threats. In addition, some premises will need policies and instructions regarding the searching of visitors and whether to allow bags to be carried through the museum.

2 Although I have mentioned five principles of security for the purposes of this paper it is only necessary to elaborate upon the first four and I shall deal with them in the same order as above.

3 Physical defences

(a) Whilst experience has shown that precautions are necessary to prevent incidents of theft and damage during the hours a museum is open to the public, it is the risk of a large volume loss during the closed hours that can be diminished by protecting the building. The scale of protection will depend upon the nature of the collection. Factors to be considered include value, portability and disposability whilst not forgetting that theft may be committed to extort money or changes of policy.

(b) Particular attention must be paid to the strength of the shell of a new building. Galleries, unlike banks and jewellers' shops, do not lock their valuable items in strongrooms or safes at night. The very purpose of a gallery allows the criminally minded access to much of the premises and the opportunity to reconnoitre his target and the protective measures. The shell, comprised of the roof, the walls and the floor, must therefore be able to resist determined physical attack for at least the amount of time needed for response forces to attend.

(c) Materials such as breeze-block, foamed concrete, sheet asbestos, aluminium sheeting, plasterboard, hardboard and bitumen bonded substances are now used extensively in the construction of buildings. They do not offer the same resistance to attack as that afforded by the traditional materials such as stone, brickwork or reinforced concrete.

(d) As the building shell must be regarded as the security perimeter the number of openings should be limited to the minimum necessary for access, ventilation and natural light. These openings should then be protected to offer the degree of resistance necessary to reach the required security standard.

(e) There are a number of ways of defending doors to provide differing degrees of protection. For an exterior door the least acceptability quality is of solid hardwood or solid hardcore construction. Further strength to meet an increased risk can then be obtained by using iron or steel doors of varying thickness or laminated security doors with reinforced plastic or steel sheet insert. Glazed doors to the exterior must be regarded as weak and must be supported by a secondary door system. Secondary systems are frequently found to be cost-effective and aesthetically acceptable and can be achieved by fitting steel roller shutters, expanding steel gates or laminated security doors inside the primary door. The weak point of any door will often prove to be the locking system. Care must be taken over the choice of system and consultation with a master locksmith will be justified for high-risk premises.

(f) Windows and rooflights continue to be a major problem of security. From the security adviser's point of view the ideal gallery would have none at all. Even very high windows are often reachable from roofs or ledges and must be taken into account when deciding protection policy. Decisions taken at the design stage can provide window security to meet lower category risks. The use of glass bricks set in steel or concrete frames for rooflights can be advantageous. For windows, a locked fixed steel sash with panes not more than 23 cm. by 18 cm. or narrow windows with effective opening of no more than 18 cm. are beneficial. Nevertheless, despite such treatment the real defence of windows and rooflights will rest in secondary measures. Steel roller shutters, iron or steel bars, collapsible gates and grilles or secondary glazing using polycarbonate or laminated glass all have a useful and distinct part to play in countering a particular threat.

(g) Consideration of security measures at the design stage cannot be overstressed. It should be possible to avoid features that provide access, albeit unintentionally, to the openings in the shell. Thieves can and do take advantage of pipes, ledges and buttresses to reach windows, rooflights and doors that seem inaccessible. They can then often use an easier and quicker exit to escape at ground level taking advantage of such features as fire escape routes not secured internally during closed hours. Design should also cater for the problem of thieves who conceal themselves within premises during open hours and break out after closing time. Careful planning can avoid unused spaces, dead ends, insecure ducts and panels which can conceal the human frame. Attention must also be paid to the exterior to eliminate conditions affording concealment such as vegetation, porches, deeply recessed doors and adjacent outbuildings. Less obvious is the risk of attack from a concealed position in a non-alarmed contiguous building. In such circumstances a case can be made for a party wall of stronger construction than the outer walls of the gallery.

4 Intruder alarm systems

(a) The deterrent value of an intruder alarm system depends on whether an entry and escape can be effected before the responding authority arrives on the scene. There have been numerous examples of successful theft in circumstances where the perpetrator has been able to ignore the initiation of a signal, enter and escape within the response time. In the case of galleries public access provides the thief with the opportunity to asses the nature and extent of the alarm system and the physical defences.

(b) It is for the above reasons that stress has been laid upon the need to provide traditional mechanical forms of security such as thick walls, strong doors, good quality locks and barred windows. The intruder alarm system should then be regarded as a support to these defences and be used to signal an attack upon them. A burglar alarm cannot prevent an intrusion nor can physical defences make burglary impossible given sufficient time and the right equipment. The correct solution is combining the alarm and the defences in such a way that a successful response can occur.

(c) In order to achieve a balanced system it is important that a brief be drawn up setting out the requirement to be met by the alarm system. The details of the brief should be agreed between the gallery director, a representative of the gallery insurance company and an independent security surveyor or the crime prevention officer of the local police force. It should not be left to an installing company's surveyor as he cannot be expected to be familiar with every aspect of the customer's needs.

(d) There are some British Standard specifications dealing with intruder alarm systems and an industry-based organization supervising compliance by members with those standards. It may be that the insurance company will insist on the installing company being approved by the National Approval Council for Security Systems. However, it should not be assumed that an installing company which is not a member of this association will not work to British Standards. Insurance company surveyors and local crime prevention officers will often be conversant with the quality of work performed by non-member companies.

(e) There is insufficient space here to describe the different sensing, signalling and control devices now available for use in intruder systems. However, it is necessary to touch upon the two main descriptions commonly used in relation to automatic detection systems. The term 'perimeter protection' is generally understood to include those devices which are activated by intrusion into, or forcible attack upon, the security perimeter. 'Trap protection' is usually used to describe those devices actuated when the intruder is within the perimeter.

(f) Experience has shown that a combination of the two systems is usually the most efficient way of providing the required standard of security. The emphasis that has already been given to the need for a physically strong perimeter, however, inevitably means that an alarm system of the 'perimeter' description will be of primary importance.

5 Fire detector systems

(a) It is vital to detect fire at the earliest possible stage and arouse the necessary response. Furthermore, many galleries are devoid of people when closed and that empty period of twelve or more hours may prove disastrous if fire breaks out and remains undetected.

(b) Automatic systems based on the detection of heat and/or smoke which can arouse a response in a similar manner to an intruder alarm are available from many sources. In addition to specialist companies the major intruder alarm firms operate divisions giving appropriate advice about installations.

(c) Whilst fire detector systems have become more acceptable to gallery authorities as reliability has improved and the cost of providing night guards has escalated, there is still much resistance to the use of automatic repression systems – 'the sprinkler'. Understandably directors and keepers fear the consequences of accidental discharge of water upon collections. The facts regarding accidental discharges are difficult to obtain but there is no reason to suppose that this equipment is so unreliable that accidents are a real problem. Many systems operate a dry pipe until the detector heads indicate a fire and even then the response is curtailed to the affected zone. Those concerned in the industry point out that even in a real fire situation the amount of water dispensed by a sprinkler system at the seat of the fire will be far less than that required at a later stage to control the conflagration. It was claimed in 1986 that the British Automatic

Sprinkler Association records revealed 98 per cent of fires in premises equipped with sprinkler systems were extinguished by the operation of two or three sprinkler heads.

6 Internal security arrangements

(a) Internal design too has a part to play and consideration must be given to the siting of galleries and displays. Benefits to security may be obtained in the choice of layouts and circulation routes notwithstanding that initial consideration may emphasize the presentation of the collection and the control of visitor flow in normal and abnormal circumstances. Thus, galleries formed internally away from outside walls and above ground level may be regarded as less penetrable. Conversely it is necessary to avoid providing easy access to an intruder to circulating routes that penetrate deep within the building. Whilst some schools of thought emphasize the need to separate public routes from those areas used only by staff, some thought should be given to the benefits to be obtained of routing staff through the galleries when they need to move. The more pairs of knowledgeable eyes that pass through the collections the better the chance to identify problems.

(b) Care needs to be taken at the design stage to ensure that sufficient space is available for mechanical and electrical office equipment used by the staff. Examples have been seen of such machinery housed in store rooms thus encouraging the issue of important keys amongst too many employees. The need to give curators and keepers maximum flexibility in exhibition design will lead to changes in internal layout that will frustrate the purpose of intruder sensors and emergency routes if insufficient thought is given to the project.

29

A case study of a museum thief

Don Steward

Unfortunately, thefts do occur in museums and Don Steward's chapter provides a cautionary tale of how a number of museums were taken in by the 'respectable' credentials of a researcher, who then stole items from the collections. In addition, Steward sets out the steps museums can take to avoid losses of this nature, but recognizes that in the real world such precautions cannot always be taken.

On Friday 11 January 1985, Mr John Thomas Whitehouse pleaded guilty at Bath Magistrate's Court to stealing geological specimens from Bath Geological Museum and Gloucester Museum. He also admitted stealing material from museums at Oxford University, Peterborough, Worcester and Nottingham, and from individuals in Leicester and Bristol; asking for these to be taken into account. The case was adjourned to allow psychiatric reports to be prepared. On 6 February 1985, Mr Whitehouse was convicted of stealing the fossils, fined £75 (£40 for the theft of nine fossils from Bath Museum, and £35 for the theft of two fossils from Gloucester Museum) and ordered to pay £24 costs.

This summary of the conviction of Mr Whitehouse is the bare bones of a case that should provoke curators of any collections to assess their standards of security with regard to visitors who view reserve material. In a case that produced headlines varying from 'The fossils fanatic: collector is thief' to the more sombre 'Amateur geologist stole museum fossils' there is perhaps an unusually comprehensive cross-section of museum officers who have been involved with the activities of one miscreant and can give their recollections concerning the *modus operandi* of a (now) known thief. As the recorder for the Geological Curators' Group, I contacted those who had had dealings with Mr Whitehouse and the following is a summation of their views.

TIMETABLE OF EVENTS

The first reported contact by Mr Whitehouse with museums occurred in 1979 with a telephone call to Warwick Museum: this was apparently not followed up by a visit. The first visit to Bath Geology Museum occurred in 1981 and it is about this time that several visits were made to view the geological collection at Dudley Museum. A visit to Worcester Museum took place in February 1982, along with several museums in 1983 – Northampton (23 February), Bristol (6 July) and Stoke (29 July). By 1984, the visits positively blossomed and at some stage included Oxford University, Gloucester, Peterborough, Northampton (the last of eight visits on 1 May), Worcester (24 February, 1 and 29 November), Stoke and Nottingham (both 2 August) and Bath (23 November). Mr Whitehouse also inferred to various curators that he had viewed collections at museums in Cambridge, at the National Museum of Wales and Birmingham University.

It was after the visit to Bath Museum on 23 November that suspicions about the activities of Mr Whitehouse were aroused and after several days of checking material in (or more precisely not in) store, enough evidence was forthcoming for him to be arrested on 2 December. A search of his house on 4 December revealed specimens taken from Bath Museum and he was duly charged. An announcement of this was given at the AGM of the Geological Curators' Group at Cardiff on 7 December which effectively publicized the occurrence to geological curators who then checked their records for visits by Mr Whitehouse and, as appropriate, informed Avon Constabulary of anything that may have had a bearing on the case.

THE APPROACH

In most cases, visits to museums by Mr Whitehouse were arranged via the telephone; only Peterborough Museum reported that he had written to arrange his visits. Whether by telephone or letter, he supported his requests by inferring that his interest in the collections was for ongoing research and mentioned his calls to other museums in a style that added credence to his standing. In one instance he added that he had been taught to make sure specimens were returned to their proper storage position at the British Museum. When visiting the museums he was always courteous ('extremely polite and good natured') and was impressive with his willingness to help identify specimens with his obviously good knowledge of the subject at hand. In his earlier visits he was often accompanied by Mr Geoff Thompson, an amateur Birmingham geologist of some repute, which tended to substantiate his credentials. In fact, in many respects, he presented himself as an ideal visitor – enthusiastic ('almost schoolboy enthusiasm'), knowledgeable and considerate for the workload undertaken by museum curators.

It is only with hindsight and the ability to correlate the various remarks that he made to individuals that a truer picture of his persona can be constructed. Suspicions were aroused because he seemed too concerned that the curator '"must have other work to attend to" and he didn't want to keep me from it – and it appeared as if he wanted to be rid of my attention'. Other reminiscences include: 'I did have slight reservations as he seemed to me to be over-friendly. However, my suspicions were not strong enough to make me consider refusing him access'; 'Whitehouse was almost apologetically correct, "I am sorry to bother you – I do hope I am not taking up too much of your time,"' etc; and 'I remember his visit distinctly as he managed to break a light shade and was effusively apologetic.' In fact, in retrospect, he appeared too good to be true.

Again with hindsight, he was equivocatory about his research interests and in what capacity this research was being undertaken. To an individual the story he told was convincing and it was apparent that he must have spent some time in advance of his visits determining what should be present in the collections. Only by comparing notes does his evasiveness show through. He told most curators that he worked for Birmingham Education Department (which he did as a personnel officer in the school-meals service) but gave the impression it was in a scientific capacity. Others understood him to work at Birmingham University in a teaching capacity; to be doing research in association with Aston University; or he purported to be a teacher with only limited free time available for research. The topic of his research varied with each museum: thus at

Bath he wished to study the Jurassic fossils of the Moore Collection; at Bristol, Worcester and Stoke, it was the Silurian fossils – particularly the Wenlockian trilobites; at Gloucester it was the Stonefield Slate fossils; at Northampton it was the bivalve molluscs and the mineral collection; and at Peterborough he showed particular interest in the Oxford Clay vertebrates.

He also had a habit of arranging an appointment and then postponing it at the last minute, often giving the excuse that work commitments made it impossible to attend on that date; he was always profusely apologetic at causing the inconvenience. Additionally, his visits to several places were rushed and significantly on two occasions at the same place, although separated by a couple of years, he had to leave early saying that he had to do some shopping and get a prescription for his mother who was ill – this has been interpreted as being a plausible excuse for having a shopping bag with him.

In all, Mr Whitehouse gave the impression to individual curators that he was particularly interested in the contents of their collection; was a knowledgeable geologist; and was doing research of a fairly high standard for an unspecified educational establishment in the Birmingham area. He let it be known in some instances that he had his own fossil collection, based on one acquired from the late Leonard Jackson of Walmley, Sutton Coldfield, and discussed the problems involved in cataloguing and conservation. Indeed, he even donated material to two museums (Nottingham and Stoke) that he felt was more relevant to their collections than his own. These factors, along with his good humour, friendliness and obvious interest in the subject, made him practically an ideal visitor to look at the reserve collections.

THE CASE FOR THE PROSECUTION

Although arranged in advance, the visit to Bath Museum on 23 November 1984 turned out to be a very inappropriate time to have any visitors. When the appointment was made at the end of October the curator, Ron Pickford, had been assured by workmen – involved with extensive alteration work inside the museum to comply with fire regulations – that they would be finished by mid-November. On 23 November, however, the workmen reappeared in order to finish off some work on the top floor where some museum material was housed. Having made the journey from Birmingham to Bath for the arranged appointment, the curator felt that it would be unfair to refuse Mr Whitehouse – a previously known visitor – access to the material he was interested in, in the basement! As the only person in the Museum, the curator then had the unenviable problem of keeping an eye on both sets of visitors at each end of the building. On one occasion when the curator returned from upstairs, Mr Whitehouse was found to be examining material not connected with his stated research, and when the workmen left and the top floor could be secured, Mr Whitehouse aroused the suspicions of the curator (who could now devote his whole attention to him) by trying to get rid of him by saying that there must be other work to attend to. Mr Whitehouse left the Museum in the late afternoon of 23 November, and because of a weekend and a day off, it was not until 27 November, that the collections could be fully examined. Telephone calls to curators at Bristol and Warwick unearthed rumours that a group of Birmingham collectors had a certain notoriety for excessive pillaging of Sites of Special Scientific Interest and that, by association, Mr Whitehouse should be treated with caution. To ensure that specimens were actually missing, rather than being replaced in the wrong box, each one in the collection was checked – a process which took almost four days. (Although not mentioned in court, staff at another museum involved have a strong suspicion that a larger specimen in store was deliberately broken in two so that a box from which an object was stolen was not empty on casual inspection as it contained a large fragment of a fossil similar in nature to the one expected to be there.) Finally on Friday 30 November the theft was reported, via the Director of Libraries, to the police. Mr Whitehouse was arrested on Sunday 2 December and detained for two days until his collections at home could be examined by Mr Pickford and the police. The charge was initially denied, but after several hours of searching, a fossilized snail shell was recognized by the curator and, although the registration number had been practically erased, enough ink had settled into the matrix for positive identification to be made. At this point Mr Whitehouse confessed, but it took a while longer for the full extent of his activities to be admitted as specimens were hidden in various places around his and his mother's house. Although the confession of Mr Whitehouse significantly aided the prosecution, it should be noted that is greatly to Mr Pickford's credit that he knew exactly which specimens were missing and was able to recognize them even after the registration numbers had been removed.

At the court hearing on 11 January 1985, the prosecution went through the motions of describing the occurrence of the theft and the significance of the specimens – describing them as 'irreplaceable and it is impossible to put a price on the stolen items. However, they would be of considerable value for the right people.' In an apparently brief synopsis, no doubt abated by the guilty plea, it was stated that Mr Whitehouse had a strong interest in fossils and had abused the trust given to him by museum staff. It was also said that the defendant had simply put the items in his pocket and walked out with them.

THE CASE FOR THE DEFENCE

The defence described the case as being most unusual and bizarre, and concentrated on the previous good character of Mr Whitehouse. The offences were described as inexplicable and it was inferred that some sort of mental breakdown had occurred due to pressures at work and home. It was stated that 'He [Mr Whitehouse] has been for many years an avid collector and an honest collector of items of this description and is an expert in his field. What has happened – and he finds this difficult to understand and he has been referred to a psychiatrist to help him – is the collection has taken over the collector. It has overtaken his normally unblemished character and trustworthiness. It was his avid determination that his collection should be completed.' It was said that Mr Whitehouse deeply regretted the abuse of the curators' trust and that it had been his ambition to improve his own collection, even though many of the stolen fossils duplicated his own material. This ambition to improve his collection had been rekindled at a time when he had problems at home and at work and as the problems got greater, he spent more and more time on his collection, classifying it. It was apparent from visiting the home of the defendant that he did go to great lengths to ensure that his collections were stored in a suitable environment and were well maintained.

It was stated that all the stolen fossils had been recovered; that the police had received full co-operation; that Mr Whitehouse no longer had any enthusiasm to collect fossils; and that he wanted to donate his collection to a suitable museum. The defence noted that the thefts were not for any monetary gain and it was supposed that they had occurred during the last visits rather than being spread over the full period of contact with the museums.

THE SENTENCE

The magistrates, taking into account the apparent remorse shown by the defendant, his offer to give his collections to a museum, his questionable mental state at the time of the thefts, and his demotion at work (he had been suspended from his post as senior personnel and staffing assistant in the school-meals service of Birmingham City Council and had been demoted to clerical officer in the same department, with an ensuing loss of salary of about £2,500 per annum), decided on the relatively lenient fine of £75.

THE LESSONS FOR MUSEUM SECURITY

Most of the curators involved offered the view that this sort of theft is effectively impossible to prevent. The person involved built up a reliable reputation over several years, was knowledgeable and helpful, and in general presented a very plausible attitude when visiting museums. Practically all the museums involved were able to supply exact dates when he had visited their collections, indicating that they possessed some sort of visitor log-book. Once in the storage areas problems appear to have arisen mainly because of the lack of personnel constantly available to oversee an individual. It should be stressed that even with the best of systems interruptions such as telephone calls can leave an individual unguarded for a time. Given that the person was also an apparently trustworthy character, it is almost rudeness to constantly be looking over his or her shoulder.

Without going to the extremes of banning all visitors from seeing the reserve collections or standing over the researcher (possibly for hours) while they examine material, what can be done to improve security arrangements? Obviously in an ideal world the following would apply:

- Each specimen should be fully catalogued and securely marked with its unique number.
- Each specimen should have a photographic record.
- Each specimen should have some sort of secret security mark, possibly using ultraviolet ink.
- References should be taken up before the research worker is allowed access to the collections.
- A separate study room should be available to bring requested specimens to the researcher.
- Somebody to be available to supervise the researcher on a one-to-one basis; and make arrangements not to be called away while with a visitor

However, most, if not all, museums do not have the space, time, finance or personnel to carry out all of these safeguards. Nearly all museum collections contain a backlog of material that needs cataloguing and it is one of the ever-present jobs of the curators to reduce the deficit as time becomes available. A problem, particularly in smaller museums, is that the staff may not be expert in all fields that the collections cover. So what can be done?

HOW TO AVOID IT HAPPENING TO YOU

Most museums already have an appointment-only system to visit reserve collections. This means that a record of a visit is available and the curator can at least be prepared for the visitor. A useful ploy when the visitor arrives is to have a place, away from the stores, for them to hang their coat and leave items such as bags and lunch boxes – thus minimizing the number of pockets, and so on, that items can be hidden in. The small expense of a laboratory coat, particularly of the type dentists wear, could be value for money; if the visitor is given one of these to wear before entering the stores, it makes it even more difficult to hide specimens about their person whilst the excuse that it is to protect their clothes from dust can be given. Stores may be able to be arranged so that access from one category of specimens is separated from others by some security device, for example, locked doors – thus negating the possibility of items unrelated to the stated visit being purloined. Cataloguing of the collections should proceed as a priority. Manpower Services schemes in several museums have been in operation to contend with backlogs and most of these incorporate some facility to have material photographed. Additionally, with the present financial restrictions seriously imposing staff limitations, it could be argued that the short-term use of peripatetic curators – possibly via the area museum services – would help to clear the cataloguing backlog. Checks should be made that items studied have been returned to their rightful place immediately after the visitor has left. On no account allow anyone to let visitors have access to the stores without your permission. The recent case of the stolen eggs from the Hancock Museum, Newcastle upon Tyne shows how persistent individuals can brow-beat non-curatorial staff into letting them have access. Warn your staff that they should not let this happen to them; the collections are your responsibility and you should honour this commitment. Conversely, be wary of individuals who rush and try to confuse you during their visit – no matter how apologetic they may be for taking up your valuable time. The case also poses the problem of whether the initial visits to the museums were for reconnaissance with the intention of finding out what was worth stealing in advance, or – as the defence implied – these first contacts were out of genuine interest only later to be used as data when the mental breakdown occurred. It is impossible to tell whether the defendant was trustworthy to begin with, or feigned trustworthiness to build up a good relationship with the curators.

Finally, do not be afraid to contact curators at other museums if you have any doubts about visitors. Coffee-break discussions at Specialist Group, Federation, Museum Association and Museum Professional Group meetings can often lead to a pooling of suspicions and, although the gossip may be only rumour, does highlight the names of suspect individuals.

ACKNOWLEDGEMENTS

The following have greatly aided the production of this piece by their verbal and written communications that I hope have been collated to their satisfaction: T. Besterman, Plymouth (formerly of Warwick); G. Chancellor, Peterborough; M. Curtis, Bristol; D. Darenall, Gloucester; M. Fendall, Worcester; M. Howe, Peterborough; S. Jusypiw, NCC; R. Moore, Northampton; P. Osbourne, Birmingham University; J. Owens, Nottingham; R. Pickford, Bath; P. Powell, Oxford University; R. Roden, WMAGS; J. Round, Dudley; and a variety of national and local newspaper reports of the trial. Specifically, special thanks should go to Ron Pickford and David Dartnall for their thoughtful contributions, to Gordon Chancellor for providing the photograph [not included here], and to Linda Frayling and Carol Weston for transcribing the erratic handwritten original on to the word processor.

POSTSCRIPT

The author has attempted to contact Mr Whitehouse since sentencing, to ask him for his views on museum security! Given his remorse in court, this seemed to present an opportunity for him, in some way, to reinstate his standing amongst the profession in a situation analogous to that of the poacher turned gamekeeper. No reply has yet been received.

One of the major points highlighted by the defence was that Mr Whitehouse intended to give up his interest in collecting specimens and donate his collection to a museum. The author is not aware of any such donation having taken place.

Several museums have reported that further geological specimens have been found to be missing from their collections as a result of checks inspired by the publicity accompanying this prosecution. It may be coincidental that Mr Whitehouse visited these museums and the suspicions may be unfounded, but in years to come the 'Whitehouse factor' may become the 1980s equivalent of 'lost due to war damage' for untraced items.

The attitude of the police during the case was one of, almost, amusement (why would anyone want to steal fossils anyway?), but if it happens to you make sure you get any information about their investigation during the course of their enquiries. Afterwards they do not have the manpower themselves to be able to provide details of their evidence and their security recommendations for reports such as this. It would seem that monetary value alone acts as a catalyst for action rather than the crime itself.

30

Protection, security and conservation of collections

ICOM and the International Security Committee

This chapter discusses the wide range of protection measures to ensure that collections are not harmed, including the role of the institutional protection manager.

> The heart of a museum is its collections . . . [with] the first obligation of a museum . . . to recognize and assume the responsibilities inherent in the possession of its collections, which are held in trust for the benefit of the present and future citizens of the community.[1]

Every cultural institution manager accepts responsibility for the cultural collections under the care of that institution. The institution manager, collection manager or registrar, and the protection manager work together to provide a collection protection programme for institutional care. The programme combines the administrative care of record-keeping and inventory with that of physical care, including conservation, environmental controls, personal access, property movement control, staff checks and loss prevention programmes.

Persons know about losses of cultural property as newspapers and the electronic media report them. Those reports are usually the unusual and high-value losses from fire, burglary, theft from exhibits during the day and a few famous news incidents of 'smash and runs,' 'grab and runs' and surprising hold-ups. Persons do not think about internal losses. Some managers report only the first kind. Other managers do not report either kind.

For this reason local, national and international reports of cultural losses are incomplete and not fully representative. The full amount of cultural property loss is larger than reported figures. The exact amount of cultural property loss is unknown. The International Council of Museums publishes a few of those reported to the International Police Organization or Interpol in an article entitled 'Protecting our heritage' in every quarterly bulletin *ICOM News*.

More often, cultural property losses are accidental and unreported. These result from improper handling, environmental damage, lack of conservation or security, misplacement and neglect. Losses result from accidental and deliberate causes, including internal loss caused by staff. When staff promptly report a loss, the probability of assistance and recovery is much greater. When managers report a theft, for example, they have a greater opportunity for recovery because of public pressure and publicity.

Cultural institution staff practise good housekeeping and collection control in the building. The staff practise good collection care and use. Good collection management is part of the basic protection services at cultural institutions. Staff who handle collections work seriously and carefully. Managers and staff alert each other when there is a problem and take emergency action to protect institution collections.

Managers understand that the protection and conservation of collections is the concern of everyone. This is one of the themes of this chapter. Those caring for collections should provide at least a minimum level of consistent care for collections and prepare for every thinkable emergency when outside support is available and when it is not. This is very critical during short-term and long-term emergencies.

The protection manager is a physical security or protection officer who works with the institution manager, collection manager or registrar, curators, conservators, exhibit designers and others to protect the cultural collections. The protection manager learns the nature of a cultural institution and understands how to serve it well. The protection manager participates in developing the security and emergency portions of the collection management policy, the record keeping and inventory system, the numbering and marking system, safe handling procedures, conservation practices and internal control of collections. The protection manager must participate in these programmes to assist in enforcing them and protecting the collections.

PRIMARY COLLECTION SECURITY AND PROTECTION

Institution collection managers or registrars develop and maintain a current, honest record of collection objects at the institution. The staff inventory both permanent collections and new arrivals that still require sorting. Curatorial staff examine, identify, record and inventory the newly arrived cultural objects.

The institution manager and collection manager or registrar decide what to accept into the collection and how to return what they do not accept into the collection. They decide to accept some objects and return others or recommend sending them to another cultural institution. They develop and follow a collection management policy which they form to be consistent with the Code of Ethics of the International Council of Museums.

Collection managers, registrars, and curators use good judgement in protecting objects that they send on loan to another institution. This includes the use of facility reports.

The institution collection manager establishes an arrival registry processing centre. The centre staff make each entry in a register that no one is able to change, and record every collection item that arrives. They securely store incompletely processed objects in sealed containers in a secure area, and secure the records of collections in the process of accession at that location and secure a copy of the record at a second location.

The collection manager or registrar and staff:

- Accession or register and mark each object that managers accept into the collection.
- Follow institution procedure and professional guidelines to record and mark the objects entering their collection.
- Use the records to prove ownership, to record the history or provenance of the object, to uniquely identify the object, to connect the object to an accession number used for internal inventory, to record additional information about the object and to locate the object at a later time.
- Keep these records as one file or keep partial files maintained for different purposes

cross-indexed. Accession or registration records require high-security protection in a locked, fire-resistant cabinet.

- Keep a copy of these records in a storage safe at another location such as a bank vault. The second copy might be a photographic copy.
- Supervise collection records and check the accession and de-accession system, inventories and movement of objects internally and externally.
- Maintain a file to locate and inventory every item correctly.
- Approve collection handling procedures and check the actual handling procedures.
- Call a conservator when a collection object requires maintenance, restoration, repair or specialized attention.
- Process loan agreements and usually require some insurance coverage when they send an object out of the institution, such as on loan. Institution managers and insurance specialists determine the degree of risk to the collection object and protect the institution against major financial loss. Insurance protection is not physical protection.

Collection managers and registrars realize that everyday operations are constant threats to collections. The handling, moving, processing, exhibiting and long-term storing of exhibits are all everyday threats to the collection. Managers evaluate the integrity of their staff and require special training standards and checks. For control purposes, volunteers, researchers and special guests must be part of the protection programme.

When internal controls are effective, there is less threat of internal loss from improper handling, disappearance and internal theft. The protection manager keeps records of staff who handle collections. They check the background history of every prospective staff member who might handle collections before they have access to any collections.

In emergencies the collection manager or registrar must have an accurate record of the collections and assist the protection manager in protecting the collections. With planning, collection managers or registrars reduce losses. During times of emergency when no outside resources are available, collection managers must prepare to direct internal resources and materials to provide emergency conservation care. Collection managers and protection managers work together to limit what damage might occur and return to routine operations.

Physical collection protection uses a perimeter system. There are programmes for bag and parcel check, a removal registry, key control and identity cards for persons in limited access areas. Curators and collection managers or registrars respect access control protection programmes, fire control programmes and emergency planning programmes. Cultural institution staff develop a collection management and protection programme when problems occur. They develop a systematic collection protection programme.

COLLECTION MANAGEMENT POLICY

Every institution collection has a collection management policy. Institution and collection managers or registrars must put that policy in writing. A collection management policy is a detailed written statement that explains why an institution collects cultural property and how it plans to manage the collection. The policy makes reference to legal and professional standards on cultural objects left in its care. A sample collection management policy in outline appears as Appendix I.

The collection policy often defines the limits that the institution uses to collect, sometimes called a mandate. It defines the reasons for and means for collecting and disposing of collections. This might repeat the requirement to care for and provide access to the collections. It might provide authority to a collection manager or registrar to supervise the collection. The policy defines requirements for record-keeping, acquisition, disposal, care and maintenance, access, risk management, security, inventory, temporary custody, and lending and borrowing of collections.

RECORD-KEEPING

Collection objects have more value when the records referring to them are available and when staff easily find the objects and records. Collection managers or registrars maintain records for object registration and cataloguing, proof of ownership, condition and treatment reports, inventory and location. Some managers maintain these as separate files and others maintain these as combined files. Collection managers use the records to organize and manage the collections. Others use these records for research, study and sometimes for public access.

The staff isolate newly arrived collections for environmental, administrative and security reasons. The institution manager designates an arrival registry point, process, or centre. The staff make an entry record in a bound book that no one changes. When the staff do not complete the recording process, they inventory, account for and secure these objects separately. The staff secure the records of collections during accessioning on site and secure a copy in a second location.

Many cultural institutions use an initial temporary accession record and numbering system, different from permanent accession records and numbering, to inventory newly arrived objects, boxes or cases. The staff follow institution procedure and professional guidelines to record and mark the objects entering their collection. The staff make notes of object conservation requirements and condition on arrival. They prepare boxes and crates of artefacts for marking and opening by checking requirements for customs inspection, climate adjustment, fumigation and pest control. They photograph and record them the same way by distributing them over a flat surface and repack them when appropriate.

Collection managers and registrars mark temporary accessioned collection objects for handling and storage in a manner so that no one confuses them with those of the permanent collection. Staff often use excellent quality but inexpensive 35 mm. colour negative film for record-keeping identity. This kind of film negative is commonly available in most parts of the world and is very easy to store safely and reproduce when required. The staff close unprocessed boxes and crates of valuable objects with security seals in secure containers. They record every item received and secure the records, with a copy secured at a second location.

Collection managers or registrars keep accession records accurately and consistently. The record-keeping or registration style and format varies by institution according to institution procedure and professional guidelines. Some collection managers maintain simple files on stiff file cards of relatively small size. These contain location information with the accession number, a commonly understandable name for the object and the current location in the building. Others use a bound book register and others maintain accession location files on a computer file.

The International Council of Museums and others find these kinds of data useful to keep for each collection object:

- Identity number and any other identifying numbers.
- Name of museum or institution.
- Name of administrative body or department.
- General classification.
- Object location within the institution.
- Geographical origin of the object.
- Nomenclature or designation of the object.
- Name of author, artist or craftsman or scientific classification.
- Material composition.
- Date, method, source, and place of acquisition.
- Estimated value or price paid.
- Name of collector or expedition.
- Cultural or ethnic group classification.
- Operation or use of the object.
- Character, traditional value, or significance of the object.
- Ownership previous to acquisition (provenance).
- Chronological data.
- Artistic style, school or influences
- Historical background.
- Descriptive narration.
- Photographs from various directions.
- Identification of known parts or related pieces.
- Identification details including photographs and negative numbers and narrative including dimensions, markings, weight, material, colour and texture, unusual features and distinctive elements.
- Catalogue where featured.
- Reference to other files containing institution ownership records.
- Close-up photograph of unique markings known only to the institution.
- Condition and preservation record.
- Institution notes.
- Bibliographical notes.

Collection managers or registrars describe objects in simple terms for easy recognition, avoiding the use of specialized technical or historical terms. Protection managers authenticate what items appear to be but cannot verify actual identities of objects. Accession records have sufficient detail so that persons uniquely and easily distinguish each object from any other object of a similar kind. Managers provide accession records to researchers for study, to insurance appraisers to set the cost of insurance for a loaned object and to protection managers to prove legal ownership when law enforcement officers might question this. Managers use paper, inks, and photographic chemicals and papers that withstand extreme conditions of temperature and humidity. Managers store photographs in acid-free folders, polyester film envelopes or mylar envelopes.

Photographs are critically important for the identification of objects. Collection managers or registrars quickly and easily identify objects in records by keeping photographs of the objects in the file. Photographs are useful for positive legal identification. Staff find missing objects more easily when searchers use a photograph during the search. Photographs are more useful when the photograph includes the object accession or identification number. Archaeological photographs include measuring sticks and object number boards. Often an object photographed in place contains a site marker and a north direction arrow. Some photographs contain a colour chart for correct colour reference or a code bar for electronic scanning.

Collection managers or registrars photograph objects entering and leaving on loan and when on exhibit to assist in accounting for them and providing good identification of them in case of loss. Collection managers without extensive photographic equipment prepare carefully drawn sketches. When no record-keeping exists for an entire shelf of materials, for example, a reasonably detailed photograph of the shelf full of objects provides an immediate accountability for the objects until managers prepare more extensive records. Collection managers use good detailed photography for positive identification of unique markings found in the photographs.

Protection and law enforcement authorities use photographs in public notices of stolen cultural objects. Managers cross-reference photographs used for different purposes in catalogues and records. Managers photograph high-value, highly portable and highly marketable objects from a variety of directions for good identification. Protection managers use close-up photographs of obscure surfaces to uniquely and legally identify objects when no one else knows of the photographs or kind of photographs or has access to them.

Collection managers or registrars must keep records safe from fire, theft and tampering. Managers protect official ownership files as sensitive file information. This includes information about monetary worth, and donor or source information. Many managers mark these as 'administratively confidential' and limit access to them. Managers limit access to sensitive files on an official requirement to know or use.

Managers consider using traditional paper files. Managers who use a bound registry book for record ensure the permanence of the record but risk losing the entire original record book. Managers who use separate cards risk losing cards without obvious notice of the loss or having a person remove a card without obvious notice. Managers who use a computerized record risk easy electronic loss by demagnetization or decay of the electronic file and risk unauthorized access and easy change by a skilled person.

Managers require that staff lock collection files. Collection managers do not keep records in the same place as the objects where one person might affect the object and the record together without an outside check. Often a person collects what appears to be innocent information from different common files which together amount to sensitive information normally kept under higher security. Managers who use record books inventory the books daily and copy the registry book by film when each registry book is full. Managers who use separate cards for each object maintain a duplicate record summary on one page. They require authorized persons who remove records to sign for them on removal and return. Managers who use computers closely limit what information they keep as computer records and limit access to the information as much as possible. No computer information is completely safe.

Collection managers or registrars keep highly sensitive and valuable files in a locked, fire-resistant cabinet, safe or vault. They choose a container on the basis of its security protection rating, which varies, and its fire-resistance rating, usually stated as a certain number of hours of fire protection at various temperature fires. Combination locks are usually more protective than key locks.

Managers use a reliable locksmith to install these and set their own combination regularly. The users of combinations do not write the combination down on anything that they carry or leave near the container. The users of combinations do not use easily obtained numbers as personal birth dates, birth dates of family members, licence numbers or identity numbers. Users of combinations who use a 'day lock' on their container, by unlocking the container by all numbers except the last combination number, do not use a day lock for protection at night. Users of combinations thoroughly spin the dial at the end of each day to erase any day lock condition on their containers.

Managers prepare the more important object records such as inventories in two or three copies, with each copy located in a separate place. Some managers make a computer record copy that they easily place in a secret place on a regular basis. Collection managers keep a safe copy of important records such as inventories at another location and replace them with a new copy periodically, such as monthly or yearly. Managers make changes to records in a manner that records the authorization and date of the change.

Managers of libraries and archives face the expanding use of electronic information access, including audio visual access, and the decline of a requirement to access original books and manuscripts, except by researchers. The great volume of older books and manuscripts will be part of reference libraries but not part of general circulation to visitors.

INVENTORIES

Collection managers or registrars take a regular collection inventory. They do not delay it because of its low priority or because of the large amount of work. A regular inventory is every year, every two years or every five years. Inventory checks include objects on loan.

Managers use an inventory team on a full-time basis to conduct a large inventory with accuracy and consistency. The staff divide a large inventory into smaller parts conducted by qualified and trusted museum professionals. Collection managers assign each staff member with a specific inventory or area and require that the individual conduct an area inventory periodically. Managers conduct high inventories in pairs of persons.

Managers often inventory more often items such as high-value objects and objects that are highly susceptible to theft. This inventory method resembles the tips of the iceberg that stands out of the water. It permits a collection manager to check the top ten objects at risk personally every day, to check second level collection objects every month, and to check the remainder of the collection only on regular inventories.

Managers must realize that internal theft is a tremendous threat to every institution. Managers protect inventory records from external and internal manipulation. Managers consider using an outside audit agency to conduct an occasional check of the inventory and inventory system. This system is important for offices that accept cash, issue bank checks and credits and handle valuable tickets, receipts or vouchers.

ACQUISITIONS AND DE-ACCESSIONS

The process of acquisition and de-accession of cultural objects varies according to custom, tradition, and law, as defined by the museum collection policy. Managers encourage cultural institution staff to follow their professional guidelines. Collection managers compare the excerpts from the International Council of Museums Code of Ethics, in Appendix II, with their institution collections management policy, especially in the area of acquisition and de-accession.

The institution collection management policy details the institution acquisition and de-accession policy. In its policy on acquisition, the institution managers might base acquisitions on certain elements:

- quality
- rarity
- intellectual value
- cultural diversity
- attribution of provenance
- size, volume or quantity of the collection
- price
- cost of conservation, storage and maintenance
- limits of use
- potential for use in exhibition and research

Institution managers might base disposal and de-accessioning on other factors:

- intellectual addition
- cultural origin
- research potentials
- attribution and provenance
- condition, quality and quantity of the collection
- price
- cost of conservation, storage and maintenance
- limits of use

The disposal and de-accessioning process requires sufficient consideration before action, with any money realized from disposal of collections made available for additional collection acquisition. The policy defines methods of disposition and requires managers to keep records for ever. Libraries, for example, mark all books removed from their inventory with such a stamp.

Managers remember to protect accession and de-accession records from external and internal manipulation. Like inventory records, managers consider using an outside auditing agency to conduct an occasional check of the inventory and inventory system.

NUMBERING, MARKING AND OTHER METHODS OF IDENTIFICATION

Collection managers or registrars account for every cultural object inside the institution and record its location. Managers register or record each object brought into the institution and assign it an accession identity number or code marking for internal collection control. The staff separate unprocessed objects and protect them until accessioning or registration and numbering or marking is complete. Collection managers distinguish between a temporarily accepted object with one numbering system and permanently accessioned objects with a different numbering system.

Collection managers or registrars require a collection marking that is safe to the object and is reversible. Reversibility is the ability to remove the marking without leaving any damage on the object. The staff place the numbering or marking so that it does not detract from the appearance or the value of the object. Conservators usually agree on a safe marking system for each kind of institution object. Some conservation organizations develop guidelines for numbering or marking. Many institutions use a latex base paint background with a strong India-type ink for numbering. They use a background with a strong contrast colour to the collection object. Managers use labels for textiles and pencil markings for archival papers and postage stamps.

Institution numbering and marking systems are for internal inventory numbering and marking. Collection managers consider them permanent inventory identification markings. Protection managers do not consider them permanent security markings because of their reversibility. Most persons might easily and safely remove this marking. The staff do not rely on the numbering or marking system for identification once the article has been stolen from the institution unless analysed by laboratory. Law enforcement officers normally use the accession number for inventory and for reference. Many law enforcement officers do not know cultural property terminology or marking systems. Staff might use the terminology in the Interpol reporting form. Collection managers simplify object descriptions and provide a clear means of identification. They use photographs, detailed written descriptions, records of restoration or conservation and extremely detailed close-up photographs of surface variations in the object to identify the object uniquely, as with stamps and coins.

INTERNAL COLLECTION PROTECTION

Cultural institution managers do no protect adequately against the threat to collections and operations from internal elements. These losses are usually from internal error and accident as well from intentional theft or deterioration. The cultural institution manager protects the institution from these threats with a strong institution protection policy. Protection managers develop a protection prevention programme using training materials.

Institution, collection and protection managers realize that much collection loss is internal, from misplacement, improper handling and internal theft. The persons who cause major losses are those who physically handle collection objects. Institution managers limit those who process and handle collection objects and consider their positions as sensitive ones that require greater supervision and more thorough background investigations.

Managers avoid hiring staff who dramatically increase the risk of loss. Managers evaluate where significant losses might occur in the institution and consider what staff positions present the most risk. Managers require greater pre-work checks of persons entering these positions and require greater supervision of this work at the institution. In most institutions these sensitive positions requiring greater scrutiny before and after hiring include those who handle collections, purchases, contracts and accounts, high value objects and negotiables.

Managers who hire persons or permit persons to work with collections at a cultural institution require that the person complete an application for record and provide several references. Managers obtain a check of personal identification from a reputable source such as government records or personally volunteered and checked information. In some places no one requests personal information because of legal rules. Institution managers require that applicants personally obtain official records about themselves and deliver it to the institution as part of the application process. Managers require that any deliberate falsification of information or failure to provide information are cause for immediate dismissal for lack of trustworthiness.

Managers who hire persons or permit persons to work in a sensitive position for a cultural institution require an application for record, several references, and an identity check. They ask for more extensive information such as that listed in Appendix III. In some places local statutes might limit organizations from collecting or storing certain information such as military record information or fingerprints. Cultural staff managers must check with legal authorities to determine what limits exist.

Managers might collect background information for an immediate simplified background check or for a later more extensive check. They might be successful in conducting random checks when complete checks are impossible. Managers who conduct preliminary random checks complete their checks later. They avoid using telephone reference checks because the person answering the given telephone number might not actually be the reference listed on the application.

Managers avoid accepting applications not completed in their presence because applicants might request others to interview and complete applications for them.

Managers often detect mistakes on applications when the interviewer requires the applicant to complete a second application without access to the first application and without advance notice. Managers compare the two applications in private to look for inconsistencies or discrepancies that an applicant forgot to falsify consistently.

Protection managers review applicants to eliminate applicants who falsify information, who are not who they say they are and who have high risk records such as convictions for major crimes, theft or child abuse; dangerous emotional, psychological or mental disorders; or experiences of drug or alcohol abuse that might continue without treatment and control.

Protection managers protect their institutions from major loss by developing an internal theft prevention programme similar to the one listed in Appendix IV. Its major elements are common protection programme elements such as accountability for property, access control and property control.

A major element of every internal theft prevention programme is orientation and training of staff, including motivation. Often a poor work attitude or personal attitude towards management is the first step in the development of more serious abuse of authority or procedures, such as misuse, misappropriation or theft. Managers must show staff by example that everyone cares for and values the collection. Managers must directly show the staff that theft is a cause for immediate dismissal. Managers inform staff and others who have access to collections that law, institution procedures and professional ethical policies protect collections. Protection managers provide a positive attitude to staff and develop regular reminders for staff to keep their protection efforts on a conscious level.

SAFE AND SECURE HANDLING

Managers control the internal movement and handling of the collection. They move collection objects from storage to exhibit, to an office or to a room for study or work. Losses are accidental or intentional. Institution managers, collection managers and protection managers limit the number of persons who have contact with the objects. They check them and train them to move and transport the objects securely and safely.

Many staff steal collection objects and other valuables from their own institutions because they require money for their personal lives. They take anything possible to sell for value locally. Money-hungry staff look for small, portable items that they hide and remove, which they understand that they sell locally. Collection managers take special care to protect these items and inventory them more often.

Some persons who might not initially plan to steal begin to steal when someone provides them the opportunity to steal with a low risk of exposure. Curatorial and protection staff provide a consistent level of physical protection to objects when they travel inside the building. The staff send a trained person with every object that they require to be moved. The staff do not leave an object unattended and unsecured. The staff do not leave storage and exhibit case doors open or unlocked for their own convenience. There are many good guidelines for internal object security:

- Require an authorization to move each collection object, preferably by signature.
- Make one person responsible for each move.
- Attend or secure every object regularly.
- Avoid doing anything that might threaten the object or escort.
- Go directly according to plan.
- Do not discuss the value of collection objects openly.
- Cover objects being moved so no one is tempted into action.
- Follow safe object handling procedures.
- Avoid moving objects in public areas during open hours.
- Sign in and out objects properly in storage and in exhibit areas.
- Co-ordinate exhibit removals with the vigilance or protection staff.
- Leave an official receipt or exhibit removal card when removing items from exhibit

Collection managers or registrars designate the staff who physically handle cultural objects and train them to avoid stressing or damaging objects. Curators and conservators establish an institution object handling procedure. The staff learn to avoid unnecessary handling. Managers provide internal object movers with basic instructions:

- Do not hurry.
- Plan what to do before doing it.
- Handle one object at a time, no matter how small.
- When possible work as a team with one person in charge.
- Avoid using unfamiliar or poorly operating mechanical equipment.
- Use covered hands or gloves regularly.
- Handle objects as little and infrequently as possible.
- Do not leave objects sitting on the floor.
- Do not drag objects, especially furniture.
- Rest objects on padded surfaces regularly.
- Hold framed objects carefully by the frame only.
- Do not handle or lift sculpture by a projecting member such as an arm or head.
- Do not smoke while handling objects or while in the same room with them.
- Do not walk backwards in the vicinity of objects.
- Report damage to objects immediately.
- Treat every object as the most important and valuable item in the collection

Managers consider training protection staff how to handle objects, especially in an emergency. When managers provide protection staff with simple moving techniques and procedures for emergency movement only, the protection staff rescue collections more successfully.

CONSERVATION PROTECTION

Cultural managers and staff attempt to preserve collection objects in superior condition for as long as possible. Every collection object finally changes. With a good conservation programme, managers extend the time that the object remains in good condition and extend its useful life for the purposes of exhibit, research, and education. Collection objects often change significantly because of natural environmental causes such as sunlight, rain and biological changes. Each member of the staff including the vigilance or protection staff who watch the collections daily, looks for the first signs of serious deterioration or damage in collection objects.

Air pollutants and the lack of screens are primary causes of collection loss. Vigilance or protection staff are on guard against damage to collections from the surrounding air. The unchecked air, dust and dirt, with local climatic extremes of temperature and humidity, dirty and stress collection objects. Most museums in hot, dry, or humid environments answering the ICMS questionnaire in the Action Guide reported that they keep windows open during operating hours.

Managers of institutions with open and unscreened windows train staff to detect the subtle darkening of collection objects and blurring of their colours. The staff check collections for flyspecks that are very difficult to remove. They look for traces of local insects that might feed or nest in the institution or on the objects themselves. Institution managers install screens on openings that must remain open for cooling and circulation. They treat parts of the building as compartments in order to prevent movement of pests from one part of the building to another. By using compartments inside, pest extermination programmes do not chase pests from one area to another. Managers and vigilance staff install pest collecting and killing equipment and check the numbers and kinds of pests caught.

Institution managers require a daily cleaning and dusting of exposed collections to remove any accumulations. Contractors apply epoxy sealers and paints to interior cement surfaces to decrease powder and dust. Curators request that designers enclose more sensitive objects in a vitrine or exhibit case of polycarbonate glass or plastic acrylic laminate such as Lexan or Plexiglas. Exhibit designers cover exhibit areas with light-weight linen fabric on wooden frames to protect exhibits directly from incoming dirt and dust and from direct light. Designers make the fabric part of the exhibit or match it to the colour of the wall to limit any distraction from the exhibit itself.

Every institution manager with a cultural collection hires a conservator on staff or has direct and immediate access to one. The conservator provides immediate care for objects under emergency conditions, applies or calls for special conservation procedures as required, and conducts collection surveys for preventive protection.

The conservator restores objects to their former condition when requested, such as in the repair of broken ceramic or stone or the restoration of damaged machinery. In other cases the conservator stabilizes a damaged object instead of repairing it to an earlier condition. In some cases the work of the conservator appears simple and direct, such as correcting excessive dryness or dampness. In other cases the remedy is not obvious. Every cultural institution manager requires the assistance of a conservator for the environmental protection of its collection.

Major temperature and relative humidity changes deteriorate collections. Vigilance and protection staff might notice that a collection object contracts in dryness and expands in humidity. The staff might notice that when a collection object composed of two kinds of materials changes temperature or humidity, the two objects expand or contract at different rates. This causes the objects to separate.

The staff look for and report any water or moisture from a leak during rainy weather that might damage cultural objects. In many cases the staff act to move cultural objects out of danger from running or rising water. Institution managers want to waterproof and insulate their buildings to provide the safest place possible for cultural collections. The staff are especially watchful when water moisture leads to chemical deterioration and when moisture with higher temperatures leads to the growth of mould, mildew, and live infestations.

Institution managers, curators, and conservators use thermometers and hygrometers to measure and record temperature and humidity changes. Large changes threaten the life of collections. Managers install this equipment in storage and exhibit areas and require staff to maintain a record of the changes. The greater the change, the more dangerous is the environment for the collection. The warmer the temperature, the more moisture the atmosphere might hold and the more susceptible it is to growths and infestations.

Conservators often plan to maintain an ideal temperature of 70 to 75 degrees Fahrenheit (21 to 24 degrees Celsius) with an allowable variation of 2 degrees above or below, and an ideal relative humidity of 55 per cent, with an allowable variation of 5 per cent above or below. When managers maintain these conditions, the cultural institution manager provides the safest environmental controls possible for the collection, and extends the life of the collection.

Managers often ask staff such as the vigilance or protection staff to perform these environmental checks and alert officials when there is an extreme reading. Managers train staff how to check equipment such as the hydrothermograph. This records the temperature and the humidity on graph paper. Often any readings of dangerous extremes are easy to notice when recordings cross red barrier lines on the graph paper.

When there is an extreme of temperature or humidity, managers take action to reverse the reading to maintain a temperature and humidity stabilization. In very warm exhibit areas without air conditioning, staff rely on ceiling fans to cool the area. In very cold areas, staff start heaters, especially to avoid the damaging effects of freezing on collections. When dampness in collection areas continues, managers, conservators and exhibit designers consider putting collections in sealed cabinets or cases that maintain lower humidity ranges. When low humidity occurs, staff install humidifying machines.

Conservators often consider a vitrine, cabinet, plastic bag or exhibit case a safer, more stabilized micro-environment for exhibit objects. They often place silica gel in exhibit cases to absorb moisture. Staff redry the gel in a warm oven, to reuse it many times. Conservators protect exposed objects such as large iron objects, with a coating of micro-crystalline wax and wood or textiles with a coating of mystox (alfa) with 1 per cent alcohol to prevent mould and mildew.

Managers avoid putting collection objects in natural sunlight or under unfiltered incandescent lamp bulbs because these light sources contain an ultraviolet wave-length of energy that fades colours and deteriorates paper. Designers plan their use of the fabric part of the exhibit design or match it to the colour of the wall to limit any distraction from the exhibit itself. Vigilance and protection staff check that direct sunlight coming in windows and doors does not shine directly on any sensitive exhibit item. Staff check the use of lighting to change any hot spots and unfiltered light bulbs.

Conservators determine the safe level of lighting required for a cultural exhibition.

Many conservators recommend that no more than 5 lumens or foot candles of visible light should fall on sensitive objects. These include textiles, costumes, watercolours, prints, other works on paper, manuscripts, miniatures, painting in tempera media, wallpapers, dyed leather and most natural history exhibits, including botanical specimens. Conservators recommend that no more than 15 lumens should fall on painted wood, oil and tempera painting, undyed leather, horn and oriental lacquer. There is no maximum illumination for metal, stone, glass, ceramics, stained glass, jewellery, enamel and bone.

Vigilance and protection staff on patrol in exhibit and storage areas often are the most consistent observers of general collection care. Staff often notice insect and pest damage first. Managers train them to inspect for damage during their routine patrols.

Patrolling and inspecting staff look for the droppings of insects and pests under each collection object. The staff look for cockroaches on wool, leather and mounted insects; moths on mammals, skins, wool and ethnological objects; termites on wood objects including wood structures; beetles on timber, books, textiles, furs, hides, feathers and plants; ants on mounted insects; and house mice just about anywhere. The staff become familiar with local insects and their habits. Staff find silverfish, for example, which inhabit textiles and paper, by startling them into moving by quickly shining a light in their direction. Clothes moths flutter and leave round holes. Powder post beetles leave a trail of dust under their work area and neat round holes where they penetrate material.

Vigilance and protection staff regularly report their environmental observations in collection areas, including reporting what insects or pests they see. Conservators often set insect traps and check the results regularly. When the institution staff maintain good housekeeping and respond to minor environmental requirements, they avoid fumigating. Safety specialists consider many cultural collection fumigants dangerous and recommend other response measures first. Some fumigants are as dangerous to the collection as they are to insects or human beings. Managers understand that the first response for staff is good housekeeping.

Fire is the number one threat. Fire prevention starts with good housekeeping. Managers do not overload storage and other areas. Managers prohibit smoking as much as possible, especially near collections. The staff regularly remove extra combustible materials and refuse. Managers do not leave electrical equipment plugged in and unattended. The staff regularly check lights and audio-visual equipment in exhibit areas. Protection staff install smoke detectors in every part of the institution and test them regularly.

INSURANCE, RISK MANAGEMENT AND LOANS

Risk management is a management system of identifying, reviewing and evaluating risks in order to select the better way to proceed without having great loss. Institution managers avoid risks and reduce those risks that are unavoidable. Everyone practises risk management when they protect their valuables and takes precautions to avoid losses. The risk manager considers these alternatives in a certain order:

1 Eliminate the risk.
2 Transfer the risk away.
3 Reduce the risk.
4 Insure against loss.

Institution managers, legal advisers, collection managers or registrars, building managers and protection managers have major risk management responsibilities in the institution. They manage the collections and other institution assets to prevent loss. The staff evaluate their own work to determine their principles of valuable protection and risk management.

Cultural institution managers who extend loans and receive loans rely on loan agreements. Insurance organizations often support good loan and transport practices. The lending and receiving institution often insure the same set of travelling collection objects.

Collection loan agreements include:

- A formal written loan agreement.
- Description of the objects, a condition report, identifying marks and three-sided photographs of the objects.
- Periodic check and inventory to check each presence of the object. For long-term loans, agreements might call for periodic submission of photographs to the lender or periodic checks of the loaned items by the lender.
- Exhibition checklists to be used by both the protection and curatorial staff.
- Proper packing and inventory and periodic checking of objects in transit.
- Proper training for staff acting as security escorts for international shipments of collections.
- Insurance requirements against loss.
- Responsibilities for each step of the move.

Institution managers collect information for loan agreements by asking for the completion of a facility report. This describes the conditions of the loaning institution. Collection managers rely on the facility report, the loan agreement and insurance coverage for objects on loan.

SUMMARY

The collection management policy defines how it provides public access to the collections, from the public visitor to the school child to the research scholar. It might define its lending and borrowing policy and its responsibility to care for and maintain objects in its care.

Most collectors of cultural property cherish what they collect. They preserve and protect it for the many lessons that it provides mankind. Cultural institution staff do the same, in the name of the public for which they hold the property. Everyone regrets the loss of a collection item whether it occurs from deterioration, sale, fire or theft. Institution staff, as stewards of the public trust, preserve and protect the collections in their care.

The staff must realize that both collection objects and other objects are susceptible to internal loss, neglect, vandalism and theft. Managers care for the collections with professionally accepted standards. Collection managers account for collections by recording them and by controlling their condition, use and location. Managers call conservators to provide physical care for collection objects. Collection managers and protection managers manage both incoming and outgoing loans.

Protection staff check the storage, exhibition and movement of collections in the building and often assist in safely moving collections going on loan to another institution. Protection staff physically spend more time with the collections than managers do and require a clear understanding of their duties in protecting the objects. Protection staff are of much greater assistance in institutions when protection staff learn and appreciate the work of the institution.

Institution staff inappropriately take collection items for money, for the pleasure of having an object, for the challenge of skilfully taking it and for political or psychological reasons. Internal collection theft occurs in storage, work areas, offices, transit and even on exhibit. The staff report collection loss from internal theft the least while it is the most dangerous. Managers must report every loss when it occurs.

Protection managers assist in the process by providing physical building controls. Protection managers understand the internal process of managing and accounting for collection items. The protection manager represents these procedures to local police officials when they report a loss. The protection staff are often the important link to the physical protection of collections and recovery of lost or stolen objects.

NOTE

1 Guthe, C. E. (1953) *So You Want a Good Museum – Guide to the Management of Small Museums*, Washington, D.C.: American Association of Museums: 34.

REFERENCES

Dudley, D. H., Wilkinson, I. B. *et al.* (1979) *Museum Registration Methods*, 3rd edn, Washington, D.C.: American Association of Museums.
Fall, F. K. (1972) *Art Objects: Their Care and Preservation*, La Jolla, CA.
ICOM (1990) *Code of Ethics*, Paris: International Council of Museums.
Messenger, P. (1989) (ed.) *The Ethics of Collecting Cultural Property: Whose Culture? Whose Property?*, Albuquerque, NM: University of New Mexico Press.
Oddon, M. (n.d.) *Guide for the Cataloguing and Analysis of Collections in General Museums*, Paris: International Council of Museums.
Plenderlieth, H. J. (1966) *The Conservation of Antiquities and Works of Art*, Oxford: Oxford University Press.
Reibel, D. B. (1978) *Registration Methods for the Small Museum. A Guide for Historical Collections*, Nashville, TN: American Association for State and Local History.
Shelley, M. (1987) *The Care and Handling of Art Objects*, New York: Metropolitan Museum of Art.
Smithsonian Institution (1990) *Collection Management Policy*, Staff Handbook 688, Washington, D.C.: Smithsonian Institution.
Thompson, G. (1986) *The Museum Environment*, 2nd edn, London: Butterworth.
Unesco (1968) *The Conservation of Cultural Property with Special Reference to Tropical Conditions*, Paris: Museums and Monuments Series No. XI.

APPENDIX I:

Collection management policy guide for museums and other cultural institutions

1.0 *Explanation of the format of this policy*
1.1 Policy outline
1.2 Policy implementation
1.3 Other

2.0 *Purpose and scope of this policy for each collection entity*

3.0 *Acquisition policy*
3.1 Criteria for acquisition

3.2 Gift and bequest policy
3.3 Donor limit policy
3.4 Purchase policy
3.5 Accession policy
3.6 Acquisition authority
3.7 Whole collections offering policy
3.8 Appraisal policy
3.9 Record-keeping policy
3.10 Collection exchange policy
3.11 Personal collection policy
3.12 Copyright law interpretation

4.0 *Policy for removal from accessions*
4.1 Policy for decisions for removal or disposition
4.2 Criteria for decision-making
4.3 Policy for authority for removal
4.4 Policy on disposition channels
4.5 Prohibitions for removal and disposition
4.6 Selling policy
4.7 Record-keeping policy

5.0 *Loan policy*
5.1 Incoming loan policy
5.2 Outgoing loan policy
5.3 Authority to make loans
5.4 Condition report policy
5.5 Facilities report policy
5.6 Record-keeping policy

6.0 *Policy for objects left in institution custody*
6.1 Policy for acceptable circumstances
6.2 Record-keeping policy
6.3 Disposition policy

7.0 *Care and control policy*
7.1 Responsibilities
7.2 Record-keeping policy

8.0 *Collection access policy*
8.1 Basic policy
8.2 Access requirements policy

9.0 *Insurance policy*
9.1 Policy for objects that are owned
9.2 Policy for objects in custody
9.3 Policy for incoming loans
9.4 Policy for items in transit
9.5 Loss and damage reporting policy
9.6 Record-keeping policy

10.0 *Inventorying policy*

NOTE

Adapted from Smithsonian Institution (1990).

APPENDIX II:
Professional collection ethics policy guide for museums and other cultural institutions

Professional and collection ethics are an extension of standards of conduct. Many professions add to these basic policies for colleagues in the cultural property world. The handling of collection information, like the handling of collections themselves, applies to all staff. Readers may add to these policy guides according to profession and local practice. These policy guides do not intend to encourage the violation of local law.

A collecting policy

- '[A]dopt and publish a written statement of its collecting policy.' (Paragraph 3.1).
- '[R]eview [its collecting policy] from time to time . . . at least once very five years' (Paragraph 3.1).
- Make acquisitions 'relevant to the purpose and activities of the museum' (Paragraph 3.1).
- Only 'acquire material that the museum is [likely] . . . to catalog, conserve, store, or exhibit, as appropriate, in a proper manner' (Paragraph 3.1).
- '[D]evelop policies that allow it to conduct its activities within appropriate national and international laws and treaty obligations' (Paragraph 3.3).
- Develop policies [so that] 'its approach is consistent with the spirit and intent of both national and international efforts' (Paragraph 3.3).
- Apply 'moneys received [from de-accession and disposal] for the purchase of additions to the collections' (Paragraph 4.5).

Legal requirements for purchasing and studying

- Do not acquire 'any object unless the governing body and responsible officers are satisfied that the museum can acquire a valid title' (Paragraph 3.2).
- Accompany purchases with 'evidence of a valid legal title' (Paragraph 3.1).
- Clearly describe 'any conditions or limitations relating to an acquisition' (Paragraph 3.1).
- Ensure that the acquisition 'has not been acquired in, or exported from, its country of origin and/or any intermediate country in which it may have been legally owned, in violation of that country's laws' (Paragraph 3.2).
- Avoid acquiring 'biological and geological material' that has been 'collected sold or otherwise transferred in contravention of any national or international law or treaty' (Paragraph 3.2).
- '[A]scertain if the proposed [field study and collecting] activity is both legal and justifiable on academic and scientific grounds' (Paragraph 3.3).
- Do not acquire excavated material or accept loans for exhibition or other purposes 'where . . . [there is] reasonable cause to believe that their recovery involved . . . destruction or damage . . . or involved a failure to disclose the finds to the owner or occupier of the land, or to proper government authorities' (Paragraph 3.2).
- Conduct the field study and collecting 'in such a way that all participants act legally and responsibly in acquiring specimens and data, and that they discourage by all practical means unethical and destructive practices' (Paragraph 3.3).

A fairness in collecting among colleagues

- Precede all field studies and collection 'by investigation, disclosure, and consultation' with colleagues (Paragraph 3.3).

- '[R]espect the boundaries of the recognised collection areas of other museums' (Paragraph 3.4).
- '[S]eek to consult with such other institutions where a conflict of interest is thought possible' (Paragraph 3.4).
- '[A]void acquiring material . . . from the collecting area of another museum without due notification of intent' (Paragraph 3.4).
- '[D]iscourage by all practical means unethical, illegal, and destructive practice' (Paragraph 3.3).

De-accession by proper authorities and by proper manner

- '[T]here must always be a strong presumption against the disposal of specimens to which a museum has assumed formal title' (Paragraph 4.1).
- Make de-accessioning 'the exercise of a high order of curatorial judgment' (Paragraph 4.1).
- Take the decision to sell or dispose only 'after due consideration' (Paragraph 4 3).
- Make disposal decisions 'the responsibility of the governing body of the museum' (Paragraph 4.1).
- Have each disposal 'approved by the governing body' 'only after full expert and legal advice has been taken' (Paragraph 4.1).
- Keep 'full records . . . of all such [disposal] decisions and objects involved' (Paragraph 4.3).
- '[M]ake . . . proper arrangements . . . for the preparation [and] for the preservation and/or transfer of the record-keeping relating to the object . . . including photographic records' (Paragraph 4.3).

Avoidance of exhausting the supply of specimens

- '[E]nsure that the activities of the institution are not detrimental to the long-term survival of examples of the material studied, displaced, or used (Paragraph 4.1).
- Apply 'special considerations [of de-accession and disposal] in . . . institutions . . . such as "living" or "working" museums and some teaching and other educational museums where they find it necessary to regard at least part of the collection as "fungible" [replaceable and renewable]' (Paragraph 4.1).
- Offer disposals first 'by exchange, gift, or private treaty sale to other museums' (Paragraph 4.3).

Legal disposal

- Fully comply with the 'legal or other [original acquisition] requirements and procedures . . . unless it can be clearly shown that adherence to such restrictions is impossible or substantially detrimental to the institution' (Paragraph 4.2).
- '[O]nly be relieved from such [original acquisition] restrictions through appropriate legal procedures' (Paragraph 4.2).

Avoidance of personal advantage

- Ensure that no person 'take advantage of privileged information received because of his or her position' (Paragraph 3.7).
- Only give 'written certificates of authenticity or valuation (appraisals) and opinions on monetary value of objects . . . [on official request] from other museums or

competent legal, governmental or other responsible public authorities' (Paragraph 8.5).

- '[E]nsure that no person involved in the policy or management of the museum compete with the museum for objects' (Paragraph 3.7).
- Permit the interests 'of the museum to prevail' 'should a conflict of interest develop' (Paragraph 3.7).
- '[N]either members of staff, nor members of the governing bodies, or members of their families or close associates should ever be permitted to purchase objects' (Paragraph 4.3).
- '[N]o such person should be permitted to appropriate in any other way items from the museum collections' (Paragraph 4.3).
- Respect rules not permitting 'private collections of any kind' where such rules exist (Paragraph 6.8).
- '[D]o not accept any gift, hospitality, or any form of reward from any dealer, auctioneer, or other person as an improper inducement in respect of the purchase or disposal of museum items' (Paragraph 8.6).
- Not 'accept gifts, favours, loans or other dispensations or things of value that may be offered . . . in connection with their duties for the museum' (Paragraph 5.2).
- Accept gifts, bequests and loans only 'if they conform to the stated collection and exhibition policies' (Paragraph 3.5).
- Reject gifts, bequests and loans 'if the conditions proposed are judged to be contrary to the long-term interests of the museum and its public' (Paragraph 3.5).

Illicitly acquired objects and requests for repatriation

- '[T]he museum should, if legally freed to do so, take responsible steps to cooperate in the return of the object to the country of origin' . . . 'if a museum comes into possession of an object that can be demonstrated to have been exported or otherwise transferred in violation of the principles of the Convention on the Means of Prohibiting and Preventing the Illicit Import, Export and Transfer of Ownership (1970) (see p. 113) and the country of origin seeks its return and demonstrates that it is part of the country's cultural heritage' (Paragraph 4.4).
- Be prepared to initiate dialogues 'in the case of requests for the return of cultural property to the country of origin' (Paragraph 4.4).
- Explore 'the possibility of developing bi-lateral or multilateral cooperations to assist museums in countries which are considered to have lost a significant part of their cultural heritage' (Paragraph 4.4).
- '[R]espect fully the terms of the Convention for the Protection of Cultural Property in the Event of Armed Conflict (1954)' (Paragraph 4.4).
- '[S]hould abstain from purchasing or otherwise appropriating or acquiring cultural objects from any occupied country' (Paragraph 4.4)

General work conditions

- '[B]e conversant with both any national or any local laws, and any conditions of employment, concerning corrupt practices, and . . . at all times avoid any situation which could rightly or wrongly be construed as corrupt or improper conduct of any kind' (Paragraph 8.6).
- Follow 'all legal and employment contract conditions scrupulously' (Paragraph 8 4).
- Take 'great care . . . to ensure that . . . outside interests do not interfere in any way with the proper discharge of official duties and responsibilities' (Paragraph 8.4).

- Divulge frankly and in confidence all information relevant to consideration of their [work] application' (Paragraph 5.2).
- Avoid taking 'paid employment or accept[ance of] outside commission without the express consent of the governing body of the museum' (Paragraph 5.2).
- '[R]efrain from all acts or activities which may be construed as a conflict of interest' (Paragraph 8.4).
- '[R]eport [any potential conflict of interest] immediately to an appropriate superior officer or the museum governing body' (Paragraph 8.4).
- Urge 'the governing body . . . and members of the museum profession . . . [to comply with] the ICOM Code and any other Codes or statements on Museum Ethics whenever existing' (Paragraph 5.1)

NOTE:

From International Council of Museums (1990) *Code of Professional Ethics*, Paris: ICOM.

APPENDIX III:
Work consideration elements from background checks for museums and other cultural institutions

1.0 *Personal identification check*
The applicant either provides the organization with the following information during the application process or delivers official checks of any of these records from official record offices.
1.1 Full name and other names used.
1.2 Date and place of birth.
1.3 Full name of spouses, date and place of each spouse's birth, and date and place of marriages and divorces.
1.4 Any identification numbers issued for military service, passport or immigration, and licences.

2.0 *Activity check*
The applicant either provides the organization with the following information during the application process or delivers official checks of any of these records from official record offices.
2.1 Addresses of residences used and dates during which they were used for the last ten years.
2.2 Membership in national organizations other than religious and political.
2.3 Full names and addresses of employers, dates of work for the last ten years.

3.0 *Negative record check*
The applicant either provides the organization with the following information during the application process or delivers official checks of any of these records from official record offices.
3.1 Complete list of law enforcement detentions, arrests, charges or convictions by any law enforcement authority for any violation. Do not list car parking violations. For each incident, describe the circumstances, date, location, charge, court and action taken. Convictions for major criminal violations, especially concerning theft, violence and misuse of property, or socially unacceptable crimes against other persons, including children, might be cause for an applicant's unacceptability.

Records of falsification of records, lying and the abuse of alcohol or drugs are noted but must follow local recommendations.

3.2 Complete list of work discharges, dismissals, removals and requests for resignations in the past five years. For each incident, describe any important details.

4.0 *Disposition in case of error or incompleteness*
The applicant is processed according to public law and organizational policy. The following suggestions are reviewed by a legal adviser.

4.1 Each applicant who submits incomplete or minor inaccurate information must correct the information before full acceptance of the application.

4.2 Each applicant whose position requires a more complete background check might be conditionally accepted pending completion of the acceptability of the more extensive investigation. Such applicants might be provided limited access until completion of such an investigation.

4.3 Each applicant who submits a major error or deliberate falsification of this information, or similar verbal statement in an interview, might be immediately discharged for falsification of records.

NOTE

From the Office of Protection services, Smithsonian Institution, Washington, D.C.

APPENDIX IV:
Internal theft prevention programme guide for museums and other cultural institutions

1.0 *Staff record checks*
1.1 General record check at hiring.
1.2 Additional record check for those in a sensitive position.
1.3 Recurring record checks for those in a sensitive position.

2.0 *Property accountability*
2.1 Regular inventory and check of inventory procedure.
2.2 Marking of inventory items including collection items.
2.3 Limited access to inventory records.
2.4 Property pass and sign out systems for property going out.
2.5 Bag and parcel check for visitors and staff on departure.
2.6 Personal responsibility for each object with mandatory receipting systems.
2.7 Property sign in and out at storage and on display, with displayed removal authorization with signature.
2.8 Separate, duplicate check and record to maintain an audit trail of events.

3.0 *Reduction of object accessibility by personal access control*
3.1 Identification or identity check required for persons on entry to non-public or closed areas.
3.2 Limited access for everyone at least by lock and key or by keycard.
3.3 Limited access for everyone to collection and alarmed areas.
3.4 Visitor and staff escort requirements, monitoring requirements and record-keeping requirements.
3.5 High-security area access by authorized list with registry or keycard records.

4.0 *Special theft prevention programmes*
4.1 Reduction of large-value targets or concentrations of targets in one area.

4.2 Identification of and additional protection measures given to items of general high value and high monetary value.

4.3 Identification of and additional protection measures given to items of high loss or high potential loss.

4.4 Establishment of a full authority internal investigation procedure.

4.5 Analysis of losses including motivation, opportunity and means of loss.

4.6 Analysis of property flow systems and controls, including loss vulnerabilities.

4.7 Central loss reporting system and reasons that thieves give for their actions.

4.8 Tests of control or prevention systems.

4.9 Internal and external audit procedures of cash, cheque and ticket operations.

4.10 Consideration of the use of undercover operations and informants.

4.11 Use of external investigations and audits.

4.12 Determination of means of loss, popularly used subterfuges and intelligence on actual loss events.

4.13 Consideration of the use of a reward and an anonymous information turn-in programme.

4.14 Special communication links among security, staff, audits and money-holding departments.

4.15 Computer information protection programme.

4.16 Pilferage loss prevention programme.

4.17 White-collar crime loss prevention programme.

4.18 Internal movement control including storage, exhibits and overnight temporary storage.

5.0 *Loss prevention orientation programme*

5.1 Orientation loss prevention programme for staff including the requirement of no thefts to be tolerated.

5.2 Management's announcement of a positive programme towards staff.

5.3 Publication of national, regional and municipal laws, rules and codes; organizational rules and codes, including ethics; and professional codes, including ethics.

5.4 Announcements, posters, stickers and letters as reminders of rules.

5.5 Special reminders for computer operators, persons handling valuables and persons handling highly marketable items or common pilferage items.

5.6 Prosecution of violators and recovery of losses without providing opportunities to resign.

NOTE

From the Office of Protection Services, Smithsonian Institution, Washington, D.C.

Part 7
Insurance and indemnity

31

Liability risk management for museums

Elizabeth A. Griffith

This chapter presents the concept of risk management for museums in terms of identify-ing risks for insurance purposes. Insurance is an expensive business and museums need to look around for the best possible packages. An assessment of possible risks within the museum environment will allow museum managers to make realistic decisions about their insurance requirements.

In a violent windstorm, visitors to the historic house take cover. A woman ventures into the open and is struck by the branch of a tree, sustaining minor but permanent brain damage. She sues the museum and six of its employees for negligence, asking $5 million in damages. The woman's lawyers uncover no sign of negligence. However, in order to avoid a jury trial (and the possibility of a large 'sympathy settlement'), the museum's insurers settle out of court for $500,000, and give notice that they will not renew insurance coverage at any price.

This story is true. It happened at Monticello, the home of Thomas Jefferson in Virginia, and a similar accident could happen at any museum with high visitation, jeopardizing its ability to obtain insurance and stay open.

THE INSURANCE CRISIS AND MUSEUMS

The insurance crisis is here, and it is striking hardest at service industries and organi-zations which have contact with large numbers of people. Hotels, restaurants, hospitals, transit systems, retailers, city governments – these are some of the businesses that are seeing premiums increase four and five times for coverage decreases of up to 90 per cent. Museums, despite their lack of clear hazards, are thrown into the same category by underwriters who see only large numbers of people and their propensity to slip and fall. In the present era of conservative underwriting, even museums with good safety records are subject to large premium increases, penalized by an environment in which the public is increasingly likely to sue the owners of the property on which they sustain life's inevitable minor accidents.

Most museum administrators, when they think of insurance at all, think in terms of coverage for their collections and loan items. Fine arts insurance, however, is just one part of the total insurance coverage a museum should carry. Coverage should include:

1 A package policy, which insures the buildings and contents (exclusive of the collec-tion) against loss or damage.

2 A fine arts policy, which insures the collection and loan items, both at home and in transit.
3 A liability policy, which protects the museum's assets and staff against suits arising from personal injury or property damage sustained by visitors to the museum.
4 An umbrella policy, which extends the liability coverage to higher limits in the event of extremely large claims.
5 Workers' compensation coverage, for claims by employees for injuries sustained on the job.
6 Automobile coverage, for any museum-owned vehicles.
7 Directors' and officers' coverage, which protects the directors and officers against suits arising from personal injury or property damage sustained by visitors to the museum.

The components of this package most adversely affected by the insurance crisis are the liability, umbrella and directors' and officers' coverage.

Museums unable to obtain such coverage face an unpleasant choice: closing their doors to visitors, or remaining open without coverage – 'going bare' as it is known in the business. Museums without coverage leave their assets open to claims by accident sufferers; one large claim could, in the worst case, force liquidation of the collection and endowment for payment. An alternative to closing, often considered by museums and other businesses unable to obtain liability coverage, is that of requiring visitors to sign claims waiver forms. Experience has shown, however, that these forms often fail to hold up in court. Once a museum has sustained a large claim, it has a serious insurance problem; the best it can hope for is a large premium increase. More likely, as in the case of Monticello, it will face discontinuation of coverage by its current carrier, and a lack of interest from other carriers. In the absence of convincing evidence to the contrary, other carriers will assume that the circumstances leading up to the first claim still exist, leaving them open to similar losses.

A PRIMER ON INSURANCE

The insurance business began in earnest in Venice, during the Renaissance, to protect the fortunes of the great merchant shippers. The practice of insuring gradually spread to cover land-bound activities. From this came the term, still used, inland–marine insurance, used to signify the insurance of goods against loss or damage, and often applied to fine arts policies. Businesses today purchase insurance from an underwriter or carrier, which insures many types of businesses. Coverage is rarely purchased directly, however; most often a business goes through an agency, or broker, whose business it is to know the insured's business and assist with loss control and the filing of claims. Agents can range from an individual licensed to do business with one or two carriers to an international firm able to tap many markets, the term often used by agents to refer to carriers. Carriers evaluate the desirability of a given account by evaluating its risk experience and loss history. The risk experience of a business is a summary of any claims filed against it, usually for the past five years. The risk experience summary will include claims for which no payments were made, as well as claims which resulted in payments. A firm's loss history consists of just those claims which resulted in payments by the carrier.

From the loss history and the policy premiums the loss ratio derived. The loss ratio is the most important single factor in determining a firm's desirability to an insurer. It equals the premium paid for a given year, divided by the claims paid during that year. Loss ratios of less than one represent a net loss to the carrier and render coverage extremely difficult to obtain. Ideally, a museum will bid out its business once every three years, to assure a competitive price. To do this, it submits a summary of the coverage it wishes to obtain to one or more agents for circulation to interested underwriters. This list should include:

1 An appraisal of its collection.
2 Valuations of its buildings at current replacement costs.
3 A list of all its non-collection property at current replacement costs.
4 A list of vehicles and drivers.
5 The names of all directors and officers.
6 Information on visitation, sales and other activities.
7 Premiums paid for the past five years.
8 Its risk experience and loss history for the past five years.

THE INSURANCE MARKET AND MUSEUMS

Museums with excellent loss histories, low loss ratios and little claims potential should be able to use the bidding system to their advantage, with a number of carriers competing for their business on the basis of price. Other museums – those with unattractive loss histories, high loss ratios or simply the potential for large claims by virtue of high visitation and a large physical plant – may find themselves in the position of trying to interest just one or two carriers in their business. Their managers must present their operations in the most favourable light just to obtain a quote. Waiting until an accident occurs to begin an accident prevention and response programme is a serious mistake. Such programmes established after an accident occurs are far less convincing to the carrier, and can sometimes increase the likelihood of an unfavourable settlement by implying negligence on the part of the management. Instead, preventing and responding to accidents should be an ongoing part of your museum's operations. To begin, ask yourself two questions about your museum's operations:

- How would your museum look to an insurer who is thinking about assuming your risk?
- How would your museum look to a court deciding a personal injury case in which you are the defendant?

RISK MANAGEMENT

What can a museum do to avoid a liability disaster? It can, and should, manage its risk. An understanding of the concept of risk management by the director and staff is necessary for any museum which seeks to reduce its liability exposure. Many organizations regard accidents, such as the one described above, as uncontrollable events. 'That's why we have insurance,' they say. Insurers, however, do not see it quite that way, and have begun to avoid writing policies for organizations guided by this belief. Insurers today insist on seeing an attitude of risk management among their insured clients. They rightly see themselves in business to insure pure risk – not the risk occasioned by sloppy maintenance of a heavily visited site or the indifferent attitude of management.

Insurers do not demand risk-free environments. They simply want to know that a museum is doing its best to reduce its manageable risk – they will insure the rest. Likewise, courts do not decide cases from a zero-risk standpoint. While a few cases involving high settlements on spurious grounds have been widely publicized, most cases are decided using the 'reasonable man' principle; organizations which take steps a reasonable man would be expected to take to reduce its guests' risk are usually found not liable for negligence. How can museum managers apply the 'reasonable man' rule to their museum's operations? A good first step is to survey other, similar museums and see what they do to minimize *their* risk. If you can demonstrate that you are doing as much or more than other museums, chances are courts will find that you are acting as a 'reasonable man' would.

Two kinds of risk

Risk experts understand that there are essentially two kinds of risk, which I call manageable risk and pure risk. By pure risk I mean the risk which cannot be reasonably avoided or diminished. Manageable risk, on the other hand, can and should be diminished as far as it is possible to do so. The incident of the tree branch offers a good example. 'Pure risk!' many would say. But is it? Clearly the windstorm is a pure risk, but other aspects of this incident are arguably manageable, such as the maintenance of trees and the training of employees to deal with extreme weather conditions, crowd control and first aid. This experience caused the staff at Monticello to think long and hard about visitor safety and to implement a number of changes, many of them surprisingly inexpensive, to achieve a higher level of safety. Other sites can learn from this experience, so do not wait for disaster to strike before taking preventive measures!

THREE STEPS TO GREATER PROTECTION

To carry out an accident prevention and response programme, museums must:

1   Identify their areas of greatest liability.
2   Prioritize their needs.
3   Implement the programme.

Identifying risk areas

Identifying areas of greatest liability can begin with the director of security, grounds or maintenance, clipboard in hand, taking a walk around the property. Where could visitors slip and fall? Hit their heads? Stumble in the dark or in inclement weather? Taking a look at the premises through a loss-control expert's glasses is a simple but effective way to identify areas of risk. Once a liability risk management programme is in effect, the best method of identifying high-risk areas is through accidents reports. These reports should include space for:

1   The name, address, phone number and age of the injured person.
2   A specific description of the area in which the accident took place.
3   The weather conditions at the time of the accident (particularly if it took place outside the building).
4   Names, addresses and phone numbers of eyewitnesses.
5   Staff response.
6   Rescue unit and hospital response.
7   Comments at the scene from the accident sufferer and eyewitnesses.
8   Comments from the staff.

Clear patterns will often emerge, leading to clear solutions. For example, reports at

Monticello during the first year of its programme showed that the majority of accidents were taking place on a certain walking trail during rain. Closing the trail on wet days has effectively reduced these slip-and-fall incidents.

Prioritizing risk projects

A museum assessing its liability risk for the first time will be faced with a daunting list of things to do. To keep the list from overwhelming the staff, realistic priorities need to be set. By the time it reaches the prioritization stage, a museum's administration is usually ready to articulate an accident prevention and response policy. This is an important step to securing the support of the staff and board.

Implementing a risk programme

Implementing a risk reduction plan is, in the long run, often less costly than a manager might expect. Expenditures fall into one of these categories:

1 Major, one-time capital expenditures.
2 Minor training costs incurred at regular intervals; or
3 Minor, ongoing costs of stepped-up maintenance.

A frequent pattern is for the initial liability survey to turn up one or two major items requiring capital expenditures. Once these expenditures have been made, however, future surveys are likely to reveal procedural matters which cost little or nothing to implement. It is easy to be overwhelmed by an initial survey which indicates the need, for example, to spend $25,000 on fire detection/suppression hardware. Museum managers, however, must guard against this tendency. While insurers would ideally like to see well-protected properties, they are most interested in seeing a commitment to safety, and recognize, especially in the case of not-for-profit organizations, the need to phase in large capital items.

It is important for managers to take a long-term look at their risk management programme. One-time purchases of necessary equipment, regular training and ongoing stepped-up maintenance are all part of a good prevention programme. Each of these activities should be monitored regularly by a committee composed of the director, the directors of grounds, security and maintenance and the person responsible for administering the insurance programme.

ACCIDENT RESPONSE AT MONTICELLO

While accident prevention at Monticello is the responsibility of all the staff, accident response centres around a few, select individuals who comprise the Accident Response Team (ART). The ART was formed by the director of security to assure prompt, professional treatment to all visitors suffering accidents or medical problems while visiting Monticello. Most members of the ART had some prior experience in accident response through working with a rescue squad, volunteer fire department or hospital emergency room. After being selected for the ART, each member received further instruction in first aid, CPR, visitor communications, accident reporting and Monticello's insurance package. Detection of an incident likely to give rise to a liability claim is an important step in accident response. Monticello employees have been taught to recognize such a situation, and to call the ART in the event of one. The ART is taught the importance of responding appropriately and consistently, always mindful of the public relations impact of their actions. Each of these elements is detailed below.

Appropriateness of response

The appropriateness of the response depends to a great extent on the laws of the jurisdiction in which the museum lies. For most American museums, first aid and CPR by trained personnel are protected by 'Good Samaritan' laws; that is, staff cannot be sued for injuries sustained during a good-faith effort to be of assistance. Further help, however, including moving the accident sufferer, is not. The director of security should investigate the location and response time of the nearest hospital and rescue squad, and should undertake to acquaint the staff of these organizations with the museum and its needs. Notices with these telephone numbers should be available to museum staff for use in time of need.

Consistency of response

Consistency of response is the best way to ensure that staff members do not lose their heads in an emergency, doing or saying something detrimental to the museum's well-being. Trained staff do not panic or make statements implying museum negligence. As in warfare, the team that is trained the best beforehand performs best in action, and the more disastrous the potential incident the more important the training. The Monticello Accident Response Team is grilled regularly on the 'worst-case' scenarios. What would you do in the case of a severe seizure? A bus accident? A sudden death? ART members must learn to respond unhesitatingly with a legitimate plan of action – one that holds up under the 'reasonable man' rule. The catch is that what seems 'reasonable' to a court of law in the calm of the chambers would not necessarily occur to a young museum employee faced with disaster. Regular training and evaluation help to bridge this gap. A crucially important aspect of this training should be the recording of remarks at the site of an accident. Verbatim quotations of the accident sufferer's remarks and of those around him not only help to capture the nature of the incident to those reading the report afterwards, they often provide a solid defence in the event of future suit (and indeed forestall suits by those who remember that their candid comments were recorded).

The public relations aspect of response

The public relations content of a museum's response to an accident is crucial. It is important that the response should represent the museum well, because it will be heard by the accident sufferer's family, friends and travelling companions as well as other visitors in the location. Watching your employees in action will shape their impression of your museum at least as much as the exhibit they visited. Some museums go to great lengths to leave a favourable impression on visitors in distress. One large American historical museum actually provides any visitor needing medical attention, regardless of the circumstances, with a pass to the local emergency room to be treated at the museum's expense. Managers at this museum consider that this investment has paid off handsomely for them in goodwill and reduced lawsuits.

Commitment of top management

Like any programme that requires money and staff time, an accident response programme will not function without commitment from top management and an ongoing, closely monitored programme. Ideally, the director should circulate a memorandum to all staff on risk-reduction and -response measures as they are developed.

CONCLUSION

Risk management, as an intrinsic part of managing a museum, is here to stay. Clearly, the costs associated with operating a public facility are increasing, and insurance premiums are just one part of the picture. The expense of making a facility safe and secure for visitors, as well as for the collection, is rising as well. Museums must remember, however, that the costs of increased premiums, maintenance, personnel and training are insignificant when compared with the worst-case alternative – closing their doors to the public.

32

Insurance and indemnity
G. Stansfield

These notes provide an outline of the insurance situation for museums in the UK, including a brief explanation of the Government Indemnity Scheme.

Insurance may be defined as a contract whereby, in return for a payment, the insurer guarantees the insured that a certain sum will be paid for a specified loss.

Indemnity: under the terms of an indemnity, one body (or individual) undertakes to restore the victim of a loss to his former state. No payment (insurance premium) is usually involved.

Risk management involves the following stages:

1 IDENTIFICATION OF RISKS

Identify the nature and value of the property at risk and how loss or damage might occur. In museum terms, the nature of the property involves buildings, collections and people, and the risks might include fire, lightning, storm, explosion, tempest, flood, earthquake, subterranean fire, thunderbolt, vehicles, aircraft, articles falling from aircraft, sonic boom, burst pipes, fuel spillage, war, riot, civil commotion, nuclear radiation, theft, malicious damage and accidental damage. Risks can involve premises, collections or people.

2 MEASUREMENT OF RISK

Having identified the nature of the risk it is then necessary to assess how likely it is that the risk will materialize (probability), and how serious the risk might be (severity).

3 AVOIDANCE OR REDUCTION OF RISK

In some instances the risk may be avoided (e.g. it may be decided not to display or not to lend a specimen). Risks may be reduced by upgrading buildings, fittings, equipment and staff.

4 ACCOMMODATION OF RISKS

A museum may decide to accommodate its own risk by making budget provision for repair costs or loss. Alternatively the risk might be transferable to another party (risk transfer) by agreement, contract or indemnity (e.g. it is usual to require the borrower to accept full responsibility for items whilst they are on loan).

5 RISK TRANSFER BY INSURANCE

Here, the museum enters into a contract with an insurance company (often through a broker) whereby in return for periodic payments (premiums) the insurer undertakes to reimburse the museum in specified circumstances. There are many kinds of insurance policies dealing with risks due to fire, theft, accidental damage, personal accident, etc.

MUSEUM INSURANCE

There are some insurances which are required by law:

(a) Employers liability covering the employer against claims for injury or illness caused by negligence. The employer is required to provide a safe working environment for his employees.
(b) Third party motor liability.
(c) Inspection of plant by competent persons.
(d) Specialist cover – e.g. aeroplanes, boats, locomotives, steam vehicles, mining equipment.

Other insurances arise out of contractual obligations:

(a) Insurance on leases
(b) Hiring or loans agreements

A third category involves areas where it is prudent to insure:

(a) Public liability (really essential).
(b) Buildings and contents.
(c) Business interruption (may be important for a museum which relies on admission charges for large proportion of revenue).

PRESENT POSITION IN THE UK: BUILDINGS AND COLLECTIONS

National museums

National museums in the United Kingdom do not insure either their buildings or their collections. The government carries its own indemnity.

Buildings and collections – local authority museums

Local authority museums normally insure buildings, furniture and equipment, etc. against fire under general policies negotiated by the local authority for all its properties at a relatively low cost.

The extent to which local authorities insure museum collections depends upon the individual authority, but it is common practice for museums to take out an 'all risks' policy for collections. Such policies often give cover for objects 'temporarily removed' from the museum. There is also automatic coverage for new acquisitions providing that the insurance company is notified within a defined period. It should be noted that it is often possible to reduce premiums if security is improved. Before negotiating an insurance, the insurance company will wish to inspect the premises and review security provisions and may refuse cover or insist that security be improved.

LOANS – NATIONAL MUSEUMS

A Treasury Indemnity is provided for objects lent by national museums to other national institutions. Loans from non-national museums to the nationals are also covered by this scheme. The British Council also has this facility for loans to British Council-organized exhibitions.

GOVERNMENT INDEMNITY SCHEME

Under the terms of the National Heritage Act, 1980, it is possible for the government to indemnify against loss or damage loans to:

> a museum, art gallery or other similar institution in the United Kingdom which has as its purpose or one of the purposes the preservation for the public benefit of a collection of historic, artistic or scientific interest and which is maintained
> i) wholly or mainly out of monies provided by Parliament or out of monies appropriated by Measure; or
> ii) by a local authority or university in the United Kingdom.

Under the terms of this Act the above indemnity can be extended to national libraries, local authority libraries, the National Trust, the National Trust for Scotland and 'any other body or person for the time being approved for the purposes of this section by either of the ministers with the consent of the treasury'.

Note that private museums, private houses or dealer's exhibitions are not covered under the terms of the Act and are therefore ineligible to apply for cover under this scheme.

To meet the conditions of a government indemnity it is necessary to have premises approved by the Museums Security Adviser. Although in the past environmental conditions have not been included as a requirement for the granting of an indemnity, the MGC are now looking at setting minimum environmental standards for museums seeking indemnity.

Applications for Government Indemnity should be made to the Museums and Galleries Commission at least six months in advance of the opening of the exhibition. Recent changes in the organization of the scheme now mean that museums borrowing from the national museums should apply directly to the individual national museums for government indemnity cover and to the Museums and Galleries Commission for non-national loans.

LOANS – LOCAL AUTHORITY MUSEUMS

For loans between local authority museums and between local authority museums and private individuals and organizations not covered by the above:

(a) Travelling exhibitions – it is usual practice for each museum to insure from the time that the exhibition is dismantled in one museum to the time that it is mounted in the next (peg to peg or nail to nail). Insurance costs are sometimes included in the loan fee.
(b) For individual loans, the borrower (whether museum or individual) undertakes the responsibility for insurance and sometimes for an independent valuation.

LOANS ABROAD

Loans to exhibitions beyond the United Kingdom may be insured in a variety of ways. A common way is for the borrowing institution to arrange insurance cover with its own brokers. There are difficulties with this approach, however, particularly if the insurance certificate is written in another language. Some of the national museums now arrange cover with their own brokers who then debit the borrowing institution for the premium. This solution means that the lending institution knows exactly the extent of cover etc., and also the valuation is kept in sterling (may be problems with exchange rates if valuation is converted into another currency).

Some countries offer a government indemnity similar to the British scheme. Examples of this are the US Federal Indemnity Scheme and the Swedish scheme. These indemnities are generally acceptable to the British national museums.

VALUATION

For insurance purposes most museums produce itemized lists of objects which are valued at more than a set value (e.g. £25,000), the list being reviewed annually.

Valuations for the Government Indemnity Scheme are examined by the MGC's expert advisers.

33

Indemnity arrangements for local museums, galleries and other non-governmental bodies
Office of Arts and Libraries

The Government Indemnity Scheme is an important source of support for non-national museums attempting to organize temporary exhibitions with loans from other museums, private owners and institutions. The scheme reduces the need for museums to take out commercial insurance cover for items lent to the exhibitions, by providing an indemnity, which means that the government undertakes to provide compensation to an owner should the object they have lent be damaged or destroyed whilst on loan. Because the government is bearing the risk, there are strict conditions which must be met relating to security and environmental conditions. These are checked by the Museums and Galleries Commission, which administers the scheme on behalf of the Department of National Heritage. Government Indemnity Schemes are not unique to the United Kingdom; the United States, Germany and Sweden, to name but three, also operate such schemes. The papers included in this chapter set out the requirements for the UK Government Indemnity Scheme and provide information about applying for cover.

INTRODUCTION

1 This note, produced by the Department of National Heritage, gives guidance on the indemnity arrangements for loans to museums, galleries or libraries maintained by local authorities, university or library authorities, the National Trust, and private bodies or individuals approved by the Secretary of State for National Heritage and the Secretaries of State for Scotland and Wales (subsequently referred to as the Ministers) under the National Heritage Act, 1980. As from 1 April 1985 the procedures will be administered by the Museums and Galleries Commission. The addresses of the organizations concerned are given in Annexe A.

2 The Ministers have power under the National Heritage Act, 1980, to indemnify any individual owner or institution which falls within the terms of the Act for the loss of or damage to any object loaned to another such institution, subject to:

(a) The loan facilitating public access to the loaned object or contributing materially to public understanding or appreciation of it.

(b) Appropriate arrangements being made for the safety of the object while it is on loan.

(c) The loan being made in accordance with conditions recommended by the Commission and approved by the appropriate Minister.

THE POWER TO GRANT INDEMNITIES

3 This note describes indemnity arrangements as they apply to lenders in England, Scotland and Wales. Indemnities in Northern Ireland are at present administered by the Northern Ireland Office and are not covered in this document.

4 The location of the lender will determine the appropriate Minister for the granting of an indemnity. Loans from lenders resident overseas however will normally be considered for indemnity according to the location of the borrowing institution.

5 The power to grant an indemnity is discretionary, subject to the statutory requirements set out in paragraph 2. Details of these requirements and the criteria used in their determination are given below. It should be emphasized that even when the Minister or Secretary of State is satisfied that the statutory requirements are met, he may still refuse to grant an indemnity if, for example, this would exceed the limit on the total liability under the scheme (see paragraph 14).

STATUTORY REQUIREMENTS WHICH MUST BE SATISFIED

Public benefit

6 The National Heritage Act, 1980, requires that the Minister shall assure himself that the loan will facilitate public access to the loaned object or contribute materially to public understanding or appreciation of it. The Museums and Galleries Commission, which gives advice on this aspect, may seek views from the Royal Commission on Historical Manuscripts or whatever other source they think appropriate.

Public access to the exhibit

7 In assessing whether a loan will facilitate public access the Commission will take account of the location and accessibility to the public of the place where the object is to be exhibited, including hours of opening and admission charges where appropriate. Objects which cannot be displayed (e.g. books or items requiring a special environment) should be advertised as available for viewing by special arrangement.

Public understanding of the exhibit

8 In assessing whether a loan will contribute materially to public understanding or appreciation of the object the Commission will consider whether the object is of such quality and importance that its exhibition is likely to arouse sufficient public interest to justify the indemnity.

Security arrangements

9 The Minister must be satisfied that the security arrangements operated by the borrower for the period of the loan (including transit to and from the place of exhibition) are sufficient to secure the reasonable safety of the item on loan. The National Security Adviser, a member of the Commission's staff, will check on the adequacy of the security arrangements. The general requirements are listed at Annexes B and C; the Security Adviser may recommend further conditions as appropriate.

PROCEDURE FOR APPLICATION

10 Applications for indemnity cover may be made by the borrower or the lender, and should in all cases be sent to the Museums and Galleries Commission (see Annexe D). The information required includes: a list of the objects for which cover is sought; the names and addresses of the owner and borrower; the duration of the loan; the security arrangements to be made, including arrangements for transit; and a current valuation of the objects with supporting evidence for each individual item whose value exceeds £5,000. Applications should normally be made at least three months before indemnity cover is required to enable the Commission to take all necessary steps.

FACTORS TO BE CONSIDERED BEFORE AN INDEMNITY IS GRANTED

Valuation

11 The valuation of individual objects offered for loan should be agreed before the loan is accepted. The level of cover will be determined by the Minster in the light of the Commission's advice. Application for revision of any valuation must be accompanied by supporting evidence; otherwise the Minister may take the Commission's advice on the level of cover required.
12 Arrangements may be varied by agreement for collections of books, manuscripts or bulk archive material where the computation of individual valuations is particularly onerous.
13 In order to avoid unnecessary administrative costs over a variety of small claims, objects valued individually at £100 or less will not be indemnified.

Financial limits

14 The extent of the government's total liability requires the scheme to operate within a financial ceiling. If this ceiling is in danger of being exceeded applications may have to be refused or restrictions imposed on the liability incurred by individual institutions.

Period of indemnity

15 Loans are generally covered for a specified period of up to two years in the first instance, subject to review in the light of the total contingent liability within the financial ceiling and the Security Adviser's satisfaction with the continued security of the loan.

LOANS FROM THE ROYAL COLLECTIONS

16 For reasons of constitutional principle it is not possible for the government to provide formal indemnity under the National Heritage Act, 1980, for loans from the Royal Collections. The government has therefore given an undertaking to Her Majesty that in the event of loss of or damage to items on loan from the Royal

Collections it would be prepared to seek Parliamentary authority for compensation comparable to that available to private lenders. The borrowing institution need not therefore take out commercial insurance to cover loans from the Royal Collections.

LOANS FROM BODIES FUNDED BY GOVERNMENT DEPARTMENTS

17 The government bears its own risks when lending its property and government departments are not expected to indemnify loans between themselves or indemnify loans from bodies funded by other government departments (e.g. The Tower Armouries or the National Army Museum). It will be for the government departments concerned to decide whether to bear the risk when lending property for which they are responsible; in some cases borrowers may be required to insure such loans commercially.

LOANS TO BODIES NOT COVERED BY THE NATIONAL HERITAGE ACT, 1980

18 Objects loaned for exhibition in a commerical context (e.g. to a private gallery or an auction house) will not normally be accepted for indemnity cover under the National Heritage Act, 1980.

CONDITIONS OF INDEMNITY COVER

19 In granting an indemnity to the owner the government is relieving the borrower of the need to take out commerical insurance. It therefore requires the borrower to observe certain conditions. The lender should be given the opportunity, if he wishes, to see and approve them.

(a) As a means of encouraging continuing responsibility by borrowers in order to eliminate small claims the scheme has a minimum liability clause. The borrower is required to undertake to meet the cost of the loss of, or reparable damage to, any object on loan to him covered by indemnity under the scheme, up to the limit of:

(i) £100 for objects of value up to £4,000.
(ii) £100 plus 1 per cent of the total value of the object for objects of value over £4,000.

It is open to the borrower to insure against the possibility of having to meet this minimum liability.

(b) The borrower is required to adopt any special security measures stipulated by the Minister (on the advice of the Security Adviser) and to display the objects only in the place which has been afforded security clearance.

(c) The objects must be made accessible to the public at the agreed times.

THE OWNER'S RIGHT TO IMPOSE CONDITIONS ON A LOAN

20 The terms of the indemnity scheme do not affect the owner's and/or lender's rights to impose other reasonable conditions on the loan of the object. Nor do they affect

the owner's rights to claim compensation from the borrower where conditions imposed by the owner have been breached.

PAYMENT OF COMPENSATION

21 An undertaking given by the Minister provides a guarantee that Parliamentary authority will be sought for the provision of the necessary funds to recompense the owner for the loss of, or damage to, the object.

22 Compensation will be paid to the owner or his agent under the following terms:

(a) If the claim does not exceed the borrower's liability the borrower shall make the appropriate payment direct to the owner.

(b) For larger claims the borrower shall again pay his liability direct to the owner. Where the object has been lost or irreparably damaged, payments (including the borrower's liability) will be made on the agreed valuation. In the case of damage to the object the payment will represent the costs of such reasonable repairs as may be agreed between the owner and the institution and shall not exceed the agreed valuation; in default of agreement upon the valuation, it may be determined by an arbitrator appointed by agreement between the owner and the institution. Such payment may take into account any reduction in the market value of the object after any such repairs.

23 Compensation will be paid subject to the provisions below:

(a) In the event of loss of, or damage to, the object concerned, the borrower shall submit to the Commission sufficient evidence of the circumstances in which the loss or damage took place to enable them to assess whether the conditions of the scheme were fully complied with. If the conditions have not been observed the Minister reserves the right to recover from the borrower the amount paid in satisfaction of the indemnity.

(b) The borrowing institution is responsible for providing a level of environmental control appropriate to the care of the loaned property. It is accordingly open to the lender to impose any conditions he deems necessary for the safety of the object as compensation will not be payable under the indemnity in respect of any deterioration in the condition of the items occasioned by their being maintained in inadequate physical or environmental conditions during the period of the loan.

(c) Compensation for the loss of books, manuscripts or bulk archive material will be made in accordance with the valuation agreed between the owner and the borrowing institution or, in default of an agreement, to be determined by an arbitrator nominated by and mutually acceptable to the owner and the borrower.

(d) Compensation will not be payable in respect of loss or damage caused by a deliberate act or omission of the owner or lender, his employees or agents.

(e) In the event of loss or damage due to the specified conditions not having been observed the Minister shall be entitled to conduct in the name of the owner or lender the pursuit or settlement of a claim against the borrower or a third party or to prosecute in the name of the owner. The Minister shall have full discretion in the conduct of any proceedings or in the settlement of any claim and the owner shall give all such information and assistance as the Minister may require.

(f) If a lost object which has been the subject of an indemnity payment by the Minister is subsequently recovered it should be returned to the original owner. The owner will normally (depending on the terms under which the compensation was paid) be expected to reimburse the amount paid.

ANNEXE A: GOVERNMENT INDEMNITY SCHEME

Organizations involved

1   Statutory responsibilities

For England: Secretary of State for National Heritage
Department of National Heritage
2–4 Cockspur Street
London SW1Y 5DH
Telephone: 071 211 6000

For Scotland: Secretary of State for Scotland
Scottish Education Department
New St Andrews House
Edinburgh EH1 3SY
Telephone: 031 556 8400

For Wales: Secretary of State for Wales
Welsh Office Education Department
Cathays Park
Cardiff CF1 3NQ
Telephone: 0222 825111

2   Administering body

Museums and Galleries Commission
16 Queen Anne's Gate,
London SW1H 9AA
Telephone: 071 233 4200
Facsimile: 071 233 3686

3   Security advice

National Security Adviser
Museums and Galleries Commission
16 Queen Anne's Gate,
London SW1H 9AA
Telephone: 071 233 4200
Facsimile: 071 233 3686

ANNEXE B: GENERAL CONDITIONS FOR THE TRANSPORT OF ITEMS TO BE COVERED BY THE GOVERNMENT INDEMNITY SCHEME

1 Any transport company used to move the item(s) should be one which has experience in the transport of fragile and valuable artefacts with employees trained in the handling of such material.

2 If the material is to be sent out or brought in from abroad the company used must have considerable and appropriate experience in handling consignments of valuable and fragile material over long distances. Staff must be experienced in dealing with the necessary documentation.

3 The arrangements for the removal, packing, unpacking and transport must be supervised by senior members of the transport company and by the representative of either the lender or borrower of the material.

4 Any vehicle used for the transport of indemnified items, whether it is operated by a transport company, by a lending institution or borrowing museum and gallery, by the Arts Council or by an Area Museum Service, must conform to the specifications in paragraphs 5 and 6.

5 Vehicles used should normally be closed vans (i.e. having solid sides and roof) with a windowless freight compartment separate from the driving cab. The locking furniture for the freight compartment should conform to international standards, in particular any padlocks being of the 'close' shackle type.

6 The vehicle must be provided with fire-fighting equipment appropriate to the load and the crew experienced in its use.

7 Vehicles other than closed vans may be used in appropriate circumstances, e.g. the carriage of very large items which may demand the use of an open lorry with the load suitably sheeted. Furthermore, small consignments or single items may be carried by car, small van, train or air, in charge of a dedicated courier.

8 Whatever method of transport is necessary compliance with the operating conditions in paragraphs 9–13 is required.

9 A vehicle crew should consist of at least two persons of good character, experienced in the handling of valuable consignments, capable of reacting effectively to an emergency.

10 The route should be carefully planned and the addresses and telephone numbers of emergency services should be carried by the crews.

11 Ideally, the journey should be completed in one haul.

12 When a stopover is necessary arrangements should be made to lodge the vehicle and/or material in secure premises which are protected by a twenty-four-hour alarm system or under continuous supervision.

13 On no account should a vehicle be left unattended by the crew, even in an emergency.

14 The proposed method of transport must be included on the indemnity application form.

15 Any other conditions recommended by the National Museums Security Adviser must be complied with.

16 The borrower of the indemnified material must also comply with all conditions imposed by the lender.

17* In the event of loss or damage due to the specified conditions not having been observed, the Secretary of State shall be entitled to conduct in the name of the owner or lender the pursuit of settlement of a claim against the borrower or a third party or to prosecute in the name of the owner. The Secretary of State shall have full discretion in the conduct of any proceedings or in the settlement of any claim and the owner shall give all such information and assistance as the Secretary of State may require.

March 1989

* Amended June 1993

ANNEXE C: GENERAL SECURITY CONDITIONS WHICH APPLY UNDER THE GOVERNMENT INDEMNITY SCHEME

1 The borrower shall at all times be responsible for ensuring that the greatest possible care is taken of the material which is the subject of the indemnity.

2 The indemnified material must be displayed in a building which has strong physical security to all openings in the shell.

3 The building must have an automatic fire detector system which is regularly maintained and in good working condition.

4 When the building is closed to the public there must be either a security guard deployed or a modern intruder detector alarm system installed which is regularly maintained and in good working condition and which covers all possible entrances into the building.

5 The intruder and fire detector systems must be connected by a signalling device to the police or an alarm company central station or fire brigade unless they are monitored internally by security guards.

6 If, as the result of a bad false alarm rate, the police response to the system is withdrawn, or if there is a failure which renders the system ineffective, guarding by trained attendants must be introduced until the police response is restored or the system repaired.

7 Paintings, drawings and similar objects must be secured to walls by mirror plates and screws, or, if this is not possible for any reason, an acceptable alternative must be agreed with the National Museums Security Adviser.

8 Small pictures, i.e. less than 18 inches x 10 inches, must *not* be displayed near fire escapes, or entrances and exits.

9 The public must not be allowed to approach unglazed paintings, fragile or sensitive artefacts. Rope or other barriers must be erected at least 30 inches from the exhibits.

10 Small portable objects must be exhibited in display cases which must be fixed to the wall or floor to prevent movement. If the material consists of gold, silver, jewellery, or items which are especially valuable, the cases must be fitted with alarm devices. The cases must be secured in a manner approved by the National Museums Security Adviser.

11 Warding staff must be deployed in the exhibition rooms during the time the public is admitted and proper arrangements must be made for their relief for refreshment and other purposes. They must concentrate exclusively on the safety and security of the indemnified material.

12 When it is not possible to arrange for a gallery containing indemnified material to be properly invigilated it must be closed to the public

13 There must be a form of drill, with which every member of staff is familiar, to cater for emergencies.

14 Warding staff must be equipped with some form of device by which they can indicate to other members of staff that there is an emergency situation.

15 Food or drink must not be allowed in the area containing the indemnified material

except under arrangements approved by the National Museums Security Adviser. Smoking must not be permitted at any time.

16 The arrangements for formal openings and private viewings must comply with the above conditions.

17 Any illegal entry to, theft from or act of wilful damage at the borrowing institution, whether or not this results in any theft, damage, or hazard to the indemnified material, must be reported at once to the Museums and Galleries Commission. Any other incident hazardous to the indemnified material should also be reported.

18 Any other conditions recommended by the National Museums Security Adviser must be implemented.

19 The borrower of the indemnified material must also comply with all conditions imposed by the lender.

20* In the event of loss or damage due to the specified conditions not having been observed, the Secretary of State shall be entitled to conduct in the name of the owner or lender the pursuit of settlement of a claim against the borrower or a third party or to prosecute in the name of the owner. The Secretary of State shall have full discretion in the conduct of any proceedings or in the settlement of any claim and the owner shall give all such information and assistance as the Secretary of State may require.

March 1989

* Amended June 1993

Further reading

Audit Commission (1991) *The Road to Wigan Pier?: Managing Local Authority Museums and Galleries*, London: HMSO.

Case, M. (ed.) (1988) *Registrars on Record: Essays on Museum Collections Management*, Washington, D. C.: American Association of Museums, Registrars Committee.

Chenall, R. G. and Vance, D. (1988) *Museums Collections and Today's Computers*, New York: Greenwood Press.

Dudley, D. H., Wilkinson, J. B. *et al.*, (1979) *Museum Registration Methods*, 3rd revised edn, Washington, D.C.: American Association of Museums.

Holm, S. A. (1991) *Facts and Artefacts. How to Document a Museum Collection*, Cambridge: Museum Documentation Association.

Howie, F. (ed.) (1987) *Safety in Museums and Galleries*, London: Butterworth.

ICOM and the International Committee on Museum Security (1993) *Museum Security and Protection. A Handbook for Cultural Heritage Institutions*, London and New York: ICOM in conjunction with Routledge.

Karp, I. and Lavine, S. D. (eds) (1991) *Exhibiting Cultures – The Poetics and Politics of Museum Displays*, Washington, D. C.: Smithsonian Institution Press.

Lees, D. (ed.) (1993) *Museums and Interactive Multimedia. Proceedings of the Sixth International Conference of the MDA and The Second International Conference on Hypermedia and Interactivity in Museums (ICHIM'93)*, Cambridge: Museums Documentation Association & Archives & Museum Informatics.

Lord, B., Lord, G. D. and Nicks, J. (1989) *The Cost of Collecting. Collection Management in UK Museums – A Report Commissioned by the Office of Arts and Libraries*, London: HMSO.

Lord, B. and Lord, G. D. (eds) (1992) *The Manual of Museum Planning*, London: HMSO.

Malaro, M. (1985) *A Legal Primer on Managing Museum Collections*, Washington, D.C.: Smithsonian Institution Press.

Messenger, P. (ed.) (1989) *The Ethics of Collecting Cultural Property: Whose Ethics? Whose Property?*, Albuquerque, NM: University of New Mexico Press.

Mitchell, R. (1988) *Insurance for Independent Museums*, 2nd revised edn, Ellesmere Port: Association of Independent Museums.

National Audit Office (1988) *Management of the Collections of the English National Museums and Galleries*, London: HMSO.

Neustupny, J. (1968) *Museums and Research*, Prague: Narodni Museum.

O'Keefe, P. J. and Prott, L. V. (1984) *Law and Cultural Heritage*, Vol. 1: *Discovery and Excavation*, Oxford: Professional Books.

—— (1990) *Law and Cultural Heritage*, Vol. 3: *Movement*, Oxford: Professional Books.

Orna, E. (1987) *Information Policies for Museums*, Cambridge: Museum Documentation Association.

Roberts, D. A. (ed) (1988) *Collection Management for Museums. Proceedings of an International Conference in Cambridge in 1987*, Cambridge: Museum Documentation Association.

Solley, T. T., Williams, J. and Baden, L. (1987) *Planning for Emergencies: A Guide for Museums*, Association of Museum Directors.

Stolow, N. (1987) *Conservation and Exhibitions: Packing, Transport, Storage and Environmental Considerations*, London: Butterworth.

Thompson, J. M. (ed.) (1992) *The Manual of Curatorship*, Oxford: Butterworth-Heinemann.

Weil, S. (1985) *Beauty and the Beasts. On Museums, Art, the Law, and the Art Market*, Washington, D.C.: Smithsonian Institution Press.

Index